# LITERARY CRITICISM

For my daughter Charlotte, who told me to shut up about Aristotle

# LITERARY CRITICISM

## A NEW HISTORY

• • •

GARY DAY

Edinburgh University Press

© Gary Day, 2008

Edinburgh University Press Ltd
22 George Square, Edinburgh

Typeset in 10.25/12.5 Sabon by
Servis Filmsetting Ltd, Stockport, Cheshire, and
printed and bound in Great Britain by
Biddles Ltd, King's Lynn, Norfolk

A CIP record for this book is available from the British Library

ISBN 978 0 7486 1563 6 (hardback)

The right of Gary Day
to be identified as author of this work
has been asserted in accordance with
the Copyright, Designs and Patents Act 1988.

Cover image: © Yuriko Takata *Literature II*. Courtesy of McGaw Licensing/
The McGaw Group, LLC.

# CONTENTS

# ACKNOWLEDGEMENTS

My thanks are due to Alistair Minnis for early encouragement and interest, and for his willingness to share his immense knowledge of Medieval criticism; to Philip Smallwood, a comrade in arms, not just for his expertise in the eighteenth century but for his sustaining belief in the importance of criticism; to my colleagues Joe Phelan and Peter Shillingsburg for their suggestions about the nineteenth century; to Kevin Morris who values literature; to Peter Andrews for his care and attention in copyediting the manuscript; and, most of all, to Jackie Jones, my editor at Edinburgh, for her enormous encouragement, prodigious patience, and knowing exactly when to deliver that kick up the backside. Naturally, all the faults, lacunae and inevitable inconsistencies are entirely my own.

# PREFACE

Read not to contradict, and confute; nor to believe and take for granted; nor to find talk and discourse; but to weigh and consider. Some books are to be tasted, others to be swallowed, some few to be chewed and digested. (Francis Bacon)

The opinions prevalent in one age, as truths above the reach of controversy, are confuted and rejected in another, and rise again to reception in remoter times. Thus the human mind is kept in motion without progress. (Samuel Johnson)

To ascertain the master current in the literature of an epoch, and to distinguish this from all minor currents, is one of the critic's highest functions. (Matthew Arnold)

All books are divisible into two classes: the books of the hour and the books of all time. (John Ruskin)

I consider criticism merely a preliminary excitement, a statement of things a writer has to clear up in his own head sometime or other, probably antecedent to writing; of no value unless it come to fruit in the created work later. (Ezra Pound)

Literary criticism can be no more than a reasoned account of the feeling produced upon the critic by the book he is criticising ... We judge a work of art by its effect on our sincere and vital emotion and nothing else. (D. H. Lawrence)

Criticism is as inevitable as breathing. (T. S. Eliot)

A critic is to be judged by his quotations. (J. Middleton Murray)

There has never been a statue erected to honour a critic. (Zig Ziglar)

# POLEMICAL INTRODUCTION

It's impossible to build a mountain out of melting ice and it's even harder to write a history of criticism. That's what René Welleck (1903–95), a brilliant linguist and one of the most accomplished scholars of the twentieth century concluded after his projected seven-volume history of modern criticism. *Seven* volumes. And they only stretch from 1750 to 1950. That makes the *Cambridge History of Literary Criticism*, with mainly one volume per period, look almost frivolous.

It's not just the sheer amount of material that dooms the would-be chronicler to failure, it is also the fact that, in a sense, criticism has no history. And what I mean by that is that we can find the same concerns in Ancient Athens that we find in modern England. The worries that Plato had about the power of poetry to corrupt morals find their parallel in all those anxious articles about the bad effects of *Grand Theft Auto* on the young. The belief that literature can mould behaviour is an example of rhetorical criticism. It is one of the two strands that recur throughout the history of criticism: the other is grammatical criticism, which is mostly concerned with editing texts and establishing their authenticity.

Once we recognise this basic division, we can see that what appears to be diverse forms of criticism are merely different manifestations of these two principles. An immediate example is the supposed division between theory and traditional criticism. Those who felt it was bliss to be alive in the revolutionary 1970s and 1980s will recall the oft-repeated claim of theorists that they had a radically different view of literature to their predecessors, particularly F. R. Leavis, who was condemned for being elitist and for not justifying the assumptions underlying his criticism.[1]

But in fact there is little to choose between Leavis and, say, Terry Hawkes, one of the pioneers of cultural materialism. No doubt some will find this an outrageous claim. They will splutter that Leavis judges a work while Hawkes historicises it; that Leavis believes in a hierarchy of literary values while Hawkes shows in whose interest such hierarchies are constructed. The purpose of criticism, they will argue, is not to praise literature for making experience irresistibly real but to expose it as an ideological clash between the dominant and subordinate groups in society. Such assertions are based on an ignorance of Leavis together with an inflated view of criticism's importance.

A closer inspection reveals that both men belong to the rhetorical tradition of criticism, for each maintains that literature should play a part in the wider culture. They may read Shakespeare in different ways, Leavis for the creative power of his language, Hawkes for how power appropriates his poetry, but each claims that the bard can shape our seeing and alter our actions. Their differences, then, are complementary rather than contradictory. They stress, each in their own way, the notion that literature is a form of emancipation, that past literature has its life in the present or not at all. We should therefore try to look for points of comparison between theorists and traditionalists if we wish to do justice to recent developments in criticism. If there is a history of criticism, it is an account of variations on a theme.

A definition of the term criticism is as impossible as the history of it, as Philip Smallwood has ably shown in his beautifully argued book, *Reconstructing Criticism* (2003). I use the term to cover the following: evaluation, explanation, self-expression and a way of organising the emotions. By evaluation, I mean how works are judged; by explanation, I mean how they are determined to be genuine, how they are interpreted, glossed and put into context; by self-expression, I mean criticism as a form of autobiography; and by organising the emotions I mean how critics from Aristotle to Freud have thought of literature as a way of channelling feeling and affect. These various descriptions, which are by no means exhaustive, fall under the headings of either rhetorical or grammatical criticism.

But criticism is also an account of conceptions of literature such as literature as inspiration, as imitation, as imagination, as impressionism, as a form of ideology and as a means of affirming identity. The last, which sees literature as a means of stepping into your own rather than someone else's shoes, underpins contemporary manifestations of criticism such as feminism, postcolonialism and queer theory. It is therefore sometimes hard to disentangle concepts of criticism from those of literature, so a history of one all too readily becomes a history of the other. But that may be no bad thing because it reminds us that there is no hard dividing line between literature and criticism. Many poets were also critics, for example, Sir Philip Sidney, Coleridge and T. S. Eliot. And then there are those, like Walter Bagehot and Cyril

Connolly, whose writings for their ease, elegance and beauty could easily be classed as literature. And if that sounds as if I am defining literature in those terms, I am, though only in part. We cannot define literature in the same way that we can define logarithms, but it would be a very odd definition indeed that took no account of a writer's style.

Nevertheless that's exactly what happened in the 1980s and 1990s.[2] If the aesthetic question arose at all it was dismissed as a form of mystification, a ruse 'through which the ruling bloc exercised its hegemony' (Easthope 1991: 70). And so theorists aimed to demystify literature; to show that, since it couldn't be defined, it didn't exist;[3] to show that it was no different to other forms of writing, for they could all be discussed in terms of 'institution, sign system, ideology, gender, identification and subject-position' (ibid.: 71). Why the 'ruling bloc' did not collapse as soon as people had this pointed out to them is a source of continuing wonder. Somehow, though, it struggled on. And today it is almost confident enough to manage without literature altogether. English language and media studies are elbowing it out of its space on the timetable and, in its present form, literature is due to disappear from the school curriculum by 2011.

If this does happen – and I am talking about literature as an object of study not as a mode of writing – then what will happen to criticism? Most likely it will become a part of cultural studies. This makes sense given that, throughout its history, criticism has touched on so many other issues. It draws on ideas of human nature and social organisation and contains elements of psychology, history, philosophy, sociology and politics, to name but a few. Writing a history of criticism, if one is not careful, morphs into a history of civilisation, which is yet another reason why it proves to be such an impossible undertaking.

So why bother to write something which can't be done? The short answer is that I didn't know it couldn't be done at the time. The longer answer lies in the theory wars of the 1980s. I was a student at Essex in the 1970s when French ideas first started to trickle into English departments and I attended a few of the famous sociology of literature conferences there. My overriding impression, apart from sheer bafflement, was that a good proportion of the proponents of the new theories, Althusserian Marxism, Lacanian psychoanalysis and so on, were fundamentalists for whom disagreement was tantamount to blasphemy.

Many years later I went to the School of Critical and Cultural Theory at Cardiff which boasted some of the biggest names in English theory, Catherine Belsey, Hawkes and Christopher Norris. This was an altogether more relaxed environment, although that impression may have been owing to the fact that I was much older and less easily intimidated. Yet even there I heard complaints that so and so wasn't 'a proper post-structuralist', an extraordinary remark given that one of the tenets of post-structuralism was that there was no such thing as a 'pure' identity.

It was these sorts of inconsistencies that intrigued me. And there were others. Why were all texts granted multiple meanings, apart from those of Leavis, who could only be read in one particular way? Time to look at him again. Not surprisingly, there were tensions in his work. And then came a shock. Some of Leavis's ideas bore a passing resemblance to those expounded by English theorists.[4] How could this be? The history of modern criticism was not, it seemed, one of ruptures and radical breaks, but returns and revisions.

There was something else too. Leavis's criticism contained a number of references to money and, more puzzlingly, some of his terms echoed the idioms of scientific management. This made me think about the relations between the discourse of criticism and that of the market. I was particularly struck by the coincidence that theory came to prominence in England almost at the same time as Mrs Thatcher came to power. She was elected in 1979, Belsey's *Critical Practice* was published in 1980, Peter Widdowson's edited collection *Re-Reading English* came out in 1982 and Chris Baldick's *The Social Mission of English Criticism 1848–1932* appeared one year later. To put it crudely, changes in the conceptions of the economy, heralded by the conservative government, seemed to require changes in the conceptions of literature and criticism.

Another coincidence. The rise of management theory shadows the rise of literary theory.[5] What's more, management theorists dip into their Derrida to find new ways of motivating staff. And their tone is not dissimilar to that of some of the theorists from whom they borrowed, that of one who has seen the light and is on a mission to convert the unbeliever. Why this connection? Because in the 1980s and 1990s criticism and management were committed to change, not just in their respective fields but in society as a whole. Managerialism was – and indeed still is – identified with modernisation and it spearheaded the transformation of the workplace.

This made me question the conventional idea, stretching from Aristophanes to Arnold, that criticism is a form of social critique. It might very well be, but its association with economic discourse also makes it complicit with the very order it seeks to subvert. The alliance between criticism and economics begins in ancient Greece where we find some of the same assumptions that govern the thinking about money, also applied to the thinking about poetry. The affinities between criticism, money and, later, market and management theories lead to a problem of evaluation. Broadly speaking, there is a potential conflict between literary works, which see humans as ends in themselves, and a critical commentary which, because of its economic element, sees them as means to an end. What we witness in a critic like Leavis is a perpetual tension between the humanistic impulse of criticism and the instrumentalist tendencies of the language of scientific management, but that tension disappears from contemporary criticism which shows little consciousness of its reliance on monetary and management metaphors.

The connection between the idioms and ideas of criticism, money, the market and management has had a further consequence: it has facilitated the incorporation of business practices into the universities. The attack on literature by theorists may have been inspired by a desire to democratise the term but it also had the effect of depleting one of the few rhetorical resources that could be deployed against the spread of market values. More than that, the demand that critics should be explicit about the theory of their practice chimed nicely with the requirement that academic life should be transparent. Most of all, though, theory has become a method of reading that insulates the student from the experience of literature. Nowhere is this more apparent than in Peter Barry's *Beginning Theory* (1995) which contains a list of what a post-structuralist, a postmodern, a post-colonialist critic etc. does. The student applies the theory and, hey presto, the text reflects it back to them. Theory is the answer to the problem of assessment. It is easier to measure a student's understanding of new historicism than it is to measure the much more difficult art of them finding the words to describe their response to a work.

This history is in part an attempt to explain how this situation has come about. By doing so it suggests that criticism is a class-based discourse. This once familiar claim related to *social* not *economic* divisions though of course the two are inseparable. The finger would be pointed at those like Leavis who maintained that literature could only be appreciated by a few. Well, that's probably true; but good and especially inspiring teaching ensures it can be enjoyed by many more. To 'appreciate' literature, whatever that may mean, requires a level of interest in the subject that most students simply do not have. And that's fine. They find their calling elsewhere.

In any case, it's not literary appreciation which is the real issue, but the divided nature of the educational system. I can't be the only one to notice that those loudest in their condemnation of elitism worked in the Russell group of universities, a body that perpetuates the very inequalities against which radical theorists protested – too much methinks. That these same theorists rarely mention class is also instructive. The concept of class which refers fundamentally to a particular form of economic organisation, capitalism, vanishes from criticism at the very moment that critical vocabulary acquires an economic cast. In short, the language of criticism is implicated in capitalist economics which compromises its ability to articulate notions of human autonomy found in literature. The famed 'linguistic turn' was not from a correspondence theory of language to one which stressed its constitutive role in perception and action – that was merely a return to the rhetorical tradition – but a turn away from the idea of class when, under various conservative governments, it was becoming an increasing reality.[6]

But this history is not just concerned with the relation between criticism and the language of economics. It also focuses, from the Renaissance onwards, on English criticism. And, to the inevitable charge of provincialism, I can only say that English criticism is an amalgam of largely European influences and to talk about it is therefore to pay homage to a much wider culture. Having said that, there are two advantages to concentrating on English criticism. The first is that it avoids the pattern in other histories[7] which is a summary of various schools of thought, with important individuals highlighted, and a bit of background thrown in for good measure. It allows for a more integrated approach, to show the complex relations between, for example, the vernacular, the market, Protestantism and reading, and to trace continuities such as a preference for the plain style over time. The second advantage is that, by examining a specifically English tradition, we are able to put the achievements of theory into proper perspective. More than that, the forgotten figures of English criticism, from John Bale to G. K. Chesterton, provide a rhetorical resource for combating the reductions of the human, whether in the ideology of the market or the latest literary theory.

So, then, this 'history' is, in part, a reaction to theory. It seeks to show continuities in the 'history' of criticism, particularly in respect of a rhetorical relation with economics. And it adopts a different approach to previous histories by the focus on England. Despite this 'history' taking its cue from theory, I am very aware that I do not cover the 'linguistic turn' and its consequences in detail. There are at least two reasons for this. First, there are already many introductions to theory on the market. Second, I am not so much interested in individual theories, feminism, postcolonialism etc. as in what these theories have in common with each other; in what 'theory' has in common with 'traditional criticism', and how it relates to wider developments, in particular, to developments in the economic organisation of society.

The longstanding connection between critical and financial discourse suggests that Marx was right: we cannot finally separate base and superstructure. Culture and commerce have been opposed since the late eighteenth century[8] but their relation is, in some sense, continuous and complementary. Samuel Johnson argued that 'if there are qualities in literature which are above price, these are also to be found in the world of manufacture and finance – in that huge pyramid of loyalty which is modern industry, and that vast network of fidelity which is modern commerce' (in Gordon 1946: 12). It would be hard to make such a claim today. The relationship between culture and commerce is not equal. In any conflict, the latter always triumphs. The day when commerce makes criticism practical and criticism makes commerce philosophical lies far in the future.

Pointing to the parallels between the two is part of a much greater endeavour to put criticism in context, something that critics pride themselves on doing with literature. And so I have tried to indicate some of the conditions in which criticism arose: the festival, the forum, the Church, the court, the market, the educational institution and so on. Having said that, I am mindful of Leavis's argument that context has its limits. We have the poem in front of us, but not the social, economic and political conditions in which it was written. How, then, can we explain the poem by what isn't there? All we have are bits and pieces, scraps we have to paste together and then pick apart as new fragments are found. The context, like the poem, is always provisional, a matter of ongoing construction, and so has no privileged power of interpretation. We shouldn't ignore context but neither should we prioritise it. The artist takes dross and turns it into precious metal. It's not the job of the critic to turn it into fool's gold.

The one topic this history does not deal with is perhaps the most important, the encounter with the individual work.[9] It is there we are paid the compliment, so rarely extended elsewhere in the culture, of being intelligent, feeling beings who are asked to be open to what is in front of us and to respond as fully and honestly as we can. It is rare, though, to find a genuine response in the acres of print that pass for contemporary criticism which, to be fair, has been distorted by the demands of the Research Assessment Exercise. At the same time, critics are professionals and, like others of their kind, do not get personally involved in their work. They are scholars who communicate in a shared language but one mostly devoid of what makes the subject fascinating, compelling and desirable. And they are scholars rather than critics because, in a democratic multicultural society, it seems to be an act of supreme hubris to expect others to defer to your judgement on what is and is not worth reading.

But a criticism that does not confront the problem of value, or else takes its own values as a given, plays into the hands of a political class that is forever refining the means without ever thinking about the ends. To be competitive in a global economy. Is that really our only goal? It's the one we hear about most. The one to which everything else is subordinated. Criticism should be an exploration of values as played out in literature, not a method of imposing them on it. What we need is a critical idiom that respects the claims of both personal response and scholarly requirement but the 'history' of criticism shows that we swing from one to the other.

The problem of value is one of many that I can only mention in passing. A history like this can only dwell on the outlines, point out an interesting feature or two before moving on. But if I have not managed to cover everything, which I most certainly haven't, I hope that I have at least shown that the concerns of criticism remain fairly constant over a long period of time.[10]

Yes they are phrased differently and may receive greater emphasis in one period than in another but they remain in view if not always in focus. Many students are under the impression that English begins and ends with theory. In a sense it does because there has never been a time without it, but the term acquires a special significance in the last quarter of the twentieth century and refers mainly to the impact French thinkers have had on our understanding of literature. I believe we are in danger of forgetting our past. This history is one version of it which, like all the others, disturbs and nourishes our present.

## Notes

1. See Day 2006.
2. One notable exception is Eagleton 1990.
3. This was to take a very narrow view of what was meant by 'definition'. There are, after all, different ways of defining things. A descriptive definition, which gives the general meaning of a term, is different to a stipulative definition, where the speaker imposes a definition on the term for the purpose of a particular discussion. Then there are intensional, extensional, enumerative and ostensive definitions, to say nothing of definition by genus-differentia. In short, we need to be careful about what mode of definition we are using when we say that literature cannot be defined. Perhaps it can't, but the attempt clarifies our understanding of the concept. And the fact that literature cannot be defined means that it cannot be measured and the fact that it cannot be measured means that it cannot be controlled. It slips through the ideological mesh of managerial England to give us a glimpse of how else our lives may be lived.
4. See Day 1996: x–xi.
5. In the early 1990s, books on management theory were outselling those on sex and cookery.
6. See Day 2001: 187–204.
7. I am thinking not just of Wimsatt and Brooks 1957 but also of Habib 2005.
8. The classic work on this matter is Williams 1958.
9. Let me try to be clear about this: there are two ways we encounter a literary work, as critics and individuals. Since we are both critics and individuals, and since the critical account of a work may be quite different from the value it has for us as individuals, the reading of literature may be said to induce a mild form of schizophrenia, a complaint that students routinely make though not necessarily in these terms.

    We can write a critical history of a work, its various versions, how it has been interpreted, the influences that shaped it and so on. That will tell us something about the history of criticism but not much. The history of the reception of *Adam Bede*, for example, doesn't tell us about the approach to nineteenth century poetry, nor does it consider prior forms of criticism and how they may relate to

Eliot's novel. A history of criticism has to be general which is at once its strength and weakness.

And if we can't base the history of criticism on the treatment of single works, how much less can we base it on individual responses. They are too diverse and far reaching. Yet they can, like the critical account of a work, make some contribution to our ongoing understanding of literature. The rise of book clubs testifies to a continuing interest in, perhaps even need for, encounters with imaginative writing. One group, run by Jane Davis from the Reader Centre at the University of Liverpool, caters for those who have been ill, suffered a bereavement, or are in reduced circumstances. Recent research suggests that reading helps such people alleviate pain or mental distress though only if they read classic texts, those 'which address existential concerns, not anodyne pep-ups'. By attending to the cry of another, 'we articulate our own cries, frame them, contain them, and feel less stranded.' But great literature 'doesn't just echo our own experience, recognise, vindicate and validate it, takes us to places we hadn't imagined but which, once seen, we never forget.' These observations obviously apply to only one kind of reading group and hence illustrate how difficult it is to make generalisations about the value of reading. But at the same time they do suggest that some kinds of literature have a greater value than others which brings us back to the central problem of criticism: the determination of literary worth, and that is going to be different with each work, hence the impossibility of a history of criticism that rests on individual encounters with works. See Blake Morrison, 'The Reading Cure' *Guardian Review* 05. 01. 08 pp. 4–6, p. 6

10. I am very aware, for example, that I do not do justice to the diversity of 'theory'. My answer to this charge, and I hope Derrideans appreciate the irony of my answering it in a footnote, is to reiterate the general point that I am drawing out what various theories have in common to show how they have grown out of the various traditions of criticism. But I do regret that lack of space does not allow me to consider this issue in more detail; a conversation with a friend, for example, revealed that his idea of theory, derived from the French Marxists Louis Althusser (1918–90) and Pierre Macherey (1938–) was completely different from mine – except that we both agreed that criticism, of whatever kind, involves some sort of theory about literature. I also regret that lack of space does not allow me to analyse the different contributions of Frank Kermode and Terry Eagleton who, in their different ways, have mediated 'theory' to a wider audience and who have kept faith with the idea of criticism as part of the enlightenment project.

CHAPTER

1

# GREEKS AND ROMANS

The words 'criticism' and 'crisis' both spring from the Greek *krisis*, a feminine noun. The phrase 'criticism in crisis' enjoyed considerable vogue in the late twentieth century, mainly because of the impact of French theory. Now we see that the two terms are linked etymologically as well as circumstantially. *Krisis* has various meanings including 'separation', 'selection' and 'judgement' and refers to decisions taken in court or poetic contests. The need to decide a course of action is central to the idea of 'crisis' defined in the *Oxford Dictionary* as 'a time of great danger, difficulty or confusion when problems must be solved or important decisions must be made'. In competitions there must be a winner, in court there must be a verdict. From the very beginning, the study of literature requires the reader to choose; this work or that? Until, that is, we reach the age of deconstruction where we encounter a new claim, namely, that reading always leads to a point where it becomes impossible to choose between two equally valid but mutually incompatible interpretations.

The Greeks did not have a word for 'literature'. In fact they didn't have a word for poetry until the fifth century BC. Song was the more usual term. But, in the fifth century, a new vocabulary appears. Singers were described as 'makers' or 'poets' and songs as 'made things' or 'poems' (Ford 2002: 93). In 507, an Athenian noble by the name of Cleisthenes (fl. c. 510 BC) invented democracy (Jones 1999: 27). Is it just coincidence that this form of government appears more or less at the same time as poetry? Cleisthenes' reform of the ancient constitution built on the earlier work of Solon (638–578[?] BC) who was a poet, philosopher and politician, so there is already a connection between verse and voting.

Previously, poets had validated their work by claiming it was inspired by the Muses, the Greek goddesses who presided over the arts and sciences.

10

Hesiod (fl. 700 BC) describes how they inspired him to write his*Theogeny* (c. 700 BC), which deals with the origin and genealogy of the gods. The poet's submission to the Muses is mirrored in the people's submission to monarchic rule. The overthrow of monarchy in the eighth century led to two competing forms of government, tyranny and oligarchy, before the eventual appearance of democracy, though not in the sense that we might recognise the term. The Greek democracies, and we are mainly talking about Athens, were not representative governments. They really were run by the people – the literal meaning of democracy – the only trouble being that the people meant free male citizens. Slaves, women and foreigners had no say in the running of the city state.[1]

The change from monarchy to democracy was accompanied by a change in the conception of poetic language. A key figure here is Democritus (460–370 BC), a proponent of Greek atomic theory. He argues that words are nothing more than 'conglomerates of atoms perceived by the ear' (Ford 2002: 166). Writing a poem involves combining elementary substances into a structure that produces a specific feeling in 'the auditor's psyche' (ibid.: 164). The recognition that poets shape the language complements the democratic idea that citizens shape their state. But there is a crucial difference, at this stage, between poetry and political rhetoric. Poetry is likened to craft activities like weaving and carpentry, a comparison that reflects the poet's new economic position as a 'seller of his goods in the late archaic city' (ibid.: 135). Politicians disdained these lowly conceptions of speech, basing their view of it on medicine, 'a resolutely rational and progressive contribution to human happiness' (ibid.: 162). It won't be long, though before Aristotle (384–322 BC), tutor of Alexander the Great (356–323 BC), discerns a medicinal property in art. He says tragedy purges us of pity and fear, but the main statement of his celebrated notion of catharsis occurs not in the*Poetics* but in the*Politics* where he defines it as 'a relief accompanied by pleasure' (Russell and Winterbottom 1972: 133).[2]

### The Great Dionysia and the Master–Disciple Relation

But what about criticism? Does it too have a political dimension at this early stage? To the extent that it involves the art of decision making, the answer has to be 'yes'. The *kritikoi*, or judges, in fifth- and fourth-century Athens, of the various competitions in epic, tragedy, comedy and the dithyramb, and especially the annual international festival, the Great or City Dionysia, were all drawn from the assembly.[3] The Great Dionysia was a state festival held every spring in honour of the god Dionysus who represented the instinctual life of humans. According to Simon Goldhill, it was 'an opportunity to explore the emotional and intellectual complexities of life [and] to reflect on the inherited stories of the city, as well as to join in civic celebration' (2004: 232). Three playwrights, chosen by 'the archon, a leading state bureaucrat' (ibid.: 220), competed for the prize, a wreath of ivy. Each one had to write three tragedies and a satyr play whose themes of drunkenness, sexuality and general merriment were intended as a light relief after the pitiless universe depicted in a work like Sophocles' (c. 495–c. 406 BC) *Oedipus Rex*. During the conflict between Athens and Sparta, known as the Peloponnesian War (431–404 BC),[4] each playwright's entry also included a comedy, which was performed on the same day as the other plays.

The purpose of the Great Dionysia was to uphold the values of the city, so judging which was the best tragedy or comedy was also a means of renewing the political ideals of the Athenian state, as were the rituals which opened the festivals and the plays themselves. There were four rituals. The first was a sacrifice, the second was the award of 'an honorific crown' to those who had benefited the city in some way, the third was a display of 'bars of silver bullion', tribute from those whom Athens had conquered, and the fourth was a parade of war orphans, who were educated at the state's expense, and who swore an oath of loyalty to fight for their city as their fathers had done (ibid.: 224–6). The plays themselves show what the state should be like by showing what it should not be like. In Goldhill's words, 'both tragedy and comedy show a world ripped apart, civic foundations shattered and the noble values of citizenship turned against themselves in violence, confusion, despair and horror' (ibid.: 227). But they could also uphold ideals and offer instruction. The tragedies of Aeschylus taught the audience to be honourable, patriotic and brave, while the chorus in Aristophanes' comedy *The Frogs* (405 BC) state that playwrights 'two privileges prize: / To amuse you, citizens, and to advise' (1964: 181).[5]

If the Great Dionysia is the public face of criticism in the classical world, then the master–disciple relation is its private one, though of course its effects reach out into the wider world. Plato was Socrates' student and Aristotle was Plato's. The nature of this relation, its focus on the meaning and purpose of life, are an important ingredient in the history of criticism. George Steiner describes it in almost religious terms. The master 'is truly a bearer and communicator of life-enhancing truths, a being inspired by vision and vocation of no ordinary sort . . . To teach seriously is to lay hands on what is most vital in a human being. In part this involves an act of violence.' 'A master invades, he breaks open, he can lay waste in order to cleanse and rebuild' (2003: 14 and 18). But teaching also involves persuasion. Indeed, it is its very 'pulse' (ibid.: 26). The master 'solicits attention, agreement, and, optimally, collaborative dissent' (ibid.: 26). This description resembles F. R. Leavis's characterisation of literary criticism, which begins with the question ' "This is so, is it not" and expects the answer ' "yes but", where the "but" stands for qualifications, reservations, corrections' (1972: 62).

Steiner also claims that there is an erotic element in teaching, not a conclusion he is likely to have made from watching Leavis at the lectern, famous though the great doctor was for wearing his shirt unbuttoned. The erotic, says Steiner, is part of the power relation between master and disciple, but it is also integral to 'trust, offer and acceptance' which are equally part of that relation and which have their 'roots' in the 'sexual' (Steiner 2003: 27). The relationship between master and disciple, which culminates in a remembering of being, goes through three stages based loosely on Hegel's theory of history: thesis, antithesis, synthesis. In the first stage, the master 'destroys' the disciple; in the second, the disciple betrays or usurps the master; while the third is characterised by 'the electric arc of shared faith and paternity' (ibid.: 132).

Socrates was the paradigmatic teacher. He sought not to impart but to awaken and wrote nothing down because he believed that only what we learn by heart will 'ripen and deploy within us' (ibid.: 32). Once committed to papyrus, thought ossifies. Plato preserves the spirit of Socrates in his dialogues but Aristotle writes in continuous prose. The words of the master, even at this early stage, are turning to stone, becoming heavy with authority. By the time we get to the twenty-first century the master–disciple relation has become a relic of history. Possibly its last manifestation, in English, was Leavis (1895–1978) who brought a visionary intensity to the study of literature, a feat that won him many followers, but far more foes. The characteristic concerns of the master–disciple relation, the way it summons, unsettles and remakes us, complements great literature's exploration of the deepest issues of human existence. The master, like the literary work, never leaves us with an answer but with a question, a conjecture, a tremor in the soul. That, though, is not, in general, how we see literature today. By and large it is an object of research, not an existential encounter. It seems to have lost the power to disturb, to throw us off balance. We mostly use it to illustrate, but rarely interrogate, ideologies such as feminism or post-colonialism.

It would be untrue to say that the near disappearance of the master–disciple relation is responsible for the present, parlous state of literary studies but it is a factor in their decline. Instead of the face-to-face relation, we have distance learning; instead of extending the student experience, we validate it; and, instead of the history of truth or the mystery of being, we teach skills. Current pedagogy emphasises only one side of education, training, and ignores its other meaning of drawing or leading out. Its insistence on measurable outcomes leaves no room for the uncertain but deeply enriching experience that comes from an encounter with a mind greater than one's own. Even if they were not required to be responsive to the needs of the economy, schools and universities, by their very nature, stifle curiosity, pervert the quest for meaning and standardise the operations of the intellect. They turn living processes into outcomes and units of assessment, individual qualities into quantifiable standards. All, of course, in aid of supporting student learning.

This is by no means a modern phenomenon. It starts with the sophists in the fifth century. They are the originators of textual criticism, but they are also the first to take money for teaching wisdom. How, asks Steiner,

> is it possible to pay for the transmission of wisdom, of knowledge, of ethical doctrine, or logical insights. What monetary equivalence or rate of exchange can be calculated as between human sagacity and the bestowal of truth on the one hand and an honorarium in cash on the other? (2003: 14)

Financial considerations are as much, if not more, of a factor in shaping the character of criticism than the master–disciple relation. The fact that students have to pay for their degree and the fact that universities need to acquire funding makes the ideals of self-realisation or the pursuit of truth seem purely fanciful. Even so, such aspirations continue to influence the teaching of literature despite the increasing emphasis on skills. The language of criticism is forged in the struggle between the economy and education, a struggle in which the former is usually, but never wholly, victorious.

There are at least two things that stand out from these introductory remarks. The first is that *krisis* was integrated into the life of the polis, unlike criticism in our own time, which is largely an academic activity. One example of this integration is the close relationship between the *kritikoi* and the audience at the dramatic festivals. They all came from the same city, they all saw the same plays at the same time and they were all familiar with the stories portrayed on stage. The judges' decision may not have pleased everyone but it was made on the basis of shared values that gave Athens its identity. Again this contrasts with the contemporary situation where the critic is viewed more as a specialist than as a representative member of the community. The second thing is that the master–disciple relation highlights the personal dimension of criticism. Although this relation was more concerned with philosophy, it serves as a model for criticism because literature too raises profound questions about the nature of existence and how best to live. The conflict inherent in the master–disciple relation may offer a partial explanation for the hostility that frequently marks critical discussion. Critics inspire followers who do intellectual battle with the followers of other critics. The best example of such a critic in recent times would be, once again, Leavis.

The rivalry between different schools of thought was as much a feature of classical Greece as it is of our own times. Plato (428–347 BC), who at one time apparently trained as a wrestler, took issue with the sophist claim that there were no absolute standards in either ethics or epistemology. Anyone acquainted with even the most basic tenets of postmodernism will be familiar with such assertions. The Greeks also had their own version of the dumbing-down debate. Plato complained of popular spectacle where the whole audience voted for the most entertaining act. He disapproved of the practice on the grounds that it encouraged performers to 'pander to the mob with inappropriate or incorrect pleasures' (Ford 2002: 284). But it wasn't just the performers who abandoned their standards, so too did some judges. They made decisions according to the desire of the audience rather than their own expertise. Judges, wrote Plato, should be the 'teachers' of the audience, not their 'pupils' (Russell and Winterbottom 1972: 83). The reputedly fashion-conscious Aristotle also rejected the idea of mass appeal as a criterion for artistic excellence, but only in the case of poetry. Even then he is prepared to admit that the general public may be a better judge than the individual, 'for some judge one part, others another, and collectively they judge the whole' (in Ford 2002: 288–9). However, he has a more tolerant view of music than Plato, recommending that different types be available to cater for different tastes: 'cathartic melodies give people a harmless enjoyment [and] the vulgar too should have relaxation' (Russell and Winterbottom 1972: 133).

## Archaic Greece: Song and the Beginning of 'Criticism'

We said above that before poetry there were songs. Indeed, Gregory Nagy suggests that the major metres of Greek poetry were all 'derived from the rhythm of songs' (1997: 5).[6] There were songs for different occasions: *threnos* for funerals; an *iambos* for ritualised abuse; and *dithyrambs* for the worship of Dionysus. There were also songs that dealt with the Greek mythology. Each part of Greece had its own tradition of song, and it wasn't until the development of the city states that any attempt was made to standardise them. Songs were an integral part of public occasions like games, festivals, victory celebrations and religious ceremonies and of private ones like the symposium, or drinking party. They were usually performed in one of two ways. The first, a monody, was performed by a single professional such as a rhapsode and the second was performed by a chorus who also danced. The chorus had a leader whose 'ultimate model' was Apollo himself and the divisions in the chorus reflected divisions in society (Nagy 1997: 52 and 57). Songs were judged on their appropriateness for the occasion. It would not do to sing a song of lamentation to Apollo, for that was more proper for Hades. Since each god had their own song it would be a violation to perform for one what belonged to another. The Greek word *prepei*, 'it is fitting', governs the use of song and is one of the sources for the 'decorum' which will be a key concept in the discourse of literary criticism.

Aside from honouring the gods, the basic aim of all song was to confer fame or glory on a person, often by comparing them to the heroes of old. 'All

Greek literature', writes Nagy, 'originates in *kleos*, the act of praising famous deeds' (1997: 9). And Greek literature begins, as indeed does Western literature, with Homer. We don't know if he actually existed but works attributed to him certainly do. And in the *Odyssey*, composed in the seventh or eighth century, we find what is probably the first example of criticism. After dinner, a bard named Phemius performs a song for the wife of Odysseus, Penelope, her son Telemachus and their guests. The guests are suitors vying for Penelope's hand. She has promised to make her choice when she has finished weaving a shroud but, because she never gives up hope that Odysseus will return, she unpicks at night what she stitched during the day and so, to the frustration of her suitors, she never gets any closer to deciding between them. Phemius sings of 'The Achaeans [Greeks] Journey Home from Troy'. It is too much for Penelope and she asks him to stop.

> Phemius!
> So many other songs you know to hold us spellbound,
> works of the gods and men that singers celebrate.
> Sing one of those [and] break off this song . . . that always rends the heart
>    inside . . . me
> the unforgettable grief, it wounds me most of all. (Homer 2003: 88)

Penelope's response underlines the point that poetry celebrates great deeds but it also introduces two new elements into our understanding of song. The first is that the singer should transport his audience beyond the workaday world and hold them, as Penelope says, 'spellbound'. The second appears to contradict the first because Phemius is describing an event that 'actually happened': the return of the Greek fleet. That's why Penelope asks him to stop. She cannot bear to be reminded of the Greeks coming home because Odysseus wasn't with them. We can reconcile these two different ways of looking at song as follows. Phemius' tale is neither fact nor fantasy but the selection, shaping and heightening of an aspect of history in order for the audience to feel it more keenly. This is similar to the Russian formalist idea that the purpose of literature is to defamiliarise our habitual perceptions the world.[7] The Greeks, however, did not believe that the singer was responsible for his song and therefore he could not be a conscious artist. As Telemachus, Odysseus' son, remarks, why deny

> our devoted bard the chance to entertain us
> any way the spirit stirs him on?
> Bards are not to blame – Zeus is to blame. (Homer 2003: 88–9)

Yet at the same time we have Penelope insisting that Phemius be held accountable for his performance. So we are left with a question. Does song come from mortals or immortals? Penelope thinks it's the former, Telemachus the latter.

His reaction to her outburst draws attention to two more characteristics of criticism. The first is that it is a function of power and the second that it is a matter of fashion. Penelope may object to Phemius' song but it is Telemachus' opinion which prevails because, as a male and Odysseus' son, he is a representative of patriarchal society. He dismisses his mother, telling her to

> go back to your quarters. Tend to your own tasks,
> the distaff and the loom . . . As for giving orders,
> men will see to that, but I most of all:
> I hold the reins of power in this house. (Homer 2003: 89)

He instructs her in what he regards as the proper response to the song, namely, that it should inspire courage. 'Harden your heart', he tells her, 'Odysseus was scarcely the only one . . . / whose journey was blotted out at Troy. Others, so many others, died there too' (ibid.: 89). The purpose of song is to instil moral fibre, not to encourage emotional indulgence. But such a high-minded view of the bard's role is somewhat undermined by the observation that 'It's always the latest song, the one that echoes last / in the listeners' ears, that people praise the most' (ibid.: 89). The implication being that song is of the moment, that it has no lasting effect and that it is therefore a poor means of inculcating ethics.

But there is one further feature of this episode which deserves mention and that is its Oedipal nature. We have a son who insists on his father's death, who dismisses all his mother's suitors, 'You must leave my palace!' (ibid.: 89) and who assumes the role of her husband. It is curious that one of the first scenes of 'literary criticism' contains elements of the Oedipus complex. And they are present in Plato too. His objection to poetry is partly based on the myth of Kronos who, prompted by his mother, castrated and then killed his father. This is not a story, Socrates observes dryly, that should be told to the young men, 'even if it [were] true', for fear it may encourage them to do the same (Russell and Winterbottom 1972: 52). These two instances of the Oedipal drama, which Sophocles had made famous in his trilogy known as the Theban plays, occur in a patriarchal culture whose influence shapes the master–disciple relation. The struggle between the teacher and pupil parallels that between father and son. Is there any significance in all of this? We can only speculate. It is one of the joys of intellectual life, though an increasingly rare one in the managed environment of the modern university.

### Songs and Symposia

Andrew Ford[8] has argued that the symposium is important in the history of criticism 'because, as songs were exchanged over wine, guests were expected to react to them, sometimes in responding songs of their own' (2002: 25). We have seen, in the episode from the *Odyssey* how the hosts, if not the guests, might react to a song. Telemachus' claim, that it should make Penelope brave, is consistent with the belief that the purpose of song is 'to offer some advice or idea that was useful for life' (ibid.: 26). The symposium, which most likely reached its mature form in fifth- and fourth-century Athens,[9] originates from two kinds of gathering in the ancient world. The first was 'a feast of merit, designed to foster solidarity among a warrior class' and the second was 'a kind of male fellowship . . . dedicated at once to pleasure and the conspicuous display of excellence' (ibid.: 27). It was not the custom, in the former, for the guests to sing, as that could be seen as a sign of effeminacy. The emphasis was, therefore, on conversation, which was not just a pleasant way to pass the time: it was also a way of discovering the true nature of one's fellow guests. Hesiod proclaimed that it enabled you 'to distinguish the brave from the base' (in ibid.: 28–9). The relevance of the warrior feast to the history of criticism is probably twofold. First, it bequeathed the idea that words had to be carefully weighed before deciding on their meaning and, second, that the responsibility for such weighing lay within the confines of a small but powerful group.

The development of the city states and, in particular the growth of democracy, diminishes the influence of the warrior class. The symposium, involving anything between seven and thirty males, was still designed to reinforce the authority of the elite and to demonstrate their achievements, but these could now include the arts of peace as well as those of war. After the tables had been cleared the guests would wash, anoint themselves, don garlands and sing a paean, a hymn of thanksgiving, to show their piety. They would then choose a symposiarch, or master of ceremonies, and agree on how much wine would be drunk and its strength. Songs lay at the heart of the evening: there were old favourites and new ones improvised for the occasion. There were also toasts in verse and games. The symposium was not just a form of entertainment. It was also a training for civic life. Its commitment to order, measure and harmony helped disseminate those qualities throughout the state. More specifically, both singing and 'graceful speaking' could be seen either as 'a playful imitation of proffering one's views publicly' or as 'a kind of rehearsal for graceful concourse with citizens in the *agora*', an open space used for markets and assemblies (Ford 2002: 40).

What contribution did the symposium make to the development of criticism? At one level, it shows that discussion of song was a prerogative of the elite and that it had a role to play in preparing them for public life. At another level, it establishes the idea that song and conversation are socially unifying activities, an argument that will often be used as a justification for the study of literature. At still another level, it promotes the idea that singing and talking are essential for the development of one's humanity, and again this will be offered as a reason for reading literature. The critical commonplace that a work has different layers of meaning may also be traced to the symposium's pronounced concern with the relation between the inner and the outer person. This primarily moral matter is a reminder that the symposium was a forum 'for ethical discussion and debating wisdom' (ibid.: 41), a role which literature will inherit. And yet this development is partly countered by the transformation of some of the symposium's ethical terms into technical ones. Take the example of *metron*. In the context of the symposium, it referred to the measuring out of wine, while the phrase *huper metron* meant drinking more than the stipulated amount. The 'man of "due measure" was he who followed the *metron*' (ibid.: 43). The term had a moral dimension implying moderation in all things. But, by the fifth century, it has evolved into the word 'metre' used solely in relation to the number of syllables in a line of verse. Indeed, metre becomes poetry's defining feature. 'I hold all poetry to be speech with metre' (Russell and Winterbottom 1972: 7) writes the sophist Gorgias (483–375 BC). Above all, the symposium bequeaths to criticism its characteristic criteria of harmony, decorum and proportion, terms which lend themselves to both a qualitative and a quantitative analysis.

The concern with due measure was part of the elaborate ritual of the symposium. This has been interpreted as a form of compensation by a warrior class whose power was on the wane (Ford 2002: 32). No longer able to display its prowess so easily in battle, it sought other means to maintain its standing. Unlikely as it may seem, there is a parallel of sorts with what happened to criticism in Britain in the late twentieth century. Briefly, the election of Margaret Thatcher in 1979 began the process of spreading market values through all aspects of social life. English, like other humanities subjects, was seen to have little to contribute to the economy and so its status, which had never been high at the best of times, suffered a further drop. High theory was an attempt to restore its fortunes, to show that criticism, at any rate, could be rigorous and innovative and was therefore deserving of respect. Its success though, as I shall argue later, was largely dependent on the way it underpinned the philosophy of the free market and the new style of management which accompanied it.

So far we have been talking about song. In very general terms, it was used to praise individuals who had excelled in sport or battle. It was also used to extol the virtues of rulers of which the *enkomia* of Pindar (522–443 BC) are probably the best example. The fact that song was performed on specific

occasions gave it an ephemeral quality which may have been responsible for
the desire of tyrants to have their achievements recorded in a more durable
form. But the poet Simonides (556–469 BC) argued that no physical object,
not even stone, could 'broadcast fame so widely or so long as performance'
(Ford 2002: 99). A monument is a fixed thing and will suffer natural decay,
even if it escapes human destruction. But an 'ever-flowing' oral tradition
'makes the names of the dead sound again in time' (ibid.: 109). It is partly
thanks to Simonides that we remember the three hundred Spartans who, for
three days held off the entire Persian army at the pass of Thermopylae in 480
BC. His lines 'Go tell the Spartans, stranger passing-by / That here, in obedience to their laws, we lie' is a terse and powerful tribute to the bravery of the
men who perished on that spot. Song may be a response to an occasion but
it was also a potentially permanent record of it. Here, perhaps, is the one
source of our idea that literature transcends the period in which it was
written.

   If song was largely of the moment, epic was for all time. Unlike Pindar's
*epinikia* or victory odes, which celebrated an individual in the here and now,
the *Iliad* and the *Odyssey* recounted the achievements of heroes in the distant
past. But the singer and philosopher Xenophanes (570–480 BC) criticised
Homer for depicting the gods in a bad light. 'Homer and Hesiod have attributed to the gods every kind of behaviour that among men is the object of
reproach: stealing, adultery and cheating each other' (in Ford 2002: 47).
Xenophanes' criticism was based on his conception of divinity as a single
entity. He had no time for stories about the inhabitants of Mount Olympus,
writing that 'there is one god . . . who effortlessly sways all things with his
mind' (in ibid.: 50). He therefore recommended that songs which dealt with
the stories of the so-called immortals should be banned, as should those
which told of war, for they were a threat to peace:

> applaud him . . . who does not summon up battles of Titans, Giants
> or Centaurs – fabrications of men of old
> or violent civil strife; in such things there is no profit. (in ibid.: 55)

Xenophanes' remarks revolve around how best to organise a symposium.[10]
He gave advice concerning the rituals of purification, the order in which
guests should speak, and how much they should drink. He even recommended what deportment they should adopt on walking home: 'each must
drink only so much as to get back home without a servant guiding the way,
except if he be very old' (in ibid.: 55). Chiefly, though, he stipulated what
kinds of songs ought to be performed. They should be purged of fanciful
imagery and promote social harmony. The idea that the language should be
cleansed and that literature should heal social divisions is a constant in the

history of criticism and receives one of its most forceful expressions in England, after the Civil War.

## The Birth of Allegory

If Xenophanes wanted to condemn Homer because of his characterisation of the gods and the bellicose nature of the *Iliad* there were others who were prepared to defend his work. The sixth-century poet, Theagenes of Rhegium, is credited with the oldest known Greek treatise on allegory.[11] Unfortunately none of his work survives but he is known to have argued that the Battle of the Gods in Homer's epic could be interpreted partly as a conflict between the forces of nature and partly as warring passions in the human breast. This is one of the earliest examples of allegory which, in ancient Greek, meant 'saying other'. The appearance of allegory signals a shift from how songs are evaluated to how they are interpreted, though this does not become the dominant approach to writing until the rise of Christian commentary. The rhapsodes, who traditionally performed Homer's work, claimed to have a special knowledge of it based on the fact that it was handed down from father to son. They also embellished their performances with accounts of Homer's life. But, in the sixth century, their expertise was challenged as Homer's epics were taught in schools, discussed at dinner parties and analysed by sophists of the fifth century who made a living teaching, by example and imitation, 'modes of discourse useful in civil life or dialectical discussion' (Kennedy 1997c: 82). The sophists may be compared to the post-structuralists in that they were sceptical about the possibility of knowledge, believed that all values were relative and celebrated 'the practical utility of speech' (ibid.). Their stance was famously summed up by Protagoras (490–420 BC) who claimed that 'Man is the measure of all things' and who held that there were two opposed arguments on every issue (ibid.: 82). The man credited with the introduction of rhetoric in Greece, Gorgias, argued that 'the alliance of speech and persuasion shapes the mind as it wishes' (Russell and Winterbottom 1972: 7). If speech operates at the level of opinion, not knowledge, then there can be no definitive interpretation of a work. Different people will find different meanings in Homer, none of which is final. This is an example of what J. Tate (1934) calls 'artificial allegory', a form of reading limited neither by the author's intention nor by the signs or symbols of the work itself. The nearest parallel in contemporary criticism would be that species of deconstruction which stresses the endless play of signifiers.

Allegory makes an appearance in Book 19 of the *Odyssey*. Penelope has a dream of twenty geese but an eagle swoops down from the sky and kills them all. She asks Odysseus, whom she doesn't recognise because he is in disguise, what it means. He tells her that her husband will return and kill all her suitors. It wasn't only dreams that required interpretation, so too did omens and oracles. Again, in the *Odyssey*, two eagles attack a crowd. One character sees this as an omen of the imminent return of Odysseus, bringing 'bloody death for all these suitors here' while another scoffs at this suggestion, claiming that 'not all' bird flights 'are fraught with meaning' (Homer 2003: 98–9). Croesus of Lydia (595–546 BC), who was renowned for his great wealth, consulted the Delphic oracle about his plan to attack the Persians. He was told that a great kingdom would fall. He interpreted this to mean the kingdom of his enemies but in fact it was his own. As George A. Kennedy notes, 'oracular responses were often couched ambiguously so as to be self-validating' (1997c: 79). Such formulations exploited the fact that the same word could have different meanings. *Logos*, for example, could mean ' "word", "speech", "story", "narrative", "mention", "reputation", "conversation", "cause", "argument", "pretext", "due measure", "proportion", "principle", "the faculty of reason" ' and, most tellingly, 'it could mean both truth and lie' (ibid.: 80). The gods use omens and oracles to convey information to humans. As these are indirect forms of communication they need to be interpreted. Allegory arises first of all as a means of understanding messages from the spiritual world.

But allegory is not used solely to understand the mysterious pronouncements of divinity. It is also, as we have seen, a way of explaining the meaning of a song, or an episode in an epic. Religion and song both require allegory. The singer, like the prophet, is inspired to utter words of great import, words that must be probed and plumbed to discover their true significance. The relation between the singer and the prophet is complex. Nagy distinguishes between: the *mantis*, the person who is inspired; the prophet, who 'communicates the message of the *mantis* in a poetic medium; and the *theoros*, the person 'who is officially delegated by the city state to communicate the message of the mantis/prophet to the polis, or, in the case of athletics, the sacred message of victory' (Nagy 1997: 29). We are used to thinking of the prophet as an inspired visionary, so it's a surprise to learn that is not how he was regarded in ancient Greece. There, he was merely a messenger for those who had been divinely stirred. The point to stress, however, is that at the heart of these distinctions is a view of criticism as translation; the prophet translates the moment of inspiration, then the *theoros* translates the prophet's words into a form suitable for all.

We get our word 'theory' from *theoros*, literally, he who sees a vision (ibid.: 28). Nagy explains that, in the context of 'Archaic Greek etymological legacy . . . theory must recapture exactly what was intended by the poetry [or], to put it another way, theory must recapture the very essence of the communication between the poet and the poet's community' (ibid.: 29). How different to the conception of theory in the 1980s and 1990s which derided the notion of authorial intention and which cultivated difficulty as a barrier to understanding. At the same time, we shouldn't forget that the idea of the poet's intention was itself not enough to explain the meaning of a work, even in archaic Greece. Allegory was a recognition that, say, the *Iliad* meant more than Homer could know because he didn't compose it – the Muses did.

But why exactly is there a need for allegory in the sixth century? Why do we begin to see a shift from evaluation to interpretation? One suggestion is that allegory was necessary to understand the cryptic language of politics. In a time of internal conflicts and the constant threat of invasion, direct speech could be very dangerous. The poet Stesichorus (640–555 BC), who apparently went blind for being rude about Helen of Troy, and then had his sight restored when he was nice about her, used animal fables to predict that Phalaris (570–549 BC) of Acragas in Sicily would become a tyrant (Ford 2002: 76–8). And Plato, when he was tutoring Dionysius II (367–357 BC), said that he conveyed his views about 'just governing "not by expressing them straight out – which was not safe – but through riddles" ' (in ibid.: 77). Another suggestion for the interest in allegory is that it was a way of maintaining the status of at least a section of the elite in a period of change. The growth of democracy, particularly in fifth-century Athens, prompted the need for cultural distinctions now that political ones seemed to be disappearing. The commentator on the Derveni papyrus[12] 'repeatedly sets his allegorical interpretation against the ways of "the many", those "who do not understand"' (in ibid.: 75). His desire to reserve truth for a select few also informs the writings of Heraclitus (535–475 BC), the first western philosopher to give a metaphysical foundation to human existence and ethics. His work necessitated the creation of a new terminology to describe the world. It was designed to be understood by the few rather than the many, earning Heraclitus nicknames like 'the riddler', 'the obscure' and 'the dark'.

The shift from 'a predominantly oral to a predominantly written basis of intellectual life', which occurs in Greece from 'the mid-fifth to the mid-fourth century' (Kennedy 1997c: 87), helps to reinforce the exclusive nature of allegorical interpretation because 'only one or two people in twenty could read and write with ease' (Ford 2002: 152–3). The fact that allegorists distanced themselves from the majority and that allegory was not a fully developed art also kept it at the margins of Greek poetics. The dominant form of interpretation was rhetorical; a poet had a thought which he expressed in words (ibid.: 85). Socrates distrusted both writing and allegory. He argued that writing would destroy memory and undermine dialogue, whose open-ended form was more likely to lead to truth than a script 'which cannot answer back' (Kennedy 1997c: 88). He objected to allegory on two grounds: first, because there is no way of knowing if it yields the correct interpretation; and second, because it is 'a source of amusement and show of brilliance rather than part of a philosophical search for ethical truth' (Ford 2002: 86). Allegory contributes to literary criticism the idea that a work has different layers of meaning and this can be useful in preserving writing from earlier periods. To see the characters in the *Iliad* in terms of the air, the moon and the sun was a way of making it relevant to current ideas about nature (Kennedy 1997c: 85–6). But allegory also restricts criticism to an elite.

## The Secularisation of Song

The spread of writing changes the nature of criticism. Among other things it encouraged 're-reading with knowledge of the text as a whole, allowed a greater accuracy of citation and helped ensure a greater integrity of preservation of the original' (Kennedy 1997c: 88). It is also one of the factors responsible for a change in the conception of song. Once it is written down, song 'is no longer tied to any occasion of performance' (Ford 2002: 114). It can now be read as well as heard; it becomes a verbal artefact to be appreciated as well a lyric to please the ear. This development was accompanied by another, the growing secularisation of song. By the end of the fifth century, the connection between choral performance and the cult of various deities had been considerably weakened. The chorus was now far more likely to be found in the amphitheatre than in the temple and had, in any case, long been diverted from cults to praising the great (Nagy 1997: 20). One reason for this change was the growth of Panhellenism. The diversity of religious customs was not a good basis for the expression of a common identity for that merely emphasised the difference between the city states. What was needed was a symbol of unity, and there were a number of these ranging from the Olympic Games to the epics of Homer (ibid.: 16, 22 and 41–2). As part of the growing interest in the development of Greek culture, the 'father of history', Herodotus (484–425 BC), made a study of song traditions. He was one of a number who undertook this investigation, but the conclusions were all broadly similar: namely, that different types of song represented different stages of civilisation; that they provided information about history and culture; and that they contained religious beliefs that 'a small group of men who were good with language' imposed on the rest (Ford 2002: 144–5 and 146). Herodotus' particular contribution was to treat songs and indeed epics as 'texts, valuable for their antiquity but to be critically and closely related to other traditions and texts' (ibid.: 152). Only by comparing them could we improve our understanding of the past.

The process of secularisation meant that inspiration was no longer assumed to be the source of the poet's song. And it was at this point, in the fifth century, that we find those who composed songs called 'makers' or 'poets' (*poietai*) and clearly distinguished from 'singers' (*aoidoi*) who performed them; instead of 'singing', (*aeidein*), they are said to be engaged in 'making' or 'poetry' (*poeiesis*); finally what they produce may be called a *poiema* or 'made thing'. (Ford 2002: 131)

To put this another way, the rise of poetry is related to the decline of religion, or at least a certain view of it. The singer relies on divine prompting, the poet on himself. A new vocabulary appears that reflects this change. There is less talk of the Muses and more of making. The poet uses words like the carpenter uses wood or the weaver uses cloth, as raw material to be shaped into a finished product.

This new vocabulary also points to the changed position of the singer, or poet as we must now call him. The growing importance of money transformed the poet's relation to his audience. Pindar describes the traditional payment for a song in terms of 'the beauty and pleasure of reciprocity between the poet and the subject of his praise' but now he was to receive a wage and nothing more (Nagy 1997: 20). Nagy argues that 'the system of reciprocity within the community at large [was] breaking down . . . [poetry was] in danger of shifting from an expression of the community to an expression of the individual' (ibid.: 20). But what the community lost, Panhellenism gained. The poet's contribution to this cause was a vision of Greek history. Travelling from place to place, he was able to select what different myths had in common. In the process the word 'myth' comes to be associated with what is 'divergent', while the word 'truth' comes to be associated with what is 'convergent' (ibid.: 30). The word 'truth' in this context does not mean knowledge of facts so much as a particular kind of remembrance, one that involves the forgetting of whatever detracts from an idealised view of the progress of Greek civilisation (ibid.: 30-1). The poet shows himself a critic in selecting material to form a coherent narrative of tradition and in canonising certain tales while discarding others.

None of these developments quite eradicate the idea that a poem is the product of inspiration. In fact, Penelope Murray (1981) suggests that the opposition between inspiration and making is the invention of Plato, and Ford adds that the very concept of inspiration 'is more easily understood as arising concomitantly with this new vocabulary: it accounted for aspects of poetry that could not be comprehended under the artisanal conception of poetic making' (Ford 2002: 136). Indeed, those who held their art in high regard refused to use the new terminology which was restricted to prose and comic verse. The sole exception was Euripides (485–406 BC) who declared that 'love can teach anyone to be a poet, even the one who has never cultivated the Muses' (in ibid.: 137). If inspiration came from the gods then what the poet said must be true. But as a maker the poet produces his own truth, in the sense of remembering what stories have in common and forgetting where they differ. Ford, however, disagrees. He argues that verbal skill is now prized over other qualities such as 'wisdom, truthfulness or tact' (ibid.: 132). Technique triumphs over truth. What's more, the idea that a poem is man-made proves favourable to the development of criticism. As Ford puts it, 'expertise in poetry did not require knowing how to sing or compose, it could focus on breaking down a poem as a verbal construct' showing how it pro-duced its effect (ibid.: 132).

If we date the beginning of 'literature' to the appearance of the word 'poetry' then it begins, as most stories do, with a fall. The singer has sunk to the level of an artisan. He works for wages not for honour (Nagy 1997: 19–20). The growth of the theatre's popularity meant that not only the various genres of lyric poetry fell into disuse but so too did other genres such as hymns, laments and dithyrambs (ibid.: 66). Poets, Plato sighed, didn't even respect those genres that were left, unlike in the good old days following the Persian Wars (c. 499–448 BC).[13] And whereas in former times it was usual for educated Greeks to play the lyre, that task has now fallen to professional musicians who promote new forms, which is another factor in the disap-pearance 'of the media of song as represented by lyric poetry proper' (Nagy 1997: 71). Nor were these traditions preserved in schools where dialogue appeared to be supplanting poetry (ibid.: 75).[14] And it wasn't only the cur-riculum that was crumbling, so also were school buildings, as Herodotus records (1998: 361). But the picture is not entirely gloomy. There are some positive views of poetry. A knowledge of Homer is a mark of sophistication. It also provides opportunities for diversion and the display of wit at the sym-posia (Ford 2002: 199–200). This is poetry as private pleasure rather than public praise and, as such, is open to accusations of trivialisation. These could be countered by pointing out that poetry could be a source of information, about military strategy for example, and that it can shape a person's moral character (ibid.: 198 and 203).

## Classical Athens c. 507–400 BC

### Aristophanes' The Frogs

The assumption that poetry can produce an ethical effect underlies Aristophanes' *The Frogs* (405 BC). The play was performed in the last years of the Peloponnesian War. The Spartans were encamped a few miles outside Athens. The city could be attacked at any moment and needed good advice which its politicians had singularly failed to provide. Why not, suggests Aristophanes (c. 448–385 BC), ask one of our great poets for his opinion? And so Dionysus is dispatched to the underworld where he must decide which playwright is best qualified to help the city. The gravity of the situation and the need to choose illustrates the two meanings of *krisis* mentioned earlier, danger and judgement. Dionysus' choice is between Aeschylus (525–456 BC), often regarded as the founder of tragedy, or Euripides who focused on the inner lives of his characters. Aeschylus' outlook is religious, Euripides' is secular. Aeschylus leans to an aristocratic form of government, Euripides to a democratic one. Aeschylus provides a template for heroes, Euripides for citizens. Each poet criticises the other. Aeschylus says that Euripides uses tragic verse for 'a barn door rooster' while Euripides accuses his rival of 'craggy phrases' whose meaning is 'hard to gather' (Russell and Winterbottom 1972: 18).

Despite their differences both poets believe they have a duty to educate. Aeschylus, for instance, places himself in a tradition from Orpheus to Homer. As well as 'show[ing] us his mystical rites', Orpheus 'barred foods taken by slaughter; Musaeus 'taught cures of disease and oracular lore; and from Hesiod we have learned when to reap, when to plough', while Homer has given us valuable lessons in 'battle order', 'deeds that excel' and 'the way to bear arms' (Russell and Winterbottom 1972: 22). Aeschylus sees himself as carrying on the work of Homer; shaping himself 'to the mould of his mind', he too has 'bodied forth many patterns of greatness' which he hopes will inspire his 'fellow Athenians' to heroic deeds (ibid.: 22). He reprimands Euripides for not showing enough respect to royalty in his plays, for satirising the heroes of mythology and for introducing low themes into tragedy whose effect is to emasculate youth and encourage them to challenge their elders. Euripides defends himself by saying that he educated the audience in the art of reason, acquainted them with 'new progressive ways of keeping house' and generally improved their 'civic sense' and 'nature' (ibid.: 20–1).

The chorus is impressed by the to and fro of the discussion.

Is there a judge could make a decision
when, of the two, one throws his weight in,
yet his opponent, ably wheeling, scores a fine, sharp counter blow? (ibid.: 25)

Aeschylus proposes that his and Euripides' verse be put on a weighing machine. 'Only the scales can put our poetry to the test; / the weight of our phrases will try us and find us out' (ibid.: 35). Dionysus reluctantly agrees, comparing the process to finding which of two cheeses is the heavier. Each poet quotes several lines from his work and each time Aeschylus' words outweigh those of Euripides. Despite his clear victory, Dionysus says he 'won't decide between them. One I consider clever – and one delights me' (ibid.: 36). But Pluto, the god of the underworld, reminds him of his mission and so choose he must. Dionysus says that he will take the one who gives him the soundest advice on how Athens can be saved. But, even after hearing their advice, he is still in 'torment of indecision', for 'one has given a clever, one a lucid answer' (ibid.: 37). In the end, Dionysus decides to return with Aeschylus but not because of anything the poet actually says. Instead he chooses 'the one my soul is pleased to choose' (ibid.: 38). David Barrett's translates these lines, for the Penguin edition of the play, as 'Well, in my heart of hearts I have known all the time. No question about it' (Aristophanes 1964: 210).

I have dwelt at length on this episode from *The Frogs* because of what it tells us about criticism. The fact that a *play* deals with the problems of making a literary judgement is itself a reminder of the complementary relationship between criticism and creation. And yet the episode with the scales – a frequent image in the classical world when comparing the merits of different poets – shows that there is an enumerative element in criticism's conception of literature. It derives from measure being integral to poetry in the form of metre. The difference between one metre and another, in terms of how many syllables each involves, serves not merely as a point of comparison between two types of verse but as a reason for preferring one over the other. To put it crudely, there's an aspect of criticism that involves counting and this forms the basis of its later alliance with the idiom of finance. Not just with finance, in fact, but with theories of management too because both disciplines deal, in varying degrees, with the production of surplus – criticism in the form of meaning and management in the form of profit. Both these relationships, which are characterised by conflict as much as convergence, become evident in the twentieth century. The connection between criticism and finance, though, starts to crystallise in the eighteenth century. All the same, we shouldn't forget that, even in Aristophanes' time, monetary considerations have already altered the status of the poet and his relationship with his community.

Measurement, then does play a part in judgement. But so too do other factors, notably the idea that writers are vital to a society's wellbeing. Aeschylus is charged with no less a task than securing Athens' safety. In times of crisis, citizens turn not to their politicians, but to their playwrights. Different sorts of literature are used for different purposes and this a dramatic – in all senses of the word – example of that principle. Literature is functional. It has a variety of roles to play in the life of the polity and is therefore integral to civil life. It is valued according to the purpose it serves. We see this in the competition between Aeschylus and Euripides. The one provides models of heroes, the other of citizens. With the Spartans massing outside the city walls it is the model of the hero that is most relevant. And that is why Dionysus chooses Aeschylus. But he also resists having to make a decision. He appreciates the merits of both playwrights – 'one I consider clever and one delights me' (Russell and Winterbottom 1972: 36) – and so is torn between them. Dionysus' dilemma suggests that works can be valued beyond any function they happen to fulfil, but there are no criteria for this form of appreciation, except perhaps one: whatever pleases the soul (ibid.: 38). And this suggests that there are no real grounds for judging one work to be better than another: it is psychology which decrees whether we prefer this to that. Who and what we are determines our decisions. In the end, *The Frogs* presents us with contradictory ideas about criticism for, on the one hand, it claims there are clear criteria for judging between one writer and another while, on the other, it shows there are none.

### Plato on Poetry

In *The Frogs* Aristophanes comes close to portraying Pluto as a pub landlord: 'One for the road, gentleman, won't you come in?' (Aristophanes 1964: 210). This would not have pleased Plato who believed that poets were far too casual in their depiction of the deities. It was quite wrong, he argued, to show them as changing shape, tricking us, or causing us trouble. Nor, finally, should they appear to be fond of laughter for that too lessens our respect for them. We have heard this argument before. Xenophanes complained that Homer attributed human traits to the gods. Theagenes countered by claiming that Homer needed to be interpreted allegorically. But Plato rejects this move on the grounds that the young especially 'can't distinguish the allegorical from the non-allegorical' (Russell and Winterbottom 1972: 53). If poetry must exist, Plato seems to say, then it should be of some benefit to the community. In that respect he is in agreement with Aristophanes. But they differ on how it achieves its effect. Aristophanes believes poetry works by offering advice while Plato believes that it works by offering models for imitation.

Plato's discusses poetry in *The Republic* (360 BC), whose main subject is whether it is best to be just or unjust, particularly as the latter seem to profit more than the former. In Book 3, Plato's exploration of the effects of poetry takes the form of a dialogue between Socrates and Adimantus. He starts by discussing stories of the gods and suggests that, in the ideal city, or 'republic', children should only hear the good fables that poets compose and not the bad. They should not be exposed to tales of 'how gods war, plot and fight' (Russell and Winterbottom 1972: 52), because this will encourage them to behave in the same manner. They must learn instead that citizens should love one another and that 'readiness to hate . . . is the greatest scandal' (ibid.: 52). Out, therefore, go stories like that of Hephaestus, the god of fire and son of Zeus and Hera, who was thrown off Mount Olympus for siding with his mother against his father in a quarrel. The purpose of stories is to 'implant virtue' and one such is 'bravery' (ibid.: 53 and 58). Poets should not portray Hades as a frightful place for this will make soldiers fear death. Any poetry that weakens the warrior's nerve will be banned. That's why Plato proposes deleting the following from the *Odyssey*: 'Rather would I be bound to the soil, a thrall to another, / to a poor man at that, with no land to his portion, than be king of all the nations of the dead' (in ibid.: 58).[15] Similarly, the great men should not be shown indulging in 'lamentations and expressions of pity' (ibid.: 58) as this will sanction like behaviour in the young. If a hero weeps at the death of a son, a brother or friend, then young men will not only follow his example but also 'mourn freely, without shame or restraint, at small accidents' (ibid.: 59).

There are different kinds of poetry and, in naming them, Plato performs one of the least interesting tasks of any history of criticism, the taxonomy of literary genres. First is narrative. Here the poet tells a story in his own voice. Second is imitation, that is tragedy and comedy. Here the poet 'pretend[s] that someone else is speaking' (Russell and Winterbottom 1972: 61). Third is epic, which is a mixture of narrative and imitation. Plato then ponders which form would be most beneficial to the wellbeing of the republic. There are two problems. The first is that, in the ideal city, individuals are trained to perform one particular function. If they are moved to imitate others, who perform different functions, then their expertise will evaporate. The second problem, which Plato deals with in Book 10 of *The Republic*, is that the poet, for reasons which will become clear shortly, cannot even imitate one thing well. He cannot, for instance, copy courage correctly. Consequently, it is impossible for anyone to improve themselves by listening to poetry, particularly drama. But Plato's greatest fear, at this stage, is that if poets are allowed to operate freely, they will produce a host of inappropriate models: slaves, women, cowards, drunks whom many may be tempted to imitate. And, once they acquire a taste for imitation, they may stoop to impersonating workmen or even madmen and animals. Banning all but the most high-minded poets from the republic is the obvious way to prevent this situation from arising.

If that is not possible, then there must be careful consideration of how poetry may benefit the republic. Plato's suggestion is that epic is more ethical than tragedy or comedy because it offers less opportunity for imitation. What's more, epic has a more uniform style compared to the 'manifold variations' of drama (Russell and Winterbottom 1972: 65). It is therefore more likely to promote harmony than drama which, by encouraging identification with different characters, threatens to undermine the stable hierarchies of the republic: a smith might dream of becoming a politician and that would make him discontented with his lot. Finally, epic appeals to the elite while tragedy and comedy appeals to the multitude. We see here an early example of the divide between high and low 'literature'. The fact of the divide is a recurrent feature of critical history but, over time, works which belonged on one side can find themselves on the other, tragedy being the most obvious example. Plato's republic offers little in the way of enjoyment for the many. The only entertainment on offer is an 'austere and unpleasing poet and tale teller' (ibid.: 66). He does not aim to delight but to instruct, offering models of virtue for citizens to imitate. Any poet proposing to give pleasure will find the gates of the city locked against him.

Plato seems to view poetry almost as a form of propaganda. Its aim is to produce unquestioning obedience, to condition people from an early age to accept their lot in life and to train them in the behaviour appropriate to their station, ideas that Aldous Huxley incorporates into his dystopia, *Brave New World* (1932). Plato, it seems, has abandoned dialogue for dictatorship. And yet poetry doesn't appear to be a very effective form of social control because the good man will want to identify himself with his counterpart in poetry, while the bad man will want to do the same. Indeed, 'the worse he is, the readier he will be to imitate everything' (Russell and Winterbottom 1972: 65). Poetry doesn't change a person: it confirms who he or she is. It doesn't mould morality: it reinforces it. A similar inconsistency afflicts the citizen's relation with poetry. On the one hand, it must draw people together by providing instances of goodfellowship while, on the other, it must make them 'self-sufficient' with little need for anyone else (ibid.: 52 and 59). Perhaps it was problems such as these that made Plato doubt the power of poetry to promote good behaviour. In Book 10, Socrates is talking to Glaucon. 'If Homer had been able to help men acquire virtue', he asks, 'would his contemporaries have let him wander around reciting poetry? Would they not have held onto him more eagerly than gold and forced him to stay at home with them?' (ibid.: 69). And the reason poets don't 'help men to acquire virtue' is that they imitate images of goodness 'without any contact with the truth' (ibid.: 69).

Plato is very big on truth. What else can we expect? He is a philosopher and philosophy means the love of wisdom. And we can't have wisdom without truth. All this is perfectly clear. What is not so clear is why Plato endorses lying. Yes, that's right. Lying. To be fair he does distinguish between a real falsehood, 'the mental ignorance of the deceived', and a verbal falsehood, 'a representation of the mental situation, a subsequent image, not real' (Russell and Winterbottom 1972: 56), but the distinction is questionable. Can we really say that the representation of an untruth is less of an offence than the untruth itself? And how on earth can we distinguish one from the other? No doubt there is much more to say on this matter but the relevant point is that Plato's position on truth is a trifle inconsistent. He condemns poetry for its 'lack of contact with truth' while condoning the use of falsehood, at least in certain instances; for example, 'dealing with enemies' and for deterring friends 'when they try to do something bad' (ibid.: 56). Rulers are also permitted to lie 'to help the city' (ibid.: 60). Plato even seems to grant poets a licence to lie, because 'we don't know the truth about antiquity' (ibid.: 57). But they must make their falsehoods 'as like as truth as possible', a line of reasoning echoed by the American poet Wallace Stevens' (1879–1955) who said that the poet lies for the sake of truth, and so we must believe him.

It's all very confusing. And it's about to get worse. So far we have Plato dismissing poetry for its lies while at the same time claiming that, on occasion, it is alright for poetry to deceive us. But now the picture becomes more complicated because Plato bars poets from telling the truth. They must be silent on that of which they can speak. There are 'many unjust men who are happy and just men who are miserable' and, what's more, 'secret wrongdoing is profitable' (Russell and Winterbottom 1972: 60). But, declares Plato, we must 'forbid' poets from drawing attention to this state of affairs, 'and command them to compose songs and fables to the opposite effect' (ibid.: 60). As we have noted, this is unlikely to work because men only imitate what is like themselves, not what is different. The relation between poetry and truth has gone from the puzzling to the downright bewildering. Poets can't tell the truth, and yet they can, but aren't allowed to. At the same time, lying is shown to have socially desirable consequences. Sir Philip Sidney (1554–86) offers a way out of this dilemma when he defends poetry on the grounds that it neither affirms nor denies but invents.

But all we need to note for now is that Plato sets up an opposition between truth and poetry, an opposition that still affects discussion of art today. 'All imitators', he writes, are viewed as a threat to 'the listeners' minds unless they are protected by the knowledge of what really is' (Russell and Winterbottom 1972: 66). Plato first raises this issue in his short dialogue, *Ion* (360 BC). The ubiquitous Socrates interrogates the rhapsode Ion over his understanding of Homer. He soon has his hapless opponent cornered, forcing him to admit that, while he is inspired to perform Homer, he is not equipped to judge how accurately he portrays certain arts. When Socrates asks him whether a charioteer or a rhapsode should best know if Homer's descriptions of a chariot race are true, Ion confesses that it would be the charioteer. The pattern is repeated with a doctor, a fisherman, a horseman and a general. By the end, Ion's view of his profession has been shattered. Not only does he have to accept that he knows nothing of the various arts described by Homer but also that he has no real understanding of his own art. He is dependent on inspiration, not skill.

Plato seems to make knowledge the criterion for appreciating Homer. A horseman will value Homer according to how well he conveys the art of horsemanship. But how will the horseman be able to assess the details of a chariot race? Plato assumes that those who listen to Homer do so, not as individuals, but as representatives of their various professions. If this is the case then they can only value that part of his work which deals with their particular field of expertise. They have no conception of the whole and, consequently, little idea of poetic form other than as a collection of discrete units of knowledge. Moreover, by concentrating on what Ion does or does not know, Plato shows a misunderstanding of the art of performance. It does not consist of conveying information but of making the audience experience the events described. Homer needs to have sufficient knowledge of how battles are fought to make the *Iliad* convincing but to read it as a manual on the conduct of warfare would to be misunderstand its nature as epic poem. But that is precisely Plato's objection. Poetry appeals to our feelings and senses and, in so doing, destroys the rational part of our mind. It also encourages us to indulge our desires which makes us miserable, when instead it should encourage us to control them, which makes us 'better and happier people' (Russell and Winterbottom 1972: 74). Once again, this kind of thinking will be found throughout the history of criticism. It gradually becomes a discussion about the effects of different kinds of literature, rather than about the supposed superiority of philosophy to poetry. The 'ancient quarrel' between the two manifests itself today in the dumbing-down debate, and it is still no nearer a solution now than it was in the third century BC.

To summarise: Plato thinks of poetry in two way. First, as a way of shaping behaviour and, second, as a means of communicating knowledge. Initially, he seems to believe that poetry can make a contribution to both but, eventually, he concludes that it can neither improve nor enlighten us. The reason lies in poetry's mode of expression, imitation. Plato argues that there is a realm of ideal forms, then there is our world, which is an imitation of that realm, and finally there is art, which is an imitation of an imitation. Or, to put it another way, poetry is a poor copy of this world which itself is a poor copy of a perfect world. The realm of ideal forms is also the realm of truth which Plato conceives of in mathematical terms: it is a matter of 'measurement and calculation' (Russell and Winterbottom 1972: 70). Plato illustrates the relation between the three levels of existence with the example of a bed. There is an ideal bed made by God, an actual bed made by a carpenter and the image of a bed made by a painter. The beds in this world are deviations, in one way or another, from the perfect bed and a picture of a bed represents a further falling away from its ideal form. This threefold relation doesn't explain Plato's contradictory attitude to lying, noted earlier, but it does clarify why poets are both capable and incapable of telling the truth. They are capable of telling a partial truth, that the wicked prosper, but they mistake it for a whole one. This misleads their audience and so their work should be banned. And they are incapable of telling the truth because the nature of imitation, on which they rely, is to remove us ever further from it. In copying this world, poets compound its errors. They do not hold the mirror up to nature but to another mirror, the endless reflections showing truth forever receding. The answer to one question, though, leads to others. How does wickedness enter our world if it is a copy of a perfect world where, by definition, no wickedness could exist? Is Plato saying that wickedness has an ideal form of which wickedness in our world is but a poor shadow? And if poets should then copy this poor shadow, how could so weak a thing possibly have the strength to lead listeners into imitation? Or is he saying that wickedness only arises in our world? If it has features unique to itself, then it can't be regarded as simply a copy of another world.

Further problems arise when we consider Plato's characterisation of truth in terms of number and measure. While that may be appropriate for mathematics, it is not so for human experience. There is no formula for happiness, no equation for success. In Plato's philosophy truth belongs to one order, human life to another. But the division is not as clear cut as he suggests. If truth is based on number then, by Plato's own admission, so too is poetry. It qualifies as a type of truth because it requires 'the skill of arithmetic' (Russell and Winterbottom 1972: 41). To the extent that poetry relies on the counting of syllables, it partakes of Plato's conception of truth. The presence of numbers in poetry also shows that they are part of human experience, not attributes of some other world. Whatever Plato may say to the contrary, *The Republic* presents a view of poetry which combines the perfection of number with the perception of our living in an imperfect world. At the same time, by defining truth exclusively in terms of measurement and calculation, Plato prepares the ground for economists to claim that they have a privileged understanding of human behaviour which is best expressed in quantitative terms.

Plato's theory of forms has emptied poetry of any useful content. It cannot tell the truth because it is a copy of a copy. It also erodes the idea of poetic form. We have already seen how viewing poetry according to how well it conveys knowledge of the various arts leads to a valuation of it in terms of the part rather than the whole. The existence of a realm of ideal forms also undermines the idea of poetic unity, for it implies that all other forms are in some sense incomplete or broken. For all that, poetry contains numbers and remains potentially useful as a model of good behaviour.

Plato's theory of imitation also introduces a new element into criticism. Before then poetry was seen in terms of praise and blame. And, when it portrayed the gods, it also called for interpretation. Now, though, it is to be judged in terms of how well it represents the world. What's more, imitation is connected to sensations. 'Imitation imitates men performing actions . . . and feeling pain or pleasure as a result' (Russell and Winterbottom 1972: 71). The perception of art in physical terms points the way towards aesthetic appreciation of art though this does not become a factor in criticism until the eighteenth century, and then mostly in Germany.[16] Plato may have a low opinion of poetry, but he opens up new ways of talking about it. And we have been talking about it ever since.

### Aristotle on Tragedy

Plato regards poetry in moral terms, Aristotle in formal terms. There is a great deal of truth in this conventional distinction, though it has recently been challenged by Stephen Halliwell who argues that both philosophers view tragedy as a drama about human responsibility rather than 'fate, chance, or divine causation (Halliwell 2006: 136). Plato and Aristotle also have similar views of imitation. Stories should be strictly censored and, 'for the most part', writes Aristotle, children should only be allowed to hear 'imitations of the occupations which they will hereafter pursue'.[17] But then a difference begins to emerge. True, both thinkers believe that poetry is a form of imitation but they diverge in their use of that term, mainly because Plato understands it from the philosophic point of view and Aristotle from the poetic one. In general, Plato does not think that mimesis, the Greek word for imitation, can teach us very much but Aristotle argues that it is a medium of learning and enjoyment. It 'is innate in human beings from childhood . . . [we make] our first steps in learning through it – and pleasure in instances of mimesis is equally general . . . [we] like to look at . . . pictures, because in looking at them [we] come to understand something' (Russell and Winterbottom 1972: 94).

Plato views mimesis in relation to an ideal reality, Aristotle in relation to a largely empirical one, an idea he develops in the *Poetics* (350 BC), possibly the most influential work of literary criticism in Western literature. 'The object of mimesis', he writes, 'must always be one of three things; what was or is, what is commonly said and thought to be the case, and what should be the case' (Russell and Winterbottom 1972: 127). Occasionally the element of idealism, 'what should be', comes to the fore. The representation of character, for example, 'should be life-like' but, 'first and foremost', he or she 'should be morally good' (ibid.: 110). However, it is not the representation of character which is central to tragedy, the main subject of the *Poetics*, but action. 'A tragedy', writes Aristotle, 'is a mimesis not of people but of their actions and life' (ibid.: 98). Action forms the basis of plot, 'the principle of life in tragedy', to which the mimesis of character comes 'second in importance' (ibid.: 99). Hence, Aristotle's celebrated definition of tragedy as 'a mimesis of a complete, that is a whole action [and by] "whole" I mean with a beginning, middle and end' (ibid.: 100).

Tragedy doesn't just imitate any action, only those actions which arouse pity and fear. In other words, it produces a quite specific effect. As Aristotle notes, 'one should look to tragedy for its own pleasure, not just any pleasure' (ibid.: 108). It may seem rather perverse to claim that feelings of pity and fear are a source of delight, but psychoanalysis has taught us that there is no such thing as a simple pleasure. The point here, though, is that Aristotle says poetry gives pleasure, and this is another difference from Plato who says that it should mould morality. A further difference is that, while Plato says poetry should not appeal to the emotions, Aristotle says it should. Plato thinks that poetry weakens us by encouraging us to indulge our emotions but Aristotle argues that it strengthens us by exciting then expelling them – a process that has obvious parallels with the sexual act.

Particular types of poetry call forth particular types of emotion. There is, in other words, an intimate relation between feeling and poetic form. In philosophical terms, Aristotle's idea of form is very different from that of Plato. He believes that it does not exist independently of content, or what he calls substance; that it exists only in the shape of this table, that chair and so on. Moreover, form is bound up with function. A chair has a seat and four legs because we sit on it. What is true of physical objects is also true of poetry. Tragedy is defined through its six component parts: plot, character, diction, thought, spectacle and song. Without these it has no existence. They give tragedy its particular form and purpose, which is to arouse pity and fear. As we noted above, plot is pre-eminent and it is the imitation of a whole action. The action must have a beginning, middle and end; it must be neither too short nor too long; and it must have unity. There should also be a probable or necessary connection between the different parts of the action. Aristotle's care for the shape of plot, that it should have 'beauty' (Russell and Winterbottom 1972: 101), shows that poetry is to be admired for its formal properties as well as its powers of mimesis. Indeed Aristotle makes mimesis continuous with harmony and rhythm because they are all 'natural to us' (ibid.: 94).

Aristotle mentions three further features of plot: peripeteia, recognition and pathos. Peripeteia refers to a surprise development in the action, recognition to a move from ignorance to knowledge and pathos to 'an act involving destruction or pain' (Russell and Winterbottom, 1972: 105). There are two basic kinds of plot, simple, which involves neither peripeteia nor recognition, and complex, which involves either or both. At its best, tragedy should be 'complex' and should 'present a mimesis of things that arouse fear and pity' (ibid.: 106). The tragic plot charts a change in fortune from good to bad. The poet should not show this happening to virtuous men as that does not arouse pity and fear, only outrage. And Aristotle echoes Plato when he says that no-one should portray vicious men passing from bad to good fortune but only because it fails to produce the right response, not because it is an incitement to vice. What guarantees our pity and fear is the story of a man 'not pre-eminent in moral virtue, who passes to bad fortune not through wickedness, but because of some piece of ignorance, and who is of high repute and great good fortune, like Oedipus' (ibid.: 106).

That name again. It is a reminder that 'the best tragedies are about a few families only, for example, Alcmaeon, Orestes, Meleager, Thysetes, Telephus, and others whose lot it was to suffer or commit fearful acts' (Russell and Winterbottom 1972: 107). Aristotle distinguishes between those who know what they are doing and to whom and those who do not. Medea falls into the first category because she knows she is killing her children while Oedipus falls into the second because he does not know, until later, that he has killed his father and slept with his mother. The worst kind of tragedy is where a character knows what to do and intends to do it, but doesn't. So, by that criterion *Hamlet*, another Oedipal drama, is a failure. Euripides' play *Cresphontes* (425 BC) is an example of the best kind of tragedy. Why? Because 'Merope means to kill her son and does not, but recognises him instead' (ibid.: 109). In other words, the best kind of tragedy is one that has a happy ending. Which again rules out *Hamlet*. But that hardly matters compared to this extraordinary claim: the best tragedies are those that end happily. Aristotle actually says that. And, what's more, it doesn't undermine his theory of tragedy, for Merope's intention can certainly cause us to feel pity and fear. In fact the happy ending may explain why tragedy can be pleasurable. We enjoy the removal of the threat that made us so afraid for ourselves as well as for the characters.

Tragedy, like comedy, originates in mimesis and takes its first shape in the dithyramb, a hymn sung to Dionysus. Tragedy and comedy were also associated with phallic songs. These, like the dithyrambs, represented a unified view of mind and body which fractured as tragedy and comedy were gradually differentiated. According to Aristotle, this was due to the personalities of poets themselves. The more serious poet represents noble actions of noble men while the less serious represents those of 'low-class people' (Russell and Winterbottom 1972: 94). In keeping with this division, tragedy praises gods and men whereas comedy 'at first produce[s] invectives' (ibid.: 94). The growing difference between tragedy and comedy can be seen as an early expression of the division between mind and body. Oedipus answers a riddle, Xanthius, in *The Frogs*, talks about farting. Of course the difference is not absolute – how could it be when the best tragedies are those which end happily? – but it does point to a dualism at the heart of the human which we will encounter many times during the course of this history, and which is the basis of the divide between high and low culture. Until the eighteenth century writers think largely in terms of a conflict between mind and body but the philosophy of Immanuel Kant (1724–1804) places that opposition within the mind itself, separating it into three distinct but related categories covering epistemology, ethics and aesthetics. Later comes Sigmund Freud (1856–1939) who makes the split between the conscious and the unconscious the foundation of all human behaviour.

We shall never know Aristotle's further thoughts on comedy because that part of his work is lost. But we do know how he thinks tragedy progresses. First, Aeschylus increased the number of actors from one to two; second, the plot evolved from a 'satyr-style' (Russell and Winterbottom 1972: 95) to something more sophisticated; and, finally, the iambic trimeter replaced the trochaic tetrameter which itself had replaced the dithyramb. Tragedy relies on music as well as metre and this distinguishes it from epic which relies on its particular use of metre, the heroic, alone. Epic and tragedy are similar to the extent that they are imitations in verse of noble personages, and both can be divided into four 'species'; that is, the plot can be simple or complex, and the story can be one of character or pathos. But there are major differences between the two genres, the most obvious being narrative form and length. Epic is a mixture of narration and dialogue whereas tragedy is dialogue alone. The action of tragedy should last no longer than a day while that of epic stretches over the years. Moreover, action is not as central to epic as it is to tragedy. Aristotle claims epic is similar to history because it 'give[s] a report of a single period, not of a unified action' (ibid.: 123). Finally, epic is 'more tolerant of the irrational' than tragedy though preferably it should not make use of it 'at all' (ibid.: 126).

Aristotle asks which is better, tragedy or epic? Some argue that epic is superior because, unlike tragedy, it does not rely on gesture. Epic, they say, is 'directed to a cultivated audience', tragedy to a 'low-class one' (Russell and Winterbottom 1972: 131). Aristotle rebuts this charge by saying that the criticism of gesture is directed against the performer, not the poet. And anyway, he adds, 'one can be over-emphatic in reciting epic as well' (ibid.: 131). Tragedy doesn't depend on movement, but its use of music and spectacle make it a far more vivid pleasure than anything epic has to offer. In addition, tragedy has a greater variety of metre, it is more unified and achieves its effect more quickly than epic. But if, for all these reasons, tragedy is to be preferred to epic, there remains a question mark about its relation to comedy. We only have Aristotle's incidental remarks on this genre, but one is especially striking. He compares poetry to philosophy because it deals in general truths, unlike history which merely records what happens. By this reasoning, epic is a very inferior form of poetry because it resembles history. But so too is tragedy because it 'still stick[s] to actual names' (ibid.: 102). The one genre which does 'aim at generality', by which Aristotle means 'what sort of man would, probably or necessarily, say or do what sort of thing' is comedy (ibid.: 102). And since Aristotle does not add anything to that intriguing suggestion that comedy is closer to philosophy than tragedy, neither will we.

What, then, is Aristotle's contribution to the history of criticism? He gives poetry value by putting it on a par with philosophy. He rescues mimesis from Plato and makes it central to poetry by rooting it in human nature. It is about what may happen and therefore encourages us to see the world differently. So poetry is not just a form of imitation, it is also a stimulus to imagine. Aristotle delves into the origin of literary genres, describing their formal features, comparing their different qualities and making judgements about their respective merits. He shows that different kinds of poetry produce different kinds of pleasure, an idea that would have horrified Plato. With Aristotle, therefore, we inch away from poetry as ethics towards poetry as aesthetics. All this shows that he has a greater understanding of the *properties* of poetry than Plato. Nowhere more so, perhaps, than in making metaphor the sign of the true poet for it is the one part of composition which cannot be learned (Russell and Winterbottom 1972: 122). Aristotle defines metaphor as 'the transferred use of a term that properly belongs to something else' and to use metaphor 'is to perceive resemblance' (ibid.: 119 and 122). It is a definition that can be applied to money. Money like metaphor involves an exchange, coin for commodity; and money, like metaphor, is based on resemblance. It is used to purchase goods all of which have in common the labour power that produced them. The amount needed to produce olive oil will be different from that used to produce a brooch, and money measures that difference.

We think of an economy broadly as an integrated system of production, distribution and consumption, but the Greek meaning of the word referred to household management. Nevertheless, Aristotle is writing at a time when money, which had been introduced into mainland Greece in the fifth century, is being used ever more extensively. The introduction of coinage occurs at roughly the same time as the appearance of the word poetry which, as we know from Pindar, soon becomes part of a cash transaction. The point is not that poetry and money are the same, only that we cannot view them as entirely separate. It is not just that poetry has entered the marketplace but that the very term, which means 'making', associates the writing of verse with other forms of craftsmanship. The meaning of poetry implies the idea of economic activity. A poet shapes words as a potter does clay. So, when Aristotle places metaphor, not metre, at the heart of poetry, we are prompted to ask if this too has any connection with money. Trade was expanding and money was playing an increasingly important part in its development.[18] Again, there is no causal relationship between the growth of money and Aristotle's valuation of metaphor, but there is a link. At the very simplest level money and words are both forms of substitution. Money stands for goods as words stand for things. This similarity is one of many we will encounter between criticism and finance.

Highlighting them counters a persistent postmodern orthodoxy, that we cannot compare what Jean-François Lyotard (1924–88) called different 'phrase-regimes', much less use one to explain another. Thus, we cannot discuss conceptual art in any terms other than those which strictly apply to it, otherwise we are in danger of losing our focus and, worse, of committing an 'injustice' by applying the standards of, say, morality to painting or sculpture. But this is to deny ourselves the opportunity to see how one 'phrase-regime' may illuminate another. Not only that, but we live in a world where budget decisions in one country can mean clean water in another. The power of multinationals connects one part of the globe to another and so it seems strange to argue that, in intellectual life, we can only understand a 'phrase-regime' on its own terms. The motto of postmodernism could be: 'only disconnect'. A further reason for spotlighting the affinities between criticism and finance is that it makes us more wary of claims by professors of literature that they are helping to subvert the social order by post-structuralist readings of Shakespeare. If the concepts of criticism are to some degree continuous with those of capitalism such claims are, to say the least, problematic. The relationship between criticism and commerce begins in classical Athens (507–400 BC). Terms like 'making' and tropes like 'metaphor' have an economic dimension, relating either to production or to the operation of money. And so too does Plato's writing on poetry. Doesn't he say that it requires 'the skill of arithmetic'? Halliwell was right; Plato and Aristotle are not so different after all. But not just in the way he imagines.

### The Hellenistic Age 323–31 BC

The Hellenistic age[19] begins with the death, either from murder or misadventure, of Alexander the Great (356–323 BC). His father, Philip of Macedon (382–336 BC), had brought the Greek city states under his rule in 338 BC before being assassinated at his daughter's wedding by, of all people, his bodyguard. Alexander extended the Macedonian empire through Asia Minor, Egypt, Mesopotamia and the Middle East and, with it, the Greek language, literature and religion. Alexander's conquests, which stretched as far as India, made the Eastern world the centre of political, cultural and commercial activity. The growth of monarchy in these regions meant that the writer had to seek patronage to survive and skill in flattery to flourish. A famous example is Callimachus' elegy on the apotheosis of the 'Lock of Berenice', Queen of Egypt, the ancestor of Pope's 'Rape of the Lock' (Kennedy 1997b: 200). Callimachus (305–240 BC) drew his inspiration from Philetas of Cos (330–270 BC) who was apparently so thin people used to joke that he needed lead in his shoes to prevent him from being blown away.

As a poet, though, Philetas was decidedly heavyweight. Two thousand years before the romantics he rejects public culture for private passion. He discards epic, tragedy and comedy for elegies, epigrams and poems in praise of his mistress, one Battis. Philetas became a model for other poets, not just Callimachus, who was famous for sayings such as 'a big book is a big evil' and 'I abhor all common things', but also Theocritus (310–245 BC), the creator of pastoral poetry. Theocritus' descriptions of shepherds in an idyllic landscape is one of several new subjects that enter poetry at this time. Others include 'myths not previously given classical treatment, "scientific subjects"' such as the constellations, religion 'and occasionally urban social life'

(Kennedy 1997b: 201–2). With these new subjects came new techniques. Callimachus, for instance, 'made significant innovations in narrative technique, including variations in tempo and the insertion of tales within tales' (ibid.: 202).

The move away from traditional genres, the introduction of new subject matter and the creation of new styles of writing meant that poetry could no longer be judged simply in terms of ethics or how it processed emotion. These criteria belonged to a conception of poetry as a public art but now it was intended for private audiences drawn from the court. The emphasis was on the appreciation of small works of 'artistic perfection' by 'an educated and sophisticated readership' (ibid.: 201). 'Judge poetry by its craft and not the Persian League' (in ibid.: 203), declares Callimachus. The themes of the classic poets belong to another age, as does their highly inflated language. Poetry should be slimmed down, a physiological metaphor that is often found in later Greek and Latin discussions of style. Callimachus' recommendations were not welcomed by all. For instance, Neoptolemus of Parium, whose work formed the basis for Horace's *Ars Poetica* (c. 19 BC), stressed the moral function of poetry, saying 'the complete poet must benefit the audience in regard to virtue, with the enchantment of the soul' (ibid.: 204). Others, though, like the Epicurean philosopher Philodemus (fl. 110 BC), asserted that poetry was purely for pleasure. Philodemus was also one of the first to argue for the unity of form and content, to say that a poem should be judged as a whole. This was in opposition to the standard view, which would prevail for many centuries, that style was merely an adornment to subject matter.

Callimachus worked at the great library of Alexandria which had been created by Ptolemy I Soter (367–283 BC), one of Alexander's generals. We do not how many scrolls, and later parchment codices, the library contained but Mark Antony (83–30 BC) was reputed to have given Cleopatra (69–30 BC) 200,000 as a wedding gift. The library is important to the history of criticism for many reasons, not least because its staff collected, collated, edited and interpreted classical works. Callimachus began a catalogue of all the books in the library. They were organised by genre or subject and authors were listed alphabetically within each category. Looking down the list, the casual observer would also find brief biographical sketches and the first line of each work. In part the librarians drew on the Peripatetic School, founded by Aristotle, for their information about authors. The philosophers of this school saw an author's work as a reflection of his ideas and interests, and even incidents from his life. According to one source, Euripides being attacked by hunting dogs became Pentheus being torn apart by women in *The Bacchae* (405 BC). The main focus of Alexandrian scholars, though, was not biography but philology, basically the study of the structure and history of language. The greatest of these scholars, men like Aristophanes of Byzantium (257–180 BC), Aristarchus

(220–143 BC) and Zenodotus (fl. 280 BC), were concerned with the integrity of the text rather than its ethics.

Zenodotus, who is regarded as the father of textual criticism, became the first head of the library in about 284 BC. He sought to establish an authoritative version of Homer. If he doubted the authenticity of a line he did not remove it, but drew attention to it by a mark in the margin. He also complied a *Homeric Glossary*. Aristophanes became head librarian around 200 BC. He further developed the marginal sign by the introduction of an asterisk to denote the repetition of a line from another context and he is also credited with the invention of punctuation. Aristophanes also wrote a dictionary detailing the changing meaning of words over time. He was succeeded by Aristarchus, who must have been a fearsome individual because a shortened version of his name, aristarch, is a term for a 'judgemental critic'. He was certainly prepared to take authors to task if he thought their work inferior. Aristarchus is important in the history of criticism because he began the process of running commentaries. He also established the principle that 'each author is his own best interpreter' (Kennedy 1997b: 208). If the sense was unclear, then it should be checked against other passages in the work to clarify the meaning. This technique was used by biblical commentators in the Middle Ages to interpret passages of Scripture. Alexandrian scholars thus pioneered methods of reading that would help Medieval man understand the word of God.

Aristophanes and Aristarchus did more than merely comment on ancient manuscripts. Their greatest achievement was to create a literary canon which was accepted by Roman and Renaissance scholars, and which still shapes ideas about literature today. It is to the efforts of these two men, mostly forgotten, that Homer, Aeschylus, Sophocles and Euripides owe their place in Western literature. Since they did not include any contemporary writers in their list, Aristophanes and Aristarchus seemed to believe that 'the greatest literary works were the creations of the past' (Kennedy 1997b: 207). Only those poems and plays which had stood the test of time could be included. Of all human constructs, the canon comes closest to giving us a glimpse of what immortality might look like: an ongoing gathering of riches. But who decides which works will survive and which won't? And on what basis? Unless the canon operates on a principle akin to natural selection, it is the result of choices based on a variety of considerations, not all literary, by those with the power to enforce them.[20] Aristophanes and Aristarchus certainly did not use ethics as a criterion for their selection. They were more interested in the linguistic features of a work.

And here we encounter, for the first time, the great rift that runs through the history of criticism – that between rhetoric and grammar. Broadly speaking, a rhetorical critic focuses on how a work expresses or shapes values and

behaviour, while a grammatical critic establishes its authenticity, glosses difficult passages and places it in its proper context. Although the two are not
mutually exclusive, one is often emphasised at the expense of the other. It is
probably true to say that most critical disputes are a manifestation, in one form
or another, of this basic division between rhetoric and grammar. Occasionally,
rhetorical critics will continue criticism's civil war among themselves. The clash
between traditionalists and theorists in the last quarter of the twentieth century
falls into this category. What was at stake for both combatants was the right
to use literature for their own particular version of human emancipation.
Grammarians can also quarrel with one another, but their conflicts tend not to
be so colourful or dramatic. Don't think, though, that those who occupy themselves with the formal properties of texts are dull. At least one branch of the
family is quite outrageous. I am thinking of the nineteenth-century aesthetes,
to whom art's integrity was far more important than its morality.

In general, the Hellenistic period is characterised by a much more technical approach to literature. As Kennedy puts it, 'teachers of grammar and
rhetoric concentrated on describing the stylistic phenomena of classical texts
and encouraging their imitation' (1997b: 219). But Philodemus had his
doubts about modelling poetry on that of his predecessors. If we consider imitation valuable, then how are we to judge originality? By this argument, those
who copy Homer are to be admired more than Homer himself. The increasingly technical character of criticism is evident in Stoicism, a philosophy
founded by Zeno of Citium (333–264 BC) which taught, among other things,
that true happiness was the result of moral and intellectual perfection. Based
on their belief that eloquence and wisdom were inseparable, the Stoics developed a theory of grammar in which we ascend through six stages from
reading aloud to the criticism of poetry. In addition, they devised a system of
allegory whereby the 'name of the god may be a metonymy for a thing that
comes from god as Ceres for grain' and they also believed that 'myths could
represent scientific facts: Kronos eating his sons means that time eats up the
years' (ibid.: 212). Here was the basis of a materialist poetics. Although the
Stoics viewed poetry as a form of imitation, they were also aware of the power
of imagination. Philostratus (AD 172–250), referring to Stoic philosophy in
his *Life of Apollonius of Tyana* (c. 215 AD), distinguished between copying
what is seen and creating what is not seen, for which he uses the term *phantasia*. It is a distinction that will loom ever larger in talk about literature, cul-
minating in the triumph of romanticism in the late eighteenth century.

## Roman Criticism: Horace, Longinus and Others

I am using the term 'Roman criticism' to refer to commentators, of whatever
nationality, who wrote during the period of Rome's ascendancy. In 146 BC, the

Romans had turned Greece into a province because of its support for Carthage in the Punic Wars (264–202 BC). And, after the battle of Actium in 31 BC, when Julius Caesar's great nephew, Octavian (63 BC–AD 14), defeated Mark Antony and Cleopatra, Rome's status as a great power was confirmed. Octavian became the first emperor and, in 27 BC, the senate conferred on him the title Augustus, which symbolised authority over man and nature. In that capacity he issued an amnesty to all who had fought against him. One of those was the poet Horace (65–8 BC) who had sided with Brutus against Octavian, as he then was, at the Battle of Philippi (42 BC). Horace became the foremost lyric poet of Augustus' reign and, in 17 BC, the emperor commissioned him to write the hymn *Carmen saeculare* (Song of Ages) for the secular games. Horace also wrote Augustus a letter about the history and nature of poetry. The Roman variety, for example, began with 'Fescennine verses'. These were originally ribald songs performed at weddings which then developed into dialogues of mutual insults 'until the joking became [too] savage', and a law was introduced 'forbidding anyone to be attacked in a malicious manner' (Russell and Winterbottom 1972: 276).

Horace has a more diffuse conception of poetry than either Plato or Aristotle. While they regarded it as a form of ethical training or emotional management, he saw it as covering everything from promoting eloquence to placating the gods. Poetry was now so much more than metre. Such diversity of purpose suggests that it plays an integral part in the life of society but, equally, it indicates a desire to compensate for the fact that it may not have a clearly defined role to play in the empire. Perhaps that explains why Ovid (43 BC–AD 17) chose to write of love, for it marked out a sphere poetry could call its own. But private passions have public consequences. Augustus banished Ovid in 8 AD, apparently because he was offended by something in *Metamorphoses* (2–8 AD),[21] a work which was heavily censured when published. But Ovid was also suspected of having an affair with one of Augustus' female relatives, which may have been a more likely reason for his exile at Tomis on the Black Sea coast. Whatever the reason, it led Ovid to make a distinction between the writer and his work, which has since become a commonplace of criticism. 'Believe me, my character is different from my poetry: my life is decent, my Muse sportive' (Russell and Winterbottom 1972: 293). This distinction was implicit in the notion of inspiration and the theory of genres – the poet spoke in his own voice in narrative, less so in epic and least in tragedy and comedy – but Ovid makes it the cornerstone of his defence as he pleads to be allowed back to Rome. He also challenges the Greek idea that poetry should preserve the names of great men for posterity, declaring that he writes for his own 'everlasting fame' (ibid.: 297). Horace disagrees. 'We and our works are a debt owed to death' (ibid.: 281), he writes. But it will be a long time before people accept the idea that poetry does not confer immortality, that time can dull the brightest words.

Horace has a more deferential view of the Greeks than Ovid. 'Greece', he famously wrote in his letter to Augustus, 'took captive its wild conqueror, and introduced the arts to rural Latium' (Russell and Winterbottom 1972: 272). For the arts to be introduced was one thing, for them to become established was another. The Roman temperament, sighs Horace, makes it difficult for poetry to flourish. The Greeks loved the Muse, the Romans money; the Greeks sought praise, the Romans reward. Ovid's father advised him against becoming a poet, calling it 'a useless pursuit', adding that 'Homer himself had no money to leave in his will' (ibid.: 292). Horace argues that poets who care more for money than fame had let 'cash taint . . . their soul', with the result that hardly any contemporary work was worth 'preserving' (ibid.: 288). But Horace's distinction between the Greeks and the Romans is not sustainable for, as we saw earlier, the Greeks themselves complained about money corrupting the Muse. Moreover, the fact that counting is integral to poetry, and that metaphor operates like money, means that we cannot finally distinguish between the two. Horace himself unwittingly acknowledges their affinity when he notes that words, like coins, can be 'stamped with the current mark' (ibid.: 281). He will not be the last to make that connection.

Horace detests playgoers. 'Stupid and illiterate', they are only interested in spectacle; even their betters have now 'transferred all their pleasure from the ear to the shifting and empty delights of the eye' (ibid.: 281). Horace's sentiments recall Plato's and, to a certain extent, Aristotle's disapproval of those who aim to please the audience rather than educate them. Ovid too complained about the Roman stage. 'It's not enough their ears should be besmirched by unchaste language', he writes, 'their eyes have [got] used to seeing much that is improper' (ibid.: 295). Another Roman poet, Petronius (AD 27–66), who was one of the emperor Nero's (AD 37–68) favourite courtiers, advised poets to avoid 'all cheapness of vocabulary' and to choose only words 'that are remote from the mob' (ibid.: 299), The motto of the true poet, said Horace, should be 'I hate the profane crowd and keep it at a distance' (ibid.: 299); a motto that could also serve for many modernist poets.

Horace's attitude to what he calls 'the sweaty mob' (Russell and Winterbottom 1972: 268) provides one context for *Ars poetica*, which, apparently, was first translated into English by Elizabeth I. Another is his fear that writing has degenerated into a fashionable pastime producing a flood of mediocre works. 'Boys and dignified fathers alike dine with leaves in their hair and dictate poetry' (ibid.: 275), he complains. The actual occasion for the work, though, is to give advice to two brothers, the Pisos, on how to compose a successful tragedy. *Ars poetica* thus belongs in the tradition of prescriptive criticism established by Aristotle. First and foremost, the aspiring writer must aim at nature. This will give his work unity and simplicity. 'Imagine a painter combining a horse's neck with a human head' (ibid.: 279), writes Horace, it would make you laugh out loud. Similarly the would-be playwright must 'mark the manners of each time of life and assign the appropriate part to changing natures and ages' (ibid.: 283). In addition to imitating nature, the young hopeful must adhere to decorum; that is, he must use the right metre for the right genre; iambus, for example, is best for drama because it is 'suitable for dialogue and intended by nature for a life of action' (ibid.: 281). These are the two main pieces of advice. There are others, such as not portraying violence on stage or making 'good speed towards the end of the story' (ibid.: 283), but they all illustrate, in one way or another, the principle that poetic compositions should be well-organised wholes that are true to life. A good way of summing up the first section of *Ars poetica* would be to say, 'nature and propriety are all'.

The second section deals with how the poet can achieve perfection. 'Wisdom is the starting point of correct writing' (Russell and Winterbottom 1972: 288). Keep an eye on life but also 'study Greek models night and day' (ibid.: 286), a precept that highlights one of the main themes of this history, namely, the relation to tradition. To ignore it means you don't learn from it and so you produce works of inferior quality, while to idealise it leads to imitation which retards the progress of your own literature. Horace stands somewhere between these two extremes. Poets should admire their predecessors, but not to excess. 'If the Greeks had hated novelty as much as we, what would exist now to be ranked as old'? (ibid.: 274), he asks. Another piece of advice is to 'keep the eraser busy' if you 'want to write something worth reading' (ibid.: 271). Relying on whatever talent you may have is not enough; art and nature 'need each other's help, and work together in friendship' (ibid.: 290). Interspersed with these injunctions are reflections on the history and use of poetry. It is responsible for bringing humans out of nature and into society. It is the foundation of law and it sharpens 'masculine hearts for war' (ibid.: 290). It is also the stuff of oracles, the persuader of kings and 'entertainment' after 'long labour' (ibid.: 290).

And it is in Horace that we find one of the most famous of all quotations about poets, that 'they aim either to do good or to give pleasure – or thirdly to say things which are both pleasing and serviceable for life' (Russell and Winterbottom 1972: 288). That statement has lasted so long because no-one has come up with a better. And there is something else in *Ars poetica* that has lasted a long time too, the scales image. Horace follows Aristophanes in using it to measure literary worth: 'if one weighs Roman writers in the same scale [as the Greeks] there is not much to say' (ibid.: 273). It is an image that connects poetry with commerce. Horace also implicates poetry in the division between public and private property (ibid.: 290) and this association between the two crops up again in eighteenth-century discussions of taste.

All of which is to say that there are two ways of looking at Horace's contribution to criticism. The first concentrates on the prescriptive character of

*Ars poetica*, its advice on how to write, its view of tradition and its pithy definition of poets. This is the most familiar account of Horace's epistle. The second is less well known and concentrates on his contempt for the crowd, his worry about the effect of money on the nature of poetry, and the significance of his imagery in so far as it relates to coins or the marketplace. 'My books aren't to be found in shops and stalls to be clutched by the sweaty hands of the mob . . . I give recitations to no-one but friends' (ibid.: 268). This remark reveals an anxiety about poetry's place in society and an attempt to rescue it from the taint of trade. But when literary worth is weighed, when a poet's talent[22] is expressed in terms of 'land and investments' (ibid.: 290), the taint begins to look like a permanent blemish.

Longinus,[23] author of another key work of Roman criticism, *On Sublimity*, written during the first century AD, was also worried about the fate of poetry, wondering if its fallen condition could be blamed on the change from a republican to a monarchical system of government. 'Are we to believe', he asked, 'the common explanation . . . that great writers flourished with democracy and died with it?' (Russell and Winterbottom 1972: 501). Longinus is not convinced. He argues that 'avarice' and 'the love of pleasure' are more likely to be responsible for the decline in literary standards. Like the 'desire for novelty which is all the rage today', they divert men's minds from 'rightness and nobility' and blind them to 'things of permanent value' (ibid.: 466 and 503). The market, Longinus implies, offers a diminished conception of man. If we want a higher view of him we must go to literature. It is at this point that Longinus differs from Horace. Both agree that commerce corrupts poet and playwright alike, that its reductive logic insinuates itself into the very act of writing, but they differ in how to combat this situation. Horace advises poets to aim for technical perfection, Longinus for greatness of thought which is, rather perplexingly, both a cause and an effect of the sublime.

Longinus defines the sublime primarily in terms of oratory, a reminder of the close connection between literature and rhetoric in the classical world. The sublime 'is a kind of eminence or excellence in discourse' and produces 'ecstasy rather than persuasion in the hearer' (Russell and Winterbottom 1972: 462). In literary terms it is

> the understanding that nature made man to be no humble or lowly creature, but brought him into the life and into the universe as into a great festival to be both a spectator and an enthusiastic contestant in its competitions. She implanted in our minds from the start an irresistible desire for anything which is great and, in relation to ourselves, supernatural. (ibid.: 494)

An example of the sublime in literature is the beginning of the book of Genesis (ibid.: 470) which shows that parts of the Old Testament must have been known and, indeed, admired in the Roman world. There are five ways to achieve the sublime; great thoughts; strong and inspired emotions; and figures, for instance, polysyndeton, the use of conjunctions to connect a series of clauses. The aim of figures is to make style 'more emotional and exciting [because] emotion is an essential part of sublimity' (ibid.: 489). The two remaining ways of achieving sublimity are by 'noble diction' and 'dignified and elevated word arrangement' (ibid.: 467).

Although Longinus states that metaphors, which come under diction, are 'conducive to sublimity', he stipulates that they should be used with caution; 'no more than two or three at most may be used of the same subject' (Russell and Winterbottom 1972: 490–1). It is strange that Longinus urges restraint in pursuit of the sublime whose very nature inclines to infinity, but he acknowledges that his suggestion is not practical, since a rush of genuine sublimity doesn't give the hearer pause to count the metaphors. Nevertheless, there is an anxiety about the unbounded nature of the sublime. It approaches chaos. One of the faults a writer may commit in striving for the sublime is to create a 'meaningless' or 'immoderate emotion' (ibid.: 464). Centuries after Longinus, critics are still trying to come to terms with the sublime. T. S. Eliot (1888–1965) says that *Hamlet* suffers from its eponymous hero being 'dominated by an emotion which is inexpressible, because it is in excess of the facts as they appear' (Eliot 1976: 145).

What Eliot finds troubling about *Hamlet* is, for the French critic Roland Barthes (1915–80), an instance of the highest intensity that reading can offer. He distinguishes between the text of pleasure and the text of bliss. We enjoy the one because it confirms our sense of identity, and the other because it unsettles our ideas, values and tastes, tips us into loss. 'Pleasure', Barthes states, 'can be expressed in words, bliss cannot' (1975: 21). He uses the image of the body to describe both books and the experience of reading them. The text is 'an anagram of our erotic body' while the various delights of reading arise from 'that moment when my body pursues its own ideas – for my body does not have the same needs as I do' (ibid.: 17). The image of the book as a body is traditional. Longinus stipulates that tropes should work like joints, enabling the argument to move forward, while what is 'filthy and contemptible' should be hidden away as are 'our private parts' (Russell and Winterbottom 1972: 491 and 501). But Longinus does not see reading in the nakedly sexual terms that Barthes does. For him it is a matter of spiritual aspiration not physical arousal. Both writers focus on the sense of excess but they have different attitudes towards it. This suggests that certain literary experiences endure, even if our ways of talking about them differ – as indeed they must. Barthes's distinction between pleasure and bliss, in fact, is no more than a restatement of the age-old struggle between Apollo and Dionysus, between reason and regulation, instinct and release.

Longinus argues that the sublime is the highest form of literature. This provides a means for discriminating between different kinds of writing. Those that approach the sublime are to be preferred to those which merely conform to the correct standards of composition. The sublime is the highest literary value because it is the one that most expresses our essence. 'It is our nature to be elevated and exalted by true sublimity' (Russell and Winterbottom 1972: 467), writes Longinus. Criticism, it seems, is based on a conception of human nature as much as it is on what constitutes good literature. Longinus is prepared to praise the achievements of 'uniformly beautiful writers' but, in the end, it is not they who transport us, it is not they who take our breath away with some marvellous stroke; that is the gift of a 'Pindar or Sophocles who sometimes set the world on fire with their vehemence' (ibid.: 493).

But the sublime is not the only quality that Longinus looks for in litera-ture: 'realism' (Russell and Winterbottom 1972: 471) is another. This comes across strongly in his comparison of the *Iliad* and the *Odyssey*. The former had 'abundance of imagery taken from life' but, in the latter, 'Homer is lost in the realm of the fabulous and the incredible' (ibid.: 471). Once again we are faced with an apparent contradiction in Longinus' account of the sublime. Surely the aim of realism, the representation of things as they are, conflicts with that of the sublime which 'raises us to the spiritual greatness of god' (ibid.: 494)? In fact there is no real conflict. Portraying an event accurately does not preclude having strong feelings about it. Indeed it is the element of emotion in the *Iliad* which makes it sublime. By the time he composes the *Odyssey*, though, Homer's powers are on the wane. And when that happens to a writer, he turns to 'depicting a kind of comedy of manners' (ibid.: 471). It's an intriguing idea: that the origin of comedy lies in the decline of passion.

So where does Longinus fit into the history of criticism? He follows in Aristotle's footsteps in recognising the importance of emotion in art. But where Aristotle sees literary form as organising emotion, Longinus sees it as overwhelmed by an outpouring of feeling. He compares this experience to the eruption of Etna, 'bringing up rocks and whole hills out of the depths' (Russell and Winterbottom 1972: 494). The high value Longinus places on great thoughts and powerful emotion, and his relaxed attitude to mistakes as long as they are redeemed 'by a single sublime stroke' (ibid.: 495) makes him appear very different from Horace, who thinks poetry should be useful and who worries about getting it right. 'The useful and the necessary', remarks Longinus loftily 'are readily available to man, it is the unusual that always excites our wonder' (ibid.: 495). For all that, he is not so very different from Horace. *On Sublimity*, like *Ars poetica*, is written in the form of a letter explaining how to achieve a literary effect. And, far from dismissing the idea that poetry should give pleasing precepts, Longinus glorifies it. The sublime, he writes, adds grandeur to principles of service and utility, something they can never have in the sphere of mundane existence. If Horace says poetry should be beautiful and useful, then Longinus says that it should be sublime and serviceable. Longinus' discussion of genius and decorum raises issues that will reverberate throughout the history of criticism, coming to a head in the mid eighteenth century with the romantic reaction to neoclassicism.

Finally, Longinus' account of the sublime challenges the notion that the value of a work can be expressed in numerical terms. If 'good points were totted up, not judged by their real value' Longinus declares, then we would have to say that 'Hyperides would in every way surpass Demosthenes' but the former's 'beauties, though numerous, are without grandeur' (Russell and Winterbottom 1972: 493). The sublime, in other words, counteracts the tendency of criticism to develop as a form of calculation. It is a reminder 'that something higher than human is sought in literature' (ibid.: 495). But the sublime cannot be entirely divorced from mathematical thinking. We have already seen that Longinus would like to limit the number of metaphors per subject, and the very fact that *On Sublimity* stipulates what methods must be used to achieve the sublime suggests that it is a matter of procedure as much as passion. Alexander Pope (1688–1744) certainly saw no contradiction between precept and powerful feeling. While the poet should always be guided by the rules of composition, it was still possible to 'snatch a grace beyond the reach of art' (Pope 1978: 68). And in the eighteenth century the sublime becomes a means of negotiating the seemingly limitless expansion of the market economy. For now, Longinus invokes the sublime as a corrective to the sort of pursuits associated with money: avarice and the love of pleasure. He appeals to 'posterity and human experience' (Russell and Winterbottom 1972: 495) for the soundness of his views, as indeed will many who come after him. There would be no history of criticism if some works had not stood the test of time and if we did not feel they said something about our condition that rang true.

The orator Dio 'Chrysostom' (c. 50–112 AD), whose name means 'golden-mouthed' shows no interest in the sublime, but shares Longinus' view that literature should be 'realistic'. He compares the different ways in which the Greek tragedians make their stories believable. Euripides, for example, is praised for his 'convincingness in incident, and skill in language' (Russell and Winterbottom 1972: 506). Like Dionysus in *The Frogs*, Dio cannot choose which playwright is best. 'Had I been on oath', he writes, 'I could never have come to a decision' (ibid.: 505). Aeschylus has a 'grandeur and archaic splendour' and is 'original in thought and expression'; Euripides is 'intelligent', has 'a care for detail' and treats us to the 'full force of his eloquence'; Sophocles 'comes between the two', his verse is 'dignified and grand, tragic and euphonious to the highest degree' (ibid.: 505–8). If criticism is defined as judgement then Dio is not a critic. He recognises that each author has his merits and it would be wrong to say that one is better than another, a position summed up by Pliny the Younger (AD 61–112), whose uncle, Pliny the Elder (AD 23–79) was killed trying to rescue the people of Pompeii after the eruption of Mount Vesuvius. The 'wise and acute reader', Pliny wrote, shouldn't compare different poems, but weigh each for itself, not thinking it is worse than another, if it is perfect of its own kind' (ibid.: 429). Dio does not, like Longinus, see literature as a means of improving society but as a source of consolation. He looks at literature from a private viewpoint whereas Longinus looks at it from a public one. If literature is to play a social role then we need criticism to tell us what is good and bad, but if it's a purely private pleasure there is no necessity to judge.

But, of course, this is a false opposition. Literature always has a public dimension. The Greek historian and biographer Plutarch (AD 46–127), whose *Lives* was a source for Shakespeare's Roman plays, was very well aware of this and believed that the purpose of criticism was to control reading, which he portrays in terms of eating and drinking, a reminder of its close connection to song and feasting. Since it was not possible to keep the young from poetry, a complaint not often heard today, 'they need an escort in reading even more than they do in the street' (Russell and Winterbottom 1972: 508). Plutarch believed that poetry had the potential to seduce the intellect. Poets tell lies because fiction is more enjoyable than truth. Who would not rather hear fabulous tales than sober facts? In addition to poets' 'deliberate inventions' are their 'false beliefs and opinions' which 'rub off on us' (ibid.: 511). These include falsehoods about how, for example, the gods 'breed crime in men' (ibid.: 512). And by presenting death and Hades in fearful terms, poets fill us with their own 'emotion and weakness' (ibid.: 512).

All these arguments are familiar from Plato, but Plutarch can also sound like Aristotle when he writes that 'imitation is to be commended if it achieves likeness whether of a good or bad object' (ibid.: 513). But where Aristotle says imitation should focus on the ideal, Plutarch says it should focus on the real. If imitation 'is to be truthful, it must reproduce the marks of vice and virtue along with their actions' (ibid.: 526). Plutarch tries to deal with the potential tension in his writing between mimesis and morality by separating them: 'we praise not the action represented by the imitation, but the art shown in the appropriate reproduction of the subject' (ibid.: 513). What, though, if we are faced with a painting of the real life murder of a child? Wouldn't our admiration for the artistry in some way implicate us in the act being depicted? It's important to ask this question because Plutarch's main interest is in literature as a form of ethics. Indeed, he develops techniques of reading based on that very principle.

Young people need to learn that a character's opinions are not necessarily those of the poet. When Eteocles, in Euripides' *Phoenician Women* (411–409 BC), says, 'If we must do wrong, it's best to do it to win a kingdom' (Russell and Winterbottom 1972: 514), he is voicing his own views, not those of the author. But how is the inexperienced reader to know this? How is he or she to tell that Eteocles' remark is 'wicked and false' (ibid.: 514) and not at all the kind of thing Euripides would say? One tactic is to search for signs that the poet disapproves of what is being said. For example, Homer's description of a character before or after he or she speaks shapes our attitude to what they say. If the poet does not immediately indicate what he thinks of a character, then we must look for remarks elsewhere that contradict the character's views. The fate of characters also indicates whether the poet approves or disapproves of them. Sometimes, though, the poet 'does not himself provide a resolution of his absurdities' and then it becomes necessary to refute what he says by reference to another poet or philosopher. 'There are only three things', says a character in a lost play, 'that really contribute to life – food, drink and sex. Everything else is an extra' (ibid.: 519). Socrates says the opposite: 'bad men live to eat and drink and good men eat and drink to live' (ibid.: 519).

These rhetorical forms of reading are complemented by grammatical ones. Plutarch recommends that we study the context of a character's remark. By this he doesn't mean the social and historical background, but the words surrounding what the character says: 'if some noun or verb in the context takes the edge off the compulsion we feel to interpret the passage in a bad sense, we should fasten onto it and expound its implications' (Russell and Winterbottom 1972: 520). Similarly, students should be aware of the history and meaning of words so as to prevent careless reading. Some words have more than one meaning (*biotos*, for example, is both life and money),[24] while others have contradictory meanings (*aluein*, for example, signifies distress and happiness). Most important of all students should know how poets use the name of the gods and of good and bad as these have an immediate bearing on ethical life. Zeus, for instance, sometimes means god, sometimes destiny, sometimes fortune, sometimes the first cause and so on.

Plutarch's aim is to make the young read more critically. Asking why a character says this or that will prevent them from falling into unqualified admiration for their literary heroes. By looking carefully at what the poet says, by relating remarks from one part of the work to another, by comparing different writers, and by knowing the history and meaning of words, the young will come to understand that poetry is an 'imitation of the manners and lives of men who are not perfect, pure and irreproachable, but are involved in passions, false opinions and ignorance, though they often indeed improve themselves through natural goodness' (Russell and Winterbottom 1972: 527). Plutarch has a rounded conception of character which, again, marks his difference from Aristotle, as does his view that poetry is an imitation of 'manners and lives' rather than action. His method of reading means there is no need for allegory, which he regards as a perverse form of interpretation. He laughs at those who say that Hera making herself look beautiful for Zeus symbolises the 'purifica-tion of air coming into contact with the fiery element' (ibid.: 516). As we shall see, though, the medieval church has a very different attitude to allegory.

Like Ovid, Plutarch is far less deferential in his attitude to tradition than Horace. He much prefers the New Comedy to the Old, especially when it is being read out over dinner. This underlines the earlier observation that Plutarch tends to see literature very much in relation to food and drink. The change from Old Comedy, represented by Aristophanes, to New Comedy, represented by Menander (342–291 BC), was the result of Philip of Macedon bringing the Greek city states under his rule. As writers no longer enjoyed the same freedom of expression, they began to look to everyday life for their material, something which would appeal to Plutarch with his view that liter-ature should be 'realistic'. He has little patience with either the myth-laden plots of Old Comedy or its political satire. He is also offended by its inde-cency and sexual licence. How much better was New Comedy, with its well ordered plot, its blend of 'seriousness and fun' and its 'useful and simple maxims' (Russell and Winterbottom 1972: 533).

Plutarch's opinion of the superiority of New Comedy was shared by the Roman playwrights Plautus (254–184 BC) and Terence (190–158 BC). They either translated or wrote in the style of Menander and, together, consolidated the standard comic plot of young lovers eventually being united after over-coming a series of obstacles. The passage from Old to New Comedy empha-sises how literary forms are shaped by external events. And New Comedy flourishes because its subject matter, the business of ordinary life, chimes with the ethos of republican Rome (c. 509–44 BC). But neither external events nor the character of society wholly explain the nature of literary genres. The comic plot, begun by Menander and refined by Plautus and Terence, survives in modified form today. While historical developments may account for why it came into being, they cannot account for why it should persist long after the conditions which gave rise to it have vanished. One of the tasks of criti-cism, therefore, is to try to understand why the long dead can still clutch us. That means acknowledging the claims of history and the heart.

The concerns of second- and third-century writers differ from those which preceded them mainly in detail. The grammarian Aulus Gellius (AD 125–80) argues that translators of Greek poetry should not 'go out of their way to ensure literal faithfulness' (Russell and Winterbottom 1972: 540). Gellius is an interesting figure because he criticises Virgil (70–19 BC), who will be revered by later ages. As a translator, Virgil has a knack of coming up with 'inappropriate similes', a fault that bedevils his own poetry which is full of 'harsh and improper metaphors' (ibid.: 549 and 551). But at least Virgil has a masculine style which draws us, says Aristides Quintilianus, a third-century author best known for a treatise on music, to whatever excites 'anxiety or activity', while the feminine style 'entices us to pleasure and whatever relaxes the mind' (ibid.: 554). Quintilianus' work is another example of how conceptions of human nature, here conceived along gender lines, shape ideas about literature. Very briefly, he believed that the soul was neuter but becomes either masculine or feminine when it takes bodily form, after which it seeks to be united with its opposite principle.[25] In literary terms, content is masculine and form is feminine, an idea that survives into the Renaissance.

Quintilianus' division of masculine and feminine also feeds into the conventional distinction between high culture, which is characterised by thought, and popular culture, which is characterised by feeling, a hierarchy that persists into our own day. The traditional supremacy of poetry over prose is, though, beginning to look more and more insecure as we move towards the Christian era. Plato had identified poetry with lies and now the orator Aelius Aristides (AD 117–81) questions its traditional alliance with religion. Why use poetry to praise the gods? We can do that just as well in prose which, in any case, is more natural than poetry with its reliance on metre. How is it, asks Aristides, that we use prose for 'encomia of festivals, and heroic deeds, narratives of war, inventions of fables, contests in court – but towards the gods who gave it to us, we do not think it right to use it?' (Russell and Winterbottom 1972: 559). His words show that many of the functions normally attributed to poetry have now been appropriated by prose. Which brings us to rhetoric.

### Rhetoric and Poetry

Aristides wanted to distinguish the orator, one who was proficient in public speaking and who was most likely a politician, from the poet. So too did the Roman historian Tacitus (AD 56–117). Rhetoric, the art of oratory, had a clear role in society, poetry did not. You were not likely to hear verse in the senate, the court or even the forum. The poet was 'incapable of pleading cases' (Russell and Winterbottom 1972: 433) and shied away from political debate or legal disputes. Not for him, then, the riches, esteem or fame that were heaped on the successful orator. No, he must resign himself to a life of struggle and obscurity. He must work all day and most of the night

> to knock together one volume [then] he has to go round begging . . . someone to listen to it – at a price. He has to borrow a house and equip a recital hall, hire seats and distribute advertisements. And even if the recitation is a success, the praise he wins for it is the matter of a day or two [and] swiftly gone. (ibid.: 437)

What a contrast to the orator who helps friends, comforts strangers, brings safety to the endangered and 'strikes terror into enemies and detractors' (ibid.: 434). The one compensation for being a poet rather than an orator is that you were unlikely to be murdered. That was the fate which befell Marcus Cicero (106–43 BC), the greatest Roman orator, for his opposition to Marc Antony. He was killed trying to flee Italy and his head and hands were nailed to the speaker's podium in the senate as a warning to others. It is said that Fulvia, Antony's wife, pulled out Cicero's tongue and repeatedly stabbed it with her hairpin as an act of revenge on his power of speech.

Better to be a live poet than a dead orator. You may have neither respect, reputation nor wealth but at least you were alive to lament your lack of them. Maternus, one of the characters in Tacitus' *Dialogue on Orators* (c. 81 AD), observes that he would much rather

> be carried by Virgil's "Sweet Muses" to their sacred haunts and fountains, far from troubles and cares and the daily compulsion to act against one's inclinations [than to have] truck with the mad, slippery life of the forum, trembling and pale in pursuit of fame. (Russell and Winterbottom 1972: 440)

We tend to see the poet's marginal status as a product of the romantic period, the misunderstood genius ignored by a philistine society. But that displacement now looks as if it has a much longer history. Poets just don't seem to be very important. If one is murdered, it's by accident. Helvius Cinna (fl. first century BC)was mistaken for Lucius Cornelius Cinna (fl. first century BC), one of the conspirators involved in the assassination of Julius Caesar (100–44 BC).[26]Sadly, practically nothing is known about Helvius Cinna. He was an obscure poet who wrote obscure verses and, as such, seems to typify what Tacitus said about poets generally, that they were not as well known as orators.

Cicero had a more favourable attitude to poetry than either Tacitus or Aristides and was even prepared to admit that the poet was, as he put it, 'next door to the orator' (Russell and Winterbottom 1972: 232). In many departments of embellishment, he wrote, 'he is his ally and his equal' and, in one thing, 'the freedom to wander where he likes with the same licence as the orator enjoys' he is the 'same' (ibid.: 232). But Cicero was also careful to distinguish the two. The poet is tied down by metre, he is freer in his use of words and he writes for the few rather than the many. More fundamentally, the orator strives to be the same as the one he admires whereas the poet strives to be different. 'There is no orator', writes Cicero, 'who would not wish to be like Demosthenes but Menander did not wish to be like Homer' (ibid.: 251). He also seems to push poetry and oratory further apart when he quotes, with approval, Aristotle's remark that rhetoric is a branch of logic.

Aristotle was reacting to Plato's complaint that the orator was more interested in ornament than truth. A lawyer can successfully defend a criminal even though he knows he is guilty, and an orator can advocate a course of action which he knows to be wrong. 'The rhetorician', writes Peter Dixon, 'is not seriously concerned with truth. His vaunted art is a device for persuading, an instrument of deception, a knack of producing easy gratification' (1971: 11). Aristotle, in contrast to Plato, argues that rhetoric is part of philosophy because it is primarily a mode of argument, relying more on demonstration than on decoration. The orator proves his point by using enthymeme, a form of syllogism based on probable as opposed to certain premises, and which leads to particular rather than general conclusions. Rhetoric, in short, leads us to truth not away from it.

We have been looking at the differences between rhetoric and poetry but it is clear that Plato's objection to rhetoric is similar to his objection to poetry which immediately draws the two disciplines together, as indeed do Aristotle's arguments that, in their own way, both poetry and rhetoric are associated with philosophy. They also have certain concepts in common such as propriety and the sublime. Ovid saw their relationship as entirely complementary. In a verse epistle to Salanus, a teacher of rhetoric, he writes

> Our work is different but it flows from the same source
> We are both practitioners of the liberal arts . . .
> As your eloquence gives my poetry vigour,
> So beauty flows from me into your words.
> So you're right to think verse borders on your studies,
> And the rites of mutual service should be kept.[27]

The Greek geographer, historian and philosopher Strabo (63 BC–AD24) claimed that poetry and rhetoric were united by diction. 'What is more a subject of rhetoric than diction?' he asked. 'And what is more closely connected with poetry?' (Russell and Winterbottom 1972: 302). The man credited with introducing oratory into Athens in 427 BC, Gorgias, saw rhetoric as a form of praise or blame which was one of the early functions of poetry. Marcus Quintilian (AD35–100), a teacher of rhetoric who counted among his pupils Pliny the Younger and Tacitus, recommended that the aspiring orator steep himself in writers such as Homer, Pindar and Virgil. The orator could learn much from the poet, particularly how to hold an audience. Cicero, for example, proposed that 'word-rhythm and musical measure', which poets used to delight the ear and 'defeat the monotony of speech . . . should, as far as the severity of prose [will allow] be transferred from poetry to eloquence' (ibid.: 263).

Poet and orator also share the same worries. Just as Horace complains that poets were going astray in their desire to please the plebeians, so too does Tacitus protest at orators 'aiming to tickle the palates of the uneducated mob'

(Russell and Winterbottom 1972: 386). Roman rhetoric, like Roman poetry, seems to have fallen away from the standard set by the Greeks, particularly after the death of Cicero and the rise of Imperial Rome which had less need of orators since power lay more with the emperor than with the Senate (Jones 1999: 111). By general consent, the greatest of the Greek orators was Demosthenes (384–322 BC) who inspired Athens in an ultimately doomed attempt to resist the Macedonian expansion, first under Philip and then under Alexander the Great. When Demosthenes spoke, declared Cicero, nothing was more perfect, nothing more sublime. And yet Roman writers did not simply regard Greek orators as the embodiment of an ideal. They were keenly aware that their classifications of Greek rhetoric distorted the reality of it. The basic distinction between Attic, or plain oratory, and Asiatic, or elaborate oratory, was useful but limited. 'There are many kinds of Attic orator', Cicero stated, and even Attic orators, he continued, can 'speak ornately, weightily, copiously' (ibid.: 239), thus blurring the boundary between them and their Asiatic counterparts.

Roman writers also understood that rhetoric was a matter of culture as well as decree and could vary from country to country. 'Speech has no fixed rules', Seneca wrote, 'it is controlled by the usage of a country' (ibid.: 365). If that was the case, for there were those who disagreed, then there was no one standard by which to judge rhetorical accomplishment. One type of oratory is not necessarily worse than another, Tacitus observes, it's different and we have to accept that. But this didn't mean that there was nothing to be learnt from those who had gone before, nor did it mean that one couldn't reasonably compare one's own brand of oratory with that of one's predecessors. Quintilian is exemplary in this respect, pointing out that if Latin lacks the grace of Greek, then it 'must prevail by weight' (ibid.: 410). By showing up your weaknesses, tradition challenged you to find your strengths.

There are, then, a number of affinities between poetry and rhetoric, including many we haven't mentioned, such as the use of 'lies' and achieving the right balance between art and nature. But it is perhaps Cicero's account of the aims of oratory, 'the instruction of the hearer, his being given pleasure, his being strongly moved' (Russell and Winterbottom 1972: 216), that brings out most clearly its relation with poetry. Descriptions of verse from Homer to Plutarch stress one or other of these characteristics, with Horace's view that poetry should teach and please coming the closest. A key figure in Italian Renaissance criticism, Antonio Minturno, put Horace's precepts into Ciceronian dress: 'the functions of the poet are that he should teach well, that he should delight, and that he should move' (in Gilbert 1940: 297). What the elder Seneca (54 BC–AD 39) said about oratory, that 'everything aims at the listener's improvement, at his moral welfare' (Russell and Winterbottom 1972: 370), could equally apply to poetry. By the time we reach the Middle

Ages, poetry and rhetoric are virtually indistinguishable. In the thirteenth century, for example, Geoffrey of Vinsauf discussed the poet's task in terms of three of the five parts of rhetoric, namely, invention (finding or discovering material pertinent to the cause), arrangement (the various parts of an oration, such as the proem, which catches the audience's attention, the narration, which relates the facts, and the peroration, which sums up the argument) and style (the grand, the middle and the low). The other two parts were memory (natural and the trained, 'artificial' memory) and delivery (usually divided into voice and gesture).

All five parts can be found, in one form or another, in the three branches of rhetoric: deliberative or legislative, which is used to exhort or dissuade; judicial or forensic, which is used to accuse or defend; and epideictic or ceremonial, which is used to commemorate or blame. Once again there are parallels with poetry. It is not hard to see, for instance, a connection between deliberative rhetoric and work that aims to persuade readers to adopt good models of behaviour. The word *krisis* which, as we saw at the beginning, was a judgement made in court or poetic contests links verse to judicial rhetoric. Horace said that poetry was the foundation of law, while Aristotle made a similar claim for rhetoric. If he is to be believed, then rhetoric springs from litigation. It was, says Aristotle, invented in fifth-century Sicily by those trying to recover their property after the Syracusan tyrants, who had deprived them of it, were overthrown. Rhetoric is the art of the dispossessed.

By and large there was a more sophisticated understanding of the formal properties of rhetoric than of poetry, simply because the former played a more active role in public life than the latter, whether it was senators trying to win approval for a course of action, or lawyers trying to win their case in court. There was, in other words, a political imperative behind the study of rhetoric that was missing in the case of poetry. And because of the similarities between the two disciplines, writers on poetry found that they had to rely on terms devised by rhetoricians. Hence, Geoffrey of Vinsauf's incorporation of 'invention', 'arrangement' and 'style' into his treatise on how to write verse. In one sense poetry benefited from its close connection with oratory. It was endowed with a rhetorical power that enabled it to play a part in shaping the vernacular and the values of an elite, as we shall see when we look at the development of criticism in the Renaissance.

But, in another sense, poetry was disadvantaged by the connection. The dominance of rhetorical concepts made it difficult to think about the specifically literary aspects of poetry. A good example is the relation between form and content. The distinction orators routinely make between the two encourages commentators to see them as largely separate entities. This is particularly true in the Renaissance where form is regarded as mere ornament. It is not until the late eighteenth century that it is considered an organic part of content. The relation between the two again comes to the fore in modernism, where interest is often in form at the expense of content. Indeed, the formal experimentation by some early twentieth-century artists can be seen as a manifestation of epideictic or ceremonial rhetoric.

For both Greeks and Romans the distinction between the substance of the orator's speech and his skill in delivering it made rhetoric a potentially dishonest art. Plato distrusted it. Aristotle was aware of the problem and tried to resolve it by showing that rhetoric was properly a part of philosophy. Cicero rejected the idea that oratory was merely a question of technique, arguing that the good orator must also have mastered law, ethics, history, science and all aspects of philosophy. Quintilian confronted the question of good oratory being used to bad ends. That, in his view, was impossible. 'At least one thing should be banished from our minds,' he writes, 'the idea that eloquence, fairest thing of all can be allied with vice' (Russell and Winterbottom 1972: 421). Pliny believed that the same was true for poetry and, to that end, quoted the Roman poet Catullus (84–54 BC): 'The good poet does well to be chaste himself' (Russell and Winterbottom 1972: 428). Cicero may well have spluttered into his wine if those lines had been read out over dinner, as he regarded Catullus' work as deeply amoral. Little is known about Catullus, except that he fell in love with an older woman, Clodia Metelli, the Lesbia of his poems who, after a brief period, spurned him for an associate of Cicero, which may have some bearing on the orator's dismissive attitude to the poet.

Ethics, then, was the glue that bound style and substance. Only the good man could be a good orator, only the virtuous poet could produce virtuous verse. Now fast forward to the present and what answer do we have to the problem of spin? We view those who govern us with the same suspicion that many of the ancients viewed their orators. But we lack their faith in the remedy. We are post-Freudian, post-holocaust, postmodern. Truth and goodness. It is all relative, an attitude that may now, after 9/11, be fuelling extremism. We may speak ethically but we act expediently. The ancients tried to marry method and morality but we are content with endlessly refining the former. In the absence of any deeper values we fetishise the means and forget about the ends. Nowhere more so than in education. Teaching has become a technique and learning a form of training. There is nothing wrong with equipping people with skills but there is if that's all we do. And for many in schools and increasingly universities, that *is* all we do. Literacy is not a step to literature but a substitution for it. The ancients were well aware of the dangers of rhetoric, that it rested less on the merit of the case than on the speaker's powers of manipulation, but they could appeal to certain ideals. That we are diffident about such calls is a mark of our distance from them. Or perhaps our wisdom.

Poetry and oratory are based on the idea that man is defined by speech, and that speech itself is the foundation of human society. If speech is bad, then so too is society. As Seneca noted, 'wherever a corrupt style of speech finds favour, you may be sure that morals have gone astray' (Russell and Winterbottom 1972: 365). It is an observation which will echo down the ages. Speech is not just bound up with society, it is also bound up with the economy on which that society is based. Seneca, like Longinus, relates the decay of speech to an appetite for novelty. 'Once the mind has grown accustomed to despising the normal and feeling that the usual is stale, it looks for novelty in speech too' (ibid.: 364). Or again, 'luxury in feasting and clothes are signs of an ailing society; so too is licentious speech' (ibid.: 365). The development of speech, in short, cannot be divorced from economic growth. Money and language are inextricably mixed. That social problems are cast in financial terms is a habit we can trace back to the moment when the word *metron* moved from the realm of the moral to the realm of mathematics.

And, speaking of history, we can say a little about its relation to poetry. Aristotle said that poetry was superior to history because it dealt in general truths. But poetry has many uses. One of them is to praise rulers in order to broadcast their fame to future generations, and this partly matches Cicero's description of history as the 'preservation of public records' (Russell and Winterbottom 1972: 255). Since Cicero makes memory the foundation of all the orator's other qualities (ibid.: 251), there is also a connection between history and rhetoric. Quintilian, though, thought they were different. The aim of rhetoric, he declared, was 'practical effect', but that of history was 'the enlightenment of posterity and the glory of the writer's genius' (ibid.: 385). All three discourses are moral and committed, in varying degrees, to beauty. Plutarch criticises Herodotus on ethical grounds, calling him 'unkind' for using 'hard words and expressions where more moderate ones are available: e.g. calling Nicias a fanatic, instead of "too much inclined to religious observance"' (ibid.: 535), while Dionysius of Halicarnassus (60–after 7 BC) declared that the object of the historian was to preserve 'a beautiful object forever' (ibid.: 313), a phrase that prompts comparison with Keats's claim in 'Endymion' (1818) that 'A thing of beauty is a joy forever'.

There were those, however, like the satirist Lucian of Samosata (AD 125–80), who were suspicious of the historian's interest in style. It is the old charge levelled first at poets, then at orators and now at historians. They want to dazzle instead of enlighten. 'These people', intones Lucian, 'seem to be ignorant of the distinction between the professions of poetry and poems on the one hand, and of history on the other' (Russell and Winterbottom: 537). History is not like poetry. It contains no element of pleasure, only utility. The one function of the historian 'is to relate things as they happened' (ibid.: 542), which is sadly impossible to fulfil. Despite insisting that the historian has no business with poetry, Lucian wraps up his attack by saying that the subject 'needs a poetical breeze to carry it forward' (ibid.: 543). But don't let's criticise his inconsistency too much. Such blunders are unavoidable in a world that is incorrigibly plural. If only those in charge of educational policy, of teaching and learning and quality assurance could recognise that simple truth then many more students might find the study of literature a good deal more wonderful than they do now. But of course our masters know that simple truth very well. They are not interested in promoting the joys of literature, just in controlling the students and, indeed, us. And they do it so well, pretending to care about education while systematically destroying it.

## Conclusion

This has been a long chapter, but the length has been necessary to cover the issues and ideas on which modern criticism is based. The sublime, for example, is an important feature of contemporary aesthetics. And this highlights a key argument of this book, namely, that the history of criticism is largely one of continuity, of variations on a theme. Much of the recent drama of criticism comes from a wilful ignorance of its past.

What, then, are the main points? The first is that song is judged according to its appropriateness for the occasion. This is the origin of propriety which will loom large in the history of criticism. And the fact that song is also an integral part of the symposium shows that criticism is the privilege of an elite. As we move from song to poetry attention turns to how well the work is made and, in the Great Dionysia, poetry is judged on how well it upholds the values of the city. Plato has a poor opinion of poetry, claiming it has a bad effect on behaviour and that it leads us away from truth. The irony is that he uses a poetic form, dialogue, to make that point. Aristotle concentrates on poetry as a form of imitation and a controlled arousal of emotion.

Horace is one of the first to worry about how contemporary writers deal with the burden of tradition but is more famous for his formula that poetry is both pleasing and useful. *Ars poetica*, though, is marked by an anxiety that poetry has ceased to be a central part of social life. In addition, Horace worries that the wrong kind of poetry is becoming more and more popular, one that appeals to the many rather than the few. Consequently, one task of criticism is to defend work which does not give instant gratification. Plutarch gives advice on how to read: how one should be alert to context, to the different meaning of words and how different parts of the work should be brought to bear on each other. The study of rhetoric enhances the practice of reading, for example, by the close study of how speakers achieve their effect. Indeed, rhetoric tends to eclipse poetry in the Roman world mainly because it plays such an important role in the political and legal life of the capital. Oratory is the focus of Longinus' treatise on the sublime but he is careful to show that it is closely related to poetry.

One of the recurrent themes of this history also emerges in the ancient world, the connection between language and money. We are used to hearing about literature's relation to the social order but not so much about how criticism increasingly absorbs economic terms and concepts. We saw how important scales were in the determination of literary value, how the interest in metaphor coincides with the increased use of money and how casually poets use commercial terms to describe their art. The effect of all this lies in the future but, simplifying greatly, it facilitates the institutionalisation of criticism and assimilates the experience of literature to the order of capitalism. We touch on this only slightly in the medieval period where the interest is the interpretation of the Bible. Allegory, which in general is held in low regard in the ancient world dominates the medieval world to which we now turn.

## Notes

1. For a brief account of the nature of Athenian democracy see Jones 1999: 63–9.
2. Aristotle wrote the *Politics* before the *Poetics* and said that he would explain more clearly what he meant by catharsis in the later work, though he never did.
3. For an account of how the judges were chosen see Ford 2002: 277–82.
4. The Greek historian Thucydides' account of the conflict between Athens and Sparta, known as the Peloponnesian War, is available on line at <http://classics.mit.edu/Thucydides/pelopwar.html>. For a modern overview of the conflict, see Kagan 2003.
5. For a very clear account of the rituals preceding the plays and the purpose of the plays themselves, see Goldhill 2004: 220–32.
6. These rhythms are, respectively: dactylic hexameter, used in epic; elegiac distich, used in 'wisdom' poetry; and iambic trimester, used in tragedy and comedy.
7. The best introduction to Russian formalism is still Bennett 1979.
8. I am hugely indebted to Andrew Ford's marvellous *Origins of Criticism* (2002) for this section of the chapter.
9. Descriptions of the conversations at symposia can be found in Homer but the masterpiece of the genre, if we can so call it, is Plato's *Symposium*, in which members of Athens' literary elite exchange their views on love. Menippus (fl. 3 BC) was one of a number to parody the philosophical symposium.
10. Over a thousand years later, the German philosopher Immanuel Kant (1724–1804) also had a number of recommendations for a successful dinner party. The main ones were: choose a conversation which interests everyone; don't change the topic until it has been exhausted; use humour to counter dogmatism and maintain good will even when there are serious disagreements. Both Xenophanes and Kant bring out a forgotten fact of criticism, that is, as a part of a social activity. Colin Davis goes further, saying that Kant's rules for a successful dinner party

are also rules for 'civic society, epistemological enquiry, the organization of universities, the preservation of religion and the establishment of peace between nations', in *After Post-Structuralism* (2004: 62). As we shall see, criticism touches on all these issues too.

11. But see Tate 1927. He traces the practice back to Pherecydes of Syros who was born not later than 600 BC and also to the philosopher Anaxagoras (500–428 BC).

12. The commentary was found in 1962 and was written in around 340 BC, making it Europe's oldest surviving manuscript. It engages with a poem attributed to Orpheus which deals, among other things, with the birth of the gods. The commentary opens with the line 'Close the doors, you uninitiated', and was finally published in 2006, though not without some controversy. See <http://www.atrium-media.com/rogueclassicism/Posts/00004586.html>.

13. For a lively introduction to this conflict, see Green 1998.

14. For a different view of education, see Ford 2002: 194–7.

15. Compare to Claudio in *Measure for Measure:* 'The weariest and most loathed worldly life / That age, ache, penury and imprisonment / Can lay on nature, is a paradise / To what we fear of death' (iii, i 128–31).

16. See Bowie 1990.

17. Aristotle, *Politics* online edition at <http://classics.mit.edu/Aristotle/politics.html>.

18. See Finley 1985.

19. I am indebted to Kennedy, 1997b for the information in this section.

20. For a good introduction to many of the issues involved in canon formation, see Gorak 1991; Hallberg 1984; and Kermode 2004.

21. The work is partly a history of the world from the beginning of time to Julius Caesar and partly a collection of myths with a strong emphasis on sexual passion. John Dryden's translation can be found at <http://classics.mit.edu/Ovid/metam.html>.

22. The word talent itself comes from the Latin *talea* and *talentum*. A *talea ferrea* was a bar of iron used as money in Britain. A *talentum* is a weight or sum of money.

23. In fact we are not sure who was the author of this tract. There are two possible candidates. One is Dionysius of Halicarnassus (60 – died after 7 BC), a Greek historian and teacher of rhetoric, and the other is Cassius Longinus (AD 213–73), a statesman, philosopher and critic. We can be a little more sure about the date of *On Sublimity* because of a reference, in the last chapter, to the change from republican to monarchical government, a topic which occurs frequently in writers of the first century, but not much after that. So it would seem that *On Sublimity* was written at some point during this period, when Augustus acquired the power that effectively made him king.

24. We get our word biology from *biotos* and the fact that it means both life and money is a small illustration of a recurring argument of this book, that matters of quality are inseparable from those of quantity. Of course that depends on seeing an opposition between organic life and inorganic money but the distinction,

though valid at that level, breaks down when we consider that biological systems can be described in economic terms.

25. A famous version of this myth is found in Aristophanes' speech in Plato's *Symposium* <*http://classics.mit.edu/Plato/symposium.html*>.

26. See Shakespeare's *Julius Caesar* (1600), III, iii, for a dramatisation of Cinna's death.

27. The epistle can be found at <http://www.tonykline.co.uk/PITBR/Latin/OvidEx Ponto BkTwo.htm#_Toc34217673>.

# MEDIEVAL CRITICISM

The word 'medieval' is an adjective which means 'relating to the Middle Ages'. The term 'Middle Ages' was invented by writers of the Renaissance to discredit the achievements of the period between the end of the classical age and the beginning of their own. I shall use the phrase medieval criticism throughout this chapter as it less cumbersome than 'criticism of the Middle Ages'.

One problem of dealing with this period is that, until fairly recently, many of the most interesting documents of medieval criticism were available only to specialists. Another difficulty is terminology for, while we use the words 'literature' and 'criticism' relatively freely, these terms had no currency in medieval writing about poetry or the Bible. The word 'literature' first appeared in English in the fourteenth century, near the end of the period covered in this chapter, and it meant polite learning through reading. It did not assume its modern but contested sense of creative or imaginative writing until the eighteenth century. Martin Irvine is therefore right to say that 'there was no separate category of writings designated as "literary" in medieval culture', and there was 'no set of linguistic objects valued exclusively for their aesthetic, imaginative or artistic worth' (1994: 161).

And if there were no such thing as 'literature' neither was there such a thing as criticism. This term enters the language in the early seventeenth century, later than literature, and its predominant sense was of fault-finding (Williams 1976: 85). The term commonly used in the medieval period was commentary, whose primary purpose was the explication of works, and it is with the commentary tradition that this chapter will largely be concerned for, as Vincent Gillespie has remarked, 'most medieval literary theory is found in the surviving commentaries on secular and classical authors' (2005: 146).[1] Another difference in terminology is that the medieval person studied manuscripts rather than books. Although these manuscripts may have contained the same material they would vary from one another in such matters as spelling and page layout and there was no clear distinction between text and commentary. Consequently, the medieval reader experienced everything on the page – glosses, marks, corrections, editorial interpolations – as an integral part of the meaning of the 'book'. Irvine argues that unless we 'confront the otherness of the medieval manuscript' we shall never understand 'medieval literary theory' (1994: 17). Part of that otherness, incidentally, was the absence of punctuation which does not appear to have been used in the reproduction of manuscripts before the Anglo-Saxon (c. 450–1066) and Carolingian eras (c. 768–984), though it was used to prepare them for reading aloud.

In addition to the differences in terminology there are also profound differences of outlook between the medieval period and our own creating further obstacles in coming to terms with 'criticism' from that era. For example, medieval commentators had no concept of a national literature. There was no body of English or French writing because the vernacular was not viewed as sufficiently 'literary', a situation which began to change in the late thirteenth century. The educated classes of medieval Europe spoke Latin and subscribed to 'a common heritage that included the Bible and a group of literary and rhetorical and grammatical works which had been transmitted first or second hand from antiquity' (Hardison 1976: 3). The idea of a universal culture with a common language is quite remote from contemporary approaches to literature which stress its role in creating local and national identities in a variety of idioms – though if the ever-increasing pace of globalisation ushers in a new universal culture then we may well have to rethink this view. The principle of *translatio studii*, the carrying over of ancient learning through reading and commentary, bespeaks an acceptance of authority which is quite at odds with the modern spirit of critique. Few contemporary critics would share the opinion of St Bernard of Chartres (died after 1124) who said that medieval commentators were like dwarfs on the shoulders of giants. They could see much further than their illustrious predecessors, but only because they were carried aloft by them. Instead, the attention of today's critics is focused firmly on how literary traditions are complicit with power structures that repress women, working-class, gay and ethnic groups. The medieval respect for the past has been replaced with a thoroughgoing attempt to dismantle it. But we should not be fooled into thinking that the medieval commentator was simply the passive recipient of ancient authority. It is true that many believed, along with Francesco Alegre, a man prompted by a vision of the Virgin Mary to write a version of Ovid's *Metamorphoses*, that all that was left to writers of the present day was to transmit the wisdom of our 'learned forefathers' (cited in Hanna et al. 2005: 390), but we shouldn't forget that translation, as well as rendering one language into another, is also an act of interpretation. Sometimes even appropriation. One anonymous thirteenth-century translator of Ovid turned him into a Christian which, as he died in AD 17, well before Jesus had started to preach, showed remarkable foresight on his part.

We have mentioned a number of reasons why we might find it hard to come to terms with medieval 'criticism'. Some of these, such as the inaccessibility of medieval texts, are no longer such a barrier thanks to the availability, in translation – with all that word implies – of a range of works from Proclus to Boccaccio.[2] Differences in outlook, however, remain more of a problem – though, as we shall see, some of these diminish on closer inspection. One difference lies in the organisation of knowledge. The medieval world divided it into the *trivium* – grammar, rhetoric and logic – and the *quadrivium* – arithmetic, geometry, astronomy and music. These were called the seven liberal arts, the number seven recalling 'the Seven Petitions of the Lord's Prayer, the Seven Gifts of the Holy Ghost, the Seven Sacraments, the Seven Virtues . . . the Seven Words on the Cross, the Seven Pillars of Wisdom, the Seven Heavens'.[3] They were presided over by philosophy in the classical period and theology in the medieval period, thereby providing knowledge with the sort of unifying framework lacking in our information age. Incidentally, this shift in terminology, from knowledge to information, reflects in language the move from a sacred to a secular society. Knowledge was associated with divine truth and was hierarchical, whereas information is utilitarian and democratic. But to return to the seven liberal arts, these were distinguished from the seven mechanical arts – hunting, agriculture, blacksmithing, war, weaving, medicine and navigation – because they were not geared to earning a livelihood. While the seven liberal arts may have enjoyed high prestige in the medieval period the same cannot be said of their modern manifestation, the humanities. The pursuit of truth has given way to the needs of business, and vocational subjects are now prized more than non-vocational ones.

It is through the unfamiliar lens of the *trivium* and *quadrivium* that we have to try and focus on the medieval conception of poetry – the nearest word we have for 'literature' in this period. It was variously associated with grammar, rhetoric and logic. Very occasionally, it was linked with arithmetic because meter was based on measure, and the numerical composition of verse was regarded as an imitation of the divine numbers responsible for creation. We look below at the relation between rhetoric and grammar but it is worth mentioning here that poetry was mostly associated with *grammatica*, a much broader term than our own 'grammar'. It didn't merely refer to the correct use of language but to compilations of works, commentaries on biblical and classical texts, encyclopedias and library catalogues. Above all, says Irvine, *grammatica* was 'the discipline devoted to the study of texts in manuscript form' (1994: 17). The association of poetry with grammar gave rise to three ways of looking at verse. The first was the gloss which consisted chiefly of notes on individual words and lines of the text; the second, known as the *ars metrica*, was concerned with the counting of vowels and syllables in poetry; and the third was the commentary which we will explore when we look at *grammatica* in more detail. Here, we can note that poetry was not to be enjoyed for its own sake but for its usefulness to the orator and even more to those trained by the grammarian. Thus it had a clearly defined social role, and part of the history of criticism has been the attempt to come to terms with the gradual disappearance of that role by trying to find new ones.

One measure of our remoteness from the medieval mindset is, then, the organisation of knowledge into the *trivium* and the *quadrivium* and the unfamiliar perspective this offers on poetry. Generally speaking, we do not, as commentators did in that period, subscribe to the idea that there is a canon of traditional texts, or that there is a correct way of speaking and writing. In literary terms this could lead to a highly prescriptive approach to writing. A good example is *Poetria nova* (1200–16) by Geoffrey of Vinsauf (fl. 1200) which stipulates exactly how to write poetry. But perhaps the main obstacle to the study of medieval criticism is that it was rooted in a devout belief that the Bible was the word of God. The medieval commentator lived in a largely religious age whereas we live in a largely secular one and this fundamental difference of outlook makes medieval 'criticism' seem very remote from our experience. As the word of God, the Bible stood at the apex of the medieval hierarchy of books whose diversity was generally sacrificed to make them conform to scriptural truth. The Bible explained the beginning and end of the world, the fall of man, salvation through Christ and the Last Judgement. It was an account of first and last things, it was the meaning of history and the promise of eternal bliss.

In our more sceptical age we have difficulty in accepting the medieval view that the Bible, or indeed any one book, can tell us about the purpose of life or the goal of history. We think in terms of books rather than *the* book, accepting their differences rather than forcing them to conform to one master work. Consequently, our reading practice is very different from that found in the medieval period. We defer far less to texts than did medieval readers. We do not, on the whole, read them to discover what is true and what is false nor to learn how we should behave. Instead, we are more likely to interrogate them, to place them in their context, to analyse how they reproduce or resist structures of power, and to challenge how they construct identities of class, gender, race and sexuality. Nevertheless, we still operate with the assumption that a work usually has a deeper meaning than that which appears on the surface and we can trace this idea back to at least the Neoplatonism of the third century.

The mention of this philosophy brings us to the problem of how to organise this period. Its extent and voluminous writings means clarity rather than comprehensiveness will have to be our guiding principle.[4] We will start with a brief account of the principles of *grammatica* and Neoplatonism as these were the main traditions from which Christian commentators drew their ideas about poetry, and which they eventually adapted for the study of the Gospels. Then we move on to examine the impact of Aristotle on biblical criticism before briefly reviewing ideas about poetry and drama prior to the rise of the vernacular, with which we conclude. Obviously, such a short survey will, of necessity, omit a great deal but, even so, the amount of material we do cover is quite wide ranging, and so it may be useful to bear in mind that the main development from the third to the thirteenth century is from reading works allegorically to reading them historically. We might also note the parallel between the rigid schemes of reading in the medieval period and our own approach to literature. We may not proceed, like the grammarians, by examining, in turn, the life of the author, the title of the work, the intention of the writer, the subject matter, the usefulness of the book or to what part of philosophy it belongs, but we do impose perspectives on a work – feminist, post-colonialist, queer and so forth – and read the work from that particular point of view. And then there is the whole culture of learning and teaching which promotes conformity by measuring performance against predetermined outcomes. Perhaps we are closer to the medieval world than we think. Derrida's exploration of the etymology of a word to show that its signification is never stable finds a precedent in Isidore of Seville (560–636)[5] who believed that studying the roots of words and concepts gave valuable insight into their meaning.

### Grammatica

In the classical world the study of poetry was caught up, as we noted earlier, in the disciplinary rivalry between rhetoric and grammar. In general, poetry was regarded as a model of correct speech and writing and its use of figures and ornament made for clarity and affect. But the use of metaphor could also be seen as a turning away from the normal meaning of words, therefore associating poetry with untruth. Although rhetoric and grammar were very close – without a knowledge of the correct rules of speech there was no oratory – it is fair to say that grammarians were more concerned with formal properties of language while rhetoricians were more interested in its persuasive powers. The difference is clear when we consider their respective attitudes to translation. The grammarian is faithful to a text, translating it word for word in order to conserve it, but the orator translates it 'according to sense', in order to make it comply with the needs of the present (Copeland 1995: 2). This distinction is not unlike that between the traditional critic, who wishes to preserve the canon, and the theorist, who wishes to dismantle or redeploy it. A reminder, perhaps, of the durability of critical concepts.

By the fourth century AD, the structure of civic life that had supported the ideal of oratory in Republican and early Imperial Rome had disappeared (Copeland 1995: 37–42). New procedures in the law courts, for example, debarred the opening and closing addresses which had been an important part of Roman public speaking. As rhetorical study diminished, the task of interpreting the rhetoric of texts, for example, their affective devices, increasingly fell to the grammarians. Moreover, this enlargement of their responsibilities coincided with a new and urgent need for commentary on the ancient *auctores*. In Copeland's words:

> Classical antiquity could restrict the exegetical services of the grammarian to an elementary application, largely because the Latin texts studied in the Roman schools were more or less contemporary cultural products. But by the late fourth century, the exhaustive commentaries of Servius on Virgil met a very real need for elucidating a linguistic and literary usage already archaic and unfamiliar. (ibid.: 56)

*Grammatica*'s dual role of recuperating and rhetorically analysing classic texts meant that exegesis was no longer a passive commentary but an active interpretation (ibid.: 56) and thus, like rhetoric earlier, it now had the capacity to subvert as well as preserve the text in its care.

As an art of interpretation *grammatica* was subdivided into *lectio, enarratio, emendatio* and *indicium*. *Lectio* or reading referred to the rules of reading such as how to construe a passage, how to recite it and how to punctuate it; *enarratio* or interpretation identified stylistic devices, topics for commentary, and clarified difficult passages; *emendatio* or correction was concerned with establishing the authenticity of a text and for correcting errors in its transmission or usage; while *indicium* or criticism denoted the process of evaluation, that is, what a text was worth in ethical or ideological terms. It should be clear from these divisions that, with the exception of *indicium*, the grammarian's conception of poetry was largely formal. A work was heroic not because it depicted the exploits of a Jason or a Hercules, but because it was written in dactylic hexameter. But this did not preclude an appreciation of beauty because, as we noted earlier, the meter's measure hinted at the numerical harmony of the created universe. Only when belief in divine numerology begins to fade does an opposition between quality and quantity insinuate itself into critical discourse. That opposition is particularly marked at the present time where the teaching of English is more to do with satisfying the demands of the audit culture than awakening an appreciation of literature.

Reading, interpretation, correction and criticism were subdivisions of one branch of *grammatica*, that known as *idiateron*, or exegesis and textual criticism. The two other branches were *technikon*, covering the parts of speech, and *historikon*, the study of history, which principally involved distinguishing between truth, legend and fiction. This did not mean that history was regarded only as a factual record of the past while all other accounts were seen as mere stories. On the contrary, the grammarians' idea of history resembles some postmodernist accounts of the term in that they believed its importance resided in the way it was written, not in what 'actually happened'.[6] First and foremost, *historia* was part of literary studies since it was identified with the narrative content of the classical canon. Although history, in contrast to poetry, was the 'narration of things done' and although historians wrote chronologically while poets began their tales in *media res*, the two converged on the matter of ethics since, as the man renowned for his conversion of the Goths, Isidore, noted, 'wise men have put the past deeds of men in their histories for the instruction of the present' (cited in Irvine 1994: 241). The 'truth' of history was an ideal of behaviour, not an explanation of events. Empires may rise and fall but the virtues of courage, wisdom and judgment endure forever. As the grammarians regarded the timelessness of these ideals as more important than the ephemera of history, they saw no need to explore the causes of war or debate the arts of peace. But beneath this seeming innocence lay a firm political purpose. The writing of 'history' was closely allied to the rhetoric of the panegyric, a poem in praise of the emperor. To extol either the bravery of Aeneas or the cunning of Odysseus was to promote the glory of Rome.

It is worth making the point here that most criticism takes places in schools and universities and has done since classical times. The principles of *grammatica* were institutionalised in the schools and libraries of Alexandria, Rhodes, Pergamum and other cultural centres of the Hellenistic and Roman world. While these various institutions drew together the various strands of *grammatica* into one discipline the relation between them was not always harmonious, with competition between Alexandria and Pergamum being particularly fierce. The former sought to distinguish itself from the latter, which cultivated an allegorical style of reading, by hardening the division in *grammatica* between an elementary pedagogy in reading and writing and literary scholarship and exegesis, effectively resurrecting the old quarrel between grammarians and rhetoricians within *grammatica* itself. It was the Alexandrian model of *grammatica* which dominated the late classical and early Christian era and it had four main features: the promotion of a literary canon, the correction and transmission of texts, the study of literary language and, the most highly valued function of the grammarian, exegesis and criticism.

All these features are still recognisable in criticism today. We may not promote the literary canon but, by challenging it, we preserve it. The business of correcting and transmitting texts continues to be a vital part of scholarly activity, resulting in new editions of writers' works, while the many forms of contemporary criticism testify to the subject's continuing vitality. The Russian formalists focused on literary language and teachers and lecturers still explain texts to students. Even today, many would agree with the *spirit* of Marcus Terentius Varro's (116–27 BC) remark that literature was 'the science of things said by historians, poets, and orators' (cited in Irvine 1994: 51), because they, too, reject a narrow definition of the term. Of course, Western Europe has changed tremendously since the highly influential Marcus Fabius Quintilian (30–100 AD) drew up his list of approved authors on the basis of their ethics and recommended that grammarians should study etymology, legislate for correct usage in diction and orthography, cast out 'barbarisms' and solecisms, and attend to poetic meter and figures of speech, but the similarities are evident. Even the contemporary tension between textual scholars and ideologues harks back to arguments between rhetoricians who commented on the literature and grammarians who corrected the language.

One of the key texts from late antiquity which played an important part in medieval culture was the fourth-century grammarian Aelius Donatus' two-part *Ars grammatica* which Irvine has described as 'the most successful textbook ever written' (1994: 58). It is divided into two parts: the first is an introductory guide to the parts of speech and inflection and the second, which serves as a 'grammar' of Virgil's works, is a more advanced guide to 'speech, letters, feet, accents, classes of words, barbarisms, solecisms, schemes and tropes' (ibid.: 58). Donatus' handbook was one of three basic types that emerged in late antiquity. The most common was the encyclopaedic treatise, a collection of classical and Christian writings, the second was the mainly vocational school text and the third, a guide to inflections, was not widely used until the seventh and eighth centuries. Donatus, who taught Saint Jerome (AD 340–420 ), one of the first translators of the Old Testament, provided, with his introduction to Virgil's works, a template for the study of classical authors. He introduces the poet by giving the reader a brief account of who Virgil was and when and where he lived, followed by his reason for writing – which in the case of the *Georgics*, was to imitate Theocritus, the third-century inventor of pastoral poetry, and 'to praise Caesar and other leaders through whom he had his homes and lands restored' (cited in Irvine 1994: 126). The 'reason for writing', incidentally, had nothing to do with the author's intentions. As in the 1980s and 1990s, this was not recognised as the explanatory principle of a work. It was, says Irvine, 'generic, literary and philosophical . . . a function of larger intertextual principles' (ibid.: 124–5). It is only with the rediscovery of Aristotle's works that the author starts to emerge from anonymity. Donatus' introduction served as the basis for another important grammarian, Servius, whose expanded version is described below at the beginning of the section 'Introductions to Authors: The Type B and the Type C Prologues'.

Donatus begins his discussion with the *Eclogues*, then moves to the *Georgics*, before proceeding to the *Aeneid*. He discusses the authenticity of the works, whether they are really by Virgil, and places them in the tradition of their respective genres. Donatus interprets Virgil's three poems in an allegorical fashion, each one representing a stage of human life. The *Eclogues* belongs to the pastoral period, the *Georgics* to the agricultural one and the *Aeneid* to the time of war. Donatus then shows how Virgil's works correspond to the three styles high, middle and low. The *Aeneid* is written in the high style because it deal with heroes, the *Georgics* is written in the middle style 'because of the nature and affairs of the characters', and the *Eclogues* is written in the plain style because it deals with 'country people delighting in simplicity, from whom nothing higher ought to be required' (cited in Irvine 1994: 125). The concern with the hierarchy of styles is a reminder that the grammarian was an active figure in the process of social differentiation. He was the complement of the soldier, maintaining linguistic and social distinctions while the other maintained 'the empire's political structure and its system of laws' (Kaster 1997: 18). The grammarians produced an educational programme 'which secured and promoted the interests of the dominant literate classes', and throughout the Middle Ages an expertise in *grammatica* ensured that monks and clerics could advance 'through the ranks of ecclesiastical and civil authority' (ibid.: 49). The basic division of *grammatica*, between elementary instruction in reading and writing and training in the interpretation of literary texts, is still alive in England today. All children must take literacy classes but only a few study literature.

What then, was the legacy of *grammatica*? It stipulated a hierarchy of styles, the high, the middle and the low; it defined genres such as satire; and it described modes of writing, not just distinctions between history and fable, but various types of poetry: the narrative, in which only the poet speaks; the dramatic, in which the poet does not speak; and the epic, which is a mixture of both. But its central aim was to teach correct speaking and writing and the art of interpreting, which it did by reference to a canon of works. The preservation of a body of works was central to its project and these works, particularly Virgil, were both a body of knowledge and a guide to behaviour. The grammarians developed a form of reading which consisted of an introduction that glossed such matters as the author's life and his reason for writing and a commentary which gave the meaning of words and explained difficult passages. It was this idea of reading which informed approaches to the Bible. We have seen that Donatus looked at Virgil's work in an allegorical fashion, and this is a key feature of Neoplatonism. One big difference is that while grammarians were not particularly interested in historical fact, those who commented on the Scriptures were. They attempted to base their ethics on actual events. This left them with the problem of how to deal with fictions which were not true. One answer lay with the Neoplatonists, whose metaphysical conception of allegory proved useful to Christianity.

## NeoPlatonism

The main proponents of NeoPlatonism were Plotinus (AD 204–70), his disciple and literary executor Porphyry (AD 233–309) and Proclus (AD 411–85). Like Plato, Plotinus believed that there was a real world and a world of appearances but, unlike his master, this did not lead to him devalue the experience of art. 'We must recognise', he writes, that the arts 'give no bare reproduction of the thing seen but go back to the reason principle from which nature itself derives' (in Preminger et al. 1974: 232). Put simply, this principle was the creation of the world by the One, and a proper study of that creation could lead to a communion with the One. The One communicated an 'ideal form' to matter, giving it not just shape but beauty too.

Art works in a similar way. Plotinus asks us to imagine two stones, one left alone, the other worked by a craftsman. 'It must be seen', he continues, 'that the stone brought under the artist's hand . . . is beautiful not as stone but in virtue of the form or idea introduced by the art' (in Preminger et. al. 1974: 232). This form or idea derives from the impulse of the One to bind and control matter. Inspired by the One, the artist gathers the parts of nature and orders them into a whole. In Plotinus' words, the 'the ideal form . . . rall[ies] confusion into co-operation [and makes] one harmonious coherence' (in ibid.: 229). A key mark of art, then, is unity; the bringing together of different elements to make a new totality. It is this quality that makes art beautiful. As Plotinus puts it, 'the several parts will have beauty not in themselves, but only as working together to give a comely total' (ibid.: 228). Beauty is art's gift to the world; it 'adds where nature lacks' (ibid.: 232). We do not only find beauty in art but also in action, manners and morality. Although our encounter with different kinds of beauty produces slightly different effects, they will all, to a greater or lesser degree, cause the soul to strain upwards, to long to break away from the body and to mingle with the divine. The phrase Plotinus uses to describe the feeling we get in the presence of beauty is 'Dionysiac exultation' (ibid.: 231).

Beauty for Plotinus is largely a matter of what we see and so has no direct relevance to how we perceive literature. Nevertheless, his comments about the subject do have a bearing on the history of criticism since they relate to artistic inspiration, the importance of form, and the twofold experience of beauty as ecstasy and moral uplift. It is this relation between ethics and aesthetics, though Plotinus does not use these terms, that is of particular relevance for our topic. It goes back at least to Horace who said that poets should 'aim either to benefit or please, or to combine the giving of pleasure with some useful precepts for life' (Murray and Dorch 2000: 107). The relation is always one of tension because, as Thomas Aquinas (1225–74)[7] who, because of his portly figure was nicknamed 'the dumb ox', noted, aesthetics is a matter of contemplation while ethics is a matter of action (Wimsatt and Brooks 1957: 129). We can see an example of this in different introductions to Ovid. One commentator will look at a moral, the aim of the work is 'to persuade us to help a true friend in his hour of need', while another comments on style, 'the end is for us to recognise verbal embellishments and an attractive word order' (in Minnis and Scott 2000: 26 and 28).

During this period both ethics and aesthetics derive their meaning from a metaphysical system that holds them in balance. For Plotinus, this consists of the diffuse continuity between the Creator and the created. The Creator, as the One, stands for unity while the created, as matter, stands for multiplicity. Both unity and multiplicity are simultaneously ethical and aesthetical. Unity is form and goodness while multiplicity is formless and therefore evil. But once this system starts to crumble, the tension between them comes to the fore and one is then emphasised at the expense of the other. A good example here would be the aesthetic movement of the late nineteenth century where art was seen in terms of beauty not morality. The fact that these terms were still current in the 1880s and 1890s is proof of their longevity. Indeed, they surface again in the 'theory wars' of the 1980s and 1990s where Plotinus' valuation of unity and multiplicity is reversed; unity was condemned as, if not evil, repressive, while multiplicity was praised as a good. This reversal, in part, reflects the culmination of the long process whereby politics gradually replaces religion as the basis of criticism. In the late twentieth century, ethics and aesthetics lose their authority because they were seen as symptoms of an order that needed change. But concepts with such a long history cannot simply be dismissed and what happens in the 1980s and 1990s is that they sink to the level of unexamined assumptions. Post-structuralists, for example, valued multiplicity without ever really explaining why it was a 'good'.

Apart from being the biographer and editor of Plotinus, Porphyry is also known for his revision of one Cronius' interpretation of 'The Cave of the Nymphs' in Homer's *Odyssey*. Cronius had argued that the cave did not exist but was an allegory, whereas Porphyry claimed that it did have some basis in reality and, furthermore, that it was possible to interpret the allegory in different ways.[8] This 'tolerance of polysemy', suggests D. A. Russell, 'may recommend Porphyry to modern literary theorists' (1997: 325). A fuller account of poetry can be found in Proclus – who apparently had some success as a rainmaker. He claimed there were three conditions of the soul which corresponded to three types of poetry. The first was that of union with the divine, and this produced the highest kind of poetry, a ' madness better than sanity'; the second was the intellect which traced out the divine pattern in nature, producing poetry that conveyed 'the essence of things' or else portrayed 'good and beautiful deeds'; while the third condition of the soul was approximately that of the body and this produced two types of poetry – the first imitated things realistically while the second rendered them impressionistically (ibid.: 326–7). Proclus' view that there was a continuity between the highest and the lowest form of poetry – which is another version of the grammarian's three styles – stands in stark contrast to twentieth-century views of literature, which is seen either as quite different to other forms of writing, as in high modernism, or as being no different from them at all, as in some of the more extreme versions of post-structuralism.

Proclus believed that poetry conveyed its truths in an allegorical fashion. Since it was impossible to represent divinity directly, the poet could only represent it in a coded form. But allegory didn't always have to refer to the nature of the divine. It could also be a way of conveying moral or philosophical truths. In his *Commentary on the Dream of Scipio* Macrobius (AD 360–c. 440) distinguished between fictions which were a pleasant pastime and those which served a higher purpose because they contained a philosophical truth – a useful distinction for Christians when dealing with pagan works.[9] But only the educated had the ability to detect a deeper meaning. Macrobius, who was one of the first to speculate that the earth may be round, argued that truth had to be hidden from those who couldn't understand it, a view echoed by Alexander of Hales (1186–1245).[10] 'It is most fitting,' he wrote, 'to conceal divine mysteries in elaborate language and to make inaccessible to the many that true knowledge [which] should be hallowed and hidden from view' (in Minnis and Scott 2000: 213). We have already encountered this idea in our discussion of *grammatica*. The notion that only a select few are able to appreciate the true significance of a piece of writing recurs throughout the history of criticism. The elite preserve their power by controlling the dissemination of knowledge. A later manifestation of this attitude can be found in the early twentieth century when the value of the literature we now call modernism derived, in part, from its difficulty. By then, critics had no political power only a certain and, in fact, declining cultural authority, unlike their medieval counterparts whose commentaries had the weight of the Church behind them.

The main contribution of Neoplatonism to biblical study was the emphasis it placed on allegory as access to the divine, but before Christian commentators could exploit this idea or indeed the work of the grammarians, they first had to overcome their hostility to the classical world.

## Christianity and Classical Culture

The encounter between Christianity and the classical world differed from that between the Romans and the Greeks since the Christians sought to banish the ancient authors whereas the Romans enthusiastically embraced Greek culture. But were Christianity and paganism completely antithetical as implied by Tertullian's (c. 160–c. 220 AD) famous question, 'What has Athens to do with Rome?' Or was some form of accommodation between them possible? Christians believed the grammarians were wrong to hold literary culture and polished speech in such high esteem for they were distractions from spiritual truth and right living. Unlike the grammarians who, they believed, were concerned with mere form and appearance, the illiterate and ill-educated apostles tried to save souls by preaching the gospel. Saint Augustine (AD 354–430) argued, in *De doctrina Christiana*, that true communication was not a matter of correct speech. The grammarian had argued that the style of speech depended on the importance of the subject but the Christian made no such distinction since 'everything we say is important' (Saint Augustine, cited in Kaster 1997: 83). The message of the Gospels remained the same even if its mode of delivery varied according to the needs of the audience. According to Saint Augustine, the grammarian aimed to win the good opinion of men but the Christian aimed to procure their salvation. A grounding in literary culture may be a mark of social distinction but it was powerless to save a person from hell. As Robert A. Kaster notes,

> the literary culture was a culture of the tongue, not of the heart; it invested everything in trappings meant to increase prestige among men in a world rotten with false values, and [which] cared nothing for grace, the inner truth that bound a man to God and gave a stable centre to his life and his relations with others. (1997: 71)

The debate about the substance versus the style of communication, and their relation to one another, is one which resurfaces throughout the history of criticism.

The opposition between Christianity and classical culture gradually turned into a hierarchical relationship where pagan authors were made to serve Christian ends and, by the close of the fifth century, a knowledge of Homer and Virgil was as much a feature of the Christian aristocracy as it had been of the Greek or Roman one.[11] One effect of Christianity's assimilation of classical literature was the narrowing of the canon owing to authors being excluded because of their incompatibility with Christian doctrine, and another was to reverse the chronology of world literature. Since the Hebrew writers came before the Greek ones, they must have influenced them. The

Song of Songs was possibly therefore the first epithalamium, and the book of Job the first tragedy (Preminger et al.1974: 285). The rise of Christianity initially called into question the principle of *translatio studii*, Plato should give way to Saint Paul, but ultimately that principle reasserted itself. The classical authors continued to be important not for any intrinsic value they may have but for how they could be made to conform to Christian doctrine. This rejection of tradition, followed by rereading it in the light of new ideas, will prove to be a durable element in the history of criticism.

As noted above, Christians were uneasy with if not downright hostile to the value grammarians placed on polished speech. They believed that the eloquence of Homer and Virgil inflamed the passions but others countered this objection by claiming that the rhetorical powers of classical literature were simply a means to promote 'right living'. Conrad of Hirsau (c. 1070–c. 1150) claims that the 'intention' of Virgil's *Georgics* 'is to instruct mortals in how to live the simple life, that is, a life devoted to tilling the land, so that being thus employed, they may learn their own real nature and divert their thoughts from empty idleness and pre-occupations that are positively harmful' (in Minnis and Scott 2000: 63). In any case, Christians needed the art of eloquence if they were to 'wage the wars of truth and to interpret scripture' (Preminger et al. 1974: 284). Hence we find Gratian (AD 359–83) justifying the study of poetry by pointing out that if we find in the ancients 'either the gold of wisdom or the silver of eloquence' then it should be turned to the profit of salutary learning' (cited in ibid.: 285). Conrad goes further than most when he claims that classical authors wrote so beautifully about ethics that biblical writers sometimes incorporated their expressions into Scripture.

> Where [asks Conrad] did St. Paul borrow the words 'Bad companions ruin good morals' [1 Corinthians 15: 33], if not from that most ancient of poets Menander? From what source did he take his famous testimony to his disciple Titus, 'The Cretans are always liars, evil beasts, more slothful bellies' [Titus 1: 12], if not from the pagan poet Epimenides? (in Minnis and Scott 2000: 59)

Far from being viewed as the enemy of the true faith, the ancient authors were now seen as precursors of Christian morality, even as a rhetorical resource for the writers of scripture.

The chief problem that early – and indeed many later – Christians had with classical literature was that it appeared to be so many lies when set against divine revelation. But did pagan writing only convey untruth or was it reconcilable with Holy Writ? Saint Augustine was of the opinion that

> [j]ust as the Egyptians had vessels and ornaments of gold and silver [which the Jews could] put to better use at God's command, so all the doctrines of the

pagans contain not only superstitious imaginings but also more liberal disciplines more suited to the use of truth and some most useful precepts concerning morals. (cited in Minnis and Scott 2000: 38)

Similarly, Tertullian believed not only that classical literature gave a knowledge of letters but also that it could and should be used for Christian purposes. Writing roughly at the same time, Clement of Alexandria (c. 150–c. 215 AD) argued that Greek philosophers had caught a glimpse of the true nature of God and that passages in Homer, Sophocles and Euripides seemed to imply that the pagan gods were not real.[12] His work suggested that the ancient authors could be read in a manner consistent with Christian ethics, a theme taken up by Basil the Great (AD 327–79)[13] who claimed that the ethical value of the classics aided the soul in its journey toward the true and final good. Fulgentius, a commentator of the fifth/sixth century[14], offers a concrete example of how a classical author could be read in a moral fashion. He argues that Aeneas' adventures in the *Aeneid* correspond to the different stages of life: the shipwreck in the first book 'symbolizes the perils of birth' while the defeat of Mezentius and his son Lausus in the tenth book, 'the belittlers of the gods' symbolizes 'the wise man's conquest of his own soul' (in Preminger et al. 1974: 333 and 340). But it was the work of the grammarians and the Neoplatonists, to whom we have already referred, that gave commentators the necessary techniques for reconciling the classical and Christian world. Of particular importance here is Servius,[15] a fourth-century grammarian who provided 'an interpretative model easily appropriated by Christian readers' (Irvine 1994: 133). The primary purpose of Servius' commentaries was to teach Latin grammar to adolescents. The tone of Servius' commentary was therefore prescriptive, as indeed is the culture of higher education today, where students are trained to meet objectives, not to have opinions. Servius did, however, read Virgil's works in part as an allegory of the life of the emperor Augustus. For example, 'the games celebrated in *Aeneid* 5 are taken to reflect the games given by Augustus in honour of Julius Caesar' (ibid.: 135). And if Servius could read Virgil allegorically, then so too could Christians, especially as Servius' account of Aeneas caught between good and evil spirits (ibid. 1994: 140) chimed with the Christian view of the soul. Thus the Bern commentator sees Rome's new age under Augustus, depicted in Virgil's fourth *Eclogue*, as 'symbolizing the new era of Christ' while Philargyrius states that Augustus' magnanimity towards his enemies anticipates Christ freeing us from our sins (ibid.: 151 and 153).[16]

## Introductions to Authors: The Type B and the Type C Prologues

Servius' commentary on Virgil's *Aeneid* was 'the most important and influential commentary on a classical work known in the Middle Ages' (Irvine

1994: 126). When reading Virgil's text, said Servius, the following matters are to be considered: 'the life of the poet, the title of the work, the nature of the poem, the purpose of writing, the number of books, [and] the interpretation' (cited in ibid.: 129–30). This approach to an author was known as the Type B prologue and it survived until the eleventh century. We can see what this looked like in practice by giving a quick summary of Servius' commentary on Virgil. After a brief biography of the poet and explaining that the title of the poem is derived from the name Aeneas, Servius describes the nature of the poem. It 'is in the heroic meter and is a mixed performance where the poet speaks and represents other people speaking as well' (ibid.: 131). We have already noted that meter alone determined whether a poem was heroic but Servius claims that the *Aeneid* is also heroic 'because it consists of divine and human characters containing the true and the fictive' (ibid.: 131). Truth, for Servius, was not a matter of chronology or empirical fact but of 'lofty discourse and serious meaning' (ibid.: 131) as much a matter of style as of substance. The *Aeneid* was written in the 'high' rather than 'middle' or 'low' style, thus guaranteeing the validity of its claims in respect of ethics and metaphysics. Virgil's purpose was to imitate Homer and praise Augustus which, argues Irvine, shows the aim of commentary was not only to place texts in a tradition but also to articulate and amplify their political message. While there is sometimes a problem determining the number of books which make up a work, this is not the case with the *Aeneid* which has twelve. It is their order that is contentious, and Servius is dismissive of those who believe that a writer should begin at the beginning and continue through to the end. These 'ignorant' commentators fail to appreciate that in 'poetical art', unlike in history, one may begin 'in the middle of things' (cited in ibid.: 131) without any detriment to the tale.

There are six parts to Servius' interpretation of Virgil's text. The largest, devoted to grammatical and linguistic clarification, is a reminder that the grammarian differs from the contemporary critic in that his primary function was not exegesis, but instruction in the living language.[17] Hence a great deal of Servius' commentary concerns such matters as the proper use of figure. He reminds his reader that *figurae* are a deviation from natural usage and must be strictly controlled. Servius accepts that Virgil deploys *figurae* to make his message clear but he also warns his reader against them since they are not part of correct speech. We have already encountered this anxiety about *figurae* with Plato and it proves to be a constant feature in the history of criticism. The second part of the interpretation is an allegorical account of the mythology of the *Aeneid*, a gloss of its narrative details and an elucidation of its historical and geographical references. The third part is a commentary on style and poetic language and the fourth is an exposition of unusual words, often by examining their etymology. The fifth part explains the religious and philosophical doctrine of the text and the sixth is a commentary on the literary tradition and Virgil's place in it.

Servius' influence can be seen on introductions to both pagan and Christian authors. The commentator who writes an introduction to Homer may not give us details of his life but he tells us that the title of the *Odyssey* comes from the word ode meaning praise, that it is therefore 'a laudatory poem', that its purpose is to warn against the perils of an illicit union, which in the case of Paris and Helen gave rise to the Trojan war, and that it consists of three parts (in Minnis and Scott 2000: 16–17). Servius' model is even more evident in the introduction to *Incipit Carmen Paschale* (Here begins the Easter Song) by Sedulius,[18] a Christian poet of the fifth century. The anonymous commentator says, 'we must inquire into seven things: the life of the poet, the title of the work, the nature of the verse, the number of books (the order of the books) and the explanation' (in Minnis and Scoot 2000: 19). We therefore learn that Sedulius was born a pagan but later converted and that the word 'title' comes from Titan 'that is the sun' because 'just as the rising sun gives light to the whole world, so the title illuminates the work that follows' (ibid.: 19). More specifically, the title tells us that the book deals with 'the miracles of the paschal lamb, that is Christ' (ibid.: 20). As is fitting for the deeds of the King of Kings, says the commentator, the verse is heroic, while the intention is 'to destroy the pagan religion and reveal the true path of faith' (ibid.: 20). There are four books: the first recounts the miracles in the Old Testament and the remaining three are devoted to Christ's life and works. The explanation entails 'setting out the contents of the whole book' (ibid.: 20) but it also alludes to stylistic matters, as when the commentator points to how Sedulius uses invocation and narration in his verse. As we can see from this introduction, the commentator carefully guides his reader's response to the work, which is quite different to the contemporary notion that readers are free to create their own meaning from what they see on the page. Not so in the medieval period where reading was a rule-based activity. To paraphrase Hugh of Saint-Victor (1096–1141),[19] a highly influential theologian of the period, each man should know what he ought to read, the order in which he should read it and the manner in which he should read it (Minnis and Scott 2000: 65).

By the twelfth century the Type B prologue had given way to the Type C. It derived from Boethius (c.475–524 AD) who stipulated that any philosophical text should be considered under the following headings: title, subject matter, intention, method and/or didactic treatment and use and the part of philosophy to which the work belonged (Minnis 1984: 18). The association of the Type C prologue with philosophy may be regarded as a stage in the move of poetry away from its traditional association with grammar towards logic, a result of the rediscovery of Aristotle's works. According to Hardison (Preminger et al. 1974: 274), this undermined the idea of poetry as a vehicle for moral instruction since, unlike philosophy, it was not based on true state-ments about the world.[20] Why bother to take any notice of its ethical content if the story itself is a lie? By contrast, Minnis and Scott argue that the Type C prologue 'enhanced the prestige of secular literature' (2000: 13) precisely because of its ethical orientation. It was this quality which distinguished it from the Type B prologue with its focus on the author's life, the kind of poem and type of verse (Minnis and Scott 2000: 13). An example of a Type C pro-logue is the introduction to *Distichia Catonis* (the poems or sayings of Cato). Cato wrote the book for his son 'showing him the proper way to live' (in ibid.: 15). '[P]recepts for living a good and moral life' constitute the subject matter of the book; its intention 'is to show us by what way we may reach true sal-vation, and that we should seek after it and zealously search for it,' while the book itself 'pertains to ethics for its aim is to make a useful contribution to men's morals' (ibid.: 16). The focus on morals made it comparatively easy to say what the meaning of a work was. For example, the aim of Ovid's epistles was 'to commend lawful marriage and love' (in ibid.: 21). However, Minnis insists that the Type C commentary 'does not reveal the meaning of [a] text but is a pointer to one possible meaning thereof' (1984: xvi). Thus, one com-mentator on Ovid's epistles repeatedly uses the phrase 'another interpretation is' pointing to how the author variously 'commend[s] chaste love', 'praise[s] those who write the letters for their chastity' and 'gives pleasure and prof-itable advice to all his readers' (in Minnis and Scott 2000: 22–3).

The Type C prologue was not just applied to the pagan authors, it also became 'the standard form of introduction to commentaries on the Bible serving as an introduction to and a preparation for the explication of the text which followed' (Minnis 1984: 40). Peter Abelard (1079–1142), the renowned lover of Heloise (1101–64), is believed to have been the first person to have transferred the Type C prologue from the arts to theology though there is some dispute about this (see Minnis and Scott 2000: 69). In his *Commentary on Saint Paul's Epistle to the Romans* – Peter focuses on inten-tion, subject matter and mode of treatment. The general intention of the epistle is to reinforce what the Gospels teach, namely, 'those things which are necessary for our salvation' (in Minnis and Scott 2000: 102). The more spe-cific one is to 'restore to true humility and brotherly concord the Roman con-verts from Judaism, who were pushing themselves forward in arrogant rivalry' (ibid.: 102). Paul does this by 'enlarging upon the gifts of God's grace by diminishing the merits of our works so that no-one may any longer presume to glory in his own merit', recognising instead 'that he has received whatever good quality he has' from divine benevolence (ibid.: 102). The subject matter 'is completely taken up with . . . our works and the divine grace', while the mode of treatment is to contrast the feebleness of human endeavour with God's infinite munificence (ibid.: 102).

## Signification: The Literal and the Spiritual Sense

Saint Augustine, who regarded the world as a series of signs which led to a knowledge of God, was one of the first Christians to formulate a theory of signification. He argued that the Bible differed from pagan literature not only because it contained spiritual truths but also because it was true in and of itself. The term 'ox', for example, refers to an animal of that name and 'to an evangelist, as is signified in the Scripture, according to the interpretation of the Apostle when it says "Thou shalt not muzzle the ox that treadeth out the corn"' (cited in Minnis and Scott 2000: 66). Similarly, the wood that Moses casts into bitter waters to make them sweet not only describes a real event, it also 'signifies the cross of Christ' (ibid.:66). Thomas Aquinas put the matter succinctly at the beginning of his *Summa Theologiae* (1266?): 'whereas in every other science things are signified by words, this science [Scripture] has the property that the things signified by the words have themselves also a signification' (cited in Wimsatt and Brooks 1957: 147). In short, biblical signs, whether they are words or things, may be literal and figurative, whereas pagan ones may only be figurative, and even then they cannot convey spiritual truths. Saint Augustine's theory of signification was the foundation for the view that the Bible had 'a single literal sense and a threefold spiritual sense' (Minnis and Scott 2000: 203). We are much less inclined to believe in the distinction between a literal and a spiritual sense not just because we live in a largely secular culture but also because we tend to think of all language as being metaphorical to the extent that words are substitutes for things. For the medieval commentator, the literal sense referred to actual persons and events and so it was primarily historical.

According to Henry of Ghent (1217–93), also known as 'Doctor Solemnis', presumably for his lack of humour, the three spiritual senses were the allegorical, which 'teaches us what we should believe . . . about Christ and the Church', the tropological which 'teaches us what we are to love in order to lead moral lives', namely, the 'supreme Goodness', and the anagogical, which 'teaches us what we are to hope for', namely, 'the immeasurable joy of everlasting bliss' (in Minnis and Scott 2000: 258–9). These three senses depend on a knowledge of Christian doctrine, which regulates how the world is to be interpreted. It assumes that signs need to be referred to this doctrine before they can truly signify. This knowledge is the preserve of experts who protect religious truth from 'vulgar misunderstanding' (Kennedy 1997: 334). Thomas Gallus (1183?–1246) advised his followers to 'hide holy secrets . . . from the ears and knowledge of the impure multitude' and quoted Matthew 7: 6 for his authority: 'For, according to our lord's meaning, it is not lawful to scatter before the swine the beauty of pearls visible or invisible' (in Minnis and Scott 2000: 182). The greatest strength of this system of interpretation was that it provided a master code that could explain everything but that was also its greatest weakness for, if one part was shown to be erroneous, the entire edifice was thrown into question.

The specialist knowledge required to interpret the Scriptures in their spiritual sense provided an intellectual justification for the gradations of feudal society: just as there were hierarchies of readers, so there were hierarchies of power. However, as feudalism came under pressure from the growth of a merchant class and the conflict between landlords and peasants, so the system of allegorical interpretation began to lose its authority. A person's position in society was no longer fixed by their birth, and the meaning of the Scriptures was no longer fixed by a system of interpretation. Indeed, as we shall see below, there was concern about the proliferation of allegorical readings with Saint Bonaventure advising that 'not everything should be given a mystical interpretation' (in Minnis and Scott 2000: 237). Here we encounter another constant in the history of the criticism: how to control reading so that it does not generate an excess of meaning which implicitly challenges the constraints of social and political life. The solution to this problem is either to limit the production of meaning or else to find a way of discriminating between meanings so that some are deemed more significant than others. But no solution succeeds for long: all books which deal with the big questions of human existence are bound to reach beyond the existing order of things, asking new questions of the old answers.

### Historical, Allegorical, Tropological and Anagogical Readings of the Bible

Hugh of Saint-Victor summed up the relation between the historical sense and the allegorical and the tropological one as follows: 'You have in history the means through which to admire God's deeds, in allegory the means through which to believe His mysteries, in morality the means through which to imitate his perfection' (in Minnis and Scott 2000: 77). According to Hugh, the proper way to understand the Bible was to consider it first as history, second as allegory and third as tropology. For Hugh, history 'belong[ed] to the order of time' and was 'the foundation and principle of sacred learning' (ibid.: 76 and 82). He believed there were four things to be sought for in history – defined as both 'actual deeds' and the literal rather than the figurative use of words – 'the person, the business done, the time and the place' (ibid.: 74 and 76). If history belonged to the order of time and was the foundation of learning, allegory 'belong[ed] to the order of knowledge' and was the 'superstructure' (ibid.: 78) which rendered comprehensible the mysteries of, for example, the creation, the origin of sin and the resurrection. Allegorical interpretation of the Scriptures begins with Saint Paul's account of Abraham's two sons, the one, Isaac, born to his wife Sarah and the other,

Ishmael, to a bondwoman, Hagar.[21] These two births are 'an allegory' of how humans have been set free from the flesh by being born again in the spirit (Galatians 4: 22–31). One of the functions of allegory was to make the Old and New Testament correspond with one another.[22] For example, the Italian theologian Peter Lombard (c. 1100–c. 1160), commonly known as the Lombard despite being born in Norvara, notes that the 150 songs of the Psalms can be divided into two groups of 70 and 80, the first group signifying the Old Testament, the second the New and also the resurrection: 'for while men go through six stages in their lives and the seventh stage is death, the eighth will be that of resurrection' (in Minnis and Scott 2000: 106). Allegory's main function, however, was to explain those parts of the Scripture where the literal meaning either contained 'many things which seemed to be opposed to one another, [or] to impart something which smacks of the absurd or the impossible' (ibid.: 78). By interpreting words in their figurative sense, allegory redeemed the fallen meanings of their literal one. Centred on Christ and the Church, allegory revealed spiritual truth concealed in the historical narrative.

Hugh's main point about tropology is that it pertains more to the meaning of things than to the meaning of words for it is only 'by contemplating what God has made [that] we realize ourselves what we ought to do' (Minnis and Scott 2000: 82). As we have seen, Hugh identified three ways in which Scripture conveyed meaning, but there was traditionally a fourth, anagogy, a word which derives from the Greek words *ana*, which means 'up,' and *agoge*, which means 'leading'. Alexander of Hales, called 'the unanswerable doctor' by his fellow theologians, defined anagogy as 'the means by which we are led to higher things when we intend to treat of the loftiest themes and matters celestial' (in ibid.: 218). One of the most quoted examples of these four layers of meaning was Jerusalem. It is an historical city but allegorically it signifies the Church, tropologically it signifies 'the soul of any faithful Christian' and anagogically it signifies 'the life of all heavenly beings who see God "with face uncovered"' (ibid.: 218).

## Representing God: Neoplatonism Again

Of course no-one can see God's face but that didn't stop the Dionysian scholars of the thirteenth century pondering how to represent divinity. No-one quite knows who 'Dionysius' was. The author of *The Celestial Hierarchy* flourished in the fourth century yet he claimed to be Dionysius the Areopagite, a first-century Athenian who was converted to Christianity by Saint Paul (Acts 17:34). If the anonymous author had borrowed the illustrious name of the convert to ensure the survival of his work and to increase its influence, then he was successful: the writings of 'Pseudo Dionysius' were a major factor in the revival of Neoplatonism. This does not differ greatly from its earlier manifestations in the late classical period: it is more a matter of emphasis. Proclus had focused on the various ways in which poetry conveyed a sense of the One, and later commentators drew on this tradition when seeking to understand the relationship between sacred imagery and heavenly splendour.

The human is not equipped to apprehend the divine directly and so God, in his goodness, has enveloped it 'in veils and figures, visible beauties being made to reflect the invisible beauties of heaven, sweet sensory odours being used as emblems of the intelligible teaching, and material lights serving as a likeness of the gift of immaterial enlightenment' (in Minnis and Scott 2000: 168). In the words of Gallus, one of the major commentators on *The Celestial Hierarchy*, Holy Scripture uses 'figurative inventions' to lead us 'to a knowledge of intelligible things' and 'signs and symbols' to prompt 'contemplation and imitation of the supreme celestial hierarchies' (in ibid.: 175). For the Neoplatonists, the images of Holy Scripture can only intimate divine reality they cannot represent it; hence, we can be aware of heavenly things, but never know them.

What needs to be emphasized is the enormous difference between 'the lowly nature of sensible figures [and] the invisible attributes of God and heavenly things' (Gallus in Minnis and Scott 2000: 177). Though some may fear that this 'reduces heavenly objects 'to a condition that is ignoble and dishonourable' (Minnis and Scoot 2000: 177), Gallus argues that in fact 'it begets a truer appreciation of them' (ibid.: 177). There are two ways of representing the divine realm. The first is affirmative, 'employing attributes which are like as when it is said "God is light" [1 John 1:5]' and the second is negative, 'employing attributes which are unlike and incompatible in the extreme, and seem to be highly incongruous in relation to God' (Minnis and Scott 2000: 177). Both forms of representation 'signify that God's divinity surpasses all material things' (ibid.: 178). Light, for example, may give some idea of the resplendent nature of the deity but still 'falls far short of any likeness to it' (ibid.: 178). For that reason, Gallus champions the negative form of representation as the one which, by its very distance from God's glory, comes closest to it. The four beasts around the throne of God (Revelation 4:8) should not make people think that 'the heavenly regions are filled with lions, horses and other similar animals' (Gallus in Minnis and Scott 2000: 177); rather, the very lowliness of these forms should show how far the things of heaven exceed all earthly forms of expression. Taking the argument one step further, Gallus declares that 'nothing which exists or is capable of being understood can properly be said to be of God'; hence, he is best represented by 'negations'; only by saying what God is not can we begin to sense 'His immaterial, incomprehensible, and ineffable infinity which exceeds unity itself' (ibid.: 178). At first sight, Gallus' argument concerning the inadequacy of representation seems to gesture towards

Derrida's claim that representation itself is impossible. However, there is an important difference. Derrida claims that it is the very nature of language which prevents us from being able to express reality whereas Gallus claims that it is the very nature of a supreme reality which prevents us from being able to express it. Nevertheless, we should not use that difference as a reason to dismiss the argument that there are continuities in the history of criticism, since these continuities provide a context for the discussion of current debates.

### The Recovery of Aristotle

The recovery of the works of Aristotle in the thirteenth century[23] – frequently referred to as the scholastic period – particularly his *Prior Analytics, Posterior Analytics* and *Topics*, heralded a change in the approach to the Scriptures with commentators focusing more on the literal than the allegorical signification. No longer content with 'stripping off the bark of a letter to find a deeper and more sacred meaning in the pith of the spiritual sense' (Bede cited in Atkins 1943: 49), they concentrated on the human and historical dimensions of sacred writing, rather as today we aim to put texts in context rather than to read them in isolation. The anxiety about allegorical interpretation was that it was often at variance with the more obvious meaning of a text. As early as the fourth century, Saint Jerome (c. 340–c. 420 AD)[24] had warned of the conflict between a figurative and a literal reading and, by the thirteenth century, Nicholas of Lyre's (1270–1349)[25] claim that mystical interpretations are preferred to plain sense had become the dominant view. An example is the story of David and Bathsheba (2 Samuel 11). David sees Bathsheba washing herself and is struck by her beauty. He discovers she is married and arranges to have her husband, Uriah, placed 'in the forefront of the hottest battle that he may be smitten and die' (2 Samuel 11:15). The allegorical interpretation of this event was that David was Christ, Bathsheba was the church and Uriah was the devil. But how is it possible, asked William of Auvergne (c. 1192–c. 1249)[26] 'that Uriah, a just and holy man should represent the devil?' (cited in Minnis 1984: 106) or that the adultery of David and Bathsheba could represent 'the most immaculate conjunction of Christ and the Church?' (Minnis and Scott 2000: 208). It was precisely this sort of absurdity to which commentators objected. The relentless pursuit of an allegorical meaning could completely distort the literal one, which in this case was about penitence. Read properly, the moral of the story of David and Bathsheba was, in the words of Raoul Ardent (c. 1134–c. 1200)[27], a warning that 'if we should fall into such sins, we should not despair, but, by the example of David, revert to the remedy of repentance' (cited in ibid.: 110).

The preference for a literal reading over an allegorical one was reflected in the replacement of the Type C prologue by one based on Aristotle's idea that there were four major causes which 'governed all activity and change in the universe' (Minnis 1984: 5). As this notion derived from his *Physics* and *Metaphysics*, a 'scientific' terminology was transplanted onto literary theory. In terms of the prologue, the four causes were: the efficient cause (the author); the material cause (the author's sources); the formal cause which consisted of two parts, the *forma tractandi* (the pattern imposed by the author) and the *forma tractatus* (the arrangement or organisation of the work); and the final cause (the ultimate end of the work). One example of the Aristotelian prologue is Hugh of Saint Char's introduction to Saint Mark's Gospel.

> The efficient cause is Mark himself, or the grace of God, or the request of the disciples of Peter. The material cause is Christ and his works. The formal cause or mode of treatment has few words but many profundities. The final cause is indicated by John xx. [31], where it is said, 'these things are written that you may believe, and that believing you may have life.' (cited in Minnis 1984: 79)

We shall look at the efficient cause and the formal cause as they are more relevant to a brief history of criticism than the material cause and the final cause. In any case, scholarship on sources does not have a significant impact until the Renaissance when there is a concerted attempt by philologists to study critically the manuscript tradition, to identify the oldest sources, to eradicate interpolations and remove errors. The final cause is sufficiently straightforward not to merit separate discussion.

### The Efficient Cause: The Author

Hugh cites a number of possible efficient causes for the Gospel and biblical commentators normally distinguished between two levels of authorship, *duplex causa efficiens*, the human and the divine. God was regarded as the first *auctor* and the human *auctor* as the second. The second *auctor* was both moved and mover: moved by God to write and mover of the materials that made the text.

In terms of the history of criticism, the efficient cause is important because it recognises the contribution of the human *auctor* in the creation of the books that make up the Bible. Prior to the thirteenth century, it was assumed that God was the sole *auctor* of the Scriptures and that humans were merely his instruments; he inspired them to write; and that was the extent of their involvement in the production of Holy Writ. The recovery of Aristotle's works, however, encouraged a more sophisticated conception of the *auctor*. Saint Bonaventure (c. 1217–74),[28] a leading thinker of the Franciscan order, distinguished the *auctor* from the *scriptor* (scribe), the *compilator* (compiler) and the *commentator* (commentator). The *scriptor* is someone who copies what someone else has written; the *compilator* does the same, adding what others had to say about it; the *commentator* explicates what someone else has written; while the *auctor* 'writes both his own materials and those of others' and he uses 'the materials of others for the purpose of confirming his own' (cited in Minnis 1984: 94). The Latin term *auctor* means someone who is both 'an originator, or one who gives increase', and it also derives from the Greek *autention* which means authority (Minnis 1984: 10). The term is further related to the Latin *auieo*, to tie, for poets were deemed to tie their verse together with feet and metre (ibid.: 10) These various descriptions of the act the writing are a reminder that the term 'author' has a long history and cannot be reduced to a single idea, for example, that it limits what can be said about a work to the writer's view of it, as was the case during the 'theory wars' of the last decades of the twentieth century.

The *auctor*'s contribution to biblical books was both moral and literary. We have already alluded to the former in our discussion of the story of David and Bathsheba where it was noted that the allegorical interpretation of their relationship, with David as Christ and Bathsheba as the Church, was discounted in favour of a moral one which highlighted David's repentance. Commentators were also more aware of the historical context and this made them able to distinguish between the private and the public man. David may have been an adulterer but he showed proper remorse for his actions and, in any case, this did not ultimately detract from his achievements as a king. Indeed, his 'admirable qualities and virtues' in this role made him 'a model of behaviour for his successors' (Minnis 1984: 109). Another approach to the problem of how to reconcile the shortcomings of the man with his authority as an *auctor* can be seen in the treatment of Solomon, author of the book of Ecclesiastes. How can Solomon properly be called the *auctor* of this book, asked Saint Bonaventure, when he was clearly a sinner? What authority has the word of a wicked man? But Solomon, ran the counter-argument, was not a wicked man since he composed Ecclesiastes in a state of penitence, not a state of sin. Moreover, and this is the key point, he spoke in different voices, sometimes as a wise man and sometimes as a foolish man.

Such techniques showed that authors were not merely ventriloquists but that they had their own styles which could be used to resolve disputes about who wrote what. One such concerned the authorship of the book of Revelation. Was Saint John the Evangelist the same Saint John who wrote Revelation? It was argued that they could not be the same person because the language of the Gospel was so different from the language of Revelation. One was clear, the other was convoluted; in one the message was obvious, in the other it was obscure. In the words of one anonymous commentator, 'John the Apostle wrote useful things, whereas this book [Revelation] has nothing worthy of the Apostolic gravity' (cited in Minnis 1984: 133). To look at the Bible as at least in part the work of individual *auctors* was a significant departure from the allegorical tradition which ignored stylistic differences, preferring to emphasise what the books of the Bible had in common so as to reinforce the central message of the Scriptures: that they were written 'for our learning, that we through patience and comfort of the scriptures might have hope [of salvation]' (Romans 15:4). The idea that we can recognise an author by his or her style anticipates the romantic notion that art's value lies in its being an expression of a unique personality – another reminder that critical concepts have a long history.

*The Formal Cause: The* Forma Tractandi *and the* Forma Tractatus
The various modes of biblical books were examples of the formal cause of the work, the *forma tractandi*, the pattern the *auctor* imposed on his material. Each mode worked in a different way. Odo Rigaldi (1205–75),[29] a disciple of Alexander of Hales, stated that the preceptive mode, which is found in the books of the Law and the Evangelists 'moves because of its power' while the revelatory mode, which is found in the Prophets, 'moves because of its wisdom' (cited in Minnis 1984: 124). Solomon, as the author of the sapiential books, was regarded as being proficient in at least three modes: the teaching of Proverbs, the melancholy of Ecclesiastes and the joy of the Song of Songs. Should a person fail to be affected by one particular mode, then he or she may be affected by another. In the words of Saint Bonaventure,

> if a man is not moved to hear precepts and prohibitions, he may be moved by the benefits which are pointed out to him; and if he is not moved by these, he may be moved by wise warnings, by promises which ring true, by terrifying threats; and thus be stirred to devotion and praise of God, and thereby receive grace which will guide him to the practice of virtuous works. (in Minnis and Scott 2000: 236)

The emphasis on persuading a person to act in a certain manner linked the various modes of Scripture to the classical tradition of rhetoric. The modes connected with praise and blame, for example, derive from demonstrative rhetoric, while those connected with persuading and dissuading derive from deliberative rhetoric (Minnis 1984: 125). The danger of analysing biblical books in terms of rhetoric was, as noted above, that Christian doctrine could itself appear to be no more than a species of oratory.

Or even 'literature'. According to Minnis, the attention given to the form *auctors* used in the presentation of their material during the course of the thirteenth century meant that 'the exegete's discussion of the authors' *forma tractandi* became more and more literary' (1984: 133). The various books of the Bible were now classified according to literary as well as more conventional criteria. Traditionally, the Old Testament had been divided into three major parts, the Law, the Prophets and the Psalter but now each book could be divided in turn. The books of the Prophets, for example, could be organised on the basis of how they led people to observe the Law: Isaiah working mainly by blandishment, Jeremiah mainly by threat and Ezekiel mainly by argument (ibid.: 135). The clear assumption was that *auctors* had deliberately deployed their chosen modes in order to produce the desired effects. Saint Bonaventure's stipulation that 'the mode of proceeding ought to suit the material' (in Minnis and Scott 2000: 223) eventually becomes the commonplace observation that the style should be appropriate to the subject matter.

In the medieval period, however, the relationship of form and content was conceived in terms of preaching the Word of God. According to Thomas Waleys (1293?–1350), a preacher and noted commentator on Saint Augustine's *City of God*, the task of the preacher was 'not only to stir the intelligence to what is true by means of the inevitable conclusions of arguments, but also, by means of narrative and likely persuasion, to stir the emotions to pity' (cited in Minnis 1984: 137). Those who had a preaching mission had to make sure that their sermons suited their audience, and the friars, whose vocation was to spread the gospel, played an important role in boosting the study of *forma tractandi*. The fact that sermons were devised according to the capacity of the audience is a reminder of the importance of hierarchy in the period. The use of metaphor in the Scriptures was, according to Thomas Aquinas, 'useful in stimulating serious students' to interpret the meaning and valuable as 'a defence' against those who were not fit to hear the word of God in that particular form (in Minnis and Scott 2000: 240). There may have been a diversity of literary modes but they were all geared to reinforcing the truth of the Scriptures which, in turn, underpinned the medieval social order. Nevertheless, the idea that the different books of the Bible had an individual voice ultimately implied that the three estates model of society presented a somewhat limited view of human variety. Could the medley of mankind really be reduced to aristocrats, clergy and peasants?

The term *forma tractatus* refers to the organisation of a work. As one anonymous commentator wrote in 1245, the form of a treatise 'is the form of the thing produced which consists in the separation of books and of chapters and the order thereof' (cited in Minnis 1984: 147). Following Aristotle, Aquinas distinguished two sorts of order though both closely related; the first is where the parts have a relation to each other, for example, the various parts of a house; and the second is where they are ordered towards some end, in the case of the house, warmth and shelter. With a book, we can say that sentences, paragraphs and chapter are all related to one another and that this relation exists because of the purpose for which the author wrote it. Minnis sums up this idea with his usual exemplary clarity:

> Literary *ordinatio* [ordering] involves subordination: the parts of a doctrine are subordinated to chapters, chapters are subordinated to books and individual

books are subordinated to the complete work. A text can be thought of as a
hierarchy of superior and subordinate parts. (1984: 148)

The idea that each part of a work had its proper place mirrored the belief that
each person had their proper place in the social hierarchy. One reason why
the estates model was defended so vigorously was that the Norman French
needed to consolidate their rule in England but the big economic expansion
between 1050 and 1300 exerted pressure on the various estates because it
greatly increased the opportunity for social mobility. There was, for example,
a huge rise in the number of people moving from the country to the towns.
According to one estimate, the proportion of the whole population who were
town dwellers had risen from a tenth in 1086 to a fifth in 1300 (Saul 1997:
155). Faced with such pressure on the social structure, it is tempting to draw
at least a crude parallel between the pursuit of order in commentary and the
pursuit of order in society.

In keeping with the preference for the literal or historical reading over the
allegorical one, Hugh of Saint Cher (1200–63) ordered the book of Proverbs
into four parts. The first contains those of King Solomon, the second those of
King Ezechiah and those of both kings in the third. The final part 'contains a
few things Solomon was taught by his mother' (Minnis 1984: 150). If Hugh
couldn't find a literal way of organising a work he would resort to an allegorical one. Thus, he writes of Isaiah that 'the history [is] not in orderly
fashion . . . but random according to the revelation of the Spirit' (ibid.: 150),
but Aquinas disagreed. He thought the structure quite plain. 'This book is
divided into two parts, the prohemium (introduction) and the treatise' and
these are themselves further subdivided (ibid.: 151). The second part, for
example, has two parts: the first contains the threat of divine justice for sins,
the second contains a promise of mercy. Nicholas of Lyre struggled with the
organisation of the Psalter. What drew the Psalms together? Was it authorship, titles, time of composition, or subject matter? He concluded that none
of these really worked and so the Psalms would have to be left as they were.
Nevertheless, the fact that Nicholas thought there should be some method of
organisation principle shows how important this principle had now become.

What Minnis calls the 'near obsession with textual construction' (1984:
153) was no mere formalism. The purpose of dividing and subdividing a text
was to make it easier to teach. By breaking it down into ever smaller units the
author's argument became easier to understand. This is another example of
how Aristotle's view of science influenced the commentary tradition. His proposed method of investigation, defining a subject, dividing it into parts and
then collecting propositions in order to be able to draw conclusions about
it (ibid.: 123) is clearly evident in the fourteenth-century man of letters
Giovanni del Virgilio's remark that

the form of the treatise consists of putting together and arrangement of the fifteen books in this volume and of the chapters in the aforesaid books, and of the parts within the chapters, right down to the smallest parts which essentially introduce one idea each. (in Minnis and Scott 2000: 364)

In summary, we can say that the formal cause incorporated rhetorical, 'literary' and 'scientific' elements. While this may have led to a more accurate understanding of the Holy Scriptures it risked diminishing their status as the revealed word of God. The more commentators relied on reason to establish biblical truth, the more they discovered human creation and contingency.

Up to now we have looked at the development of Christian commentary on the Bible from the various prologues to the influence of Aristotle and we have seen that the general trend has been a move away from an allegorical interpretation of Scripture to an appreciation of its more literary and historical aspects. What emerges from this survey is that biblical commentary is a crucial factor in the evolution of literary criticism. It incorporates theories of signification, different levels of reading and conceptions of authorship which help shape future ideas about literature – one of the most important being that it is a means to self-development. Reading practices produced in response to the demands of Scripture are later transferred to secular works which are viewed, for example, in terms of surface and depth and as a guide to morality. Perhaps one of the reasons why, traditionally, literature was viewed as transcendent, why it was seen as a key to understanding the human condition, is because that is how the Bible itself was read.

## Drama: From Donatus and Evanthius to Averroes

We looked at poetry when we discussed *grammatica* and Neoplatonism. The main point was that these traditions provided a framework for discussing sacred as well as secular literature. After that, our main focus was on the development of biblical prologues. Now it's time to say something about drama.

The two main commentators on tragedy and comedy were the fourth-century grammarians Evanthius and Donatus. Evanthius looks at the origins of drama, the etymology of tragedy and its difference from comedy. He also describes how the Romans adapted the forms. Donatus takes a similar approach but gives us more colourful detail. 'A pimp wears a cloak of various colours; a prostitute wears a yellow one symbolizing greed' (in Preminger et al. 1974: 308). Both writers have a strong awareness of the social context of drama, where it was performed and for what purpose, the harvest, the games and so on, and both largely concentrate on its formal features, such as the four parts of comedy, the *prologue* – which speaks for itself, the *protasis* or 'beginning of the drama', the *epitasis* or 'development and enlargement of the conflict' and the *catastrophe* or 'resolution' (ibid.: 305). The focus on the generic features of tragedy and comedy rather than on individual plays is explained by the fact that classical drama wasn't performed during the Middle Ages – which also meant neither writer had much to say about staging. Evanthius hails Terence as the most comic Latin poet; but he, like Donatus, does not respond directly to specific playwrights. Drama, like poetry, is assumed to have a moral function. Tragedy shows the kind of life that is 'to be shunned', comedy the kind of life that is 'to be sought after' (ibid.: 301). Beyond that elementary distinction, there is no clear idea of genre in the medieval period. Tragedy, for example, is often confused with epic. There were a number of conflicting views about tragedy, that it refers to singers, that it tells the story of wicked kings, that it's written in heroic meter, but the most common view, derived from Boethius, was that it teaches contempt for Fortune. This is very different to Aristotle's view of tragedy as an imitation of an action.

Evanthius and Donatus make little use of Aristotle's *Poetics* and, if echoes of that work occur in their writings, it is 'very faint' (Hardison 1974: 300). In fact Aristotle's *Poetics* was not made widely available in the West until 1256 when the wonderfully named Hermann the German, a monk living in Toledo, translated Averroes' interpretation of the work. Averroes' view of the *Poetics* prevailed for the next four centuries until, in fact, Lodovico Castelvetro's study published in 1570 (ibid.: 348).[30] Averroes (1126–98), considered to be the greatest Arab philosopher of the Middle Ages, opens his work with the remark that 'Aristotle says: Every poem, and all poetic utterance, is either praise or blame' (in Minnis and Scott 2000: 289). In fact no such statement occurs in the *Poetics*. Averroes characterisation of tragedy – or, as he mistakenly calls it, poetry – links it to epideictic rhetoric, which is concerned with praise or blame. Averroes also replaces Aristotle's idea of imitation in the definition of tragedy – the imitation of a serious action – with imagination or imagistic likening. For Averroes, imagery has a twofold function: to represent reality and to move an audience to right action. This is again different from Aristotle where the purpose of arousing the emotions of pity and fear is to purge them. Averroes' rhetorical-ethical approach to the *Poetics* also transforms at least some of Aristotle's six characteristics of tragedy. Character, for example, becomes habit or custom and thought becomes credibility. But the biggest change is plot, which Averroes construes as 'fictional language', or imagistic likening (ibid.: 286, 294–6).

Averroes says there are three forms of 'likening': the first is 'the likening of one object to another'; the second 'is when the comparison is reversed, as when you say "the sun is like this woman" not "this woman is like the sun" '; and the third 'is a compound of these two' (in Minnis and Scott 2000: 290).

Averroes tells his readers that the poet must ensure that 'the subjects which he draws on for his imitative representation actually exist in nature' (ibid.: 300). This is partly because of the pleasure we 'instinctively' feel in the representation of things, things which we might 'not enjoy when we experience them', but mainly because the goal of poetry is 'that kind of pleasure which is achieved by rousing the virtues through representation' (ibid.: 293 and 306). The virtues would not be aroused if we saw them portrayed in an unrealistic way. But Averroes' first concern is morality, not accuracy. The depiction of the world must always serve the cause of good behaviour. We have encountered this expectation of poetry and drama many times before. From Servius to Samuel Johnson the idea that literature should be an improving influence remains fairly constant.

Hardison claims that Averroes replaces Aristotle's conception of poetry as 'an imitation of action, human character/nature' with a conception of poetry as 'the skilful manipulation of similes, metaphors and analogies' (in Preminger et al. 1974: 344). And yet we could argue the opposite, that, far from removing imitation from his work, Averroes places it right at the centre. His work shows a clear commitment to the idea of representation. That is why he is so dismissive of 'invented fictions': they 'are not part of the work of the poet' (in Minnis and Scott 2000: 299). He has little time for Macrobius' idea of the *narratio fabulosa* (fabulous narrative) which uses fiction to 'draw the reader's attention to virtue' (1990: 85). The poet's job, Averroes reiterates, is to speak 'in terms of objects which exist or can exist' (in Minnis and Scott 2000: 299). This contrasts with the Neoplatonist and Christian traditions where, ultimately, 'likeness' refers to the correspondence between the Creator and his creation. Until the rediscovery of Aristotle, commentators thought of the world as a book with a hidden meaning, and that implied that its cover was dispensable. Not so Averroes. He believed that reality should be heightened for the sake of morality, not discarded for some inner truth. As such, his account of the *Poetics*, while not consistent with what Aristotle wrote, chimes nicely with the wider understanding of the philosopher as recalling commentators away from allegory to actuality.

Averroes also revived the debate about where poetry belonged. It has usually been associated with grammar and rhetoric in the *trivium*, and indeed Averroes appears to argue that poetry is rhetorical because it is about praise or blame. The two disciplines, he says, are similar 'because they are directed towards the same end, namely that virtuous acts should be pursued and vices shunned' (in Minnis and Scott 2000: 307). They are not, however, identical. One difference is that rhetoric refers to the public domain, poetry to the private one. In terms that anticipate Yeats's famous remark that 'out of the quarrel with others we make rhetoric; out of the quarrel with ourselves we make poetry', Averroes writes that rhetoric is 'more concerned with the way of living with special reference to other [people], poetry more with reference to the self' (ibid.: 311). And, because rhetoric aims at the common good, it is more important than poetry, which aims only at the individual.

In addition to outlining poetry's relationship to rhetoric, Averroes also shows that it 'constitutes a special part of logic' (ibid.: 308). His argument is rather technical but the main point is that poetry uses a mode of reasoning, the syllogism, that can be found in philosophy.[31] A syllogism has three parts (major premise, minor premise and conclusion) and, in Averroes' conception of poetry, these take the form of 'exordium' (introductory part), 'actual praise' and 'conclusion' (ibid.: 303). But where the philosophical syllogism appeals to the intellect or reason, the poetic syllogism appeals to desire or the imagination. And where the philosophical syllogism is concerned with knowledge, the poetic one is concerned with 'moral realities' (ibid.: 311). Hence philosophy is concerned with truth, poetry with 'speculation' (ibid.: 311). Poetry may be superior to sophistry,[32] where the emphasis was more on skill in argument than arriving at truth, but the fact that its end was practical rather than intellectual made it inferior to philosophy. In short, poetry was a form of knowing, not a way of knowing. More particularly, it was 'a method of treatment applicable to many things' (ibid.: 311).

This discussion about the place of art in relation to knowledge and morality recurs throughout the history of criticism and receives perhaps its most refined expression in Kant where art, far from being a variant of logic or rhetoric – in Kant's terms pure and practical reason – is, in fact, an entity in its own right; one, moreover, which reconciles these two faculties. For now we can note that, once more, poetry is not regarded as giving knowledge. This is the curse inherited by literature. We live in an age that positively fetishises information and so works of imagination must appear even more impoverished to us than to earlier ages. If they don't tell us anything, if they don't show us the truth of things, then why bother with them? At least Averroes gave poetry a central role in moral matters. It doesn't have that today. But we should note two things. First, we cannot finally divorce poetry from knowledge because poetry itself is an object of knowledge: grammarians and others seek to understand tropes, etymologies, grammatical constructions and so forth. Second, in so far as poetry raises issues of imitation, then it is relevant to questions of how we represent the world, and how accurately.

## Aristotle and the Classics

Aristotle influenced commentators on the classics as much as those on the Scriptures. William of Aragon, a somewhat shadowy figure, invoked his name in his commentary on Boethius' *Consolation of Philosophy*, itself a fairly late addition to the medieval canon. William uses Aristotle's observation that 'all

things seek the good' (in Minnis and Scott 2000: 328) as the basis of his interpretation of Boethius' work which helps us, he claims, 'to spurn transitory
goods . . . and to choose those which are permanent' (in ibid.: 330). William
illustrates this with a discussion of Boethius' treatment of the myth of
Orpheus – whose name means eloquence–arguing that it teaches us to value
good expression and learning as a way of correcting base desires. Another
thirteenth-century commentator, Giovanni del Virgilio, also famous for his
correspondence with Dante, uses Aristotle's theory of causality in his introduction to Ovid's *Metamorphoses*. He makes the conventional point that
there is a twofold efficient cause, God and Ovid, but adds that another cause
was Ovid's desire to win the affection of the emperor Octavian. The material
cause, the subject, is 'the treatment of change in things' (in ibid.: 363), while
the formal cause, that is, the treatment and organisation of the material, is
'discursive and inferential and so on' and is arranged into 'books, chapters
and parts' (ibid.: 364). The final cause is for Ovid to 'win everlasting fame'
for himself and to prove, by establishing the fact of metamorphosis, 'that it
was possible for Julius Caesar to have been a god' (ibid.: 364). On that last
point, *Metamorphoses* must be judged a failure.

Nicholas Trevet (1258–1337), author of a French chronicle believed to be
a source for Chaucer's 'The Man of Law's Tale', adopted the Aristotelian prologue for his commentary on Seneca's tragedy *The Madness of Hercules*. The
cause which brought it into being, he writes, was Seneca, the origin of the
subject matter is the madness of Hercules, the formal cause is dramatic
and the final cause is the enjoyment of the audience or, he adds, almost as an
afterthought, 'correction of behaviour by means of the examples set out
here' (Minnis and Scott 2000: 345–6). By putting pleasure above morality,
Nicholas suggests that literature is more than a means of instruction or
improvement. That is the most interesting aspect of his four causes. For surely
we don't need to be told that it's a play and that it's by Seneca? And do we
really need to be informed of the subject matter since the title makes that
abundantly clear? This particular example highlights an implicit feature of
the commentary tradition, that it contains an element of tautology. Yet so
does all criticism. Any discussion of a work, from the very good to the very
bad, reproduces it in some form or other, at best to make us see it in a new
light, at worst to smother it in darkness. But since the critic cannot reproduce
the work in its entirety, we only get a version of it. A refraction. Good criticism distorts the work so that we can see its truth. Or one of them. And a
work's truth, whatever form that may take – imaginative, verisimilitude, psychological and so on – is only part of its value.

Prior to his detailed discussion of *The Madness of Hercules*, Nicholas gives
an account of tragedy itself. This is an instance of what is called an extrinsic
prologue, which deals with a subject in general, compared to the intrinsic

prologue which deals with it in particular. As William of Conches (c. 1090–1154),[33] one of the first Christian writers to study Arab thinkers, puts it, the extrinsic prologue considers such matters as 'what the art is, its name, the reason for its name, the category within which it falls and what is its office or function' (in Minnis and Scott 2000: 130). Hence, Nicholas tells us that tragedy got its name from the practice of rewarding the best singer with a goat, 'which the Greeks call *tragos*', and, quoting Isidore of Seville, defines it as the relation of the crimes of wicked kings in 'doleful verse' (in ibid.: 344). He says that tragedy falls, like all poetry, into the category of 'mythical theology'[34] and that its purpose is to 'root out vices' and implant virtues (ibid.: 342 and 343). Something of Aristotle's idea of tragedy as catharsis hovers around Nicholas's discussion of the term for he refers to tragedians as 'wise doctors, who offer their patients bitter medicines coated with honey in order to cleanse humours and promote health' (ibid.: 342). The extrinsic prologue is then followed by the intrinsic one which stipulates the headings under which the work will be considered, in this case the four causes.

When writing the extrinsic and intrinsic prologues, the commentator is, in effect, examining the relation between the genre and the individual work. He can do this in a judgemental way, condemning the work because it does not conform to the requirements of the genre, or he can be more sensitive, exploring how far the work develops or extends the genre. If the medieval commentator places the work in its generic context, the contemporary critic places it in its ideological one. Critics study the work not so much in relation to others of the same kind, but in the context of particular theories in order to understand how it interrogates conventional representations of, say, race, gender and sexuality. In addition, the contemporary critic believes that the work is both relative to the period in which it was written and relevant to our present concerns. Despite having a particular context, its meanings can still be applied to current problems. The medieval commentator, by contrast, had no real conception of the context of a work, believing that it – particularly the Bible–was relevant in all times and places. Hence, he would not have agreed with the modern critic that meaning can be adapted for our own purposes. It was not our place to shape the work, but to be shaped by it. That is the thrust of William's account of Boethius. *The Consolation of Philosophy* 'teach[es] each of us to distinguish between the various goods and shows which good men ought to direct their hearts and minds towards' (in Minnis and Scott 2000: 330).

But beneath these differences lie certain similarities, not least the fact that, by 'christianising' the classics, medieval commentators did indeed adapt works for their own purpose. And, to that extent, they share with their modern counterpart the assumption that readers not only can, but also should bend works to their own ends, whether these be secular or spiritual. Medieval commentators also have an historical sense. This is evident in a number of ways, from their commonplace observation that classical writers have a limited idea of truth because they lived before Christ, to the increasingly nuanced understanding of types of authorship and variety of literary styles. There are, then, no absolute differences between the medieval period and our own. The idea that certain forms of writing have a central role to play in the development of humans and their society is as true today as it was then. And while we may pride ourselves on a varied critical scene, we shouldn't forget that the medieval one had its fair share of diversity. As well as propounding an author's message, commentary was expected to make a work accessible, highlight the pleasures it had to offer and even promote it as a means of achieving physical and mental health. What's more, many may feel that Nicholas' remark that 'ardour for the Muses has cooled' (in ibid.: 342) is a lament that can be heard down the ages. And, of course, commentary was taught in schools and universities as critical theory is today (Minnis 1984: 161). Whatever claims are made about literature and life, they are usually made in the seminar room.[35]

## The Rise of the Vernacular

The thirteenth and fourteenth centuries see the rise of vernacular literature. The reasons for this vary from country to country but one which was common to Europe was the 'great schism' of 1054 between the Eastern and Western Church. This precipitated the disintegration of a universal culture and prepared the ground for the emergence of a national one. Another was the growth of trade. Latin was the language of learning not commerce so, if merchants wanted to increase their wealth, it was better to study the language of those they traded with rather than pour over Cicero. In short, the impetus was with the vernacular. As the medium of business and innovation it was on the side of change, not the culture of eternal truths.[36] Ironically, by the time we get to the twentieth century, commerce and culture start to converge and we can see this in the way management gurus annex the language of literary theory. But, at this point in history, literature is aligned with politics, not economics. And politics had a religious dimension. One of the most dramatic moments in the history of the vernacular, at least in England, was the argument over whether the bible should be translated into the common tongue.

The key figure was John Wyclif (1330–84), an Oxford scholar who was asked by Edward III (1327–77) to help persuade the Church to give more financial support to his war in France. Angered by the Church's response, Wyclif began a campaign to limit its power. His followers, known as Lollards, a term which variously meant a weed, to mumble or to be lazy,[37] believed that everyone had the right to read the bible for themselves. As one said: 'If we are to be judged by Christ's word, we must learn His word and know it. Why then should not unlearned men read and write and speak His word' (cited in Hanna et al. 2005: 395). This was a direct challenge to the Church's authority so arguments about the problems of translation were also arguments about who should have access to sacred writings. The Church maintained that because English was not comparable with Latin, the meaning of the Bible would be lost in translation. But, came the reply, if it had not been lost when it was translated into Latin from Hebrew and Greek, why should it be lost when it was translated into English? What was at issue was not merely a view of translation but of biblical signification. The orthodox position was that there were different levels of scriptural meaning, the literal, the allegorical, the tropological and the anagogical but the Lollards asserted that there was only one, the literal. To argue for multiple interpretations violated the unity of the Scriptures and created hierarchies of readers – an argument that would surprise post-structuralists who associate the plurality of meaning with democracy. Because Lollard writings were perceived as a threat to the social order, they were eventually suppressed and discussion of the nature of translation suffered as a result. But the issues were revived when William Tyndale published his English bible in 1526. Ten years later he was burnt at the stake.

The vernacular begins as protest and ends as literature. The Lollards wanted an English Bible and the leaders of the Peasants' Revolt in 1381 wrote their demands in English to a largely French-speaking land-owning class. But English was becoming the language of rule as well as rebellion. Henry IV (1367–1413) used it to win support for his claim to the throne after usurping Richard II (1367–1400). This policy was continued by his son, Henry V (1387–1422). He spoke English when addressing the citizens of London prior to his campaign to recover territory in France (1415–20). Once there, he took the unprecedented step of writing to his chancellor in English and, from that time until his death, 'he used English in nearly all his correspondence with the government and citizens of London and other English cities' (Fisher 1996: 22). In short, Henry IV and Henry V promoted English as a means of securing their right to the throne and of ensuring obedience to their rule. They astutely used English rather than French – the language of the Norman invaders – to win support for the House of Lancaster as an English monarchy.

The efforts of the poet John Lydgate (1371–1449) to create a native literary tradition, with Chaucer (1343–1400) at its head, was part of this process. Chaucer was chosen for political rather than literary reasons. It's true he was an important technical innovator – the first to use the decasyllabic couplet for narrative poetry – but his real significance lay in his association with Richard's court. By praising Chaucer, the Lancastrians could assert their continuity with all that was best of the deposed monarch's culture – its style, learning and energetic literary vernacular. What's more, Chaucer was a fairly neutral figure. He was not a spokesman for any particular part of society and, comments Nicholas

Watson, 'he was unusual among late fourteenth-century writers in the degree to which he avoided direct discussion of his times' (1999: 349). This contrasts strongly with William Langland (c. 1332–1400) who, in his great work *Piers the Ploughman* (1379), looks at English society through the eyes of a labourer and also John Gower (c. 1325–1408) whose *Vox clamantis* (c. 1379–81) offers advice to Church and Crown from the perspective of the commons. The critical spirit of both these works meant they could not be recruited to the cause of national unity. *The Canterbury Tales*, however, could. Instead of revealing England's divisions, it revelled in its diversity. Born of a political need, English writing eventually shrinks to a private pleasure, despite the best efforts of contemporary critics to make it more relevant to everyday life.

There still remained the matter of how vernacular literature compared to ancient writing. Was its subject matter as serious? Was its style as lofty? The great gain of the vernacular was that it dealt with common subjects in common language. It was concrete where Latin was abstract, it was experiential where Latin was bookish. But Latin had the sanction of centuries, the gravitas of tradition and the approval of the authorities. No wonder vernacular authors were anxious. One who confronted this problem head on was Dante Alighieri (1265–1321). He conceded that Latin was superior to the vernacular. It could express more and was not subject to change. But, he continued, the vernacular had one advantage which Latin lacked. It was the original language of human beings. Adam and Eve spoke Hebrew. The vernacular was therefore more spiritual than Latin. It is also more natural because that was what people learn to speak first. Cecil Grayson brings out a further dimension of this comparison when he draws a parallel between virtue and the vernacular: 'just as natural human virtue can be fostered and can bring forth its fruits and aspire to greater perfection, so can the natural vernacular be trained and cultivated by art' (1965: 76). This conception of the vernacular potentially links it with a middle class who determine their own destiny. The idea is implicit in Dante's distinction between the nobility of the soul, which belongs to the vernacular, and the nobility of rank, which belongs to Latin, if only because it gestures towards the individualism that will underpin the rise of capitalism.

Aside from general discussions of the vernacular, authors sought to raise its status by modelling it on the forms of Scripture. Gower, for example, likened his *Vox clamantis* to Saint John's vision of the Apocalypse. Both deal with contemporary events, John with the sufferings and corruption of the Church, Gower with the general sufferings and corruption of the three estates; both write in sorrow rather than anger; and both counsel patience and warn of impending divine vengeance (Minnis 1984: 170–1). Gower even divides his work into seven parts to mirror the seven seals on the book depicted by Saint John (Apocalypse 5:1). He also adopted the Aristotelian prologue for his *Confessio amantis* (1390), a book he claimed to have written 'for Engelondes sake' (cited in Minnis 1984: 177), while his characterisation of its style as 'between ernest and game' (ibid.: 186) shows that, even then, irony was integral to English. Framing vernacular writing with the kind of commentary that usually accompanied classical and Christian literature was, in fact, the most common way of dignifying it. If a poem required interpretation, then it was respectable. Another example is Guido da Pisa's prologue to the *Divine Comedy* (c. 1314–20). He starts off by informing the reader that several events in the Old Testament predict Dante's great work. The three parts to Noah's ark miraculously anticipate the three books of the *Comedy*. After more of the same, Guido eventually turns to the work itself, stating that there are six things to examine: the material cause, the formal cause, the efficient cause and the final cause. In addition, we should ask, 'under what kind of philosophy this *Comedy* should be included; and lastly [we should consider] the title of the book' (in Minnis and Scott 2000: 471).

Dante, like Gower, liked to tell the reader what his work meant; no more so than in *Il Convivio* (1304–7) or 'banquet' which was originally intended to provide a commentary to fourteen of his *canzoni*, but which he abandoned after analysing only three. One canzone, *Voi che 'ntendendo*, deals with earthly and heavenly love and is a further exploration of Dante's relationshipwith Beatrice, first described in *Vita nuova* (1293). Minnis and Scott have observed that love is one of the first subjects of vernacular literature (2000: 377) and we get a strong sense of the speaker's pain and confusion at the loss of the beloved. Dante claims, in *Il Convivio*, that vernacular literature has four senses, the literal, the allegorical, the moral and the anagogical. He begins by dividing each *canzone* into its various parts so that 'its meaning will then be easy to see' (in Minnis and Scott 2000: 398). He also invokes Aristotle's theory of causality, as when he talks about 'the final cause of my ascending up there [heaven]' (ibid.: 402). As Dante moves from the literal to the allegorical level the sense of authentic human experience diminishes. The 'truth hidden beneath the beautiful falsehood' (in ibid.: 396) in *Voi che 'ntendendo* is that the lady who comforted Dante after the death of Beatrice 'is Philosophy, who is truly a lady full of sweetness, embellished with dignity, wondrous in knowledge and glorious in freedom' (ibid.: 411).

The complexity of Dante's condition, his grief, longing and self-division, is, in the end, ill served by the conventions of commentary with their demand for a Christian message. This is an instance of what Minnis and Scott call the 'central dilemma' of the commentary on vernacular love poetry:

> how could scholastic interpretative method, a product of a world view wherein *amor* (the love between a man and a woman) was at best regarded as a limited and a transitory good that had to give way to *caritas* (the superior

love of God and one's neighbour), come to terms with a poetry that had human love as its main subject and professed that woman was man's joy and all his bliss? (2000: 378)

The main answer, as we have just seen, is to replace the beloved with a personification of wisdom. This solution derives from Socrates' speech on the nature of love in Plato's *The Symposium* (c. 416 BC). It starts with the contemplation of physical beauty and, passing through a series of stages, which include contemplating the beauties of morality and science, it ascends to absolute and eternal beauty (Plato 1980: 92–5). Once again, classical philosophy proves useful to the Christian religion. They combine to provide a frame that standardises the meaning of love and loss.[38] Dante may want to determine how his poems are read, yet what he writes is itself determined by a tradition which he applies into the vernacular but fails to develop.

Chaucer offers an alternative way for an author to present his work. This is in the form of compilations. These were collections of sayings from Christian and classical sources. The technical term was *florilegia*, meaning culling flowers, the Latin name sweetly signifying the delight that Horace attributed to poetry. In contrast to the commentary tradition, which tries to relate all literature to the Bible so that all books become, in effect, one book, compilations are made up of extracts from different books and are juxtaposed in a manner reminiscent of a modernist collage. The compiler does not claim the authority of an author, he is merely someone who arranges the material of others. Thus Chaucer presents himself as the organiser of *The Canterbury Tales*, not the originator. Of course, the compiler was being disingenuous by deferring to an author's words for his ordering of his material inevitably imposed an interpretation on it. Some, like John Trevisa (1326–1412) who was possibly associated with Wyclif, 'delivered his own opinions and sometimes criticised his sources' (Minnis 1984: 200). By disclaiming responsibility for the precepts and observations, the complier left his audience free to decide what they meant and how they applied it to their own lives, and this reflects a new emphasis on 'the reader's response as a legitimate and central part of the hermeneutic process' (Gillespie 2005: 148). This was a worry in relation to pagan literature but it could be defended by an appeal to Romans 15: 4 where Saint Paul did not say that all that is written is true, just that it was written for our doctrine. Giovanni Boccaccio (1313–75), the great promoter of Dante, used this argument in his prologue to *The Decameron* (1348–53), a collection of traditional stories, justifying the inclusion of immoral episodes by saying that they will help the reader to 'learn to recognise what should be avoided and likewise what should be pursued' (Gillespie 2005: 148).

But Boccaccio is not just interested in the morally improving qualities of literature. The tales were also intended to provide 'succour and diversion' for women in love (cited in Minnis 1984: 203). Furthermore, they are told in gardens, in places designed for amusement not instruction. Minnis comments that the force with which Boccaccio puts this point brings him 'close to claiming a large measure of autonomy for pleasurable fiction' (ibid.: 203). This claim is part of a wider defence of literature in general. It seems to be a truism of critical history that poetry is always undervalued. Certainly Boccaccio thought so. Dismayed by the poor regard in which poetry was held, he set about restoring its reputation. Poetry begins as worship of a superior power, its heightened language a mark of respect for the first gods of mankind. The coming of Christianity confers an even higher status on poetry because biblical authors rely on its many techniques to convey God's word. In the modern world poetry 'veils truth in a fair and fitting garment of fiction'; 'counterfeit[s] sky, land, sea, adorn[s] maidens with flowery garlands'; 'portray[s] human character in its various phases'; in addition it can 'awake the idle, stimulate the dull, restrain the rash, subdue the criminal, and distinguish excellent men with their proper meed of praise' (Minnis and Scott 2000: 420). These and many other such, Boccaccio declares, 'are the effects of poetry' (ibid.: 420).

Although Boccaccio says that it 'proceeds from the bosom of God' (Minnis and Scott 2000: 420) and, although he draws parallels between secular and sacred writing his emphasis ultimately falls on the social and even the psychological uses of poetry or, as he sometimes refers to it, fiction. Hence, what he also calls 'exquisite discourse' arms kings, marshals them for war and launches whole fleets from their docks (ibid.: 420–1). Or, in peacetime, 'diverting stories' help to renew the minds of those engaged in 'affairs of state' (ibid.: 425). Elaborating on this theme, Boccaccio extols the therapeutic powers of fiction. It relieves adversity and 'furnish[es] consolation' (ibid.: 425). Then, suddenly, in the midst of all this praise of poetry, Boccaccio announces that it is potentially dangerous because princes use it to make people believe 'that which they wanted them to believe' (in ibid.: 494). Long before Marx, he was aware of the ideological function of art.

It is not just this insight that gives Boccaccio a contemporary resonance. So too do his comments on the difficulty of poetry. He compares it to Holy Scripture whose different levels of meaning cater for different levels of ability. The Bible 'tests out the wise and reassures the ingenious; it makes public that by which little children may be nourished, and conserves in private that by which it may keep the minds of the loftiest thinkers rapt in admiration' (in Minnis and Scott 2000: 495). In a similar way poetry 'pleases the unlearned by its external appearance' and the learned 'by its hidden truth' (ibid.: 426). Both these conceptions speak of a unified culture where high and low are integrated into a meaningful whole. This contrasts with the modern world where there is an increasing divide between majority and minority tastes. At the same time, we need to be careful about making such bold distinctions. Even in the eighth century Bede (c. 673–735) complained of those who preferred songs, romances, spectacles and drama to the holy writ, saying that they were 'addicted to laughter, jests, storytelling, gluttony and drunkenness' (cited in Olson 2005: 275), while today advertisers use high art to enhance the appeal of their goods. If the Bible brought the medieval world under the sway of a single system of signification, then capitalism does the same for the modern world. It doesn't matter whether we are talking about poetry or pornography; both must make a profit.

Boccaccio also defends the difficulty of fiction on the grounds that if readers have to work hard to discover its meaning, then they are more likely to appreciate it. Again this contrasts with our age where the emphasis on accessibility implies that those who seek knowledge need make little effort to acquire it, with the result that intellectual ideals are not held in particularly high regard. It is a short step from this to the assumption that, if an idea cannot be presented clearly, then it has no value. And to distort a difficult and demanding idea by forcing it into a simple format means that even those who are genuinely interested will have little sense of its real worth. Seen from this angle, Boccaccio's comment that poets 'veil truth with fiction' to prevent it from being 'cheapen[ed] by exposure' (Minnis and Scott 2000: 429) has much to recommend it. He also points out that if something is expressed in a less than straightforward manner, it will stimulate discussion and, quoting Saint Augustine, he observes that 'men may [then] go away the richer, because they have found that closed which might be opened in many ways, than if they could open and discover it by one interpretation' (ibid.: 430). That is a lesson which those in charge of education today still have to learn.

We have seen that the rise of the vernacular brings about a close relationship between literature and politics. But, given that the origins of poetry partly lie in the celebration of the warrior chief, this is to be expected. We have also seen a number of defences of vernacular writing, ranging from the use of commentary to its powers of consolation. What is most striking is the variety of justifications given for reading literature. We are starting to move away from idea that reading is about discovering the truth or learning how to behave. These are still – and will remain – central to any debate about reading, but they increasingly have to contend with other considerations such as it being a form of meditation, a source of information or pleasure, and a means to exercise the reason or to arouse feeling. It seems appropriate to mention here how the act of reading itself changed over the medieval period. Prior to the ninth century, it was mostly a collective experience. Romances and epics were read aloud in courts, and the Bible was read aloud in religious houses. The communal nature of reading was owing to a number of factors: most people's lives were spent in groups; there were only a tiny number of books; and the literacy rate was about one in a hundred (Fischer 2003: 142). From about the ninth century silent reading became more common, partly as a result of changes in Latin, which brought the written word closer to the spoken word, and partly because of simplified scripts (ibid.: 160–2). The rise of silent reading personalised the reader's relation to a book and it also meant that he or she was free to interpret it in his or her own way. Silent reading was potentially subversive though the power of the Church, the lack of books and widespread illiteracy ensured this was not a problem for quite some time to come. What, though, are we to make of the British Government's White Paper on education (2003),[39] which urges universities to move away from a model of research based on individual scholarly activity to one which involves collaboration with other institutions? Is this, in form at any rate, a throwback to the controlled interpretations of public reading in the medieval period? Well we, or those who come after us, will find out.

There is one other change we should mention. The late Middle Ages saw a shift of wealth and power from the nobility and clergy to affluent town dwellers. To this new class reading was 'a mark of gentility' (Taylor 1999: 363). The books they read ranged from devotional ones such as the ubiquitous book of hours – a series of short services, the Little Office of the Virgin Mary, designed to be recited at different times of the day and night – to ones dealing with manners and moral guidance. William Caxton advised that a gentleman and a gentlewoman should not confine themselves to such literature but should also read tales of chivalry. These too offered ideals of behaviour, for men 'valyaunt acts of arms and war' and for women lessons in how 'to be stedfaste and constaunt to them that they ones have promised and agreed to' (cited in ibid.: 364). The written word was still a mark of social division and even imaginative tales were judged in terms of how they influenced actions. But there is, in the fourteenth century, something new about books. Moneylenders accepted them as collateral. They were beginning to take on a commercial character. Books, says Fisher, were no longer the product of monastic scribes for ecclesiastical consumption, but were . . . mass copied . . . for commercial profit by professional copyists in the employ of booksellers and stationers' (Fischer 2003: 190). In short, books were becoming commodities. In private homes, they 'were often part of a public display when guests came to visit' (ibid.: 195). The possession of a library was a sign of wealth if not necessarily of wisdom. The development of a book market, which in turn stimulates the manufacture of 'special reading furniture' (ibid.: 194) means that the value of the written word, which formerly rested exclusively on its truth and its power to persuade the reader to right actions, is now also a matter of money.

## Conclusion

During the course of this chapter we have examined the study of literature from the third to the fourteenth century. We have seen how Christian commentators made use of pagan approaches to poetry and philosophy and how they adapted those for biblical study. We have also seen a move away from allegory to a more historical understanding of literature. That this was because of the discovery of Aristotle shows that it's not just in the Renaissance that classical authors were revived. Finally, we reviewed the rise of the vernacular, noting how it was defended and its links to power. Throughout, we noted parallels with the criticism of our own times, making the point that while there are differences there are also similarities. We still treat literature as a form of truth and a guide to behaviour, though no contemporary critic would put the matter so starkly. What needs to be stressed is that commentators do not ultimately dispense with past literature but use it to enhance their own canon whose very endurance adds a value beyond any social use it might have. This is seen most clearly in the Christian appropriation of classical literature. Of course a past work can be adapted for present purposes but its very difference from the world into which it has survived, or is made to survive, also forms part of its worth. In the late 1970s, critics talked more and more about a break from the past. The comparisons we have made between the medieval period and our own show that there are deep continuities in the history of criticism, and we need to come to terms with these if we are to understand what is at stake in the act of criticism. Ultimately, these continuities are based on ideas of what it means to be human. In the medieval period, humans were defined largely in terms of their soul, and in the Renaissance they will be defined in terms of their eloquence. But these are not mutually exclusive. As usual, it is a question of emphasis. Our relation to the past is always the same but different. Petrach (1304–74) was said to have kissed his copy of Virgil before opening it, but he cursed Cicero as a friend whose 'mistakes fill me with shame and pity' (in Minnis and Scott 2000: 416).

### Notes

1. This is a good place to acknowledge the enormous debt this chapter owes to A. J. Minnis's work on medieval literary criticism. Throughout this chapter I draw heavily on his scholarship and have benefited from his advice.

2. See Minis and Scott [1988] 2000; Preminger et al.: 264; Atkins 1943; and Wogan-Browne et al.

3. For a useful introduction to the seven liberal arts see <http://www.newadvent.org/cathen/01760a.htm>.

4. I refer the reader to Minnis and Johnson (2005) for a more detailed view of how criticism develops over the medieval period, in particular the essays by Winthrop Wetherbee (2005) and Vincent Gillespie

5. For information on Isidore see <http://www.newadvent.org/cathen/08186a.htm> and <http://www.catholic-forum.com/saints/saintio4.htm>.

6. See Jenkins 1991. For a contrary view see Evans 1997.

7. For a good introduction to Aquinas, see Copleston, (1977), and for a brief introduction to his life and works, see<http://www.utm.edu/research/iep/a/aquinas.htm>

8. For a transcript of Porphyry's disagreement with Cronius, see <http://www.prometheustrust.co.uk/TTS_Catalogue/2_-_Porphyry/2_-_porphyry.html>

9. For more detail on the relation between truth and fiction, see Minnis and Scott 113–164.

10. For a brief introduction to the life and works of Alexander of Hales, see <http://www.newadvent.org/cathen/01298a.htm>.

11. The emperor Constantine (d. AD 337) converted to Christianity after he received a sign which he believed foretold his victory over his rival Maxentius. As a result, Constantine issued the edict of Milan in AD 313 which proclaimed a toleration of all faiths. Constantine ruled over the eastern, Greek, part of the Roman empire but the two areas split apart in AD 395 as the western half was subject to increasing raids by Germanic tribes. The conversion of Clovis (c. 466–511 AD), King of the Franks, in AD 496 eventually led to Roman Christianity being dominant in Europe by the end of the seventh century. For further details, see Green 1996.

12. Kennedy 1997b: 333 and 337.

13. Basil the Great was one of the Cappadocian fathers – Gregory of Nazianus and Gregory of Nyssa were the other two – and they were noted for being men of learning who sought a synthesis of the best of classical and Christian culture. For a brief overview of the life and work of Basil, see <http://www.basilian.org/Publica/StBasil/Stbasil1.htm> and <http://www.newadvent. org/cathen/02330b.htm> See also Wilson 1986 and 1975.

14. For a brief overview of the life and work of Fulgentius, see <http://www.people.virginia.edu/~bgh2n/fulgentius.html> and <http://gondolin.hist.liv.ac.uk/~azaroth/university/orfeo/node9.html>.

15. For a brief overview of the life and work of Servius, see <http://www.nsula.edu/scholars_college/Thesis/Thesisabstracts/HSTtheses/Vaughn.html>. <http://www.romansonline.com/sources/Serv.asp> <http://virgil.org/bibliography/servius.htm>

16. The commentary tradition is a long and complex one. A useful starting point is <http://www.people.virginia.edu/~bgh2n/commentaries.html> which gives a timeline of some of the major figures.

17. See Kaster 1997. A. J. Minnis would disagree. He quotes Thierry of Chartres to the effect that grammar was not just a matter of learning how to write and speak well, its task was also 'the explication and study of all the authors' in Minnis and Scott 2000: 12.

18. For further details of Sedulius see Minnis and Scott 2000: 19, especially note 33. See, too, Sigerson 1922 and the following useful websites: <http://www.cyberhymnal.

org/bio/s/e/sedulius_c.htm> <http://www.gmu.edu/departments/fld/CLASSICS/sed ulius.html>.

19. For a brief introduction to the life and work of Hugh of Saint Victor, see <http://www.newadvent.org/cathen/07521c.htm>.

20. For a different point of view, that poetry remained central to ethics, see Allen 1982.

21. O. B. Hardison points out that by the fifth century there were five distinct systems of allegory: 'allegory as etymology, allegory as euhemerism (the theory that mythological figures are based on historical persons), allegory as doctrine related to science, ethics or religion, and allegory as divinely inspired truth concealed under a veil of fiction either to protect it from the eyes of the unenlightened or because transcendent vision can only be expressed in symbols', in Preminger et al. 1974: 265. For a detailed discussion of allegory and its development during this period, see Copeland 2005.

22. See Minnis1984: 43–59.

23. See Luscombe1997 and Copeland 2005.

24. For a brief overview of the life and work of Saint Jerome, see <http://www.newad-vent.org/cathen/08341a.htm>.

25. For a brief overview of the life and work of Nicholas of Lyre, see <http://www.newadvent.org/cathen/08341a.htm>.

26. For a brief overview of the life and work of William of Auvergne, see <http://www.newadvent.org/cathen/15631c.htm>.

27. For a brief overview of the life and work of Raoul Ardent, see <http://www.bautz.de/bbkl/r/radulfus_a.shtml>. and <http://www.ulb.ac.be/philo/urhm/ardent.html>.

28. For a brief overview of the life and work of Saint Bonaventure, see <http://www.newadvent.org/cathen/02648c.htm>.

29. For a brief overview of the life and work of Odi Rigaldi, see <http://users.bart.nl/~roestb/franciscan/franauto.htm#_Toc427588428>. Lodovico Castelvetro, c. 1505–71.

30. For a more detailed account of Averroes' view of poetry and tragedy, see: Hardison in Preminger et al. 1974: 341–8; and Minnis and Scott 2000: 277–88.

31. For a brief introduction to the medieval syllogism, see: <http://plato.stanford.edu/entries/medieval-syllogism/>; and Luscombe 1997: 18–19. For more details on Averroes' placing of poetry, see: Minnis and Scott 2000: 277–81; and Hardison in Preminger et al. 1974: 341–4.

32. For a brief account of the sophists, see: Kennedy 1997c: 82–6; Luscombe 1997: 162–3; and< http://www.uky.edu/~jjordo/Sophist.htm>.

33. For a brief overview of William's life and work, see <http://www.newadvent.org/cathen/15632b.htm>.

34. Nicholas is here drawing on Saint Augustine's distinction between three types of pagan theology: the mythical, the natural and the civil. The first relates to the theatre, the second to nature and the third to the temple. Augustine thought that the third should be banished because of its association with false gods. Augustine

was not altogether happy with mythical theology but, in the end, decided that the theatre was better than the temple because it only portrayed rites which were actually performed in the temple (in Minnis and Scott 2000: 343).

35. Though, see Gillespie 2005. Gillespie argues that because at the end of the thirteenth century grammar schools dropped morally difficult works for more didactic ones, writers like Ovid 'increasingly came to be read, assessed, contested and rewritten . . . outside the conventional venues and frameworks of academic training' (p. 173).

36. Fisher argues that English was 'standardised by government and business rather than by literary usage' (1996: 9). See also Kaye 1998. Although he does not focus on the vernacular, he does explore a related area; namely, how the 'rapid monetization of European society strongly influenced the conceptual model of the natural world' (p. 2).

37. For further discussion of the derivation of this term, see: <http://www.newadvent.org/cathen/09333a.htm>;and<http://www.lollardsociety.org/>; and <http://www.courses.fas.harvard.edu/~chaucer/special/varia/lollards/lollards.html>.

38. The interested reader might compare how Dante deals with loss of Beatrice in *Vita nuova* (1293) and *The Divine Comedy* (c. 1314–20) with how Tennyson deals with the loss of Arthur Hallam in *In Memoriam* (1850). Their different attitudes to religion are one mark of the change in sensibility from the medieval to the industrial world.

39. The White paper was the basis of the Higher Education Act 2004 and the Further Education and Training Act 2007.both are available at <http://www.opsi.gov.uk/acts2004/20040008.htm>andhttp://www.opsi.gov.uk/acts/acts2007/ukpga_2 0070025_en_1>.

# ENGLISH RENAISSANCE CRITICISM

In the late medieval period, poets sought to dignify their native language by prefacing their work with the sort of commentary normally reserved for the classics or the Scriptures. As we move into the Renaissance we can see a continuing preoccupation with the vernacular. Its steady rise eventually spells the end for a 'universal' culture based on Latin so that by 1621 we find Robert Burton, the author of *The Anatomy of Melancholy*, complaining that no publisher will print his magnum opus in that language. As Richard Waswo points out, because of

> a conscious campaign and numerous polemics, first developed in Italy, then continued in France, the results of which were simply transferred to England, the major vernacular languages of Western Europe had, by that date, effectively dislodged the monopoly held by Latin on all forms of serious, written or printed enquiry. (2001: 409)

Consequently, any history of criticism now has to focus on individual countries rather than the continent as a whole though, of course, similarities remain.[1] Accordingly, for the rest of this book, we will focus mainly on England, mentioning the work of other countries where it has an impact on the development of English criticism which, in this period, is principally a concern with the moral status of literature. In the last chapter, we saw a shift in late medieval criticism from the study of the meaning of a work to how it achieved its effects, and this sets the trend for a good deal of writing about poetry and drama in the sixteenth and early seventeenth century. The focus now falls not so much on the interpretation of literature, as on how its various features influence behaviour. This is partly because secular literature became more prominent at this time, and partly because it did not present the same difficulties of understanding that had driven theories of biblical signification.

### 'Language Most Shows A Man'

Accompanying the rise of the vernacular is a belief that man is defined by his power of speech. Roger Ascham (1515–68), who tutored Queen Elizabeth I when she was a girl and who is described as 'the father of English prose' claimed that it is 'one of the fairest and rarest gifts that God doth give to man', while Ben Jonson (1572–1637) wrote that 'no glass renders a man's form or likeness so true as his speech(in Vickers 1999: 142 and 578).[2] If man is defined by his speech then, by implication, he is also defined by literature, since that is the highest form of speech. As the poet Thomas Campion (1567–1620) notes, poetry 'is the chief beginner and maintainer of eloquence, not only helping the ear with acquaintance of sweet numbers, but also raising the mind to a more high and lofty conceit' (in ibid.: 429). The definition of man in terms of literature, and in these years that means poetry and drama, appears, at first sight, to break with the medieval view that his salient characteristic was his soul. But a closer look reveals continuity, not change. For example, the increased awareness, in the thirteenth century, of an author's individual style contributed to the high value placed on eloquence during the Renaissance, while the idea that eloquence derived from God is a feature of both eras. He bestowed the gift of speech on man, and also inspired the poet so that literature becomes the supreme sign of man's divinity, though we should also note that the part played by heavenly 'infusion' is gradually reduced as writers stress the importance of study in order to acquire the skills necessary to produce poetry (Vickers 1999: 192 and 586–7; and Moss 2001b: 99–100).

The spiritual significance of speech helped shape attitudes to the vernacular. Most obviously, it should reflect man's exalted position in the hierarchy of God's creation. To speak badly was to betray your very essence. Here is one obvious difference between the Renaissance and our own age. We do not hold eloquence in such high regard, and therefore, perhaps, pay less attention to literary expression than Renaissance humanists did. And we – the culture generally – certainly do not think that the 'shame of speaking unskilfully' is an offence against God (Hoskyns in Vickers 1999: 399). The translation of the Bible into the vernacular dramatised these issues. The native idiom had to be good enough to receive God's word and also to communicate it effectively. Did this mean that the vernacular should be plain or refined? This question was explored in different ways by the Dutch theologian and humanist Erasmus (1469–1536) and the German monk Martin Luther (1483–1546).

Erasmus distinguished between good language and bad language. He associated the former with Christ and the latter with scholasticism. Those who aspired to speak and write well should imitate the ancients and pay close attention to the rules of rhetoric and grammar. They should always observe propriety in their choice of vocabulary and cultivate an elegant style. In this way they not only express their resemblance to the divine, they also help strengthen social ties, unlike what Erasmus called 'scholastic barbarism', where an obsession with logic and neglect of grammar shrank understanding of religion and 'divided the commonwealth into factions' (O'Rourke Boyle 2001: 48). The figure of Christ is crucial to Erasmus' argument, for he had renewed the word of God just as the humanist would renew the word of man. And just as Christ's word promised to transform man's relation to God, so the humanist's word promised to transform society. Moreover, Christ was a figure around whom all could unite. Not all could be erudite, but all could be pious, and so, Erasmus declared, 'no-one is prevented from being a theologian' (in ibid.: 49). This was reflected in his translation of the New Testament, particularly the Gospel of John. Saint Jerome (AD 347–420) had translated the first line of this book as 'In the beginning was the word' but Erasmus translated it as 'In the beginning was the conversation'. The difference hinged on the Greek term 'logos' which had variety of meanings ranging from word, speech, and reason to Christ himself. 'The Word', John writes, 'was made flesh, and dwelt among us' (1:14). Erasmus' democratic gloss angered both Church and civic powers, forcing him to retract his claim that theology was open to all and to restrict it to the learned; for only they understood the relation of 'good language' to the Scriptures.

Luther took the opposite view. This was the man who, on 31 October 1517, nailed his 95 theses to the door of the Castle Church in Wittenburg and began the Protestant Reformation. Among its many causes were the growth of nation states, which challenged the power of the pope, divisions within the papacy itself, and the development of humanism which undermined the intellectual foundations of Catholic doctrine.[3] Another cause was the corruption of the Church, for instance, the selling of indulgences which allowed people to pay for the removal of their sins instead of confessing and doing penance for them. Luther believed that such behaviour showed the Church had lost sight of Christianity's central truth, that man cannot be saved by his own efforts, only by faith in God's grace. And the best way to obtain that faith, Luther claimed, was to read the Bible. He therefore supported its translation into the vernacular languages of Europe, his own version becoming the mainstay of the central and northern German presses. The availability of the Scriptures, at least to a small literate section of the population of Europe, was a further blow to the authority of the Church. Not only was Catholic doctrine now openly questioned, but also people could make up their own minds about the Bible without the priest telling them what to believe. Luther's argument that the message of the Gospels was largely self-evident meant that there was no need to interpret them. They were open to all. Learned commentary was redundant because the sense was plain. In fact, it interfered with the true transmission of the word and was therefore, like anything that did so, 'human dung' (in O'Rourke Boyle 2001: 51).

Erasmus and Luther, then, present two distinct attitudes to the vernacular. Each develops his idea of it in relation to the problem of translating the Bible. For Erasmus, the vernacular is the property of the erudite; for Luther, it is the property of all though he, like Erasmus, eventually retreated from this position, worried that commoners might misinterpret holy writ. To prevent this he authorised his followers 'to disseminate the official creeds of state churches and to inculcate orthodoxy in the public by memorization and recital' (O'Rourke Boyle 2001: 51). The struggle for the control of the vernacular in the translation of the Bible is part of the wider struggle for what counts as the correct use of the vernacular in social life. Is its diversity to be embraced or disciplined? This argument is important for literary criticism because, as we shall see, the idea of literary language is based on a particular view of the vernacular, which it continually refines. And we shouldn't forget that, in very general terms, literary analysis itself is always an act of translation, an attempt to render the language of literature into the language of criticism. It is also a comment on the work, part explanation and part evaluation. The relation of the translation to commentary ought to be complementary, for how we describe our experience of a work expresses our valuation of it as much, if not more, than a direct statement of its worth. But, too often, this is not the case. Fashion, peer group pressure or career politics usually mean that practising critics, and those hoping to enter the profession, have to adopt the current orthodoxy which then exempts them from their own individual encounter with the work, the starting point of true criticism.

## Protestantism, the English Vernacular and Criticism

The Protestant Reformation took a slightly different course in England. Henry VIII (1491–1547) was initially opposed to it, employing the finest theologians of the day to counter the doctrines of Luther. The pope was so grateful that he gave Henry the title 'defender of the faith'. But when Henry's marriage to Catharine of Aragon (1485–1536) failed to produce a male heir, Henry decided to divorce her and marry Anne Boleyn (1502?–36) whom he had previously pursued, unsuccessfully, as a mistress. The pope refused to grant Henry an annulment on the grounds that it was contrary to the teaching of the Catholic church. Henry therefore turned to the Archbishop of Canterbury, the recently appointed Thomas Cranmer (1489–1556), for permission to divorce and then, in 1534, he appointed himself the supreme head of the English church, after which he dissolved the monasteries keeping the property for the

Crown. Despite the different context for the Reformation in England, the same issues of biblical translation and the individual's right to read God's word for themselves were as applicable there as they were elsewhere in Europe.

Between the publication of William Tyndale's version in 1526 and the King James Bible in 1611 there were fifty different translations of the Scriptures. Tyndale wanted God's word to be available to everyone, even 'the boy who plows the field' (in Crystal 2004: 273). He had realised, he said, 'that it was impossible to stablysh the laye people in any truth, excepte the scriptures were playnly layde before their eyes in their mother tonge, that they might se the processe, ordre and meaning of the texte' (ibid.: 273). Tyndale trusted that everyone would see the same truth. He did not take into account the possibility of different interpretations of the Scriptures, nor how these could become the basis for questioning political and religious authority. It cost him his life. He was strangled to death on 6 October 1536 and his corpse was burnt at the stake. His last word were 'Lord, open the King of England's eyes' (in Fischer 2003: 229). That king was Henry. He may have defied the pope but he was not yet prepared to let his own people make up their own minds about the Bible.

Melvyn Bragg has written movingly of Tyndale's contribution to the vernacular. He wasn't just bringing the word of God to the people, he was 'bringing in words which carried ideas, described feelings, gave voice to emotions, expanded the way we could describe how we lived' (2004: 110). He introduced words, Bragg continues,

> which tell us about the inner nature of our condition; words which, as in the Beatitudes, express as never before or since, the great loving dream of a moral life which applies to everyone and which challenges every ruling description of society from the beginning until today. (ibid.: 110)

In short, Tyndale's translation provided an idiom for the inner life and for protest at injustice, an idiom which helped shape not just the English vernacular, but also English literature. Tyndale's rendition of the Scriptures gave continuity to the language and, in the process, consolidated it. Most of the King James Bible is based on his translation. The fact that this masterpiece was, as it says on its title page, 'appointed to be read in churches' gave it 'a national presence and level of prestige which would prove to be more widespread and longer lasting than any Bible of the previous century' (Crystal 2004: 275). Its influence on the vernacular was enormous, contributing more to English than Shakespeare, even though his works contain a greater variety of words (ibid.: 276).

The development of the language is thus greatly indebted to Tyndale's translation of the Bible. His efforts gave English rhythm, range, richness and

*Literary Criticism*

resonance, but that is not the whole story. Tyndale's limited lexicon did little to develop the linguistic resources of the language while his priority of making English deliver the message of the Scriptures perhaps predisposed it towards conservatism in expression and thought. I say 'perhaps' because the Bible could be used to challenge power as well as sanctify it. As England gradually becomes a more secular society the spiritual dimension of the language is in danger of being lost because of its association with a largely discredited idea of divinity. Our scientific understanding makes us question whether the prophet Ezekiel really saw a creature in the likeness of a man, with four faces, four wings and feet 'like the soul of a calf's foot' (1:5–13),[4] while even a cursory reading of the Gospels makes us sceptical of their claims. Jesus describes the end of the world and says it will happen in the disciples' lifetime. 'Verily I say unto you, This generation shall not pass away, till all be fulfilled' (Luke 21:32). But it would be a mistake to say that, because we look to science rather than Scripture to understand ourselves and the world, we don't need a sense of the significance of human life; we do. And language can provide it because it is the link between the mundane and the marvellous. That was the Tyndale's great achievement. He married domesticity with divinity, the baker's loaf with the bread of life. The challenge for literary artists today is to make a similar connection between our own concerns and the larger forces of life, rooting us in a new relation to the cosmos. Tyndale's Bible is no longer big enough or true enough to comprehend its beauties.

What's the relevance of this for literary criticism? Protestantism's main contribution is the idea that readers should decide for themselves what a work means. This emphasis on individual response makes it difficult to establish a critical community that can command any authority. If we are all capable of determining a work's significance, why do we need critics or criticism? This is a strong argument but since it fails to acknowledge that some readers, either through expertise or experience, are better than others, it is in danger of lapsing into Philistinism. The idea that everyone's opinion is of equal value is a nonsense. Those that are based on reason and evidence are manifestly more valuable than those based on prejudice and hearsay. It is more difficult to describe the effects of Tyndale's translation on the development of criticism. Bragg noted how he sounded the inner life and gave a vision of social justice. And we added that he joined earth and heaven, perhaps even fused them together in his homely but ringing prose: 'let there be light'; 'the truth shall make you free'; and 'blessed are the pure in heart, for they shall see God'. All these elements enter English literature which means that criticism must take note of them. Another way of saying this is that criticism needs to be attuned to inwardness, justice and the timbre of writing, for these were planted in the language by one who believed that reading was vital to life.

Tyndale's execution is a reminder that, during this period, writing was subject to strict censorship. It wasn't just religious opinion that was strictly controlled, so too was the expression of political views. In 1538, Henry VIII issued a royal proclamation forbidding the publication of any book lacking the written permission of the Privy Council and this principle of prior censorship was upheld by Edward VI (1537–53) and Elizabeth I (1533–1603) (Fischer 2003: 222–3). If writers managed to evade this process, others procedures came into play. In 1599, the authorities ordered the satires of John Marston (1576–1634), Everard Guilpin (1572–1608) and Joseph Hall (1574–1656) and others to be burned. These men were not part of the court circle and, to judge from these lines from Guilpin's *Skialetheia* (1598), they were more interested in making a name for themselves than in pleasing the powerful.

> My lord most court-like lyes in bed till noone,
> Then, all high stomackt riseth to his dinner,
> Falls straight to Dice, before his meate be downe,
> Or to digest, walks to some femall sinner.
> Perhaps fore-tyrde he gets him to a play,
> Comes home to supper, and then falls to dice,
> There his deuotion wakes till it be day,
> And so to bed, where vntill noone he lies.[5]

The usual defence of satire was that it aimed to cure society's ills but these writers positively seemed to embody them. They were 'pathological', 'uncharitably furious', 'sex obsessed', 'xenophobic', 'misogynistic' and 'contemptuous' (Prescott 2001: 289). But they were lucky. It was only their works that were consigned to the flames. Tyndale was burnt because of his translation while, in 1484, the poet William Collingbourne had been hung, drawn and quartered because he had dared to criticise Richard III and his ministers Lord Lovell, Sir Richard Radclyffe and Sir William Catesby in the lines 'The rat, the Catte, and Lovell our dogge / Rule all Englande under the hogge' (in Vickers 1999: 129). William Baldwin (1518–63) used this incident in his poem 'Death of the Poet Collingbourne' (1563) to mourn the passing of 'ancient liberties' and to advise poets 'not to meddle with magistrate's affairs' (Vickers 1999: 135 and 139). Censorship is the extreme form of criticism. It does not aim to improve expression but to silence it. But it need not be entirely oppressive. As Michael Schoenfeldt has pointed out, censorship is also 'a practice that generates frequently productive parameters of literary utterance' (2001: 371). Baldwin's poem, for instance, can be read as a clever plea for poetic freedom: Elizabeth, as the guardian of English freedoms, would never behave as Richard had done, surely?

### From Feudalism to Capitalism: Some Issues

We have looked at the vernacular in a religious context and we now need to consider how it was affected by political and economic imperatives, which also involves a brief examination of the relation between feudalism and capitalism as this was a key feature of the period. Looking at the vernacular from a political point of view means focusing on feudalism, especially the court, looking at it from an economic point of view means focusing on capitalism, especially commerce. Since the court is mostly the province of the aristocracy, and since commerce is mostly the province of merchants, traders, manufacturers and skilled craftsman, the question of class inevitably arises. This is not something we can consider in any detail here except to say that the period witnesses the build up of tensions – social, political, religious and economic which eventually explode in the English Civil War (1642–8).[6] The friction between a feudal aristocracy based on land and a broad alliance of groups based on trade, is dramatised in a number of plays in the period. In *King Lear* (1605–6), for example, Kent represents the idea of service and Edmund individual ambition. One of the main tenets of feudal society is that a person must remain in the station into which they are born, while the expectation in capitalist society is that a person can – and should – improve their lot by hard work. Again, in very simple terms, feudalism has a more social conception of man, whereas capitalism has a more economic one. In the one, people are located in a hierarchy with mutual obligations to those above and below them, in the other, they are located in a market where they must sell their labour power to survive.

It is hard to reconcile either of these notions with the ideal of the 'Renaissance man' that near-mythical figure who was knight, courtier, musician, poet, scholar and statesman. He does not appear to be a part of the feudal order because he is defined more by his relation to himself than his relation to others. And, because he fulfils many roles, he stands in stark contrast to the feudal principle that 'some are fit to make divines, some poets, some lawyers, some physicians, some to be sent to the plough and trades' (Jonson in Vickers 1999: 562). The idea of 'Renaissance man' points more towards the values that will underpin the development of capitalism. He is an individual who makes the most of his various capacities. But he cannot be identified too closely with the emerging market because the capacities he develops are social rather than economic which suggests, contrary to Hobbes, that 'the value or worth of a man' is not simply his 'price' (Hobbes 1985: 2). In short, a person like Sir Philip Sidney (1554–86), that ideal of Renaissance manhood, or Sir Thomas Smith (1513–77), author, ambassador, statesman and vice chancellor of Cambridge University, and a 'polymathic humanist' with interests in 'astronomy, architecture, natural phenomena, drugs and medicine'

(Dewar 1964: 15), are strange compounds of both feudal and capitalist characteristics.

And just as feudalism and capitalism have contrary views of man, so have they of art. Once more we must resort to very basic distinctions for the sake of clarity. The feudal preoccupation with rank and status is mirrored in the concern with decorum and the hierarchy of genres in literature. At its simplest, decorum refers to the proper relation between subject and style, grand words for a grand occasion. The author of the first systematic account of rhetoric in English, Thomas Wilson (1523–81), illustrates the principle when he writes that just 'as French hoods do not become Lords, so Parliament robes are unfitting for ladies' (Vickers 1999: 124). His references to nationalism, to the House of Commons and the House of Lords and finally to the idea that women are not made to govern show the intertwining of literary and political issues.

Moreover, the use of gender to ground the distinctions of decorum is a commonplace of the period; that's why there is outrage in some quarters over boys dressing as women in the drama. 'You ought not', declares one contemporary, 'to confound the habits of either sex as to let your boys wear the attires of virgins' (Vickers: 488). The playwright Thomas Heywood (c. 1575–1650) claims that this is merely a convention of the stage not a sign of immorality; furthermore, he asks, 'do not the universities, the fountains and well-springs of all good arts, learning, and documents, admit the like [tragedies and comedies] in their colleges?' (ibid.: 489). Acting, he continues, prepares youthful scholars for the public exercise of their various arts, dialectic, rhetoric, ethics and so on. Poetry does not seem to generate the same sort of concerns about gender as drama. There, the distinction between male and female is expressed in the division between form and content and supports the ideal of decorum. Puttenham, for example, compares poetic ornament to the 'crimson taint . . . laid upon a lady's lips' (in ibid.: 221). The use of figure, like the use of lipstick, must be neither too little nor too much otherwise it 'spoils the whole workmanship, taking away all beauty and good liking from it' (ibid.:221). The substance of a work is masculine, its adornments feminine. The distinction between the sexes must be absolute. If there is confusion over male and female there will be confusion over social rank for which the shorthand term was degree; take that away, wrote Shakespeare, 'untune that string and hark what discord follows' (*Troilus and Cressida* I, iii, 109–10). Masculine supremacy is reinforced by Sidney placing heroic poetry at the top of the generic hierarchy. Its subject is war and it moves the reader to adopt the virtues of the warrior, 'truth', 'action' and 'magnanimity' (in Vickers 1999: 365). Heroic poetry expresses the military values of the upper class and its foremost position visa vis other genres reflects the power of the aristocracy in society and government.

The broad symmetry between art and the social structure comes under strain with the development of the market. This was not a sudden process. The English economy had been growing since at least the thirteenth century. Urban industries, commodity production and the increased use of money all put pressure on a social structure deemed to be immutable because ordained by God. Further expansion in the Renaissance suggested that change, not continuity, was the basis of society. If feudalism was a closed social order, capitalism was an open one. Its philosophy of progress, its dynamic of innovation and its impatience with restraint influenced thinking about literature. For example, Dudley North (1581–1666), who apparently discovered the curative power of spring water, fears that writing is 'endless' (in Vickers 1999: 509) but, by the time we get to the late twentieth century, this has become one of its most desirable and celebrated qualities.

The point, in terms of criticism, is that its various categories are intimately related to broader conceptions of the social order. There is a reciprocal relationship between a concern with decorum in literature and the gradations of status in society, and, in our own time, between a delight in the free play of meaning and the free play of market forces. Both affirm, refine, extend and legitimise one another. It is important to remember this obvious truth because there is a tendency to treat criticism as a transcendent discourse, one that stands outside the work and claims to know it better than it knows itself, relating its silences, repressions, exclusions, blind spots and ideological complicities to those of the wider order. This is criticism as critical, but its practitioners can only truly perform this function if they are aware of the extent to which many of their ideas and idioms are themselves implicated in the rhetoric of power. Otherwise its claims to be oppositional, so frequently trumpeted in the late twentieth century, are merely otiose.

We have contrasted the different characteristics of feudalism and capitalism, as if they were distinct entities. They are, but not completely. Both involve a form of exploitation based on ownership. The peasants rarely owned the land on which they worked and were required to give their lord rent, labour and a portion of their produce on pain of fines or eviction. The industrial worker does not own the factory in which he works and his pay is based on how much it costs to keep him alive, not on how much his labour earns for the owner of the plant in which he toils. One difference is that the industrial worker relies solely on selling his labour power to survive, whereas the peasant at least has some claim to the land, enabling him to feed himself and his family. Just as there are economic continuities between feudalism and capitalism so there are social ones. For example, the feudal idea that everyone has their own particular function is very similar to the capitalist idea of the division of labour, where a simple task like pin making can be broken down into a number of different parts each performed by different people in order to increase productivity. So, although we can point to contrasts between the two systems, such as the change in the idea of learning from that which made you good to that which brought you gain, from that which made you perfect to that which brought you profit (see Sydney and Jonson in Vickers 1999: 347–9 and 568), there are also points of comparison. The courtier is similar to the merchant because they both want to improve themselves, but they are different because the courtier does this by realising his various capacities, the merchant by accruing wealth.

The differences between feudal and capitalist ideas sometimes inform writing about literature. Sidney's famous *A Defence of Poetry* (1595) offers an example. As a form of reproduction that transmits ancient learning, poetry belongs more to the feudal order, but as a form of production that invents 'forms such as never were in nature', it belongs more to the capitalist one (Vickers 1999: 338–9 and 343), though of course any social order needs to reproduce itself and to engage in new production if it is to survive. Sidney believed that art made nature 'better', and Jonson took this one step further declaring that art perfected nature: 'to nature . . . art must be added to make all . . . perfect' (ibid.: 343 and 586). It is true that we can find similar views in, for example, Horace, who said that good poetry depended on the cooperation of 'genius' and 'talent' (in Russell and Winterbottom 1972: 290) and this again underlines the persistence of certain issues throughout critical history. But when they are mentioned in a different context, these matters take on a new resonance. The doctrine that art improves nature seems peculiarly apt in an age when landlords began to exploit the productive capacity of their estates, evicting peasants from their holdings and commons, so they could increase cultivation or raise sheep.

Equally, there is aversion to affectation in speech and writing in both the ancient and Elizabethan world. Demetrius of Phaleron (d. 280 BC), who worked at the great library of Alexandria, regards affectation as a 'perversion' (in Russell and Winterbottom 1972: 206) while Bacon calls it an 'excess', an interest 'more [in] words than matter' (in Vickers 1999: 459). Again, though, the social connotations are different in each period. The work ethic of the new trading and manufacturing classes, stressing thrift and self-denial, means that criticism of luxury in literary style has a class dimension, the virtue of middle-class restraint against the vice of aristocratic extravagance. There are clear parallels with the inkhorn controversy, discussed below, and we can find similar debates in theatre and philosophy. The dramatist John Ford (1586–1640) praised his fellow playwright John Fletcher (1579–1625) for purging the stage of the ornament (ibid.: 544) while humanists rejected the abstractions of scholasticism in favour of more concrete forms of expression (Norbrook 2005: 53). These arguments have an intra- as well as an inter-class dimension. Debora Shuger suggests that 'both Sidney's Arcadian rhetoric and *The Fairie*

*Queen*'s "gothic" archaisms seem to insinuate a defence of aristocratic privilege against the encroachments of centralised monarchy whose official style . . . was conspicuously brief, plain, sententious' (2001: 184). The preference for the particular over the general in the growth of the vernacular cannot be divorced from the development of production. Language becomes more material as manufacture gathers pace in, for example, iron foundries, mining, textiles, metal wares, ship building, brewing, glass and lace making. The exigencies of trade demand a robust, practical idiom, not a delicate, decorative one. In short, commerce may influence the character of the vernacular as much, if not more than, the court. To find out how politics and economics affected the vernacular and, by extension, ideas of literature and criticism, it is best to examine each of them separately.

### The Vernacular and Criticism: A Political Context

In looking at how politics shaped the character of criticism, we need to distinguish between the ambitious claims made about poetry and its actual use. The vigorous defence of poetry in this period is an attempt to reverse its declining importance in the political sphere and to counter claims of its corrupting influence. Sir Thomas Elyot (1490?–1546), one of the first men to introduce Italian humanism into Britain, rebutted the charge that poetry 'was nothing but bawdry' on the grounds that, where such material could be found, its purpose was to deter readers from indulging in such behaviour themselves (in Vickers 1999: 65). That model of Renaissance manhood, Sir Philip Sidney, also feels compelled to clear poetry from such calumnies as that 'it is the mother of lies' and 'the nurse of abuse' (ibid.: 369). The poet cannot lie, says Sidney, because he's not claiming to tell us the truth. He doesn't aim to show us how things are but how they should be (ibid.: 370). And he dismisses the idea that poetry infects men's wit, 'training it to wanton sinfulness and lustful love' by saying that there is nothing wrong with poetry itself, it's how people read it. Poetry does not 'abuseth man's wit', he argues, it is man's wit that 'abuseth poetry' (ibid.: 371).

But it was poetry's loss of status in the political sphere that was the main concern. Puttenham complained that 'in this iron and malicious age, Princes are less delighted in [poetry] being over-earnestly bent and affected to the affairs of empire and ambition' (in Vickers 1999: 202). He sought to restore it to its proper place in social life by first reminding his readers that it 'was the original cause and occasion' of human society (ibid.: 196). This view was eventually discarded in the seventeenth century when Thomas Hobbes (1588–1679) and John Locke (1632–1704) argued that man emerged from the state of nature to protect either himself or his property.[7] Since poetry was regarded as the very foundation of society it was not surprising to find it at the heart of the political process. Among its various functions George Puttenham (1528–90), author of *The Arte of English Poesie* (1589), included: recording the deeds of monarchs; promoting the arts of peace; celebrating victories; fashioning courtiers; and dignifying feats, coronations 'and instalments of honourable orders' (Vickers 1999: 205, 235). Most of the functions in this list are examples of 'demonstrative' or 'epideictic' rhetoric, whose purpose is 'the ceremonial praise of rulers and patrons' (Norbrook and Woudhuysen 2005: 13).

But the tradition of deliberative rhetoric, or the art of political persuasion, which dwindled when Rome became an empire, was still detectable in other conceptions of poetry (Norbrook and Woudhuysen 2005: 13). Francis Bacon (1561–1626),[8] best known for his *The Advancement of Learning* (1605), believed that poetry was necessary to avert the threat of rebellion (in Vickers 1999: 462–3), while Thomas Wilson made poetry a prop of hierarchy: 'what man I pray you . . . would not rather look to rule like a lord than to live like an underling, if he were not persuaded by art and eloquence, that it behooveth every man, and not to seek any higher room whereunto he was at the first appointed?' (in ibid.: 75). Jonson said that the poet created a commonwealth, 'governing it with counsels, strengthening it with laws, correcting it with judgements and informing it with religion and morals'; in short, it 'disposes us to all civil offices of society' (in ibid.: 569 and 583). Jonson's remark illustrates the humanist belief that poetry had an important part to play in improving society. But this was not an easy thing to do. Civic humanists opposed the enclosure movement but also encouraged it by their support of the wool trade. They also believed everyone should take an active part in public life but disapproved of popular resistance to the fencing off of common land. Episodes such as that in 1549, when Robert Kett led his rebels to occupy the Earl of Surrey's mansion outside Norwich in protest at the family's 'notorious resistance to freeing their feudally subordinated bondmen' convinced many that they should abandon their attempts to educate the masses and control them instead (Norbrook and Woudhuysen 2005: 18). The ambiguities in the humanists' attitude to reform are reflected in poetry. One sort, that which belonged to demonstrative rhetoric, was conservative because it celebrated the status quo, while the other sort, that which belonged to deliberative rhetoric, was progressive because it encouraged change.

Perhaps the most tangible contribution poets made to the transformation of society was by making the vernacular more elegant and expressive. Gascoigne advised them to 'avoid prolixity and tediousness' since 'brevity is most commendable' (Vickers 1999: 170–1), while Thomas Heywood claimed that drama 'polished' the language, making it whole and 'perfect' (ibid.: 235 and 494). Poets and dramatists should elevate English, and part of this process involved the creation of a native literary tradition which could bear comparison not just with England's European neighbours but with ancient Greece and Rome. A Cambridge don by the name of William Covell (c. 1570–1613) went further, saying not just that 'a pantheon of poetic heroes might help to raise the nation's stature abroad' but also that it might 'quell dissent at home' (Ross 2000: 89), a reminder that, throughout the history of criticism, literature is often expected to fulfil a political function for which it is not really equipped. Unlike princes, writers do not have the power to pass laws nor do they have armies to enforce their will.

The role of poetry and drama was to refine the language, but that was part of the larger political project of linguistic unity. Henry V had begun the process when he ordered clerks of the Signet Office, whose function was to write personal letters on behalf of the monarch, to use only English in their correspondence. But which English? The different dialects across the country meant that the language was far from uniform. One contemporary berated the inhabitants of York for their 'harsh', 'piercing', 'grating' and even 'formless' speech which 'we southern men can hardly understand' (in Crystal 2004: 216). Nearly a thousand years after the arrival of the Anglo-Saxons, 'a man from Northumberland could still have difficulty understanding a man from Kent' (Bragg 2004: 96). There were, for example, huge differences in pronunciation. The word stone in the south was 'ston' and in the north it was 'stane' (ibid.: 97). Spelling was even more varied. Take the word church. This was used in the south but it could be spelled in at least eighteen different ways ranging from 'cherge' to 'sscherch', while in the north the word for church was 'kirk' whose various spellings included 'kryk', 'kerk' and 'kyrke' (ibid.: 97). One reason for this linguistic variety, was the dominance of French and Latin as the written languages of the British Isles.[9] For three hundred years, they had been the medium of State, Church and scholarship. They had slowed the evolution of written English with the result that there was no common agreement on matters of spelling or grammar.

But this changed in the fourteenth century. The scribes in Chancery, the office responsible for the paperwork of the whole kingdom, attempted to bring some order to the glorious confusion that was English.[10] They took the East Midlands version as their norm, partly because of the prosperity of the region, partly because of its proximity to London, and partly because it was the idiom of important literary works such as the Auchinleck manuscript (c. 1330), a large collection of religious, historical and literary texts which also contained several romances such as *Guy of Warwick* and *Sir Orfeo*.[11] A standardised version of the language began to appear in the fifteenth century but debate about what constituted correct English continued into the sixteenth century and, according to Crystal, did not die down until the eighteenth century, 'when an unprecedented concern for correctness in usage led to the composing of explicit prescriptions about usage which were universally taught in schools' (2004: 254). It is hard not be reminded here of the grammarians of late antiquity, and their determination to instil in their pupils the correct use of speaking and writing.

The drive to establish 'standard' English was symptomatic of the way in which people in the Elizabethan age 'began to think about norms, for the term turns up in a wide variety of contexts, such as alchemy and religion' (Crystal 2004: 263). Derived from old French, 'standard' originally meant 'a military or naval ensign' (ibid.: 263). From the twelfth century, the term underwent various changes and then, in the sixteenth century, was applied to language, in the sense of a norm, and also to money where it signified 'a legal rate for the intrinsic value of coins' (ibid.: 263). The educated class's concern for norms manifested itself in literature in debates about decorum. But it is the yoking together of language and money by that word 'standard' which will prove decisive in the evolution of criticism. We can measure the amount of precious metal in a coin but we can't use scales to weigh the value of a literary work. Nevertheless, the fact we can count syllables in a line of poetry and partly identify its various genres by their meter show that there is a quantitative aspect to literary analysis (Hallyn 2001: 443). This element is reinforced by the link between money and language, a link which will increasingly inform conceptions of literature. As we shall see below, it is in this period that monetary terms start to be applied to poetry.

For now, it is the upper class who stipulate the standard for English. Sir Thomas Elyot who, among his other accomplishments, tried to persuade the pope to give Henry VIII his divorce, stipulated that spoken English should be 'cleane, polite, perfectly and articulately pronounced' (in Crystal 2004: 270). His attitude was typical of an aristocracy which attempted to limit the language to a particular model of English that finds its most complete expression in the literature of the court. Puttenham says that English should be based on what 'is spoken in the king's courts, or in the good towns and cities of the land' (in Vickers 1999: 226). The notion that it should it take its cue from the borders, port towns or villages is an anathema to him, as is the idea that peasants, craftsmen or merchants should help shape the language. His remarks show that the vernacular could be as much a mark of social distinction as Latin. To be able to read Cicero and Quintilian was a status symbol. It marked the cultured person off from the rest. Those who thought these divisions would disappear if the native culture was in English, and if the best of other cultures were available in translation, were disappointed. Puttenham's stipulation that 'ye shall take the usual speech of the court, and that of London and the shires lying about London within sixty miles, and not much above' demonstrates that those who did not adopt that model were condemned as 'rustic', 'barbarous' and 'ill disposed', whose speech it was 'not possible to understand without an interpreter' (ibid.: 226 and 280).

There were some who had their doubts about the courtly idiom, including Puttenham himself. The very profession of a courtier, he writes, 'is to be able to dissemble' (Vickers 1999: 291). This statement calls into question his view that the best English is spoken at court for that implies that it is nothing more than a form of falsehood. One of the reasons courtiers need to be able to dissemble is so that they can disguise their social origins. The courtier, having risen from humble beginnings, must not show that he was once a 'craftsman' otherwise he will be 'sent back to the shop or other place of his first calling with scorn' (ibid.: 291). Puttenham's warning is evidence of at least limited social mobility in the period, but that carried with it the risk of instability in language and society.[12] What value had the courtly idiom if it was used to strike a pose, and if it could be infected by words and expressions from lower down the social scale?[13] The lawyer and writer John Hoskyns (1566–1638) was more forthright in his criticism, complaining that courtiers had no mind for anything in their studies except fashion, with the result that there was no agreed standard of eloquence. And he does not exclude himself from blame, confessing that he was guilty of having 'used and outworn six several styles [of speech] since I was First Fellow of New College' (in Vickers 1999: 418). He also disapproves of the habit of punning among 'gentlewomen', seeing this kind of 'play' as an offence against God who gave us speech that we might 'apprehend the consequences of things' (ibid.: 399 and 410).

That early advocate for a scientific understanding of the universe, Francis Bacon, agreed. The purpose of 'discourse', he wrote, lay in 'discerning what was true' (Vickers 1999: 92). This was the province of scholars but Puttenham felt they betrayed their vocation by indulging in 'much peevish affectation of words' (in ibid.: 226). Thomas Wilson, a student of Roger Ascham, advised scholars not to 'affect any strange inkhorn terms', a reference to the introduction of mainly Latin and learned terms into English (in ibid.: 120). They entered the language because there weren't enough words to describe the new experiences of the age: the effects of the Reformation, scientific discoveries and the explorations of Africa, the Americas and the Far East. The word inkhorn itself was intended as an insult and derived from the horn pot which held ink for quills. Since these imported terms were rather lengthy it also referred to the amount of ink used in writing them. Shakespeare satirises those who pride themselves on their use of classical words in the character of Holofernes in *Love's Labour's Lost* (1598). 'The deer was, as you know – *sanguis* – in blood, ripe as the pomewater who now hangeth like a jewel in the ear of *caelo* the sky, the welkin, the heaven, and anon falleth like a crab on the face of *terra*, the soil, the land, the earth' (IV, ii, 3–7). But it wasn't only scholars who spoke in this pretentious manner. 'Every science, every profession', wrote Daniel, 'must be so wrapped up in unnecessary intrications, as if it were not to fashion but to confound the understanding' (in Vickers 1999: 446). Even the 'mechanical', as Thomas Nashe notes, 'abhhorres the english he was born too, and plucks with solemn periphrasis his *vt vales* [how are you?] from the inkhorne' (in Crystal 2004: 291). This wasn't just a stylistic matter. Latin was the language of the Catholic Church and therefore any attempts to incorporate it into English threatened the Protestant character of the country. Those who resisted the Italian influence weren't just lauding the virtues of the vernacular, they were identifying England as a Protestant nation quite different from most of the rest of Europe.[14]

The poet Richard Carew (1555–1620), who at the age of eleven engaged in public debate with Sidney, demonstrated what we have come to see as the English capacity for compromise when he wrote that 'the longe wordes that wee borrowe, being intermingled with the shorte of our owne store, make vp a perfitt harmony' (in Crystal 2004: 294). But his was the minority view, at least until the end of the sixteenth century (ibid.: 294). The language, riddled with foreign terms and weighed down with elaborate expressions, had to be purified, lightened. 'Eschew prolixity', urges George Gascoigne (1539–78),[15] 'since brevity is most commendable' (in Vickers 1999: 171). This cry rings down the centuries. There is an echo of it in the 'theory wars' of the 1980s when traditionalists complained, with some justification, about the jargon-ridden language of post-structuralism, and it is also manifest in the impatience with management-speak.[16] There were various suggestions for reforming the language in the Renaissance. The most common was to aim for transparency in speech and writing. Dudley North, one of whose hobbies was jousting, prayed that he might 'write clearly and strongly rather than finely and artificially' (in ibid.: 510). Gascoigne, a former mercenary, identifies clarity and simplicity with Englishness itself. 'The most ancient English words are of one syllable, so that the more monosyllables you use, the truer Englishman you will seem' (in Crystal 2004: 292). Sir John Cheke (1514–57)[17] made the same connection in a letter to Thomas Hoby (1530–66), diplomat and translator of one of the most famous books of this period, Baldassare Castliglione's *The Book of the Courtier* (1561).[18] 'I am of the opinion', Cheke wrote, that 'our tung shold be written cleane and pure, vnmixt and vnmangled with borowing of other tunges' (in Crystal 2004: 292). Alas, the man whom Milton called 'the learnedest of Englishmen', did not seem to realise that he had used four words of Latin or French origin in that very sentence: 'opinion', 'mix', 'mangle' and 'pure' (ibid.: 292). To paraphrase Oscar Wilde on truth, English was never pure and hardly ever simple.

Nevertheless, there is a definite sense that the best English consists of plain terms and direct statement. What are the implications for literary criticism? In the first place, it encourages a preference for clear writing, with ornament being judged not as product of invention but on how it enhances communication. The purpose of ornament is not to be striking or self-referential but, as Hoskyns says, to 'amplify' and 'illustrate' (in Vickers 1999: 411). In the second place, the demand for a straightforward style may incline the language more towards the requirements of scientific rather artistic discourse, promoting an instrumental view of literature. Ann Blair, for example, claims the Renaissance was 'the heyday' of scientific poetry, a genre dedicated to communicating new discoveries in a memorable manner (2001: 454). By contrast, Debora Shuger argues that it was 'the affective and expressive ends' of English which triumphed over its 'cognitive and aesthetic aims' (2001: 183). Those particular powers helped to promote a sense of nationhood as, at a more refined level, did the hostility to the importation of foreign words. This was further enhanced by writers who praised the expansiveness of English compared to other European languages. Sidney declared that, more than any other 'vulgar language', English could embrace both ancient verse based on 'the quantity of each syllable' and modern verse based on rhyme (in Vickers 1999: 388). In patriotic fashion he lists the defects of Italian, 'full of vowels'; of Dutch, full of 'consonants'; and of French, 'not one word that hath his accent in the last syllable saving two' (ibid.: 389). The dramatist, translator and poet George Chapman (1559?–1634) takes up the fight, asserting that:

> . . . no tongue hath the Muses' utterance heard
> For verse, and that sweet music to the ear
> Struck out of rhyme so naturally as this.
> Our monosyllables so kindly fall
> And meet, opposed in rhyme as they did kiss;
> French and Italian, most immetrical,
> Their many syllables in hard collision
> Fall as they break their necks, their bastard rhymes
> Saluting as they justl'd in transition,
> And sets our teeth on edge, nor tunes nor times
> Kept in their falls. And, methinks, their long words
> Show in short verse as in a narrow place
> Two opposites should meet with two-handed swords
> Unwieldy, without use or grace. (in ibid.: 516)

If it is to be the speech of all, the vernacular can never be merely local; dialect may bind a community but not a society. Puttenham argued that the vernacular should be modelled on the court but this involved the repression of other forms of speech. By contrast, Jonson believed that we should continually adjust our speech according to whom we are speaking and according to what we are speaking about for, he writes, 'some are of the camp, some of the council board, some of the shop, some of the sheepcote, some of the pulpit, some of the bar, etc.' (in Vickers 1999: 574). Jonson offers a more inclusive view of the vernacular than Puttenham, but it remained the province of the privileged as only they would have enjoyed the education that enabled them to be so adept in social intercourse. 'The custom of speech,' writes Jonson, 'is the consent of the learned' (ibid.: 576). Once that is understood and accepted, then speech can indeed be 'the instrument of society' (ibid.: 574).

We have seen that the preference for plain expression has implications for literary criticism. It posits the idea that literature should communicate clearly. If it does, it is good, if it doesn't, it is bad. In fact, the situation is not as simple as that because, as we have seen, poetry has a variety of uses, from promoting peace to praising God. The point here, though, is that there are parallels between Puttenham's and Jonson's conception of the vernacular and ideas about poetry and drama. The court was the model for poetry as it was for spoken English, while drama demonstrated how different speakers could be accommodated within a single linguistic structure. Poetry complements the institutional base of the vernacular, while drama complements the idea of the vernacular as hierarchy of different voices. In short, there is a synergy between ideals of English and ideals of art. Like the vernacular, literature is at once for everyone yet restricted to the few, which means that it can be exploited by those espousing either equality or elitism.

## The Vernacular: An Economic Context

The political attempt to control the vernacular was countered by economic developments. The growth of commerce and the spread of printing caused it to expand in unpredictable ways. England's strong navy, demonstrated by the defeat of the Spanish armada in 1588, meant that the country was able to establish yet more trade routes, with the result that many new words were introduced into the language. Richard Mulcaster (1531–1611),[19] headmaster of Merchant Taylor's School, wrote that 'diversity of trade, make both matter for our speech, and mean to enlarge it' (in Crystal 2004: 296). We can see the effect of colonialism in John Donne's description of his mistress as 'my America, my mine of precious stones' (Donne 1971: 125) and also in Sidney's comparison of affectation in writing with 'those Indians not content to wear earrings at the fit and natural places of the ears, but they will thrust jewels through their nose and lips, because they will sure to be fine' (in Vickers 1999: 386). Bragg claims that, during the Elizabethan and Jacobean periods, trade, along with travel and borrowings from French and Latin, added some ten to twelve thousand words to the language (2004: 117).[20]

Most of these came from Latin, the medium of scholarship, so it is reasonable to assume that this would give English an academic cast. In fact, it acquired a commercial one. Here is one possible explanation for the commonplace notion that the English are not intellectual. Their language inclines more to cash than to culture. Poets readily resorted to metaphors of trade, partly because they lived, as Samuel Daniel (1562–1619) wrote, in 'a profit-seeking age' (in Norbrook and Woudhuysen 2005: 715) and partly because, as we saw above, words like 'standard' drew monetary and linguistic value closer together, a connection evident in Jonson's remark that 'custom is the most certain mistress of language as the public stamp makes the current money' (in Vickers 1999: 575). The change in the meaning of the word 'profit' from 'a general sense of benefit to a narrower sense of personal financial advantage' (in Norbrook and Woudhuysen 2005: 5) shows how the social dimension of language contracts to an economic one which then imposes itself not just on art, but on the whole range of affective experience. Raymond Southall argues that the speaker in love poetry 'weighs up his profits and losses like a businessman preparing a balance sheet' (1973: 61). Thomas Carew (c. 1594–1640) describes how the 'fresh invention' of John Donne (1572–1631) paid 'the debts of our penurious bankrupt age' (in Vickers 1999: 555), while Jonson talks of 'letters' being 'the bank of words'(ibid.: 573). The monetary theme is also there in Sidney's references to philosophers who 'set up shop' and poets who 'show the price' (ibid.: 375, 377).

Steven Fischer has memorably stated that, with Johannes Gutenberg's invention of printing in 1450, 'the age of parchment symbolically folded before the age of paper' (2003: 205). The number of books increased and so did their availability. In 1450, there was one printing press in Europe. By 1500, there were 1,750 of them publishing about 27,000 titles and, by the mid sixteenth century, this number had leapt to eight million (ibid.: 207 and 227). Most of the titles were calendars, almanacs, grammars, the classics, the Bible, books of hours and the lives of saints. The first book to be published in the English language was a translation of the *The Recuyell of the Historyes of Troye* in 1476. It came from the press of William Caxton (c. 1420–91) who helped to inaugurate a sense of national literature with his publication of works by Chaucer, Gower, Lydgate and Thomas Malory (1405–71), a man with a reputation for violent crime and author of *Le Morte D'Arthur* (1485), one of the most enduring tales in the English canon. The arrival of print, which Fischer claims 'has been as important to human society as the controlled use of fire and the wheel' (2003: 213), altered attitudes to the written word. Previously greeted with awe and reverence, the availability of multiple copies of a work made it appear almost mundane. The mystery of writing, emblazoned on parchment, the preserve of the Church and the rich, was dissipated by the comparative ubiquity of books. People were less deferential. They now folded down the corners of the page where they had finished reading. 'Virtually unknown with the expensive parchment books of the middle ages,' writes Fischer, '"dog-ears" became commonplace in the sixteenth century' (ibid.: 232). But if books lost one kind of authority, they acquired another. Before the advent of print, they were copied by hand and this led to additions, inaccuracies, corrections and interpolations so that no two versions of a work were exactly the same. By contrast, the printed book was 'petrified, immutable, final' (ibid.: 218). The reader was no longer able contribute to its transmission but he or she was free to interpret it in their own way, particularly as books were not published with 'marginal commentaries or interlineal glosses to steer [them] to the one "correct" reading' (ibid.: 218).

The rise of Protestantism and the invention of the printing press both undermined the traditional hierarchy of reading. Critics would have to find a new basis for their authority now that the commentary tradition was in decline. Another factor in its demise was the increase in literacy. Henry VIII's redistribution of land confiscated from the Catholic Church during the Reformation tripled the number of landed gentry who, with their new-found wealth, took a keen interest in education. 'Schools', writes Fischer, 'sprang up virtually everywhere, and widespread literacy was the immediate result' (2003: 242). We need to be careful here. The number of those who were able to read was greater in towns than in the country, but to say that around 60 per cent of those in conurbations could write their names compared with between 20 and 30 per cent in rural parishes does not tell us how closely that 60 per cent could follow the printed word (ibid.: 215–16 and 243). And there were others determined to remain illiterate. We get a flavour of this in Shakespeare's *Henry VI Part Two* (c. 1590–1) when the clothier and rebel Jack Cade cries, 'Thou hast most traitorously corrupted the youth of the realm in erecting a grammar school; and whereas before, our forefathers had no other books but the score and the tally, thou hast caused printing to be used and . . . thou hast built a paper mill' (IV, vii, 30–4). He sees books as a form of subjugation, not a means of liberation. They are of course both. The printed word is a threat to oral culture. It devalues it and labels its partici-pants as backward. At the same time print changed the scholar's role. As well as relaying existing knowledge, he should also add to it (Fischer 2003: 206). This development was complemented in literature by a new emphasis on the imagination. We have already noted that Sidney defends poetry because it creates new worlds, an idea echoed by Puttenham who says it is that 'inven-tive part of the mind without [which] no man can devise any new or rare thing', while for Bacon it is the power to 'join that which nature hath severed, and sever that which nature hath joined' (in Vickers 1999: 201 and 461). Dreaming up new worlds and new discoveries go hand in hand. And they both belong to an economic order committed to commodity production.[21]

One such commodity is, of course, the book itself. It might contain useful knowledge, it might improve behaviour but, most of all, it had to make a profit. Printers, says Fischer, 'were foremost merchants who had to earn their own

way' (2003: 210). A reduction in book size and large initial print runs generated good returns. This was the method of Aldus Manutius (1449–1515)[22]
whose motto was *festina lente*, hurry up slowly, and who produced a series of
books that were 'scholarly, compact, handy and cheap' (Fischer 2003: 211).
Aldus bridges the gap between the medieval and the Renaissance worlds. On
the one hand he is committed to the traditional hierarchy of knowledge, on the
other he wants to make money. By the mid sixteenth century the commercial
imperative has come to predominate. Publishers were 'no longer concerned
with patronising the world of letters but merely sought to publish books whose
sale was guaranteed' (ibid.: 233). And so they targeted 'a relatively well educated lay readership of public officials, merchants and, for the first time,
women' (ibid.: 219). Epics, romances, ballads and eventually novels competed
with the serious reading matter of theology, the classics, law and the sciences.

Contemporaries recognised a distinction, which is one of the dynamics of
critical debate, between good and bad literature. Part of the function of the literary canon was to distinguish between the two so that, in the words of one
contemporary, 'not every bald ballader to prejudice of art may pass current
with a Poet's name' (in Ross 2000: 87). This was an argument within the ranks
of the literate, and did not concern the vast majority, some fifty million in
Europe, who relied on an oral culture, and whose numbers would gradually
shrink before the march of print. Since books were ideally the source of knowledge and self-improvement, readers should not waste their time on those offering mere entertainment. The poet and critic William Webbe (1550–1607?)
complained of the 'innumerable sortes of Englyshe Bookes, and infinite fardels
of printed pamphlets, wherewith thys Countrey is pestered, all shoppes
stuffed, and every study furnished' (in Ross 2000: 72). One of the fears was
that the circulation of popular literature would sanction diverse modes of
expression, thereby undermining the authority not just of courtly English but
the court itself. The connection between the disruption of language and the
disruption of society is evident in the rant of one contemporary who furiously
condemned 'the swarming of lascivious, idle, and unprofitable bookes,
Playebookes and Ballades . . . in disgrace of Religion, &c. to the increase of
Vice' (in ibid.: 80). Ascham picks up this theme in his criticism of romances,
a 'bastard sort of history' (in Ross 2000: 81). They waste time, they delude the
affections and they stuff the mind with 'ridiculous chimeras' (ibid.: 81). In
short, they encourage the reader to focus more on himself than on his society
with possibly dire consequences for social cohesion. These various fulmina-
tions underline two conflicting ways of looking at literature, either as a source
of morality or as a source of money. As a source of morality literature is above
market imperatives but, as a source of money, ethics matter less than profits.

It was all very well to say that the aim of drama was 'to persuade men to
humanity and good life, to instruct them in civility and good manners,

showing them the fruits of honesty and the ends of villainy' (Heywood, in Vickers 1999: 495) but first it had to attract an audience. The theatre existed in competition with other forms of entertainment such as 'fencing matches, acrobatic displays, fireworks and bear baiting' and so it had to 'offer moments of surprise, wonder, passion and excitement' which might possibly conflict with its ethical intent (Hunter 2001: 249). Moreover the customers – that is the right word – wanted to feel that plays were relevant to their own lives and, in a good number of cases, this meant paying little regard to either the unities or the purity of genres. Doubtless it was works like the anonymous *A Warning for Fair Women* (1599),[23] where personifications of tragedy, comedy and history bicker over who will put on the play, that Sidney had in mind when he asserted that dramatists should maintain the strict division between types of plays and apply Aristotle's dictum that 'the stage should always represent but one place and the uttermost time presupposed in it should be . . . but one day' (in Vickers 1999: 381).

Once poetry and drama are commercialised, they acquire an economic meaning which may conflict with their political or social ones. Philip Massinger (1583–1640) dramatises this issue in his play *The Roman Actor: A Tragedy* (1629). Aesopus and Paris are discussing the purpose of theatre. Aesopus says ,'For the profits, Paris, / And more mercenary gain, they are things beneath us', and Paris agrees, 'Our aim is glory, and to leave our names to aftertimes' (in Vickers 1999: 548). Many worried that, instead of inspiring action, poetry pandered to the imagination. Sydney approved of the power of invention only if it led to virtue. Anything else and it weakened the nation. 'Before poets began to be in price', he wrote, 'our nation had set their heart's delight upon action, not imagination' (in Vickers 1999: 372). The coming of print alters the relation between author and audience. As Sidney's reference to the imagination suggests, this is becoming a private rather than a public affair, with consequences for both parties. The author had to adjust to the demands of the market rather than his peers, while the audience were free to respond to poetry at a personal rather than social level.

To distinguish himself from his competitors, the poet had to develop a distinctive style. As Elizabeth L. Einstein notes,

> few authors failed to give high priority to publicising themselves. The art of puffery, the writing of blurbs and other familiar promotional devices were also exploited by early printers who worked aggressively to obtain public recognition for the authors and artists whose products they hoped to sell. (1979: 229)

Although poets still relied more on the support of patrons than on the marketing strategies of publishers, there were signs that they were beginning to distance themselves from this traditional social relationship. There is, for example, a change in how poets were portrayed on the frontispieces of their collections. Up to 1580, they were commonly drawn kneeling and presenting their books to their patrons but, after that date, they were more likely to be depicted at the centre of 'a complex of mythological symbols whose meaning they ruled, from the laurels they commanded as poets to the gods and muses their work invoked' (Ross 2000: 98). Poets presided over and controlled the meaning of cultural capital; the irony is that this capital was diminishing in value.

Poets also became much more conscious of their relation to their predecessors. They set out to construct a pantheon of national poets, partly to chart the progress of the vernacular and partly to enhance their own prestige. Ascham praises Chaucer for his skill in developing English but condemns him for his use of 'barbarous and rude rhyming' (in Vickers 1999: 157) and, while Puttenham accepts that Chaucer and Gower 'may justly be said the first reformers of our English meter and style', he nevertheless advises poets not to follow them for 'their language is now out of use with us' (in ibid.: 210 and 226). This represents a new conception of tradition. Broadly speaking, its guiding principle in the medieval period was *translatio studii*, the transmission of ancient learning. That still remained true but, as we noted earlier, the scholar was now expected to add to the body of knowledge as well. Similarly, the poet no longer defines himself primarily in relation to classical authors but to those of his own country whom he seeks to surpass. The construction of a literary tradition is poor compensation for the poet's loss of political function. Print culture may give him an individual identity but it comes with a reduced social influence. The poet is not quite an entertainer but neither is he quite the authority on morals and truths that he once was.

The change – and it must be stressed it is a very slow one – in the status of the author has at least two potential consequences for literary criticism; first, a focus on what is distinctive about a poet and, second, a focus on poetic innovation. We must remember, though, that the term 'literary criticism' did not exist in this period, even if some of the various elements of which it is composed did. Jonson sums up one view of criticism at this time when he writes that

> the office of a true critic or censor is not to throw by a letter anywhere, or damn an innocent syllable, but lay the words together and amend them; judge sincerely of the author and his matter, which is the sign of a solid and perfect learning in a man. (in Vickers 1999: 588)

Criticism as a correction. Criticism as a part of the creative process. This cooperative vision will eventually vanish as criticism develops into a discipline in its own right.

Here, though, we are less interested in the definitions of criticism than in the conditions which shape it. The critic who comments on an individual work does so in a language shaped by events that are often far from literary, but which nevertheless have a bearing on how we understand and value a poem, novel or play. Criticism is always local but there's a whole history in the words that convey art's significance or otherwise. At the same time, we shouldn't forget that discussion of particular works raises its own problems. Jonson's view of John Donne (1572–1631)[24] is a case in point. It illustrates another difficulty that bedevils any history of criticism, namely, that there is no necessary connection between a critical principle and the perception of a given work. Jonson claimed it was more important to experiment in writing poetry than to follow the rules (in Vickers 1999: 571) and this is precisely what Donne does, prompting Jonson to remark that he was too difficult to understand and therefore would 'perish' (ibid.: 532). But this mismatch between philosophy and practice is less revealing than the suggestion that poets should innovate, for this represents a recognition that success in the literary market in part depends on cultivating a distinctive style. Of course everyone is individual but that only becomes a decisive factor in literary life when the writer moves from the political to the economic sphere. In the former he had a role, in the latter he has to find one.

As we said above, the change in the conditions of authorship alters the writer's attitude to tradition: he is now more likely to define himself against it instead of taking his place within it and one way in which he can do that is to write about personal experience, as Donne does. One consequence for criticism is that the author becomes as important an object of study as the work which, in turn, is valued less as an expression of truth than as a revelation of its creator. This approach does not mature until the late eighteenth century but its seeds are there in the sixteenth. The trend for authors to defy tradition also suggests that criticism is more likely to embrace works of the present than the past. But neither poets nor critics, at this stage, quite become imbibed with the spirit of progress. A number of elegies on the death of Donne state that his poetry was so perfect that writers could only either imitate it or put down their pens forever (Ross 2000: 126–32).

We have seen how the author was affected by the coming of print but what about the audience? If writers were more isolated, so too were readers. They did not have to consider, as they did formerly, such matters as their obligation to the author or the moral design of his work. On the contrary, they could use books as they pleased, as a stimulus to fancy, a means of diversion or a source of enrichment. The audience may have enjoyed their new-found freedoms, but authors worried that it would undermine the literary hierarchy. This was evident in Richard Tottel's address to the reader at the beginning of his famous miscellany, the *Songes and Sonettes* (1557), when he asked his 'learned' readers 'to defend their learned frendes, the authors of this work' (in Ross 2000: 64). Clearly he felt that the reputation of poets like Thomas Wyatt (1503–42),[25] who introduced the sonnet into English, would diminish in the new climate of diverse reader response.

Tottel's appeal to the learned reader, which anticipates the twentieth-century critic F. R. Leavis's address to an 'educated public', is not just an attempt to protect an emerging English canon, it is also an attempt to recreate, in the marketplace, the intimate nature of poetry at court. The close relationship between the author and his audience is captured in the call to the discerning reader, while the shared values of court culture are evoked in the assumption that readers assent to the excellence of anthologised work. John Bodenham (c. 1563–1621), in his canonical miscellany *Belvidere, or the Garden of the Muses* (1600), writes that it would be 'needless' for him to defend 'so many singular mens workes' because their 'worth' has already been 'approoved' (in Ross 2000: 74). The purpose of such remarks, Ross suggests, was 'to create a situation where criticism was seen as unnecessary because all agents participated in a consensus of value' (ibid.: 74). We might put this another way and say that criticism tries to restore, at the level of the book, the community of author and audience that was being eroded by market forces.

The community that anthologists try to create is a very small one. In Jonson's terms, it consists not of 'ordinary' but of 'extraordinary' readers (in Ross 2000: 74). By distinguishing between the two types, men like Tottel and Bodenham provided a another variation on the age-old distinction between those who were capable of construing a work properly and those who were not. The previous context for this distinction was the Church where commentators determined the true meaning of the Scriptures while others had to be content with their surface sense, and another was the court where, according to Puttenham, all poetry was a form of dissembling which only the initiated could understand (Vickers 1999: 27–52 and 291). The present context is the marketplace where the division is now between writing that promotes harmony through a respect for hierarchy and writing that, according to Sir Nicholas Bacon (1510–79), foster father of Francis Bacon, 'maketh men's minds to be at variance with one another', eventually resulting in the 'utter ruin and destruction of [their] bodies, goods and lands' (in Vickers 1999: 78). And if one sort of writing promotes eloquence and aims at the betterment of man and society, another sort, ballads, romances and the like, has no regard for expression and aims only to please the senses (see Elyot, in Vickers 1999: 63–5).

The anthologies aimed to promote the vernacular, to 'publish the honour of the Englishe tong' (Tottel, in Ross 2000: 64), but this supposedly common language was, in the hands of some, a means of dividing the nation. Those not attuned to the beauties of English verse were little better than beasts but they did not have to remain so; a little poetry would 'purge' them of their 'swinelike grossenesse' (ibid.: 64). Poetry was no longer confined, in the words of Edmund Spenser (1552–99),[26] author of *The Faerie Queene* (1590 and 1596), to 'fashion[ing] a gentleman or noble person in virtuous and gentle discipline' (in Vickers 1999: 298); it was now the means by which we come into our humanity, a humanity defined in terms of the intellect. 'What else is man,' asks Puttenham, 'but his mind?' (in Vickers 1999: 253). The idea that literature is integral to our sense of who we are, that it is a means of refining us, continues into the eighteenth century, with this difference. In place of Ben Jonson's distinction between the ordinary and extraordinary reader, we have Samuel Johnson's idea of the 'common reader'. This mythical creature has been democratised – but only up to a point. He remains male and is largely middle class.

Ross's claim that the authors like Tottel and Bodenham sought to stifle criticism with their assumption that we can all agree about what constitutes good poetry characterises it as the arena of potential dissent, diversity and difference. We may pursue true judgement, but we will never be able to arrive at it. The arrival of print and the dispersal of a cohesive literary community condemned readers to, at best, fruitful disagreement and, at worst, entrenched discord. It was relatively easy, within the narrow confines of the court, to come to some agreement about the value of a work based on how well or how badly it strengthened social relations, but once literature entered the marketplace there was no institution devoted to its study, nor any clear criteria for determining its worth. As Lawrence Manley points out, literary culture in Tudor–Stuart London 'was a product of many intersecting influences', including 'the English ruling class, and nobility, scholars and diplomats from throughout Europe' (2001: 339). There was also 'a wealthy and socially mobile merchant class receptive to learning' as well as an 'urban gentry for whom investment in culture was among the least expensive forms of conspicuous consumption' (ibid.: 339). Furthermore, the migration of literature from the court to the city led to the development of new genres, notably, the epigram, essay, elegy, epistle and ode. These, in some measure, reflected the more relaxed relations between reader and writer than had obtained at court, since they tended 'towards the privatised domains of self, friends, distinctive place, and occasion' (ibid.: 346). They were also 'specially adapted to the discriminating choices demanded by the burgeoning pace and scale of metropolitan life' (ibid.: 346). What you chose revealed what you were. To opt to be part of a growing culture of clubs, private collections, poetry and indoor theatre was a way of displaying your refinement (ibid.: 347). In this context, criticism was less an expression of community than an element of social distinction.

### Politics, Economics and Decorum

The tension between the court's desire to promote a particular model of English and the influx of terms from trade, travel and, of course, French and Latin is manifested in debates about decorum. This was a key term in Renaissance literary theory and, as we have already seen, it referred mainly to the match of subject and style. Puttenham sums up this by now familiar idea when he writes that there are three styles, 'high, mean [middle] and base', and 'it behoveth the maker or poet to follow the nature of his subject; that is, if his matter be high and lofty, that the style be so too; if mean, the style also to be mean; if base, the style humble and base accordingly' (in Vickers 1999: 228). Puttenham is thinking primarily of public speech, such as in a law court, but the same principle is found in writing about poetry and drama. Sidney rebukes those who mix the distinct genres of comedy and tragedy, 'mingling kings and clowns', while George Gascoigne, author, according to Vickers, of the first work of literary criticism in English, writes that 'royal rhyme' serves 'a grave discourse' and 'riding rhyme a merry tale' (in ibid.: 7, 171 and 383).

The preoccupation with decorum, other terms for it are 'beauty, proportion, comeliness' (Puttenham, in Vickers 1999: 286), suggests that it needed defending. When Jonson complains that Battista Guarini's (1538–1612) *Il Pastor Fido* (*The Faithful Shepherd*, 1598) 'kept not decorum, in making shepherds speak as well as himself' (in ibid.: 530), he voices a widespread concern that the unity of style and subject matter is no longer axiomatic. The desire to maintain decorum, and a growing awareness that this may not be possible, characterises John Hoskyns's *Sidney's Arcadia and the Rhetoric of English Prose* (1599). He carefully distinguishes between emblem, allegory, similitude and fable but he increasingly recognises that all these figures overlap. Allegory, for example, shades into metaphor while catachresis merges into irony (ibid.: 400 and 404). Puttenham makes the same discovery. Allegory, metaphor, irony and enigma all seem variations of one another (ibid.: 232). There are even times when a word turns into its opposite, 'diminution goes for amplification' (ibid.: 415). And, of course, there was the usual worry about metaphor leading readers astray. Far-fetched, affected, mixed, there were so many ways it could endanger understanding (ibid.: 575). This was a worry, for it was a commonplace among the educated that the state of language reflected the state of society and vice versa. 'We may conclude,' says Jonson that 'wheresoever manners and fashions are corrupted, language is. It imitates the public riot' (ibid.: 567). A failure to respect the rules of rhetoric may lead to a failure to respect the gradations of social rank. Hoskyns reflects this anxiety when he writes, 'see to what preferment a figure may aspire if it once get in credit in a world that hath not much true rhetoric?' (ibid.: 410). If figures can move from their allotted place, so can people, especially at a time when the developing capitalist economy is sending shock-waves through the feudal social structure.

Puttenham suggests that the best way to restore order is to appeal to the idea of decorum, 'the matter resteth much in the definition and acceptance of this word *decorum*' (in Vickers 1999: 232–3). But this is a not a convincing argument. Decorum has broken down, so appeal to decorum? Even if a definition could be agreed on, there is the further problem that decorum is 'very much alterable and subject to variety' (ibid.: 287). It is a matter of discretion but not everyone has 'a learned and experienced discretion' so those 'who can make the best and most differences of things [are] to be the fittest judge' of decorum (ibid.: 287). Puttenham is offering a view of decorum based on custom which is contrary to his other view that it is based on nature. 'This lovely conformity between the sense and the sensible hath nature herself first most carefully observed in all her own works, then also by kind graft it in the appetites of every other creature . . . and of man chiefly as well in his speeches as in every other part of his behaviour' (ibid.: 286–7). If decorum is seen as part of nature then it has an authority which it lacks if it is simply seen as conventional. Puttenham holds both views but his emphasis falls on decorum as a social rather than a natural phenomenon.

The concept of decorum is destabilised as it passes from the realm of nature to that of culture. There, it is danger from women who, according to Hoskyns, are given to 'that kind of breaking words into another meaning' which corrupts speech (Vickers 1999: 410). The increase in English vocabulary is a more likely cause of the disruptions of decorum than female punning since it places a heavy demand on linguistic structures of all kinds to absorb the new words. Nevertheless, we should not overlook the fact that women were seen as a threat to the purity of the vernacular. The attempt to refine the language was almost exclusively a masculine enterprise. Sidney begins his *A Defence of Poetry* with an anecdote about horsemanship which provides a military context for his discussion. Poetry 'is the companion of camps' and the highest kind is heroic poetry which 'inflames the mind with desire to be worthy' (in ibid.: 365 and 373). The connection between poetry and warfare, which goes back to Homer, means that when Sidney asserts that the English language is superior to French, Italian and Spanish, he is also making a point about England's superiority in arms and there is no place for women in this sort of rhetoric. They are perceived as a menace to the masculine ideal of poetry and, by extension, to a martial view of the nation. But they are also, as we saw earlier, a means of illustrating the correct use of ornament in poetry. In any case, the greater danger lies in the swelling of the lexicon. The flood of new words undermines traditional hierarchies of signification which, in turn, threaten ideas about the social order and people's place in it, at least from the point of view of an aristocratic class dimly aware that their control of language and their command of its various arts is under attack from developments in the wider society. Puttenham writes *The Arte of Englishe Poesie* (1589) to enable courtiers, ladies and young gentlewomen 'to become skilful in their mother tongue' (ibid.: 235), but there are many more who speak that tongue, and its growth is fast outstripping the formalities that he would like to govern its utterance.

Any discussion of criticism in this period, then, needs to take account of the development of the vernacular. Criticism contributes to this development in at least two ways. First, it is committed to promoting the type of English spoken at court and, since this is offered as the model for the rest of the nation, then criticism is implicated in the project of linguistic unity. Second, there are numerous treatises on poetry. These are mostly prescriptive and deal with the aim of poetry, to produce good behaviour, and the proper use of figure, to adorn and illustrate. Since poetry was seen as an exemplary use of the vernacular, this was another way criticism contributed to its development. In both these examples, criticism is an active force. But it is also shaped by wider events. The translation of the Bible into the vernacular undermined the authority of the commentator and this process was accelerated as, particularly poetry, passed from the court to the marketplace. It would be too much to say that this created a division between 'high' and 'low' literature; nevertheless, contemporaries are beginning to think in those terms and, from now on, criticism will be compelled to take account of this problem. Indeed, it will perpetuate and compound it.

And there is a further issue. The fact that books are for sale gives them an economic value which exists in some tension with their social one. Publishers may make more profit from a popular work that is considered to have a bad effect on social harmony than from a work of 'proper' literature which promotes it. But there's more to this than a mere conflict of values. A book has to meet market demands before it can be praised for its visionary gleams. Here, the relationship between economic and social value is more complementary. Nevertheless, a book's ability to transcend material considerations by offering truth or moral guidance is still compromised by its status as a commodity – that alone endures, while everything else changes. Criticism gives us the opportunity to think through this tangle of social and economic relations which are too often presented as simply opposed. To do that properly we must be aware of how the discourse of criticism is itself shaped by the wider society. It must reflect on its own idiom as well as that of literature. And part of that idiom, the counting of syllables, the rules governing the use of figure, is consistent with the sort of quantitative thinking that characterises the marketplace. As capitalism develops, this element is increasingly emphasised with the result that, today, criticism is little more than an unthinking application of technique. The point now, though, is the very obvious one that a book cannot be criticised if it has not been published, and the first consideration in deciding whether to publish it is not is this good, true or beautiful, but will it make money?

### The Problems of Tradition

Until the mid years of the sixteenth century, poetry had been regarded as a repository of knowledge about philosophy, mythology, the natural world and so on. The publication Francis Bacon's *The Advancement of Learning* (1605) began to change all that. He argued that knowledge could only be discovered by observing the world around us.[27] This was an age of scientific discovery. Copernicus (1473–1543) had shown that earth revolved around the sun and William Harvey (1578–1657) discovered the circulation of the blood. Numerous reference books on plants and animals were also becoming available and they, too, undermined poetry's status as a source of learning. The humanist response to this development, whose effects can still be seen today in the rather dismissive attitude to the study of literature in the knowledge economy, was to stress the specialist nature of their work. This took two forms, the recovery of ancient manuscripts and a focus on the rhetorical character rather than the knowledge content of literature.

What mainly prompted the return *ad fontes*, or 'to the sources', was a dissatisfaction with the quality of the medieval Latin translations of the Bible and classical literature. Renaissance scholars wanted to examine these texts in their original Hebrew and Greek. A number were brought to Italy by those fleeing from the sack of Constantinople in 1453.[28] Studying ancient manuscripts made scholars aware of how language changed over time. The work of Lorenzo Valla (1406–57), an Italian humanist, provides an illustration. He exposed the forgery known as the 'Donation of Constantine', a document purporting to give Pope Sylvester (c. 280–335 AD), and his descendants, rule over Italy. Valla showed that the style of the supposedly fourth-century document could not have existed before the eighth or ninth century. The identification of changes in diction, grammar and idiom helped to establish the discipline of philology and to create 'a powerful sense of language itself as a historical phenomenon' (Waswo 2001: 27).

Amazing as it may seem to us, the idea that the past was different to the present was quite new in the Renaissance. As Michel Jeanneret notes: 'For the first time, a sense of alterity and loss – an acknowledgement that the past was gone and that cultures were transient – was shifting the process of reading into the field of historical enquiry' (2001: 39). We have seen some of the changes that prompted this awareness, the growth of trade, for example, but it was also related to the discovery of perspective which was 'a means of ordering the visual field in painting and of coming to intellectual terms with the past in historiography' (Damon 1967: 29). The basic principle of perspective in art, invented by the architect Filippo Brunelleschi (1377–1446), is that objects appear to diminish in size as they recede from view. This gives the spectator the god-like illusion that he has a perfect view of the scene. In fact this an effect of geometry. Michael Baxandall explains: 'Parallel lines receding from the plane of the picture surface appear to meet at a single point on the horizon, the vanishing point; lines parallel with the picture plane do not converge' (1988: 126). Just as poetry was designed to produce specific effects, so too was perspective. According to Leon Battista Alberti (1404–72), the 'pleasing ordering of planes rendering bodies and their relations' was geared to 'moving the soul's passions' (in Reiss 2001: 515). The geometry of perspective and the mathematics of meter were not primarily intended to represent the world but to show it as it should be, their harmonies inspiring virtue – which usually meant acquiescence in aristocratic rule.

The implication of pictorial perspective for historical study was that it organised the past into a sequence of events from the most near to the most far, each laid bare to our gaze. In terms of criticism, this meant studying works in their context, clearing them of corruptions, distortions and embellishments so as to restore their original sense. No longer do scholars just transmit the past, they recover or even reconstitute it. The focus now is more on the textual differences between, say, classical and Christian literature than on their supposed continuities of meaning. As allegory gives way to philology, attention shifts from interpreting the text to establishing its integrity. Of course both go together but, in the medieval period, the emphasis was more on the message while in the Renaissance it was more on the medium. The many meanings celebrated by the allegorist, argued the philologist, were the result of mistakes which would disappear once the work was properly edited. Only by returning to the original works, expunging error, comparing different versions and clearing away the clutter of commentary would the truth be revealed. At this point, criticism was more a matter of careful editing than subtle reading. It was the culmination of a trend that had been gathering pace since the thirteenth century when, under the influence of Aristotle, scholars concerned themselves more with the literary and historical aspects of a work than with its various allegorical meanings. Not that allegory disappears altogether. The Jesuits strongly influenced the study of Latin poetry. Their commitment to Christian truth not only led to censorship but also rehabilitated 'allegorical interpretation as a way of saving ancient fictions for truth' (Moss 2001b: 105). Once again it appears that the history of criticism consists of a series of elements which are more or less constant but which receive different emphases in different periods.

Perhaps a more sophisticated way of stating this principle is to put it in terms of Raymond Williams's model of the dominant, emergent and residual.

The first refers to the current regime of meanings and values; the second to those which are coming into being; and the third to those which continue to exert an influence, even though they are on the wane (1977: 121–7). Thus philology would be an example of the dominant and allegory of the residual. An example of 'emergent' would be the new emphasis on personal experience in writing which eventually becomes dominant in romanticism. The relation between these various levels of development help constitute the idea of tradition. In the medieval world, tradition was largely a principle of continuity, the expression of a universal culture. But that idea was beginning to change owing to a host of factors such as the rise of Protestantism, the development of the vernacular and the growth of trade. Tradition was still a principle of continuity but should this be based on the native or the classical tradition?

Many thought that vernacular literature should conform to ancient models. Hence, Spenser uses 'the antique poets' as a guide for his *The Fairie Queene* and Jonson advises the aspiring poet to read the best 'among whom Horace, and he that taught him, Aristotle, deserve to be the first in estimation' (in Vickers 1999: 298 and 587). Meanwhile, Sir John Harington (1561–1612) who, despite being Queen Elizabeth's godson, was banished from court for his crude verses on the invention of the water closet, defended the text of the Italian writer Ludovico Ariosto's *Orlando Furioso* (1532 trans. 1591), a chivalric epic, by comparing it to Virgil's *Aeneid* (ibid.: 314). But respect for the classical tradition is tempered by an awareness that it belongs to a specific period of history and therefore its achievements, no matter how glorious, are strictly relative. As Ascham puts it, 'no perfection is durable' (ibid.: 154). The light of a Euripides or a Virgil may still continue to shine but it cannot illuminate all areas of human experience. 'Let Aristotle and others have their due', writes Jonson, 'but we can make farther discoveries of truth and fitness than they' (ibid.: 580), while, in a more strident vein, Samuel Daniel asks why we should 'yeeld our consents captive to the authoritie of Antiquitie . . . We are the children of Nature as well as they' (in Burrow 2001: 490).

Some of the tensions between a native and a classic tradition were played out in the debate over the use of rhyme in poetry. The main argument was that, since the ancient writers did not use rhyme, neither should modern ones. The objections to rhyme ranged from Roger Ascham who called it 'barbarous' to Thomas Campion who thought it apt to distract the reader from the matter of the poem (in Vickers 1999: 161 and 432), to John Milton (1608–74) who argued that 'rhyme arrests meaning in a way analogous to the process by which monarchs suppress their subjects' (Schoenfeldt 2001: 377). Quantity of syllables was a better foundation for English poetry than 'artificial' rhyme, because numbers corresponded to natural speech and because feet contained a greater capacity for symmetry and proportion than rhyme (ibid.: 161, 429–30 and 435). These charges were met head on by Samuel

Daniel who countered that rhyme was 'natural' and supplied 'a harmony far happier than any antiquity could ever show us' (ibid.: 442–3). He further argued that we cannot make 'counting' the basis of poetry because English is different to the classical languages. 'For as Greek and Latin verses consist of number and quantity of syllables, so doth English verse of measure and accent' (ibid.: 443). He also defended rhyme on the grounds that it required more skill than metrics, while Sidney claimed that it was an aid to memory (ibid.: 368 and 446). Finally, far from being oppressive, rhyme was rooted in English common law and custom (ibid.: 442). It was quantitative syllables that curtailed freedom because they were associated with 'Roman law absolutism' (Shuger 2001: 184). Verse, as rhyme was sometimes called, was a mere ornament of poetry whose defining characteristic was, Sidney pronounced, to 'feign . . . notable images' for the purpose of teaching the beauty of virtue and the wickedness of vice (Vickers 1999: 347 and see Jonson on 585). But go into most schools and colleges today and the students will think that poetry should rhyme. As in the English Civil War, Milton supported the wrong side. Rhyme and monarchy eventually triumphed.

We mentioned earlier that poets were drawing up a national tradition and the process began with the dissolution of the monasteries.[29] John Leland (1506–52), the only person ever to hold the title Royal Antiquary, and John Bale (1495–1563), who earned the nickname 'foul-mouthed Bale' for the crudity with which he attacked his Catholic opponents, both endeavoured to produce an inventory of the contents of monastic libraries but, despite their best efforts, they failed. Too many had been partially or wholly destroyed and too many books had disappeared abroad. The vandalism drove Bale to tears, and Leland to madness. Nevertheless, they still managed to compile a number of catalogues which Ross calls 'the first comprehensive objectifications of the canon of British letters' (2000: 52). The historical circumstances surrounding their collections underline the earlier point that criticism now takes cognisance of the *pastness* of the past. Hence, Bale and Leland do not merely list dispersed writings, they also try to answer the question of how works can retain their value once their historical moment has passed. Both argued that their efforts helped to legitimise the Tudor claim to the throne and to put England on the same cultural footing as other countries in Europe. The Tudors, especially Henry VII (1457–1509), declared that they were directly descended from King Arthur and other semi-legendary figures from the past so any literature supporting that assertion was good propaganda. Gabriel Harvey (1545–1630), who rose from being the son of a rope maker to Professor of Rhetoric at Cambridge, asked why France, Italy and Spain seemed able to develop a national literature, but not England. Were native writers too much in thrall to the classical tradition? The labours of Bale and Leland might give them the confidence to think otherwise.

Beyond these broad justifications, the two antiquaries display slightly different attitudes to their undertaking. Bale believes that we need a knowledge of past religious works because they would help justify the Reformation, while Leland believes that we need a knowledge of past literary works so that we can measure the progress of the vernacular. Bale believes that past authors ought to speak in their own words 'without bewtie of speche' (in Ross 2000: 60), while Leland wants to rewrite them so they can be more easily understood. It is arguable which of them invests more in the project. Bale goes back to the Celtic roots of Christianity to liberate an indigenous spirituality that had been subjugated by Rome. In his view, 'the English had to save their literature to save themselves' (ibid.: 59). Leland 'hopes to erect a pantheon to honour king and empire' (ibid.: 55) by rescuing the country's chronicles from the darkness of medieval expression. One writer addresses problems of religion, another problems of the State though, as these are finally inseparable, it is more a question of emphasising one rather than the other. But both use the past to vindicate the present.

Whether they demonstrate how a work can still be significant long after it was written is another matter. At one level this involves giving an accurate description of past literature but Bale makes a number of errors, for example, stating that John Wyclif (1330–84), not William Langland (c. 1332–1400), wrote *Piers the Ploughman* (1379). By making a religious leader the author of a work which attacks the abuses of the Catholic Church, Bale advances his argument for the existence of a native tradition of robust spirituality. But his error reveals a truth: that we may only be able to make the past serve the present if we distort it. And distortion is inevitable, if only because we can never know the past in its entirety. Selection is forced upon us, though there is still plenty of scope to choose from the material that has survived and some misrepresentations are more fruitful than others. Here we come to the next level. Can we give an account of how the worth of any given work alters over time? We do not find any such account in Bale. The meaning he attributes to early religious writings stands outside time. His 'transcendent logos', writes Ross, 'was not an image of survival because it fixed the source of value outside change, beyond the historicity of authors and their works' (2000: 61).

Neither do we get a satisfactory answer to this question from Leland. He judges literary works in terms of their eloquence, and since those of the past are less eloquent than those of the present they are not as valuable. The value of the past is a constantly diminishing quality, it does not endure. Not everyone agreed with this analysis. The one time MP for Bedford, George Gascoigne, takes the opposite view, declaring that English verse has declined since the time of Chaucer (Vickers 1999: 165). But Puttenham probably speaks for most when he writes that the rough rhymes of Chaucer, Gower and Langland are surpassed by 'the sweet and stately measures' (in Vickers 1999:

210) of Wyatt and Henry Earl of Surrey (1517–47). The purpose of eloquence was to refine the language but in poetry it was also to persuade the audience to act rightly. As such it was a form of rhetoric. The relation between the two has a long history. The poet and the orator are akin but they are not identical. Poetry, for example, should be more difficult and is bound by metrical constraints which rhetoric is not. The difference between them is summed up by the man known in his lifetime as the 'prince of poets' Pierre de Ronsard (1524–85) who said that 'while the aim of the orator is to persuade, that of the poet is to imitate, to invent and to represent those things that are, or can be verisimilar' (in Greene 2001: 223). Nevertheless, as we noted earlier, poetry is both a species of deliberative rhetoric because it seeks to influence behaviour and a type of demonstrative rhetoric because of its use of ornate language.[30]

The form of poetry is thus practically more important than its content which somewhat undermines one standard defence of it in this period, that it is a source of truth and knowledge. But again, as we have seen, the growth of science was proving a more reliable guide to nature's secrets than Virgil. If poetry was to lay claim to learning it had to be of a moral rather than a factual nature. For Sidney, it brought us as near as possible to perfection, while for Jonson it made 'a full man' (in Vickers 1999: 347–8 and 586). This exalted conception of learning, which contrasts favourably with our debased idea of it, was confined to the aristocracy. They were educated to appreciate the arts but the children of the mercantile class had to learn practical skills (Elsky 2001: 407). Not that learning about the arts didn't have its practical side. The ideal of learning was not as disinterested as particularly Jonson suggests. Thomas Elyot, for example, argued that the study of poetry offered a good grounding in public speaking which was very useful for those born to govern (Vickers 1999: 57–69). A similar division exists today. Those who occupy positions of power have generally enjoyed a private school education followed by three years at a Russell group university whereas the rest are taught in institutions which train them to service the economy.

Most discussion of literary form focuses on the use of ornament, how it illustrates an argument or inspires an action. But these same ornaments can also be a distraction. We have already mentioned that figure in poetry is feminised and contemporaries strongly implied that it had the power to seduce readers from the true sense of a work. Puttenham says that it 'deceives the ear and also the mind, drawing it from plainness and simplicity to a certain doubleness' (in Vickers 1999: 232). At the same time, he seems happy to accept that ambiguity. The ability to dissemble is as key to the poet's art as acting is to the orator's (ibid.: 118 and 292). Clarity should not be confused with sincerity. Ornament also has a class dimension. Poetry should be clothed in figure to keep it 'from the capacity of vulgar judgement' (ibid.:

220). 'Poesy', writes George Chapman, 'is the flower of the sun and disdains to open to the eye of a candle' (ibid.: 518). Ornament is designed to obscure, to protect art from 'the frontless detractions of some stupid ignorants' (ibid.: 518). We have been here before. In the last chapter, for example, we mentioned Thomas Gallus (1183?–1246) who advised his followers to 'hide holy secrets . . . from the ears and knowledge of the impure multitude' (Minnis and Scott 2000: 182). It is another constant in the history of criticism. Ornament is almost the condition of being heard. Sir John Harington confesses that unless his ploughmen speak like Virgil he never really listens to them. 'I was never yet so good husband to take any delight to hear one of my ploughmen tell how an acre of wheat must be fallowed . . . but when I hear Virgil . . . I could find in my heart to drive the plough' (in Vickers 1999: 310–11). Finally, ornament is used to distinguish poetry from ordinary language. Its various rhetorical devices or 'fresh colours', writes Puttenham, make it far more eloquent 'than the ordinary prose which we use in our daily talk' (in Vickers 1999: 196).

Literary form is treated almost as if it were separate from content. A fault-line runs between them. All the attention paid to balance, harmony and proportion in discussions of decorum suggests these qualities were more absent than present. This points to a certain unease in the conception of literature. Leland based his idea of tradition on the evolution of eloquence which means devaluing earlier efforts. His notion of tradition fails to account for why some works continue to speak to later generations and others do not. Even the idea of a national tradition is not straightforward. It is true that, in the 1550s and 60s:

> England was mapped, described and chorographically related to its Roman and Medieval past; the voyages of the English nation were gathered and printed and an ideological base was laid for England's colonial and mercantile expansion; English history was staged before thousands by newly founded professional acting companies performing in newly constructed playhouses . . . and finally a church of England was established, challenged and defended with unprecedented authority and sophistication. (Helgerson 1992: 299–300)

But while there is certainly a consciousness of English writing in relation to Greek and Roman literature, and that of other European countries, it is by no means a coherent one. First, the many different kinds of writing about England, historical, scientific, ecclesiastical, legal and literary, militate against a uniform expression of the nation and, second, there are differences of opinion even among poets and playwrights as to the nature of the country. 'There are those', writes Kumar, 'such as Spenser, Shakespeare and Hooker who lean towards the state and monarchy . . . and there are others, such as

Drayton, Coke and Hakluyt who seem to evoke in a more populist and inclusive mode, the spirit of the nation, the people as a whole' (2003: 117). And of course we shouldn't forget that only very few participated in the making of English national identity. The discussion did not include the illiterate nor extend to the regions.

The notion of tradition is, then, plagued by problems. It addresses a rupture in the relations between past and present and tries to repair them. The dissolution of the monasteries was one such rupture and another was the shift of literary production and reception from the politics of the court to the economics of the market. This generates anxieties about the nature of literature: how to differentiate it from other forms of writing, the siren-like nature of ornament, and the fear of it being contaminated through contact with the common people. One response to these worries is to emphasise continuity by putting English poetry and drama in the context of the classical tradition, and another is to acknowledge the break with that tradition and create a new one. Both solutions assume that literary value resides in the poet's learning or his ability to shape behaviour. But the first has been superseded by the growth of natural science and the second by literature's move into a commercial environment where its influence on action is secondary to how well it sells. Despite the grandiose claims still made on behalf of literature, criticism is really now the more humble activity of editing ancient texts. The drift to professional scholarship has begun.

### Morality and Nature

As we saw earlier, Jonson defines criticism as 'correction'. So, for instance, criticism helps to establish vernacular literature by promoting the proper use of English. But there were many activities that we might describe as 'criticism' in this period, even if that term is not used to describe them. And they all take place within certain contexts. The main ones are Protestantism, the vernacular, the court and the market. Others, to which we have only made brief reference, include patronage and censorship. Each, in their different way, impinge on what the poet can and cannot write. It is hard to know how such things affect what a critic does but he or she should at least be aware of them, if only because they are a reminder that a work is not simply the product of an artist's skill or vision. Give them too much weight, however, and the idea of art as a craft, which is central to how we value it, is fatally undermined.

Jonson's definition of criticism is highly prescriptive. And that applies to many of those mentioned in this chapter. Their aim is to teach their readers how to write well. We find the same ambition in the tradition of *grammatica*, and the pedagogic aspect is a reminder that what we call criticism often has an institutional location. One of the pioneers of the English Reformation,

John Colet (1467–1519)[31] founded Saint Paul's grammar school in c. 1512, and a central part of the curriculum was 'the creation of a canon of model ancient authors to exemplify literary excellence', a canon, moreover, that was seen as the 'basis for the active life of citizenship' (Manley 2001: 340–1). Another aspect of criticism is therefore concerned with the moral value of literature. Heywood lists the ways in which drama is a force for good: it polishes the language, it teaches proper speech, it imparts a knowledge of English history, it inspires noble actions, it commends virtue and condemns vice, it is 'a brief epitome of the time' and it is means of self-knowledge (in Vickers 1999: 475–98). All these make it a much better form of recreation than drinking in a tavern. Tragedies warn tyrants of the dreadful fate that will befall them if they abuse their power, while comedies 'refresh such weary spirits as are tired with labour or study, that they may return to their trades and faculties with more zeal and earnestness' (ibid.: 495). Drama can even bring murderers to justice. Heywood recounts the tale of a Norfolk woman who was startled into confessing that she had murdered her husband after watching a play on the same theme (ibid.: 498). Hamlet's staging of *The Mousetrap* to discover whether his uncle really did kill his father (II, ii, 596–606) no longer seems so idiosyncratic.

Heywood's vigorous defence of drama on moral and indeed cultural grounds is in part a response to the decline of literature as a medium of knowledge. So too is the emphasis on editing. If he is not promoting poetry as an ethical force, the scholar is purifying ancient writings. Moreover, Lorenzo Valla's studies had shown that language changed over time. The meaning of words came not from their correspondence to things in the world, but from the context in which they were used. As we saw earlier, this has profound consequences for criticism: allegory gives way to philology.[32] The metaphor of reading is no longer an unveiling of transcendent truth but a reconstruction of a historical document. Evoking the tradition of *grammatica*, scholars analyse words and grammar, gloss difficult passages, identify the Greek sources for Latin works and explain social, political and geographical allusions. It might be thought that such detailed investigation undermines literature's moral status; in fact it enhances it. Why? Because philology focuses on the formal properties of a work, those very features which are seen to influence behaviour rather than tell the truth. It thus complements the notion that the value of literature lies in its power to persuade us to do good. Once more, the traditions of rhetoric and grammar are closely entwined.

The commentator on literature also has to deal with the scientist claiming nature as his special object of study. How would this affect poetry? In part it involves readjusting poetry's relation to the other arts and sciences, and we have already seen one such adjustment with rhetoric. In the medieval world, poetry was associated with grammar, rhetoric and logic and occasionally with arithmetic. But this changes in the Renaissance with the rise of science. Not being seen as a source of knowledge about the natural world, poetry is more closely aligned with history and philosophy. Sidney claims it is superior to both. The philosophers teach by precept, the historians by example. Only 'the peerless poet . . . coupleth the general notion with the particular [instance]' (in Vickers 1999: 351). The high status Sidney gives to poetry contrasts with the generally low esteem in which it was held for much of the medieval period, but the sense that the study of poetry still needs to be justified remains the same. Sidney just prosecutes his case more vigorously.

If one way of coping with the threat to poetry's status from science is to group it with history and philosophy, another is to make poetry's separation from nature its defining feature. All other arts, argues Sidney, have nature for their 'principal object'. Only the poet, 'disdaining to be tied to any such subjection, lifted up with the vigour of his own invention, doth grow in effect another nature, in making things either better bringeth forth or, quite anew, forms such as never were in nature' (in Vickers 1999: 343). Were it not for the slightly dismissive attitude to nature, that could almost be a manifesto for the romantic idea of the imagination.[33] But the key word for poetic production in the Renaissance is imitation, not imagination which, in this period, is a 'passive faculty that recombines sense impressions, and so generates dreams and delusive composites such as the mythical chimera, part lion, part goat, part snake' (Burrow 2001: 488). As we have seen, imitation refers not to the natural world, but to men as they should be. This implies a fairly simplistic idea of human psychology, one which is still current in debates about the influence of television, cinema and computer games on the behaviour of young people. Imitation can thus be a focus for concerns about the social order, and the centrality of the term in Renaissance literary criticism is in part explained by the threat to traditional ideas of society from, for example, the expansion of commerce and the enclosure movement. To encourage people to imitate, as Roger Ascham does when he advises would-be writers to imitate 'the best authors' (in Vickers 1999: 145), is to discourage them from being individuals.

Part of the art of poetry now lies in imitating other poets and the reader's pleasure comes from recognising which poets are being imitated. Such a response acknowledges that literature is an autonomous entity which may only have a minimal relation to the real world. Yes, the end of rhetoric is the reform of manners but that cannot be measured; the primary experience of verse lies in the richness of its figures, the variety of its tropes. The densely worked surface not the distant effect best describes the encounter with poetry. We are a long way from the doctrine of art for art's sake, which flourishes in the last years of the nineteenth century, but the germ is present in the sixteenth. First, the development of science has reduced poetry's role as a source of knowledge. Second, poetry's move from the political to the economic sphere leaves it without a clear sense of purpose, which opens the way for it to be valued in and for itself, a development illustrated by the growing interest in form rather than content. Third, there is a connection between rhetoric and aesthetics: one is the study of how speech affects our mind and emotions, the other with how art affects our senses.[34] And when Puttenham talks about 'auricular figures', those 'which work alteration in the ear by sound, accent, time, and slipper [smooth] and volubility in utterance' (in Vickers 1999: 237), we can see just how close rhetoric comes to aesthetics.

Art, then, is seen as separate from nature. As a form of invention it produces things which aren't found in nature, while as a form of imitation its concern is with human perfection or poetic excellence. But, despite assertions like Thomas Wilson's that 'art is a surer guide than nature' or Samuel Daniel's that 'nature is above all art' (in Vickers 1999: 79 and 442), the relation between them is not one of simple opposition. Ideally, they should complement one another. 'The true artificer', writes Jonson, 'will not run away from nature', while Puttenham reserves his highest praise for the poet who can make his art appear entirely natural (ibid.: 564 and 296). More specifically, Puttenham identifies four ways in which art interacts with nature. Art is an 'aid' to nature, as when 'the good gardener seasons his soil by sundry sorts of compost'; art improves nature as when the physician 'by the use of cordials' not only 'restores the decayed spirits of his patient . . . but also prolongs his life' beyond its natural span; art in the form of painting and sculpture is 'a bare imitator of nature's works'; and, finally, art is 'contrary' to nature, producing things 'that she never would nor could have done of herself' such as 'the carpenter that builds a house, the joiner that makes a table or a bedstead, the tailor a garment, the smith a lock or key' (ibid.: 292–4).

Puttenham offers a novel conception of nature vis-a-vis art. It is mud, minerals, flowers and flesh, not moral perfection. This is the result of a more scientific outlook, one that abandons the idea of a nature in sympathy with human affairs whereby disturbance in one sphere is reflected in the other, as when the assassination of Julius Caesar is foretold by omens such as 'the bird of night sit[ing] / Even at noonday upon the market place, / Hooting and shrieking' (1599: 1, 3, 26–8), to one which examines its general laws, the better to exploit them. The writer is now faced with a new challenge. Should he represent nature and, if so, how; or should he seek to outdo it? Despite Hamlet's recommendation that the players 'hold as 'twere the mirror up to nature' (1602: III, ii, 22) neither drama nor poetry were equipped, either by tradition or convention, to convey a sense of empirical reality. That would come with the novel. The ideal of decorum denies the expansive nature of existence in a way that the more open-ended form of fiction does not. Meanwhile, the melancholy essayist Michel de Montaigne (1533–92), who broke new ground in making himself the subject of his writings, believed that the reality of art trumps that of life. 'Poetry', he wrote, can 'show us love with an air more loving than Love itself. Venus is never as beautiful stark naked, quick and panting, as she is here in Virgil' (1991: 958).

The problems poetry faced in portraying nature result in it beginning to shift from a mode of imitation to a mode of expression. This is reflected in a change of subject matter, which occurred as a result of poetry's move from the court to the marketplace. Accordingly, we don't hear so much about poetry praising the ruler, justifying the social hierarchy, promoting courtly English, imparting knowledge, or inculcating standards of behaviour; rather we hear about it as a source of delight, a diversion, a nobility of feeling, a compensation for the disappointments of life, and a satisfaction of our need for grandeur (see Vickers 1999: 442, 461–2 and 583). Dudley North sums up this change from public to private when he remarks that poetry is best enjoyed after we have discharged all our duties to God, nature, 'authority, learning, wealth, policy and . . . profit' (Vickers 1999: 509).

The difference in subject matter is matched by the difference in style. Indeed, the word 'style' starts to be used because it is more personal than 'ornament'. A poet can apply ornament correctly if he studies one of the many handbooks of rhetoric but style is 'natural to the writer' and cannot be 'alter[ed] into any other' (Puttenham, in Vickers 1999: 227). Where previously difficulty in poetry had been defended on the grounds that it discouraged the vulgar, or was commensurate with the riches to be had from it, 'wit, high conceit and figure' were now seen as mere affectation. Far preferable to these elaborate tropes were 'a natural spirit and a moving air' (Vickers 1999: 227). Authenticity not artifice became the criterion for certain types of poetry, most notably that which dealt with love. But it should not be thought that the play between imitation and expression is as clear cut as described here. We are only able to discern this development, one among many, with the benefit of hindsight. And it is useful because it throws into relief the change in the attitude to tradition, from imitating the classics to expressing the nation.

## Conclusion

One of the major problems faced by criticism in this period was that it lacked the necessary vocabulary either to analyse or appreciate the various changes in literature we have described. It promoted the vernacular, it argued that poetry led to perfection and it evolved techniques of editing ancient texts. But it had little sense of how literature was affected by wider developments and, as Colin Burrow notes, it had 'no stable language in which to praise literature, let alone describe the intricacies of literary structure' (2001: 487–8). Perhaps that explains why most of the criticism in this period remains at the level of general statement; rarely do we encounter a sustained engagement with an individual author. Even when we do, we get little sense of the particularities of his or her work. Virgil is lost in a mist of vague, impressionistic words like 'grace', 'delight', 'subtlety' and 'perfection' (Gray 2001: 274–5).

If criticism was to defend poetry it had to develop an idiom capable of conveying its unique as well as its universal qualities. Puttenham tried to address the problem by finding an English equivalent for Greek and Latin terms for the various figures of speech and, when he couldn't, he retained the original (Vickers 1999: 234–5). But this was more an exercise in rhetorical classification than critical appreciation and so did not prove a satisfactory solution. Neither did Bacon's advice on how to study: 'Read not to contradict and confute; nor to believe and take for granted, nor to find talk and discourse; but to weigh and consider' (1997: 138), for this still assumed that poetry was a source of truth. His words do, however, mark a difference of emphasis between criticism in the medieval period and criticism in the Renaissance. Authority was not to be taken on trust but tested.

## Notes

1. The starting point for any comparison of criticism in different countries in this period is Norton 2001.
2. Ben Jonson, in Vickers 1999: 578. This superb volume, which collects together many of the major English writers on poetry and rhetoric in the period, is indispensable for anyone who wants to study literary criticism in this country during the Renaissance.
3. For a good introduction to the Reformation, see Euan 1991.
4. We noted in the last chapter that the Bible was read metaphorically but the advance of science diminishes the need for such readings.
5. The full poem is available at <http://www.shu.ac.uk/emls/iemls/resour/ mirrors/ rbear/guilpin.html>.
6. See Day 2001: 64–88.
7. See Locke (1988) and Hobbes (1996). A summary of Locke's text is available at <http://www.fordham.edu/halsall/mod/1690locke-sel.html> or there is a full online version at <http://www.lonang.com/exlibris/locke/>. There is a full online version of Hobbes's text at <http://oregonstate.edu/instruct/phl302/texts/hobbes/ leviathan-contents.html>.
8. For a brief overview of Bacon's life and work see <http://www.luminarium.org/ sevenlit/bacon/>.
9. Another more obvious reason was that different parts of England had been invaded by various groups. The Angles, the Jutes, the Saxons, the Danes and the Normans had each colonised different parts of England so that the language was bound to evolve idiosyncratically according to region.

10. For a history of this process, see Bragg 2004: 94–104 and Crystal 2004: 222–48.

11. The manuscript has now been put on line. It can be found at <http://www.nls.uk /auchinleck/contents.html>.

12. On the question of social mobility, see Kumar 2003: 95–100.

13. Puttenham's argument is more complicated than I have suggested. It is true he says that the courtier is a dissembler but he ultimately identifies him with the poet whose ability to dissemble is a virtue since that is part of his art. Even so, this does not quite redeem the courtier from the taint of falsehood. See Vickers 1999: 291–2.

14. But see Kumar's point that the English Reformation divided the nation rather than united it. Moreover, Protestants identified with their fellow Protestants at home and abroad more than they did with their 'nation' (Kumar 2003: 111–14).

15. For a brief overview of Gascoigne's life and work, see <http://www.luminar-ium.org/renlit/gascbio.htm>.

16. See Wheen 2004.

17. For a brief overview of Cheke's life and work, see <http://www.moonzstuff.com/ Cheek/origin-p2.html>.

18. The entire text of this work is available online at <http://darkwing.uoregon. edu/~rbear/courtier/courtier.html>.

19. For a brief overview of Mulcaster's life and work, see <http://www.britannica. com/ebi/article-9054201>. Among other things, he believed that the curriculum should be tailored to children's individual needs and that football had educational benefits. The full text of his treatise, *Positions Concerning the Training Up of Children* (1581), can be found at <http://www.ucs.mun.ca/~wbarker /posi-tions.html>.

20. Many English artists, scholars and aristocrats visited Italy, returning with new words, for example, 'balcony, fresco and villa' (Bragg 2004: 119–20). The main source of new words, though, was Latin (ibid.: 120–1).

21. See Wrightson 2002: especially chapters 7 and 8.

22. For a brief overview of Manutius' life and work, see <http://en.wikipedia. org/wiki/Aldus_Manutius>.

23. See <http://www.oup.co.uk/pdf/0-19-871172-7.pdf#search='a%20warning%20 for%20fair%20women'> for a full discussion of the significance of this work.

24. The fact that Donne had at least two patrons, Sir Thomas Egerton and Sir Robert Dury, is a reminder that the distinction between the court and the city is not clear cut. For a brief review of Donne's life and career, see <http://www.britannica. com/eb/article-1884>.

25. For a brief overview of Wyatt's life and work, see <http://www.luminarium. org/renlit/wyatt.htm>.

26. For a brief overview of Spenser's life and work with links to his writings, see <http://www.english.cam.ac.uk/spenser/main.htm>.

27. The full text of *The Advancement of Learning* is available at <http://darkwing. uoregon.edu/~rbear/adv1.htm>.

28. For a brief over view of this event and its importance to the development of Renaissance thought, see <http://en.wikipedia.org/wiki/Fall_of_Constantinople>.
29. I am indebted to Ross 2000: 51–64 for this section.
30. Again I am simplifying for the sake of clarity. Vickers discusses the relation between poetry and rhetoric in his introduction (1999: 10–22). See also Vickers 1997. See too Ward 2001; Kennedy 2001; and Moss 2001a.
31. For a brief overview of Colet's life and work see <http://www.greatsite.com/time-line-english-bible-history/john-colet.html>.
32. I am heavily indebted to Jeanneret 2001 for the remainder of this paragraph.
33. Invention was a rhetorical term meaning the collection of material suitable to your proposed topic either from your own ideas or other sources (see Vickers 1999: 162).
34. The word aesthetic has a number of derivations. The nouns *aisthetki*, the science of how things are known by the senses, and *aisthema*, the sensation of any object; the verbs *aisthanomai*, to perceive or apprehend, and *aesthesis*, perceptive by sense or feeling. See Liddell and Scott 1869.

# ENGLISH ENLIGHTENMENT AND EARLY ROMANTIC CRITICISM

One Renaissance commonplace was that man was defined by his power of speech and, on the threshold of a new age, we find a similar sentiment echoed in John Sheffield's couplet 'Of things in which mankind does most excel/Nature's chief master-piece is writing well' (Sigworth 1971: 12). Such continuity is in part explained by the slow pace of change in English society. But that was now set to increase, for we are about to enter the modern world which, in literary terms, involves a shift from imitation to imagination. This was the period that saw the appearance of the toothbrush, washing machine and piston-operated steam engine. And, in James Boswell's *The Life of Samuel Johnson* ([1791] 1986)[1] there is reference to 'a new-invented machine which went without horses: a man who sat in it turned a handle, which worked a spring that drove it forward' (Boswell [1791] 1986: 147). Is this the first mention of a car in English literature? No matter. For this was also the century when our modern notions of literature and criticism appeared. The two terms are interdependent. Without criticism there is no literature, and without literature there is no criticism. That is why a history of criticism is inevitably, in part, a history of literature.

But this creates a problem of focus. How do we distinguish between a critical and a literary statement? For example, literary imitation and imagination, which we examine below, are themselves forms of criticism to the extent that they find fault with the existing order but, equally, criticism is a form of imitation since it must partly reproduce the work on which it comments and it is also a form of imagination since it must recreate the work if it is not merely to reproduce it. Another problem is that, when we comment on a poem or a play, we touch on matters that range from the meaning of words to the nature of man. The fact that literature embraces so many interests makes a history of criticism an even more daunting prospect than it already is. And when we consider how criticism itself shapes and is shaped by social, economic, political and cultural issues, the task starts to look well nigh impossible. But let's proceed anyway.

## Imitation, Imagination and Criticism

It is a commonplace that, during the eighteenth century, the meaning of literature changed from 'polite learning' to 'imaginative writing' (Atkins 1966: 27; Patey 1997b: 7; and Williams 1976: 184). But wait. Hadn't Sir Philip Sidney, nearly two hundred years earlier, described the poet's special art as one of invention? Here is yet another example of continuity in the history of criticism. Taken together these continuities disrupt its division into neat periods and rob revolutionary sounding claims of much of their drama. The romantic imagination did not simply spring into life as a reaction against early eighteenth century reason or as a protest against the dehumanising effects of industrial civilisation. Its antecedents can be traced at least as far back as Philostratus (c. 170–247 AD) who, in his *Life of Apollonius of Tyana* (c. 215 AD), distinguishes between imitation which 'can only create what it has seen' and *phantasia* which 'creates what it has not seen' (in Kennedy 1997b: 211). An awareness of the durability of certain concepts helps us to discriminate between ideas which are genuinely new and those which are manifestations of earlier ones.

It was only after 1750 that the imagination begins to occupy a central place in thinking about literature. Writing in 1756, the curate, schoolmaster and sometime poet Joseph Warton (1722–1800) declares that 'it is a creative and glowing imagination alone' that makes a poet (Sigworth 1971: 291). Prior to that time, poets and playwrights were expected to copy this world, not create a new one. Their task, said Sir William Davenant (1606–68), who boosted the status of his own writings by claiming he was Shakespeare's son, is to 'represent the World's true image', while John Sheffield (1648–1721) declared, in his *An Essay on Poetry* (1682), that to depart from nature was 'monstrous' (in Spingarn [1908] 1957: 3 and 293). George Granville (1667–1735) in his *Essay Upon Unnatural Flights in Poetry* (1701) also censures those who do not 'copy' what they see around them since this leads to the creation of 'gigantick forms / Which Nature shockt, disdains to own' (in Sigworth 1971: 81). The first duty of poet, he states, is always to be 'true to resemblance' while for Charles Gildon (1665–1725) the 'essence' of poetry is 'imitation', a principle endorsed by John Brown (1715–66) for whom 'beautiful imitation' is its 'immediate and universal aim' (ibid.: 82, 163 and 247). The same is true in drama. John Dryden (1631–1700), famously dubbed by Samuel Johnson (1709–84) as 'the father of English criticism' (Greene 1984: 717), said that the definition of a play was 'the lively imitation of Nature'

(Wormersley 1997: 48), while Thomas Rymer (1641–1713) objects to *Othello* because the characters and action lack all credibility. 'Nothing is more odious in Nature', he writes, 'than an improbable lie; and certainly never was any play fraught like this of *Othello* with improbabilities' (Sigworth 1971: 32). Similarly, the use of rhyme in drama was dismissed on the grounds that, since no-one speaks like that in life, neither should they 'on the Stage' (Womersley 1997: 65).

These various views represent a slightly different idea of imitation to those found in the Renaissance. Then, the term referred mainly to the emulation of an ideal of perfection, but now it refers primarily to the world as it is. Of course the idea that art should uphold ideals for all to imitate has not disappeared. The playwright, reputed Catholic priest and butt of Dryden's satire, Richard Flecknoe (1620–78), writes that the chief end of drama 'is to render folly ridiculous, Vice odious, and Vertue and Nobleness amiable and lovely' (Spingarn [1908] 1957: 96), while John Dennis (1657–1734), whose life, to judge from his spats with contemporaries, was more spirited than his criticism, states that poetry should implant in people 'the Seeds of Virtue and publick Civility' (Womersley 1997: 142). The emphasis, though, is beginning to shift from the moral effects of art to its representation of reality. Interest focuses particularly on the new genre of the novel, which is distinguished from the romance by its claim to truth. Daniel Defoe (1660–1731) said of *Robinson Crusoe* (1719) that 'the Editor believes the thing to be a just History of Fact; neither is there any appearance of Fiction in it', while Aphra Behn (1640–89) concluded *Oroonoko; or The Royal Slave. A True History* (1688) with the words 'I was myself an eye-witness to a great part of what [is] here set down.'

Poets and dramatists use a different idiom to novelists. They do not say that they describe what really happened, they say they are imitating nature. And here the matter becomes complicated because this term had a number of meanings in the period. For Dennis, it is 'human life and the manners of Men' (Womersley 1997: 260), while for Anthony Ashley Cooper, third earl of Shaftesbury (1671–1713), it is an ideal system whose symmetry and proportion should be the model for works of art. 'The measure of rule or harmony', he writes, ought not to be 'caprice or will, humour or fashion' but the 'harmony' of nature itself (Sigworth 1971: 187). Neither man thinks of nature as a struggle for survival but as a model of perfection. The conventional comparison of poetry with painting underlines their rather static conception of the term.[2] What artists imitate is not the thing itself, but an image of it. At the same time we should acknowledge the tension between imitating men as they are and presenting them as they ought to be. This tension comes out in Johnson's account of the novel. While an author should copy human manners, that 'should not be [his] most important concern' (Greene 1984: 176). Instead, he should remember that these 'books serve as lectures of conduct, and introductions into life' and so the author should choose only the 'best example' for his readers to 'imitate' (ibid.: 176).

Simultaneously referring to the world, the manners of men and an ideal order of nature, imitation is a complex idea. It implies that the value of art lies in its correspondence to the world. Criticism thus consists of comparing the poet's view of the world with the world itself. The fact that literature imitates the world partly reconciles it to science, to which it was opposed in the Renaissance. As Michael Baridon notes: 'Artists and philosophers were in agreement over the relation between geometrical shapes to artistic expression. Beauty to them was the concordance between abstract knowledge and concrete representation' (1997: 780). But, since imitation also refers to an ideal, it further implies that the value of art lies in improving the world. This fits nicely with Ben Jonson's definition of criticism as 'correction'. Both literature and criticism are united in their mission to make the world a better place. Hence the emphasis on decorum which, as we have noticed, has a social dimension. To censure a writer for not using the style appropriate to his subject is the literary equivalent of censuring those who stray from their place in society. In both cases there is an appeal to order and harmony. More broadly, the reformation of manners and morals was the impulse behind *The Tatler* (1709–11) and *The Spectator* (1711–12).[3] Richard Steele (1672–1729), who began *The Tatler*, said that its general purpose was 'to expose the false Arts of Life, to pull off the Disguises of Cunning, Vanity, and Affectation, and to recommend a general Simplicity in our Dress, our Discourse, and our Behaviour' (Mackie 1998: 47).

The contrast Steele draws between simplicity and affectation in life is also present in art. Clarity is praised, ostentation condemned. The debate recalls the Inkhorn controversy discussed in the last chapter. Indeed, the argument over expression continues today. Each year the Campaign for Plain English (f. 1979) gives the Golden Bull award for the best example of gobbledygook in public life. And each year the choice gets harder. Back in the late seventeenth century, Sheffield dismisses 'Figures of speech, which poets think so fine' as 'Art's needless varnish, to make nature shine' (Sigworth 1971: 18). Alexander Pope (1688–1744), who because he contracted tuberculosis as a child grew to only 4 feet 6 inches tall, echoed this sentiment:

> False eloquence, like the Prismatic glass,
> Its gaudy colours spreads on every place;
> The face of nature we no more survey,
> All glares alike without distinction gay. (1978: 73)

Proving that religion and science can mix, Thomas Sprat, chaplain to Charles II (1630–85) and one of the founders of The Royal Society (1660), was altogether more belligerent, demanding that eloquence 'be banished out of all civil socities as a thing fatal to peace and good manners' (Spingarn [1908] 1957: 116). He was thinking of the 'fantastical terms' and 'outlandish phrases' used by 'religious sects' in the Civil War (1642–8) which, in his opinion, had intensified the conflict (ibid.: 113). How different from the Renaissance where the orator was seen as the origin of society, his eloquence a means of unifying the nation. The fine words that would carry us to 'a higher and more lofty conceit' have now become so much 'luxury and redundance of speech' (ibid.: 116). And in the process one aspect of criticism, that which dealt with the deployment of figures, is eroded.

In general, the plain style was associated with imitation, the figurative with imagination. The imagination had to be kept under control. Sheffield calls it 'fancy'[4] and subordinates it to both reason and judgement: 'without judgement, fancy is but mad'; 'Fancy is but the feather of the pen; / Reason is that substantial useful part, / Which gains the head, while t'other wins the heart' (Sigworth 1971: 13). In many ways this formulation goes back to the ancient idea that, while poets could be divinely inspired, they also had to learn the rules of their craft. But the point to stress is that in the late seventeenth and early eighteenth century, the fancy or imagination was seen as a disruptive force. Sprat blames the unrestrained use of figurative language for accentuating divisions in the Civil War and calls for English to be based on 'a mathematical plainness' that derives from the speech of 'Artizans, Countrymen, and Merchants, before that of Wits or Scholars' (Spingarn [1908] 1957: 118). Again, the contrast with the Renaissance is startling. Now the call is for commerce to determine the character of the language, not the court.[5] In the last chapter we noticed how monetary terms began to be applied to literature and the process continues in the late seventeenth century. Dryden, for example, uses a financial metaphor to describe the relation of the highly influential French poet and critic Nicolas Boileau-Despréaux (1636–1711) to the classical tradition: 'what he borrows from the ancients, he repays with usury of his own, in coin as good, and almost as universally valuable' (ibid.: 68). The development of capitalism depends on technology as well as money. For example, John Harrison's (1693–1776) invention of a clock that measured longitude at sea enabled a more accurate mapping of oceans which, in turn, was beneficial for trade. A language based on calculation and measurement seemed to yield knowledge of the world and its workings. Tropes stood in the way of truth.

Literary imitation endorses the values of business and enlightenment because, in principle at least, it portrays natural phenomena that the merchant wants to exploit and the scientist to understand. More importantly, it reveals the harmony at the heart of nature. How attractive this must have seemed to a society that had suffered the upheavals of civil war, was constantly fighting the Dutch for control of trade routes (1652–4; 1665–7; and 1672–4) and which, even after the Glorious Revolution of 1688 had secured the principles of Protestantism and Parliamentary government, was still troubled by fears that the Stuarts would return and restore the Catholic religion. The imagination could offer no such comforts. It sought the realms of 'high Parnassus' and its quasi-religious rhetoric, 'sacred fountains', 'vales of bliss' and 'divine repose' (Akenside, in Fairer and Gerrard 1999: 308 and 310) was a disturbing reminder of its disruptive powers. Less than half a century before, men were killing one another because they disagreed on how to get to paradise.

But it would be wrong to see imitation and imagination solely as entrenched opposites. For all his arguments about the need for judgement, Sheffield acknowleges that it is 'genius' which gives poetry its 'soul' (Sigworth 1971: 13) and Pope too accepts that art has 'nameless graces which no methods teach' (1978: 68). Dryden sums up the relation between them when he says that the 'imagination' provides the idea to be 'represented', which is shaped by 'fancy' and then put into words by 'elocution' (Sigworth 1971: 62). Similarly, both imitation and imagination aspire to a more complete understanding of reality than is found in a reproduction of its surface features. Criticism, too, uncovers concealed beauties. Edward Young (1683–1765), author of the extremely popular poem *Night Thoughts* (1742–4), says that it should discover the 'hidden graces and secret charms' of art (Sigworth 1971: 231). An adherence to the tenets of neoclassicism, which we will discuss later, means that criticism still involves 'correction' but 'the better half of it', says Pope, now consists 'in pointing out an author's excellencies' (Womersley 1997: 277). Finally, we have Joseph Addison (1672–1719) arguing that imitation is one of the pleasures of the imagination. For example, a picture of a landscape may remind us of one we have actually seen or else it may prompt us to invent our own version of one in a painting. In either case, our delight comes from the comparison (Steele and Addison 1988: 385–6).

## The Problem of Critical Language

Dryden's use of 'fancy' for 'judgement' and Sheffield's use of 'fancy' for 'imagination' picks up a point made in the last chapter, that one of the problems facing English criticism was the lack of an agreed or indeed a stable vocabulary. For example, Charles Gildon, whose career was blighted by an ill-advised criticism of Pope's *The Rape of the Lock* (1717), despaired of ever finding 'a true and just definition of wit, that is a definition that expresses all its parts and qualities' (Sigworth 1971: 165). And no wonder. Its various meanings included 'repartee', 'well defined', the 'imagining of persons, actions, passions, or things', the 'assemblage of ideas' put together with 'quickness and variety', and the putting of 'a great thought' into 'words so commonly received it is understood by the meanest apprehensions' (Sigworth 1971: 62; Womersely 1997: 36 and 297). The use of terms like 'fancy', 'wit' and 'judgement' suggests that criticism is concerned not so much with the literary qualities of a work as with the proper organisation of the mental faculties. Young voices the orthodox view in the early part of this period when he says that judgement should 'bear the supreme sway' and imagination 'should be subdued to its dominon' (Sigworth 1971: 228). The idea that literature is the medium in which the various parts of the mind are brought into balance with one another anticipates both Samuel Taylor Coleridge's claim that the art of poetry lay in the 'reconciliation of opposite or discordant qualities' (Hoffman and Hynes 1966: 49) and I. A. Richards's definition of it as the harmonising of conflicting impulses. This emphasis on the ordering of the emotions is ultimately derived from Aristotle's notion of catharsis, though here we have integration rather than expulsion. Purgation has given way to hierarchical organisation.

### Imitation, Imagination, Criticism and Money

Although imitation and imagination aim at a truth beyond appearance, their charactertistic modes of operation complement the needs of the new capitalism. In very crude terms the mechanical application of the rules of art, for example, insisting on the three unities being observed in drama, corresponds with the new mechanical conception of the human. 'What', asked the philosopher Thomas Hobbes (1588–1679), 'is the heart, but a spring; and the nerves, but so many strings; and the joints, but so many wheels, giving motion to the whole?' (Hobbes 1985: 81). This idea is very different to the view we find in Sheffield, Dryden and others. They concentrate on man's mental capacities not his physical characteristics. They also believe in the power of art to change a person by first appealing to their affections. But once you see humans as machines this is not possible. You cannot appeal to the affections of a machine nor can you treat it as a moral being with the potential to improve itself. Humans develop, machines repeat. To conflate the two is to rob criticism of its traditional function, the justification of literature in terms of its ethical effect.

Hobbes's thinking reinforces the opposition between mind and body that was always present in Christianity. In the words of Saint Paul, 'if ye live after the flesh ye shall die: but if ye through the Spirit do mortify the deeds of the body, ye shall live' (Romans 8:13). But now this opposition is expressed in economic rather than religious terms. The division of labour separates mind and body. The increasing requirement that an item of manufacture 'should pass through as many hands as it can' (Thirsk 1978: 3) suggests that those employed in the new factories, ironware, textile, clothing, and so on, make only a small contribution to the finished article. Adam Smith (1723–90) author of *The Wealth of Nations* (1776) argued that the division of labour generated greater riches for a nation than either land or large reserves of bullion because it increased productivity. Smith gives the example of manufacturing a pin which can be divided into eighteen distinct operations. If these were all performed by one person they would not make anything like the number that ten people would make. But Smith also accepted that the division of labour breeds dexterity in a particular trade 'at the expense of [a person's] intellectual, social and martial virtues' (Smith 1986: 134), a theme picked up by Marx who noted that a 'crippling of body and mind is inseparable from the division of labour in society as a whole' (Marx 1995: 224). And this is where the imagination comes in. Its habit of showing, in the poet Charlotte Smith's words, 'the beauteous rather than the true' (Fairer and Gerrard 1999: 515) is at once a symptom of the division of labour and a compensation for the damage it inflicts. The imagination is a symptom because it exalts the mind above the body, and a compensation because it distracts the mind, dulled by the routines of production, with fantasies.

There is also an association between imitation, imagination and money based on the fact that they are all forms of representation. We have already mentioned how the growth of commerce leads to the introduction of monetary terms into criticism. But the financial revolution of the 1690s which saw the establishment of credit, the foundation of the Bank of England (1694) and the recoinage of the currency, raises questions about the nature of representation, and the relation between form and content, that were formerly the province of criticism and art. These questions centre on the relationship between the value of money and how that value is to be expressed. The Recoinage Act of 1696 had reasserted the principle that, in the words of the philosopher, politician and sometime physician John Locke (1632–1704), 'the intrinsic Value of Silver and Gold . . . is nothing but their quantity' (cited in Thompson 1996: 57). In other words, the weight of precious metal in a coin was equivalent to its value. However, the growth of credit and the replacement of coin by the promissory note made it much harder to accept that the form of money coincided with its value. Paper was not precious metal; it could only represent it, though how accurately was another matter. We can see an example of how concerns about coinage affect thinking about language in William Temple's remark that the best way to take words is 'as they are most commonly spoken and meant, like Coyn as it most currantly passes in, without raising scruples about the weight or the allay unless the cheat or the defect be gross and evident' (Spingarn [1957] 1968: 73).

If value was not an intrinsic property of money and if the banknote did not correspond to a given quantity of gold or silver then how was monetary value to be determined? These anxieties are paralleled in discussions about imitation and imagination in literature. Imitation suggests that there is a correspondence between the representation and reality. Francis Hutcheson (1694–1746), whose *Inquiry into the Original of Our Ideas of Beauty and Virtue* (1725) Kivy has described as 'the first systematic philosophical treatment in English of what we would now call aesthetics' ([1976] 2003: 24), defined beauty as the 'conformity, or a kind of unity between the original and the copy' (in Singer and Dunn 2000: 16). Imitation, we might say, is the literary equivalent of the financial argument that the form of money should coincide with the content of its value. Some early theories of the imagination contained an element of imitation. The poet and physician Mark Akenside (1721–70) who, when he visited hospital, instructed a servant to walk ahead of him with a broom in order to deter patients from approaching him, described the powers of imagination as 'holding a middle place between the organs of bodily sense and the faculties of moral perception' (in Fairer and Gerrard 1999: 306). It was the task of this intermediary faculty to provide ideas of our moral likes and dislikes; in other words, to represent them. Addison, a man who resorted to the tavern to overcome his timidity, states the more common view of the imagination when he writes that it 'loves to be filled with an object, or to grasp at anything, that is too big for its capacity' (Steele and Addison 1988: 371). Such an object is sublime and completely overwhelms us. The two main sources of the sublime are nature and art. We experience the sublime in nature when we are confronted with 'an uncultivated desert, huge heaps of mountains, high rocks and precipices, or a wide expanse of water' (ibid.: 371) and in art when we read writers like Homer, an experience which Addison compares to 'travelling through a country uninhabited, where the fancy is entertained with a thousand savage prospects of vast deserts, wide uncultivated marshes [and] huge forests' (ibid.: 390). It is this concern about the gap between what we experience and our ability to express it that mirrors the concern about money, how its forms – coin, credit and promissory note – may exceed its actual worth.

That artistic and financial matters seem to mimic one another is a measure of how eighteenth-century English society is dominated by a market mentality. This is not simply a question of new factories or the growth of financial institutions or the introduction of new ways of raising revenue like the lottery, or even the frenzy of speculation surrounding the ill-fated South Sea Stock Company.[6] These are all indications of something far greater: the power of commerce to condition language and therefore thought. As early as 1690, the man who employed Jonathan Swift as his secretary, William Temple (1628–99), made the point that commerce had altered the attitude to learning. Previously, knowledge had been pursued for its own sake, now it was for gain. The search for truth 'has been fettered by the cares of the World, and disturbed by the desires of being Rich or the fears of being Poor, from which all the ancient Philosophers . . . were disentangled and free' (Spingarn [1957] 1968: 70). Hobbes's assertion that 'the value or WORTH of a man is, as of all other things his Price; that is to say, so much as would be given for the use of his Power' (1985: 45) is symptomatic of a profound change in the conception of man: he is no longer a speaking subject but a costed commodity; no longer a social being but an economic unit. And this was a good thing because commerce, unlike religion, could unify society. No-one, says Addison, is more useful to the commonwealth than merchants. They 'knit mankind together in mutual intercourse of good Offices, distribute the gifts of Nature, find Work for the Poor, add Wealth to the Rich, and Magnificence to the Great' (Steele and Addison 1988: 439). Of course, not everyone agreed with this sentiment. One anonymous contemporary asked, 'What does the merchant care, so that he be rich, how poor the public is? Let the commonwealth sink so that he gets his profits' (in Lipson 1964: 5). But, in general, there was a move from a conflict model of society, based on religious passions, to a cooperative view of society, based on commercial interests.

We know, with the benefit of hindsight, that commerce can divide a society quite as much as religion but, after the bloodshed of the Civil War, it seemed to offer a greater chance of peace than either priests or even politicians. Business would bind the broken polity. A pioneer of the closed heroic couplet, the Royalist John Denham (1615–69) believed that 'Commerce makes everything grow everywhere' (Mackie 1998: 245). In addition, the expansion of trade promoted good relations between different groups and nations, and 'soften[ed] and polish[ed] the manners of men' (Hirschman 1977: 61). The Royal Exchange, London's central financial district in Threadneedle Street which also contained 200 shops, is the setting for Addison's vision of the unity of mankind. There is nothing he 'loves so much [as] to see so rich an Assembly of Country-men and Foreigners consulting together upon the private Business of Mankind, and making this Metropolis a kind of Emporium for the whole Earth' (Mackie 1998: 203). Our relations with others too are cast in monetary terms. Are we their creditors or their debtors? Will they or won't they buy our wares? (ibid.: 206–23). The very sense of self depends on a financial idiom. The economist Nicholas Barbon (1640–98), who is credited as the founder of fire insurance, says 'trade . . . relates chiefly to man's self', while Steele remarks that 'should we look into our own hearts we should see Money engraved on them' (ibid.: 226–7 and 237). And just as humans take on the characteristics of money, so money takes on the characteristics of humans. A coin confides in Addison. 'Methoughts the shilling that lay upon the table reared itself upon its Edge, and turning the Face towards me, opened its Mouth, and in a Soft Silver sound gave me the following account of its Life and Adventures' (ibid.: 184). No wonder, then, that monetary metaphors permeate everyday talk. Johnson tells us that Addison, 'speaking of his own deficiencies in conversation, used to say of himself that, with respect to intellectual wealth, "he could draw bills for a thousand pounds but had not a guinea in his pocket" ' (Greene 1984: 662). Our ways of thinking, feeling and valuing are gradually conditioned by the logic of money. The general effect of all this is that we judge by quantity not quality. Steele's remark that 'numbers are so much the measure of everything that is valuable' (Steele and Addison 1988: 449) anticipates our own audit culture.

But what about the effects for criticism? Well, just as literary concepts like imitation and imagination are implicated in monetary matters, so too is criticism, if only because it contains elements of imitation and imagination within itself. Defoe, who once had all his civet cats, used for the manufacture of perfume, seized by creditors, believed the imagination powered the economy since it gave birth to 'exotic projects' (cited in McKeon 1988: 287). And the imagination is the medium through which Addison has his vision of the Bank of England where he describes the economy in terms normally used for art, that is, the relation between part and whole (Steele and Addison 1988: 430). Long before the imagination enjoys its exalted status in romanticism, it is compromised by money. The problems of monetary worth shape the very operation of criticism. Does it reflect the value of the work in the way that silver reflects the actual worth of the coin, or does it exceed the work in the way that credit exceeds the amount of bullion? And, as we noted earlier, criticism easily slips into a financial idiom. In his 'Preface' to the second part of Edmund Waller's poems, Francis Atterbury (1663–1732), a man with a talent for controversy and a defender of the Stuart cause, compared Waller to Spenser in precisely these terms. Waller's language, 'like the Money of that time, is as currant as ever' while Spencer's words 'are like old Coyns, one must go to an Antiquary to understand their true meaning and value' (Womersley 1997: 122).

But we can also consider criticism as a form of production and consumption. From Aristotle to Dennis criticism was largely prescriptive. Geoffrey of Vinsauf's *Poetria nova* (1200–16) and George Puttenham's *The Arte of English Poesie* (1589) were instructions for how to write well. Their purpose, in other words, was to produce poets. This tradition continues into the first half of the eighteenth century where the rules of neoclassicism can also be considered as guides to correct writing. Yet even at the beginning of the eighteenth century there are clear signs, in particular Addison's essays on *The Pleasures of the Imagination* (1712), that criticism is becoming more associated with consumption. He dramatises the connection when he describes how an acquaintance of his was able to distinguish ten different sorts of tea without seeing them, simply by sipping. That he then goes to say 'a man of taste in fine writing will discern after the same manner' (Steele and Addison

1988: 365) shows that literary appreciation is now on a par with the appreciation of other consumer goods, which were much in evidence by the mid-eighteenth century.

> Goods which had previously appeared in the inventories of only a small number of high status households – like looking glasses, earthenware, books, pictures, window curtains and table linen – became more common. And certain new goods began to appear with increasing frequency, notably clocks, china, more elaborate kitchen equipment, utensils for the preparation and consumption of hot drinks like coffee and tea, and table settings of knives and forks. (Wrightson 2002: 298)

There were two kinds of writer in the early to mid-eighteenth century, producing work that ranged from poetry to the Gothic novel. The first enjoyed the support of a patron while the second had to survive by appealing to the market, though the difference between them was blurring as patronage declined and commercial considerations came more to the fore. Johnson complained that the expansion of the press – which increased eightfold between 1712 and 1757 – was 'prejudicial to good literature, because it obliges us to read so much of what is inferior value, in order to be in fashion' (cited in Black 2005: 147). But it wasn't just the increase of newspapers it was also the explosion of magazines, poetry, novels and history that threw traditional notions of literature into crisis. Pope felt that this new breed of writer represented a threat to literary standards. They lived in Grub Street writing, according to Johnson, 'small histories, dictionaries, and temporary poems'. Pope called them 'the buzzing tribe, the pimps of literature'.[7] Criticism, in these conditions, was a question of discrimination. But how was one to tell the difference between good and bad writing, and did it matter anyway since reading was now largely a matter of recreation?

These concerns form part of the discourse of taste, which is discussed below. What needs to be stressed here is that the context for understanding literature and, by extension criticism, has changed. It no longer operates primarily in school, church or court but the market. It is customary to stress the opening up of culture in this period and, while that is no doubt true,[8] we shouldn't forget that commerce was also shaping conceptions of the human. As we noted earler, if men are seen as machines, then literature as a moral force is redundant. Indeed money, not literature or criticism, has become the new source of morality. As one correspondent to *The Spectator* wrote:

> Love of business and money is the greatest mortifier of inordinate Desire imaginable as employing the Mind continually . . . in the due Entering and Stating

of Accounts . . . and in the exact Knowledge of the State of the Market [takes up] Thought every Moment of the Day.

More starkly, 'the Love of Money prevents all immorality and Vice' (Mackie 1998: 230–1).

## Grounding Criticism

We said at the beginning of this chapter that it was during the eighteenth century that our modern notions of literature and criticism appeared. As a guide to correct writing, criticism could claim a part in literary production but now that the poet relies on the imagination he or she has less need for the rules of good writing. The central value of the imagination is the poet's vision. It is an expression of him- or herself. This represents a departure from literature's traditional role of praising virtue and condemning vice. Since criticism was primarily concerned with the moral effects of poetry and drama, its relationship with literature is again profoundly altered. Criticism must now find a new way of talking about it.

The rise of the imagination carries another consequence for criticism. Previously, literature had been defined as polite learning, a definition which included criticism to the extent that the latter required a knowledge of grammar, philology, rhetoric, history, geography and so on. But once a writer like Young characterises original genius in terms of 'unprescribed beauties and unexampled excellence' which are outside 'the pale of learning's authorities and laws' (cited in Ross 2000: 200) then the link between literature and criticism in terms of learning is considerably weakened. Matthew Arnold strengthens it when, in the following century, he declares that the romantic poets fell short of greatness because they 'didn't know enough' (1991: 192). He argues that literature, criticism and knowledge form a whole, an idea that informs the spirit of modernism. The poetry of T. S. Eliot and the novels of James Joyce fuse literature and criticism into a new and, many students would say, intimidating entity.

Sometimes a casual remark can alert us to an historical change. One such is Thomas Rymer's observation that 'till of late years England was as free from Critiks as it is from Wolves' (Spingarn [1908] 1957: 164). This suggests two things. First, that, in the late seventeenth century, criticism began to be recognised as an activity in its own right and, second, that critics were not held in particularly high esteem. If the way writers sometimes behave to one another is anything to go by, then literature seems to bring out the worst in people. John Dennis, for example, mocks Pope's physical deformity, comparing him to 'a hunch-back'd toad' (Womersley 1997: 256). It is worth mentioning the cruelty, insults and downright viciousness of literary critics because it should make us sceptical of any claim that literature makes us better people.

In the late seventeenth century, then, the critic emerges as a new figure on the public stage. He is charged with the task of defining literary value now that poetry and drama have moved from the court to the marketplace. According to Dennis, the resulting increase in 'the generality of writers' leads to 'the debauchment of taste' and a 'want of Discernment to distinguish right from wrong' (Womersley 1997: 139). Hence 'there was never more necessity for a just and impartial criticism' (ibid.: 139). Pope makes a similar point. He writes his *Essay on Criticism* in part to remedy a corrupt taste that admires the style rather than the substance, the sound rather than the sense and the name rather than the work (1978: 72–5). It was easy to see what poetic value was when poetry refined the language, or maintained hierarchy, or fashioned a gentleman, but not when it is one commodity among others. The growth of newspapers and magazines, especially with the lapse of the Licensing Act in 1695, provided a forum for the discussion of literary value. Such diversity is to be applauded but the sheer variety of opinion made the idea of literary value too vague a notion to defend with any rigour. The category of literature then decays into personal preference and our intellectual life is consequently impoverished.

## Neoclassicism

There were at least four ways of grounding literary value in this period. The first was neoclassicism, the second was taste, the third was scholarship and the fourth, the imagination, we have already discussed. One of the main characteristics of neoclassicism was decorum. Pope, for example, writes that, in the epic, 'there ought to be a difference of style observed in the speeches of human persons and those of the deities' (Sigworth 1971: 199). But the central tenant of neoclassicism was the imitation of nature. This was to be achieved by artists modelling their work on the ancients. Hence poets and dramatists were less interested in inventing new forms than in imitating the old ones of epic, eclogue, epigram, elegy, ode, satire, tragedy and comedy. Indeed, an awareness of the characteristics of each genre, and their relation to one another, was an integral feature of neoclassicism.

Neoclassicism derives from sixteenth-century Italian followers of Aristotle like Lodovico Castelvetro (1505–71), who strictly interpreted the unities of time and place, and Torquato Tasso (1544–95) whose theory of epic influenced Milton and Dryden. The work of these and various other Italian critics, most notably the very learned but very vain Julius Caesar Scaliger (1484–1558) became the basis of French neoclassicism. The Académie française, founded in 1634 by Cardinal Richelieu (1585–1642), to regulate and maintain the French language, was the institutional expression of neoclassicism, especially after its criticism of Pierre Corneille's play *Le Cid* (1637), which 'was condemned for breaches not only to the Unities, but of the rules of decorum and probability as well' (Atkins 1966: 6). Neoclassicism took its final form during the reign of Louis XIV (1638–1715) and its most illustrious exponent was Boileau, who maintained that there were standards of excellence in literature which could only be attained by following the rules of the ancients. We should not follow the ancients because of their antiquity, but because their works conformed to nature or reason. In Boileau's formulation, neoclassicism appears less like an imposition and more like a rational choice.

He set out the main principles of neoclassicism – reason, nature, decorum, moderation and unity – in *L'Art poétique* (1674), a work which influenced Pope's *Essay on Criticism* (1711). Thus Pope advises the critic to 'First follow Nature, and your judgement frame / By her just standard which is still the same', and he underlines the necessity of decorum by declaring, 'The sound must seem an Echo to the Sense.' Pope upholds the ideal of moderation by his instruction to 'Avoid Extremes; and shun the fault of such / Who are still pleased too little or too much', and endorses unity with the observation that ' 'Tis not a lip, or eye, we beauty call, / But the joint force and full result of all.' And, although Pope uses the word 'wit' more than he does reason, Boileau would certainly approve of the lines: 'If once right reason drives that cloud away, / Truth breaks upon us with resistless day' (1978: 70, 71, 74, 75, 76). But it would be wrong to read the *Essay on Criticism* merely as an illustration of French neoclassical theory. Pope points out, for example, that the rules cannot account for all the effects of art:

> Great Wits may sometimes gloriously offend,
> And rise to faults true Critics dare not mend;
> From vulgar bounds with brave disorder part,
> And snatch a grace beyond the reach of art' (ibid.: 68)

The native tradition made it difficult to adopt the principles of neoclassicism completely. Consequently, the English relation to neoclassicism was one of dialogue.

We can see this almost literally in Dryden's *An Essay on Dramatic Poesy* where speakers debate the relative merits of French and English theatre. The French observe Aristotle more carefully than the English. For example, they depict only one action whereas the English 'burden' their plays with 'underplots' (Womersley 1997: 40). The debate about the unities was in part a debate about the best way to imitate nature. But the idea of imitation is here rather literal. Shakespeare's history plays are condemned because they cram the 'business' of thirty or forty years 'into a representation of two hours and a half which is not to imitate or paint Nature, but rather to render . . . [her] ridiculous' (ibid.: 42). The English tendency to mix tragedy and comedy is again seen to flout Aristotle because the end of tragedy, compassion, is not compatible with laughter (ibid.: 41), while the French convention of narrating terrible deeds is preferred to the English one of acting them out on stage. The counter-arguments are that the French themselves have, in recent years, moved away from the strictures of Aristotle. The unities do not lead to an accurate imitation of nature for, if a play begins in 'the King's Bed-chamber', then must 'the meanest man in the tragedy . . . come and despatch his business there rather than in the lobby or the court yard (which is fitter for him) [lest] the stage should be cleared and the scenes broken' (ibid.: 55). So, if playwrights don't adhere to the unities they distort nature and if they do, well, they still distort it.

The use of underplots is defended on the basis that it is more satisfying 'to be led in a labyrinth of design, where you see some of your way before you, yet discern not the end till you arrive at it' (Womersley 1997: 52). The mixing of tragedy and comedy is justified because the one complements the other. 'Contraries', writes Dryden, 'set each other off' (ibid.: 50). The desire to include a number of different elements in a play and the interest in managing them 'so that the beauty of the whole be kept entire' (ibid.: 50) may be a way of negotiating anxieties about national unity in the still tense times after the Restoration. But it also gestures towards a psychological view of art as does the idea of contrast between mirth and compassion. Dryden seems more interested in how we experience a play than in how it represents reality. He could have argued, for example, that complicated actions and rapid changes of feeling are a normal part of human behaviour. Instead, he analyses the effects of artistic form on our minds, an issue explored in more detail by Addison in his essays on the pleasures of the imagination. The violence of the English stage is explained in terms of the national character not the rules of Aristotle, an important development in the history of criticism: 'nature has so formed [our countrymen] that they will scarcely suffer combats and other objects of horror to be taken from them' (ibid.: 53). Indeed, the English are seen as more masculine than the French (ibid.: 56) and this continues the Renaissance view of poetry as a male preserve.

Moreover, Dryden's description of himself at the beginning of *Dramatic Poesie* as 'stand[ing] desperately to my Armes, like the Foot when deserted by their Horse' (ibid.: 17) recalls the martial context of Sidney's *A Defence of Poetry*. Drama is seen in warlike terms partly because of the conventional association between the poet and the warrior and partly because of the growing tensions between England and France. Louis XIV, for example, had promised that he would help Charles II turn England Catholic and, in 1667, he supported the Dutch in their wars against the English (Fraser 2003: 370 and 372). And it is a key moment in that war, a naval engagement on 3 June 1665, that frames Dryden's *Essay*. The military metaphor continues to be a part of critical rhetoric as evidenced in the phrase 'the theory wars' which was current in the 1980s and 90s and it has recently migrated to management studies with its talk of 'mission objectives', 'strategic plans' and 'capturing relevant information'.

The sense that drama is best understood in terms of the customs and culture of the country in which it is produced informs John Dennis's *The Impartial Critic* (1693). It is a response to *A Short View of Tragedy* (1693) by that most rigid of English neoclassicists, Thomas Rymer. Dennis takes issue with Rymer's suggestion that tragedy should have a chorus because a convention based on the religious temper of the ancient Athenians would be quite out of place in a modern English theatre. Moreover, argues Dennis, the ends of tragedy, that is, the imitation of an action and the arousal of terror and compassion, can be achieved without the presence of a chorus (Spingarn 1968: 148 and 180–8). So, while Dennis largely agrees with Aristotle's view of tragedy, particularly as set forth by French neoclassicists like Anne Dacier (1654–1720), a classical commentator, famous for her translations of the *Iliad* and the *Odyssey*, he does recognise that parts of it are no longer relevant. His remark that 'to set up the Grecian method amongst us with success, it is absolutely necessary to restore not only their religion and polity but to transport us to the same climate in which Sophocles and Euripides writ' (ibid.: 148) is a recognition that art is not so much a matter of law as context.

This shift in the perception of art is partly due to the rise of science. We have seen that literature's move to the marketplace undermined its traditional rhetorical function of shaping behaviour and, since the Renaissance, science was proving a more reliable guide to nature than poetry. Neoclassicists had some affinity with scientists because they both saw order in nature, because they both believed in reason, and because they were both committed to clarity, but the nature neoclassicists imitated was an ideal not a real one. Their view of it did not yield knowledge like Robert Boyle's (1627–91) discovery that tiny particles determine the nature of matter, or Isaac Newton's (1643–1727) discovery of the laws of motion and universal gravitation. And while a poet's inventions might be deemed admirable, they could not compare with, say, Thomas Newcomen's invention of the steam engine. One immediate response was to make the study of literature more scientific by focusing on its psychological effects. How do we respond to the beautiful? What produces that sensation? This investigation of cause and effect gives criticism an objective air. But, as Addison pointed out, 'it is impossible for us to assign the necessary cause' for any pleasure we feel in a work (Steele and Addison 1988: 375). Johnson went even further, saying that, in criticism, 'there is no system, no principal and axiomatical truth that regulates subordinate positions' (Greene 1984: 454).

These remarks are a blow to the neoclassical idea that, by following certain rules, writers can produce certain effects. Rymer's claim that a correctly written tragedy will result in catharsis or Dennis's that by following 'general rules' (Womersley 1997: 143) you can write religious poetry are just not testable in the same way as is a scientific statement. Consequently, argues Douglas Lane Patey, the reading and writing of literature cannot be justified by any appeal to a scientific model. Only by a commitment to empirical inquiry, observation, experiment and the testing of hypotheses can we understand the way the world works. Since the critic has no methodology, his contribution to this process is minimal. He must find a different rationale for the study of literature which, as suggested above, comes from assimilating it to 'more general, intellectual or cultural history' (1997a: 40 and 44). Literature is on the way to becoming an expression of the nation or, as Johnson so memorably put it, 'The chief glory of every people arises from its authors' (Greene 1984: 357). This contrasts with the late medieval period where poetry was used to advance the vernacular and promote national unity among the powerful, a project that continued into the Renaissance. Now literature is more of a passive expression than an active force, an expression that ideally embraces the whole culture rather than a political class.

The rise of science prompted a debate about who knew more, the ancients or the moderns. It became known as 'the battle of the books'. The details of the conflict need not detain us. The end result was a compromise. All those activities which depended on the accumulation of knowledge, like science, were won for the moderns, while those which did not, such as the arts, 'were left securely in the hands of the ancients' (Levine 1994: 2).[9] In general terms, the relevance of the dispute for criticism is whether or not to respect or to reject the past. One choice asserts the value of tradition, the other the value of modernity though, of course, the alternatives are not mutually exclusive. Dryden, for example, believes that while the ancients excelled in heroic poetry the moderns have surpassed them in satire and tragedy (Sigworth 1971: 68). But the debate between the ancients and the moderns is most relevant for criticism on the matter of whether the letters of one Phalaris, who ruled Sicily from c. 570 to c. 554 BC, were genuine. The man was a tyrant. One of his favourite methods of execution was to seal victims in a brass bull and then roast them alive. Fittingly, that is how he met his own end after the inhabitants of the island rebelled against his cruelties and rose against him.

The discovery of his letters presented him in a different light, as a humane man, a patron of literature and the arts. This is how William Temple sees Phalaris in his *On Ancient and Modern Learning* (1690), the essay that sparked the whole debate on the relative merits of classical versus contemporary learning. 'I think the epistles of Phalaris', writes Temple, 'to have more race, more spirit, more force of wit and genius, than any others I have ever seen' (Spingarn [1957] 1968: 65). He rubbished those who thought the letters were a forgery written by the Roman satirist Lucian (AD 120–86?), dismissing their arguments as pedantry which, along with avarice, religious wrangles and the decline of patronage, had retarded the cause of learning. Unfortunately for him, the letters were indeed fake, as demonstrated by the classical scholar, theologian and critic Richard Bentley (1662–1742), whose peculiar quirk was always to wear a hat while reading. Victory to the moderns. This episode is an uncanny echo of Lorenzo Valla's exposure of the forgery known as the 'Donation of Constantine' mentioned in the previous chapter. Once again we confront two sorts of reading, one which was broadly humanistic and the other which was more scholarly. The one assumes a continuity with the past, assumes that its works are as relevant now as they were then, while the other sees the present as a break with the past whose works need to be decoded. Much of the history of criticism oscillates between these two poles which are, of course, complementary.

## Why Neoclassicism?

We have briefly looked at some of the history and characteristics of neoclassicism, but why did it take even shallow root in England since, with the exception of Ben Jonson, there was no real tradition of using the ancients as a model, particularly in drama? One reason was the distrust of figurative language for its part in intensifying the Civil War. Another was that neoclassicism appeared to provide a rationale for the existence of literature. The move from the court to the marketplace had left the 'British Muses' lying 'abject and obscure' (Shaftesbury, in Sigworth 1971: 173). Neoclassicism seemed a way of redeeming literature's fallen state. It promoted clear expression and its aim of imitating nature gave literature a renewed sense of purpose. But, needless to say, things were not so simple. Writers still believed that literature shaped moral life even as they defined it in terms of representing nature. Dryden said that the playwright's 'imitation of nature' was for 'the delight and benefit of mankind' (Womersley 1997: 48 and 73) while, as late as 1751, John Brown, whose contribution to criticism is finally being recognised,[10] was claiming that though the 'primary end' of poetry was 'imitation', 'instruction' was a 'necessary part of its character' (Sigworth 1971: 247). In fact there is a case for saying that criticism took over this latter function from literature in the late seventeenth century. Dennis, who must be the only critic in the language to demand a clause in an international treaty that referred specifically to him,[11] said that 'the business of the critic [was] to instruct' (Spingarn [1957] 1968: 157). The point, though, is that the adoption of neoclassical principles did not mark the end of the rhetorical conception of literature. Instead, it grounded that conception in the idea of literature as imitation.

Which brings us to the third reason for the appeal of neoclassicism. By trying to imitate the world as it was rather than imagine how it might be, artists may have made a tiny contribution to the cause of political stability. By demanding respect for cultural authority they may have encouraged it for the political sort. The neoclassical view of nature may also have served the cause of social order. In addition to the idea of nature as human nature or an ideal order, it is also a force that curbs our tendency to excess. Davenant said that nature has instilled in us 'the humour of imitation' in order to 'limit' our ambitions just as 'it hath ordained the shelves before the shore to restrain the rage and excesses of the sea' (Spingarn [1908] 1957: 8). Nature is also a symbol of continuity. The nature portrayed by modern writers is the same as that portrayed by the ancients. Because nature is 'the same', wrote Steele, 'it is impossible for any modern writer to paint her otherwise than the ancients have done' (Sigworth 1971: 207). Rymer agreed. 'Nature is the same and man is the same'. In London, 'he loves, grieves, hates, envies, has the same affections and passions' as he did in ancient Athens (Rymer, in Spingarn [1908] 1958: 184). This view of nature as always the same provided a reassuring contrast to a society that had just suffered the upheavals England had. Perhaps nature would be a good base for social institutions and manners if it were properly understood. And one way to understand properly was to copy it correctly.

But what was it exactly that artists were copying? Johnson, who once described criticism as 'a study by which men grow important and formidable at very small expense' (Greene 1984: 290), famously wrote in his novel *The History of Rasselas: Prince of Abyssinia* (1759) that 'The business of a poet . . . is to examine, not the individual, but the species, to remark general properties and large appearances; he does not number the streaks of the tulip or describe the different shades of verdure in the forest' (ibid.: 352). And in his 'Preface to the Plays of William Shakespeare' (1765), he declared that 'Nothing can please many and please long but just representations of general nature' (Greene 1984: 420). Although he was writing after the high watermark of neoclassicism in England, Johnson's views are more 1680 than 1750. But he captures an important aspect of the neoclassical creed, namely, that the artist should focus on what people have in common, not what separates them. This was a matter of some urgency if the tensions and resentments left over from the Civil War were to be kept in check. Johnson reports that The Royal Society 'was instituted soon after the Restoration to divert the attention of the people from public discontent' and that '*The Tatler* and *The Spectator* had the same tendency; they were published at a time when two parties . . . were agitating the nation' (ibid.: 650). The poet or dramatist wasn't simply copying nature; he or she was cauterising the wounds inflicted by the Civil War.

And the authority of the classical tradition too would help restore the sense of continuity. If the virtues of an Aeschylus (525–456 BC) or a Sophocles

(c. 495–c. 406 BC) could still be practised, then the war between king and parliament had not permanently severed the country's relations with the past. Now was the time to assert that relation. Now was the time, not just to measure English writers against the achievement of the ancients, but to urge them to follow their example. And no-one was more rigorous in this endeavour than Rymer whom Thomas Babbington Macaulay (1800–59) denounced as 'the worst critic who ever lived'.[12] Rymer declared that the shortcomings of English playwrights were due to 'their ignorance or negligence of [the] fundamental rules and laws of Aristotle' (Spingarn [1908] 1957: 167). In particular they seemed to have forgotten that plot was the 'soul of tragedy' (ibid.: 183) and this affected other elements such as the unities and the proportion between beginning, middle and end. Believing that poets grow careless if critics do not keep 'a strict eye over their miscarriages' (ibid.: 163), Rymer helpfully pointed out what he considered to be Shakespeare's many errors as exemplified in *Othello*. It might have been too late for the bard to improve since, by this time he had been dead for over fifty years, but others might profit from his mistakes.

Othello is not a proper general because he suffers from 'jealousy', Iago is not a proper soldier because he is not 'open hearted' and Desdemona is no lady because she speaks like a woman 'bred out of a pig sty' (Spingarn 1957: 248). In fact *Othello* is not a proper tragedy. The plot lacks credibility, the characters are unnatural, the thoughts are neither 'true, fine nor noble' and, as for the fourth part of tragedy, the expression, well, there is more meaning and more humanity 'in the neighing of a horse or in the growling of a mastiff' than in 'the tragical flights of Shakespeare' (ibid.: 225). But in Rymer's defence he was one of the first to highlight some of *Othello*'s improbabilities.[13] And while he decreed that 'reason is always principally to be consulted' in plays, he reversed the neoclassical hierarchy in poetry, demanding that reason 'must consent and ratify whatever by fancy is attempted' (Spingarn [1908] 1957: 185). More to the purpose, Rymer's criticisms point to an ambiguity at the heart of imitation. Is he objecting to the way Shakespeare flouts decorum or nature, and can we separate the two anyway? Rymer seems to conflate nature and culture when he describes Iago's speech to Brabantio as an offence against good breeding and as contrary to humanity: 'But besides the manners to a *Magnifico*, humanity cannot bear that an old gentleman in his misfortune should be insulted over with such a rabble of Skoundrel language when no cause or provocation' (Spingarn 1957: 227). There also seems to be an inconsistency in Rymer's view of imitation. On the one hand, he demands that plays satisfy our sense of justice, namely, that we see the good rewarded and the bad punished, while, on the other, he demands that they conform to our experience where the opposite is true, the good are punished and the bad rewarded (ibid.: 188 and 253).

It seems, then, that the concept of imitation has a number of problems which undermine its capacity to portray and therefore cement the social order. One such problem is with the object of imitation, nature, which is moving ever closer to culture. Pope tells his readers that 'All Nature is but Art unknown to thee' (1978: 249), while Shaftesbury asks, 'if natural good taste be not already formed in us, why should we not endeavour to form it and become *natural*' (Sigworth 1971: 182; italics in original). As the gap between nature and culture grows ever smaller, nature begins to be identified with the local rather the universal and thus its authority, whether as a guarantee of human nature, ideal order, restraint, or continuity, is undermined. Romanticism may be seen as an attempt to recover some of that authority by reclaiming nature from culture. But the key difficulty with imitation is that it is the mode of epic and tragedy, neither of which are suited to conveying the complexities of eighteenth-century English society. As we said earlier, the novel will inherit the task of rendering this new world where the distinctions between ranks are no longer clearly demarcated. As one contemporary noted: 'An emulous endeavour to outvie each other in the elegant accommodations of life seems to be . . . the main ambition of a vast majority . . . There is scarce anyone but seems to be ashamed . . . of living within the compass of his own proper sphere, be it either great or small' (in Brewer 1997: 72). The neoclassicist's preoccupation with the hierarchy of genres, the proper place of the elegy against the ode, reflects a preoccupation with the hierarchy of persons, the proper place of the earl against the businessman.

In the end, neoclassicism did not establish itself in England. Perhaps it smacked too much of the absolutism that was associated with the Stuart cause, or perhaps its attachment to rules clashed too much with the English temperament. Addison quipped that 'our inimitable Shakespeare is a Stumbling-block to this whole tribe of rigid Criticks' (cited in Marks 1968: 4). But, whatever the reason, we mustn't assume that neoclassicism is irrelevant to the future development of criticism. We find, for instance, the same desire to adopt French ideas about literature in the late twentieth century as we do in the late seventeenth. The English looked to Boileau to establish some continuity with the past after the upheaval of revolution and to Foucault to understand how history was a series of discontinuities after Mrs Thatcher's conservative government destroyed the post-war consensus of the mixed economy and the welfare state. Some English critics turn to France, in other words, when there is a rupture in political or cultural life. But why to France? Perhaps because the two cultures have been mixed up with one another since the Norman conquest, or at least their upper echelons have. George Orwell often made the point that the English intelligentsia sneer at their own traditions while eagerly embracing those from abroad. Such contempt may be a factor in English literary culture but it doesn't throw any more light on the choice of France. Or, indeed, on why the intelligentsia should be so dismissive of the native stock of ideas, habits of thought and imaginings. To deal with that issue we would need to examine the class structure, in particular the tension in the middle class between its cultural and business wings, but that would take us too far out of our way.[14] Another aspect of neoclassicism which survives today, but in a very different form, is the emphasis on following rules. This is most apparent in the contemporary thinking on teaching and learning. The idea that you can write a tragedy simply by adhering to the unities becomes the belief that you can write an essay simply by adhering to the assessment criteria. And just as strict neoclassicists deny that you can create art without method, so pedagogues deny that you can learn without procedures.

Neoclassicism leaves us with a question. What is the nature of literary language? Traditionally, its value lay in the communication of truth or the promotion of virtue. The rise of science severed literature's relation with truth while the ongoing transformation of literature from rhetoric to commodity undermined its moral authority. Dryden's response was to locate the value of literature in the creative use of language. The work of the poet lies in 'descriptions', 'similitudes' and 'wit' which 'heighten' and 'beautify' his subject (cited in Gelber 2002: 116). True to the spirit of his age, Dryden believed that poetry should advance along with the other arts and sciences. And he demonstrated this by comparing the literature of his own age with that of the previous one. 'Poetry was then', he writes, 'if not in its infancy among us, at least not arrived to its vigour and maturity' (1954: 98). The chief faults of writers like Shakespeare and Jonson were their 'solecisms of speech' and 'notorious flaws in sense' (ibid.: 98). Restoration writing is more refined than Renaissance writing because it has rejected 'old words' and 'phrases which are ill sounding or improper' (ibid.: 97) and it is the richer because it has received 'new words and phrases' (ibid.: 101). We have already mentioned that writers make increasing use of financial metaphors and Dryden uses another here, comparing the injection of fresh terms into the language to the 'importation of bullion' into the currency (ibid.: 101).

One characteristic of the new economy was the fluctuation in the value of money: 'expanding and shrinking values of currency actively undermined once stable values associated with blood ties . . . and a propertied stake in the economy' (Nicholson 1996: 14). The comparison of language with money implies that literary value also changes. The value of money, like the value of literature, lies in the present and in the future, not in the past. Just as traditional forms of wealth, such as land, are being replaced by new ones such as trade, so are barbaric forms of expression being replaced by refined ones. The literary past has little value in relation to the literary present and the duty of the contemporary writer is to improve on the work of those who went before him. Dryden's argument stands in stark contrast to the neoclassical claim that authors should imitate the ancients. His view of literary value, as the discarding of the past, complements capitalism's dissolution of all previous forms of production. Only the new is valuable. The equation of literary value with forms of expression that enhance the subject means that it does not endure beyond the age in which those particular forms were current. A poem's worth is only ever of the present, doomed to obsolescence like any commodity.

But that's not the only problem with Dryden's view of literary language. For the claim that it is used to heighten a subject implies that form is less important than content. Dryden suggests as much himself when he writes that 'If Shakespeare were stripped of all the bombast in his passions, we should find the beauties of his thought remaining; if his embroideries were burnt down there would still be silver at the bottom of the melting pot' (cited in Ross 2000: 159). The content of any work is 'human nature', which has a permanent value compared to form which changes over time. The actual expression of an insight is seen as dispensable. Literary language adorns a truth at which it could never arrive itself. In fact, identifying literary value with human nature proves to be as difficult as identifying it with the inventive use of language, for it was not just style that changed over time but human nature too. This was evident from comparing the medieval love of tales of chivalry, 'the extravagant amusement of the dark ages' (Hurd, in Sigworth 1971: 368), with, say, the rational delights of the modern stage. More seriously, the voyages of exploration had brought travellers into contact with different cultures. Whether such contact sparked tales of interracial love affairs such as the famous *Inkle and Yariko* (1711), or satirical pamphlets such *An Essay towards the Character of the Late Chimpanzee* (1737), or just simple curiosity as in the exhibition of Lee Boo from the Pellew Islands in the South Pacific, the effect was to question what was meant by human nature.[15] In the end, Dryden fails to anchor literary value in either the form of expression or the experience of human nature. He divorces what is said from how it is said, reducing literary language to mere decoration. What he put asunder, Coleridge will join. In the meantime, we need to look at taste. Could this be the basis of literary value?

### The Nature of Taste and the Beautiful and the Sublime

From the mid-seventeenth through the eighteenth century the exercise of reason had become increasingly prominent in the fields of religion, science and politics and, indeed, economics. The intellectual equivalent of the demand for free trade was the call for the free expression of ideas. In the first quarter of the eighteenth century, 'Parliament was persuaded to abolish many of the import duties on raw materials as well as almost all export duties' (Fraser 2003: 424). The resulting expansion of trade strengthened the 'middling sort' financially, just as the abolition of the Licensing Act (1695) and the Copyright Act (1709) and the growth of newspapers strengthened them culturally. A confident, newly enriched class were reasonably free to challenge authority, vested interest and institutional inertia. Although principally the idiom of a wealthy middle class hungry for power, reason was also the language of radicals. In *The Rights of Man* (1792), the revolutionary Tom Paine (1737–1809) argues that reason should be the foundation of society itself, not tradition, religion or a titled aristocracy. He continued his attack on religion in *The Age of Reason* (1794), where he wrote that 'The Christian theory is little else than the idolatry of the ancient Mythologists, accommodated to the purposes of power and revenue; and it yet remains to reason and philosophy to abolish the amphibious fraud.'[16] Reason was a protest against privilege, a criticism of custom, the road to knowledge and a means of improving the human condition. In this period it was applied to every area of life, leaving nothing untouched. No wonder the eighteenth century was called the age of reason.

But it is not the attitude to reason that makes the Enlightenment the entrance to the modern world. The celebration of the rational faculty had been going on since at least the time of Plato and, in the Renaissance, Puttenham asked, 'What else is man but his mind?' (Vickers 1999: 253). The significance attached to reason in the eighteenth century was no more than a culmination of this process. So it is not reason that marks the birth of the modern but taste. When Addison remarks that 'fine taste [is] the utmost perfection of an accomplished Man' (Steele and Addison 1988: 364) he signals a huge cultural shift. For the first time in history the ability to appreciate a work of art is seen to be integral to human identity. The immortal soul, the gift of speech, even the struggle to achieve virtue now slip into the background in conceptions of the human. Reason and imitation are being replaced by taste and imagination. They embrace matters such as how we perceive and how we form preferences, and they become the basis of the new view of the human.

The need to find a balance between the different elements in man occurs while the relations between king and commons are themselves being adjusted. Taste, like reason, has a political dimension. Both signify a new freedom of self-determination. The individual does not simply obey, he exercises his judgement in a rational manner and consults his feelings. Again, both reason and taste belong primarily to the propertied middle classes but taste differs from reason to the extent that it combines the value the aristocracy place on birth with the value the middle class place on achievement. 'This Faculty', writes Addison, 'must in some measure be born with us [but] there are several Methods for Cultivating and Improving it' (Steele and Addison 1988: 366). Taste is also a way of reasserting the importance of social distinction. We saw earlier that some contemporaries were concerned about the dissolution of social boundaries.

Another example occurs in Tobias Smollet's novel *The Expedition of Humphry Clinker* (1771), where the dyspeptic Matthew Bramble fulminates against the corrosive effects of wealth on traditional hierarchies.

> All these absurdities arise from the general tide of luxury, which hath over-spread the nation, and swept away all . . . men of low birth, and no breeding, have found themselves suddenly translated into a state of affluence, unknown to former ages; and no wonder that their brains should be intoxicated with pride, vanity, and presumption. Knowing no other criterion of greatness, but the ostentation of wealth, they discharge their affluence without taste or conduct, through every channel of the most absurd extravagance . . . Even the wives and daughters of low tradesmen . . . are infected with the same rage of displaying their importance . . . Such is the composition of what is called the fashionable company at Bath; where a very inconsiderable proportion of genteel people are lost in a mob of impudent plebeians, who have neither understanding nor judgment, nor the least idea of propriety and decorum; and seem to enjoy nothing so much as an opportunity of insulting their betters. (1985: 28)

The simplest way in which taste was used to restore social distinction was to divide people according to whether they were capable merely of bodily pleasures or those of the mind as well. Shaftesbury said that the natural taste of the majority of the English was for the 'baiting and slaughter' of animals while that of a gentleman of good education was for music, painting, and 'a fancy in the ordinary things of ornament and grace' (1999: 62 and 120).[17] Similarly, the first professor of Rhetoric at Edinburgh University and, in effect, the first professor of English literature in the world, Hugh Blair (1718–1800), distinguished between those whose taste was 'bold and palpable' and those who see 'distinctions and differences where others see none' (1911: 12). His fellow Scot, the judge, philosopher and literary critic, Henry Home, Lord Kames (1696–1782), put the matter more bluntly when he declared that 'those who depend on bodily labour for food are totally devoid of taste' (2005: 726). Both men made important contributions to the development of criticism in England. That they were working at the margins of English life is an accident of birth, but that they should be so influential in shaping the study of its literature illustrates the increasing separation of cultural and political life, though critics continue to assert the link.[18]

If Kames appears to suggest that taste has nothing to do with the body, he would be quite wrong. Shaftesbury, in particular, is keen to balance sensual and intellectual pleasures. The 'moderate use of appetite', indeed, helps to make the sense of taste 'more clear and intense' (1999: 202). Blair describes taste as a 'faculty . . . more nearly allied to a feeling of sense than a process of understanding' (1911: 3). This means that perceptions of works of art are now bound up with the body as much, if not more than with the mind. As Denise Gigante argues, 'whereas sight and hearing allow for a proper representative distance from the object of contemplation (hence for the regulating principles of consciousness and morality) taste . . . is bound up with the chemical physiology of the body' (2005: 3). We are starting to move away from the political aspect of taste to its association with philosophy, particularly the idea that we learn about the world through our senses.[19]

This is most famously expressed in John Locke's *An Essay Concerning Human Understanding* (1689). In contrast to the French philosopher René Descartes (1596–1650), Locke argued that we are not born with innate ideas about how the world works but learn from our experience of it.

> Let us then suppose the mind to be, as we say, white paper, void of all char-acters, without any ideas:- How comes it to be furnished? Whence comes it by that vast store which the busy and boundless fancy of man has painted on it with an almost endless variety? Whence has it all the materials of reason and knowledge? To this I answer, in one word, from EXPERIENCE.[20]

Locke distinguishes between simple ideas which come from our senses and complex ideas which are our reflections on the impressions we have received through sight, sound, taste, touch or smell. In his own words, 'when the understanding is once stored with these simple ideas, it has the power to repeat, compare, and unite them, even to an almost infinite variety, and so can make at pleasure new complex ideas.' Locke also distinguishes between primary and secondary qualities of objects. The primary qualities belong to the objects themselves and include 'solidity, extension, figure, motion or rest, and number' while the secondary qualities 'are nothing in the objects themselves but [the] power to produce various sensations in us by their primary qualities, i.e. by the bulk, figure, texture, and motion of their insensible parts, as colours, sounds, tastes, &c.' And where ideas of primary qualities resemble the object, ideas of secondary qualities do not. Locke gives the example of fire. Its primary quality is motion and this motion produces the secondary qualities in us of warmth if we are at a comfortable distance from the fire and pain if we are too close to it. Clearly the motion belongs to the fire but what we feel, warmth or pain, does not.

Locke's philosophy of perception influenced literary criticism. Addison's states that

> We cannot indeed have a single Image in the Fancy that did not make its first entrance through the Sight; but we have the Power of retaining, altering and compounding those Images, which we have once received, into all the Varieties

of Picture and Vision that are most agreeable to the Imagination. (Steele and Addison 1988: 368)

This is a summary of Locke's view of simple and complex ideas. Locke's distinction between primary and secondary qualities provides a framework for discussing taste. Again, Addison is our guide. He distinguishes between 'the Primary Pleasures of the Imagination which entirely proceed from such Objects as are before our Eyes' and the 'Secondary Pleasures which flow from the Ideas of visible Objects' (ibid.: 369). Putting this in literary terms, we can agree about the primary qualities of a book, the title, the author, the publisher, the number of pages and so on but we may very well differ about its secondary qualities, the sensations and feelings we get from reading it. These are a matter of taste. This is an important moment in the history of criticism because it signals a shift away from traditional concerns of truth, representation and rhetorical effect to the actual experience of the artwork.

There are two aspects to this experience which we have encountered before but not in this context. The first is that it focuses on pleasure and the second is that it is largely private. Traditionally, the pleasure of poetry was related to either persuasion or instruction. But, by the mid-eighteenth century, this relation can no longer be taken for granted. Dryden had earlier announced that 'his chief endeavour [was] to delight the age in which I live' (1954: 64) and, then, in 1751 John Brown declared that the 'essential end of Poetry is to *please*, of Eloquence to *persuade*, of Argument to *instruct*' (Sigworth 1971: 246). This new attitude to pleasure, at its most explicit in the court of Charles II, was a reaction to the strictures of Puritan rule but it is also an acknowledgement that the role of art is changing. It is now more of a resource for self-cultivation than a guide to moral reformation. Accordingly, critics began to take less interest in the ethics of literature than in its beauties. Addison's definition of taste as 'that faculty of the soul which discerns the beauties of an author and the imperfections with dislike' (Steele and Addison 1988: 365) is fairly typical. Blair, for example, describes taste as 'the power of receiving pleasure from the beauties of nature and art' (1911: 2) while, in very similar terms, the moral philosopher James Beattie (1735–1803) says it 'is the capacity to be easily, strongly and agreeably affected with beauty' (1783: 160). The stress on beauty suggests its separation from its traditional association with the good and the true. Protestantism questioned this connection by claiming that human art distracted attention from God's glory which, in the form of nature, carried his message to men (Donoghue 2003: 28). In protestant theology beauty lost its equal status with the good and the true to which it became subordinated. But, in the discourse of taste, it seems to have acquired a value in its own right and to have broken free from the domination of ethics and epistemology. If it is mentioned in conjunction with anything, it is mentioned in conjunction with the sublime, a term that undergoes a number of permutations in the period. The sublime fits Locke's description of experience to the extent that it is based on sensation, but its roots are in Longinus' *On Sublimity*. Although Boileau translated the work in 1674, it wasn't until Leonard Welsted's *The Works of Dionysius Longinus* in 1724, followed, in 1739, by William Smith's *Dionysius Longinus on the Sublime*, that the idea began to attract serious attention in England.

Longinus defined sublimity as 'a kind of eminence or excellence in discourse' which could be achieved by putting great thoughts in figurative language (Russell and Winterbottom 1972: 462 and 467). Sublimity is the most powerful weapon in the armoury of rhetoric because it 'produces ecstasy rather than persuasion in the hearer' and 'the combination of wonder and astonishment always proves superior to the merely pleasant and persuasive' (ibid.: 462). But these are exactly the reasons why the English, at this stage in their history, should not have wanted anything to do with the sublime. The emphasis placed on politeness, the plain style and rational argument was intended to counter the sort of excesses that runaway oratory had produced in the Civil War. So why did the sublime exercise such a fascination? We shall try to answer this below. Early mentions of Longinus praise him for his decorum, for his using the sublime style to write about the sublime. Pope salutes him as a critic 'Whose own Example strengthens all his laws, / And is himself that great Sublime he draws' (1978: 83). But soon interest shifts to the power of the sublime to astonish and overwhelm us. Addison finds this quality in nature, for example, 'an open Champian Country, a vast uncultivated Desart, of huge Heaps of Mountains, high Rocks and Precipices, or a wide Expanse of Waters' (Steele and Addison 1988: 374). Edmund Burke (1729–97), who supported the American Revolution (1775–83) but not the French one (1789–99), identifies terror as 'the ruling principle of the sublime' (1990: 54). If we do not see something clearly, it has a much greater power to terrify us and therefore the sublime relies on 'obscurity' (ibid.) for its effect. Burke cites Milton as one of the most sublime of English poets because his description of death is 'dark, uncertain, confused [and] terrible' (ibid.: 55). In a similar vein, he attributes the sublimity of a passage in the book of Job, where the speaker is visited by a spirit that he 'could not discern' (Job 4: 16), to 'the terrible uncertainty of the thing described' (ibid.: 58).

The sublime also provides a useful lexicon for describing the consequences of political discontent.

> Confounded by the complication of distempered passions, their reason is disturbed; their views become vast and perplexed; to others inexplicable; to themselves uncertain. They find, on all sides, bounds to their unprincipled ambition in any fixed order of things. Both in the fog and haze of confusion all is enlarged, and appears without any limit. (Burke 1986: 136)

Burke is here writing about the English Civil War but his main focus is the French Revolution, 'the most horrid, atrocious, and afflicting spectacle that perhaps ever was exhibited to the pity and indignation of mankind' (ibid.: 159). This, too, is rendered in terms of the sublime. The most savage passage of the Revolution known as 'the Terror', which lasted from 5 September 1793 to 28 July 1794 and which accounted for the lives of between 20,000 and 40,000 people, is the 'ruling principle' of the sublime in the shape of guillotine. The baying crowds, the parade of prisoners, the industrialised decapitations, the abolition of the monarchy and the outlawing of religion were unprecedented. How were such events to be represented? How were they to be explained? What Burke calls the 'unguarded transport' (ibid.: 165) of the Revolution was sublime to the extent that it defied all attempts to understand it. We sense him struggling to find the right words to convey the meaning of what was happening across the channel as he refers to the Revolution variously as a 'tragedy', a 'grand spectacle', 'a magnificent stage effect' and a 'profane burlesque' (ibid.: 156, 161 and 175). The idiom of drama compensates for the failure of reason. The imagination endeavours to grasp what the intellect cannot comprehend.

And this is another important moment in the history of criticism, for it marks the beginning of a convergence between art and life which eventually becomes the post-structuralist commonplace that language constitutes reality. Burke had already drawn attention to the uncertain boundary between art and life in his *Philosophical Enquiry into the Origin of Our Ideas of the Beautiful and the Sublime* (1754) when he says that people would leave off watching a tragedy to witness a live execution because they enjoy sympathising with a real victim more than a pretend one. That they do so, says Burke, reveals a confusion in our thinking. We do not, he writes, 'sufficiently distinguish what we would by no means choose to do, from what we should be eager enough to see if it was once done' (Burke 1990: 44). In very simple terms, we are happy to watch someone commit an act that we would not wish to commit ourselves. Beyond that, Burke seems to imply that we do not clearly recognise the border between reality and representation or, indeed, realise our need to do so. But once we have crossed it, once we have confused fact with fantasy, then we have lost our moral bearings and can view actual suffering as 'a grand spectacle to rouse the imagination' (1986: 161). Burke glimpses the future. He anticipates the aestheticisation of power whose most obvious example is the Third Reich (1933–45) but which is also evident in our own image-obsessed political culture. His analysis also looks forward to Baudrillard's concept of simulation and Derrida's claim that 'there is nothing outside the text' (Derrida 1976: 163). But they show little of the anxiety that he feels about this development.

In his *Philosophical Enquiry*, Burke stipulated that the sublime should be considered under the head of 'self-preservation' (1990: 35), which indirectly brings us back to the second problem of taste, that it was largely a private matter. This privacy, as we noted in the last chapter, is a consequence of the move of poetry from the court to the marketplace. But it takes on a new character in the eighteenth century. Trevor Ross, for example, suggests that the settlement of 1688 had an effect on the very nature of the self. By giving up his autonomy to those who would represent him, the individual 'became a specialised, private, even decentred [person] who refined his moral being through a sympathetic social intercourse among the increasingly complex and differentiated human relations and products that commerce could furnish' (2000: 199). One manifestation of this condition was the diversity of taste. The philosopher David Hume (1711–76), who many thought was motivated more by a love of fame than a love of truth, maintained that the great variety of taste was even 'greater in reality than in appearance' (1884: 134).

If individuals were defining themselves through their preferences in art then did that mean they were not defining themselves in relation to each other? Historically, the sense of self arose from a person's place in the social hierarchy which regulated relations between the different levels. But, as Oliver Goldsmith's *The Deserted Village* (1770) shows, the development of trade dissolves traditional communities, as indeed it had been doing since at least the thirteenth century. Yet it wasn't only commerce that threatened to undermine customary ties. So, too, according to Burke, did reason. He pointed to the French Revolution as an example of what happened when reason rather than religion becomes the basis of social life: our conception of man is impoverished. Commerce and political philosophy complement one another in banishing habits, sentiments, affections, morality and manners from their account of the human. Consequently:

> Nothing is left which engages the affections on the part of the common-wealth. On the principles of this mechanic philosophy, our institutions can never be embodied, if I may use the expression, in persons; so as to create in us love, veneration, admiration, or attachment. But that sort of reason which banishes the affections is incapable of filling their place. These public affections, combined with manners, are required sometimes as supplements, sometimes as correctives, always as aids to law. The precept given by a wise man, as well as a great critic, for the construction of poems, is equally true as to states:—*Non satis est pulchra esse poemata, dulcia sunto* There ought to be a system of manners in every nation, which a well-formed mind would be disposed to relish. To make us love our country, our country ought to be lovely.
> (Burke 1986: 182)

The Latin quote is from Horace. It means roughly, 'it is not enough for poems to be beautiful, they must also charm'. The passage as a whole leaves it open for art to recognise the complexity of human nature so summarily dismissed by trade and politics, a recognition integral to the concept of taste which, at a very simple level, endeavours to reconcile senses, sentiment and judgement. It may also explain the eighteenth-century cult of sensibility, manifested in novels such as Laurence Sterne's *Sentimental Journey* (1768) and Henry MacKenzie's *The Man of Feeling* (1771). More specifically, the parallel Burke draws between the nature of poetry and the nature of society is a reminder that we cannot separate discussions of taste from wider worries about social change.

Taste lacks the authority of neoclassicism. It is associated with sense more than reason, it varies from one person to another and it is relative to custom and country. Moreover, a number of conditions must be met before taste can be properly exercised. These include, according to Hume, 'a delicacy of imagination', 'a perfect serenity of mind', 'a recollection of thought', 'a due attention to the object', a power of comparison between 'the several species of and degrees of excellence', a 'mind free from all prejudice', and an ability to enter into the spirit of the time in which the work was made (1884: 138–9, 142 and 144). Since it is highly unlikely, as Hume acknowledges, that anyone will be able to measure up to these criteria, taste proves to be a rather poor ground for literary value. And not just literary value. The change from neoclassical rules to individual psychology also affected ideas of truth and morality. Shaftesbury is horrified at the opinion 'that all actions are naturally indifferent; that they have no note or character of good or ill in themselves; but are distinguished by mere fashion, law or arbitrary decree' (Sigworth 1971: 186).[21] That this idea is a central plank of postmodern thought is another instance of continuity in the history of criticism.

One way of combating the relativity of taste is to insist that reason has an important part to play in its formation. The 'pleasure we receive from the representations of the characters, actions, or manners of men', writes Blair, 'is founded on mere taste: but to judge whether they are properly executed belongs to the understanding which compares the copy with the original' (1911: 9). Blair deals with the problem of taste varying from one person to another by observing that if there is no standard of taste, then all tastes are equally good, which is an absurdity. 'Is there anyone who will seriously maintain that the taste of a Hottentot or a Laplander is as delicate and correct as that of a Longinus or an Addison?' (ibid.: 16). Well, yes, if taste is relative to the country in which it is practised. In any case, Blair does not distinguish between those societies where art is a lived experience and those where it is an object of contemplation. Hume has a more nuanced understanding of the matter. He accepts that while we may enjoy art from other cultures this is because it resembles that which is found in our own age and country. Criticism, it would seem, is only comfortable with the known. Which is, of course, never fully known and that is one of the reasons for revisiting a work. Hume also makes a distinction between superficial barriers that prevent us from enjoying work from other times and places and more substantial bars to our pleasures. The first, for which we can easily make an adjustment, includes manners, fashions, sentiments and even opinions but the second, which turns on moral principles, is finally insurmountable:

> [W]here the ideas of morality and decency alter from one age to another, and where vicious manners are described, without being marked without the proper characters of blame and disapprobation, this must be allowed to disfigure the poem, and to be a real deformity. (Hume 1884: 147)

Ethics has become the criterion of art again but it does not fix the standard of taste since, as Hume implies, what counts as good and bad behaviour differs from one age to another.

We can, then, reconcile reason and taste but only up to a point, and it is much more difficult to establish a standard of taste that holds true for all times and places. Most discussion of taste in this period is dedicated to minimising its socially disruptive effects. The idea that taste differs from person to person threatens the unity of the polity because it signifies what separates them, not what they have in common. This, in fact, is the tension between civic and commercial humanism.[22] The former focuses on the citizen's duty in promoting virtue and valour to maintain the integrity of the State while the latter focuses on the cultivation of manners and pleasures. The struggle to establish taste either on an idea of human nature – 'a child born with an aversion to its mother's milk is a wonder' (Kames 2005b: 721) – or on the premise that 'there are certain qualities in objects which are fitted by nature to produce [feelings of beauty]' (Hume 1884: 139) is the struggle to find a balance between the individualism of commercial humanism and the community of civic humanism.

We can almost see those staples of discussion about taste, the beautiful and the sublime, in the same terms. The social aspect of these categories emerges during the course of the century. Addison, who identifies them as pleasures of the imagination, is one of the first to describe them in any detail. A beautiful sight is one that pleases us and 'consists either in the Gaiety or Variety of Colours, in the Symmetry and proportion of Parts, in the Arrangement and Disposition of Bodies, or in just Mixture and Concurrence of all together' (1988: 374). A sublime or what Addison calls a 'great' sight is not simply the 'Bulk of any single Object, but the Largeness of a Whole View' (ibid.: 371). Even at this early stage, the terms 'great' and 'beautiful' have more than a merely aesthetic meaning. A 'spacious Horizon', for example, has a political resonance for it is an 'image of liberty' while the beautiful impinges on gender relations because it is a stimulus to reproduction (ibid.: 371 and 376). Another pleasure of the imagination is in what is 'new or uncommon', because 'it fills the Soul with an agreeable Surprise, gratifies its Curiosity and gives it an Idea of which it was not before possest' (ibid.: 372). We saw in the last chapter that writers were beginning to strive for novelty as a way of competing with one another in the emerging marketplace and, by the time we reach the beginning of the eighteenth century, a high value is being placed on the new. It is very much a feature of the developing consumer society with its variety of shops, advertisements and 'Things that were never [before] heard of' (Addison, in Mackie 1998: 71).

The social and political dimensions of the sublime and the beautiful become more pronounced as the century progresses. The qualities of beauty themselves mirror the ideal social order, proportion, regularity and order. Burke says the beautiful 'cause[s] love or some passion similar to it' (1990: 83) while Kames notes that one of the qualities of the beautiful, 'simplicity', 'has an enchanting effect and never fails to gain our affection' when it is an ingredient in 'behaviour and manners' (Kames 2005a: 147). Both men believe that the sublime plays or should play an important part in the social order. It should be part of the symbolism of the political and religious establishment thereby ensuring submission to its authority. This is a reminder that power, and indeed terror, are central to our understanding of the sublime. Burke observes that when we try to contemplate the deity 'we shrink into the minuteness of our own nature, and are, in a manner, annihilated before him' (1990: 63). The power to terrify also characterises 'kings and commanders' and that is why sovereigns 'are frequently addressed with the title of *dread majesty*' (ibid.: 62) Kames says that 'the robes of state are made large and full to draw respect' (Kames 2005a: 150) and that a regiment 'where the men are all in one livery and the horses of one colour, makes a grand appearance, and consequently strikes terror' into the spectator (ibid.: 152).

The beautiful, for Burke, relates mainly to society and the sublime mainly to the self, for fear rouses our instinct of 'self-preservation' (1990: 36), thereby underlining our earlier point that these categories approximate to those of civic and commercial humanism. Burke's distinction opens a rift between individual and society that will become a major preoccupation of the nineteenth-century novel. We can understand this rift partly in gender terms. The qualities of the beautiful, such as softness and delicacy, are associated with the feminine while those of the sublime, such as power and strength, are associated with masculinity. But the rift is best understood in terms of a split between the social and economic spheres. As trade and industry continue to develop, they destroy traditional social relations. The most obvious example is the drift from the field to factory, from the personal relations of the village to the impersonal ones of the town. As commerce thrives, community declines.

But the real significance of the sublime is that it captures the spirit of capitalism in two ways. First, its focus on the individual is consonant with Adam Smith's conception of an economy driven by self-interest and, second, it dramatises the power of market forces over the individual. The eighteenth century saw a shift from a moral economy characterised by paternalism to one where price was determined by the mechanism of the market with possibly devastating effects on people's lives.[23] Developments in agriculture forced many off the land, compelling them to seek work in a system where the poverty of the majority was seen to be 'essential not only to sustain the privileges of a few' but also to maintain 'national greatness' (Wrightson 2002: 320). The power of capitalism seemed every bit as great as that of Burke's 'dread' monarch. Moreover, capitalism admits no principle of limitation, it is marked by excess, it cannot be clearly conceived and so partakes of that obscurity which is one of the sublime's sources of terror.

Now we have our answer as to why the sublime, although it was an aesthetic of discord, exercised such a fascination. It was a way of coming to terms with the loss of feudalism and the power of market forces. 'The age of chivalry is gone', cried Burke melodramatically, and 'that of sophisters, economists, and calculators, has succeeded' (1986: 172). The sublimity that characterised the displays of monarchical power has become a feature of the economy which, like God, seems omnipotent, and which, like God, cannot be grasped. Even beauty, the idiom of the social, is having to bend to the market. Kames argues that 'the perception of beauty greatly promotes industry; being to us a strong additional incitement to enrich our fields and improve our manufactures' (Kames 2005a: 149). The focus on the sublime and the beautiful suggests that the conception of literature is now more aesthetic than ethical. At the same time, the categories of the sublime and the beautiful are ways of thinking about social and economic forms, though not in an analytical manner. The language of art is not the language of politics, and yet they seem to obey a similar logic. This certainly appears to be the case if we look at taste and property.

Addison establishes an initial connection. 'A man of polite imagination', that is, a man of taste, 'can converse with a Picture, and find an agreeable Companion in a statue . . . It gives him, indeed, a kind of property in everything he sees' (Steele and Addison 1988: 369). Another connection, strangely enough, concerns the idea of evacuation. The contemporary medical obsession with this particular bodily function provided a metaphor for understanding the workings of taste. A person's physical health depended on the timely evacuation of 'system clogging dregs' (Gigante 2005: 48) just as their mental development depended on expelling all kinds of rudeness, coarseness and prejudice. The disposal of waste matter was a necessary prelude to cultivation and we can find a similar argument for the seizure of property. Lawyer to the Earl of Salisbury, Sir John Davies (1569–1626) wrote that the English had a right to evict the Irish from their land because it 'doth now lie waste' whereas the settlers, by ensuring that it is 'fully stocked and matured', will greatly increase its value; '500 acres will be worth more than 5000 are now' (cited in Wood 2002: 160). Locke makes the same point when writing about the American Indians. He states that individuals acquire a right to property by mixing it with their labour. They add value to the land by working it. Since the American Indian has not worked the land they have little or no right to it. The colonist may therefore in good conscience appropriate the land and make it more profitable. There is, then, an affinity between theories of bodily evacuation, the cultivation of taste and a labour-based theory of property. The logic in each case is to increase production by the elimination of waste. A man's taste improves the more he rids himself of all that inhibits its development just as the colonist improves the land by making sure that none of it lies idle. The connection may be far fetched. But here's an interesting coincidence. Kames was a property lawyer before he became a literary critic.

## Scholarship, Englishness and the Canon

Neither taste nor neoclassicism prove able to ground criticism. What, then, can scholarship offer? This seems a more promising route because it was during the eighteenth century 'that English literary scholarship established itself, formally, culturally, institutionally and commercially' (Walsh 2001: 191). But what is meant by scholarship? In very simple terms, it is part of the tradition of *grammatica*. It seeks to establish the authenticity of a work, to gloss difficult passages and to explain references and allusions. If this suggests that scholarship is a specialised activity, it is. And that's its point of departure from taste. Taste is potentially democratic because it is a faculty common to all whereas scholarship, by its very nature, is the province of a few. The rise of the trained expert suggests that only those who are truly qualified can practise criticism. But that it is to look ahead. In the early part of the century the lines between taste and scholarship were not so clearly drawn.

We can see this in Pope's 'Preface' to *The Works of Shakespeare* (1725) which combines a predominantly neoclassical taste with straightforward scholarly concerns, such as the order of scenes and speeches being put into the mouths of the wrong characters. Pope thinks very much in terms of the 'beauties' and 'faults' of Shakespeare's plays. The beauties consist of Shakespeare's originality, the individual nature of his characters, his 'power over our passions', and his 'amazing' ability to 'hit upon that particular point on which the bent of each argument turns, or the force of each motive depends' (Wormersley 1997: 266). His faults include comedies that 'have their Scene among Tradesmen and Mechanicks' and tragedies packed with 'unnatural Events and Incidents; the most exaggerated Thoughts; the most verbose and bombastic Expression; the most pompous Rhymes, and thundering Versifications' (ibid.: 267). In tragedy in particular, Shakespeare offends against the neoclassical principles of probability and decorum.

But Pope comes to praise Shakespeare not to bury him. And, in doing so, he encourages his readers to think beyond neoclassical norms. True, Shakespeare does not imitate nature but that is because he is nature. His characters, for instance, 'are so much Nature herself, that "tis a sort of injury to call them by so distant name as Copies of her' (Wormersley 1997: 268). Pope then points out that it is wrong to judge Shakespeare by Aristotle's rules, partly because Renaissance authors were not particularly well acquainted with the ancients and partly because it 'is like trying a man by the Laws of one Country, who acted under those of another' (ibid.: 268). Pope urges us to see Shakespeare in context. His crudities and verbal exuberance were due to his having to 'please the Populace' on whom the success of his plays depended (ibid.: 227). No doubt Pope has in mind how the literature of his own day is being affected by commercial considerations. It was, after all, one of the main preoccupations of *The Dunciad* (1728, 1729, 1742 and 1743), Pope's attack on all those who slandered him over the years: 'Sense, speech, and measure, living tongues and dead, / Let all give way – and Morris may be read' (1978: 535). In Book Four particularly, he complains of those who rhyme for hire, who pass off cheap verse as valuable jewels and generally prostitute every artistic principle for gain (ibid.: 555, 568 and 577). Of course we hear exactly the same complaints today. Pope's attack on Dullness prefigures our own on dumbing down.

The charge that Shakespeare was ill educated was more serious because of the high regard in which learning was held in the neoclassical creed. Pope therefore rolls out a number of arguments to show that Shakespeare was indeed well read. The fact that he had little Latin and no Greek did not matter a jot, says Pope. What did matter was whether he had knowledge and Shakespeare certainly had. 'Nothing is more evident than that he had a taste of natural Philosophy, Mechanicks, ancient and modern History, Poetical learning and Mythology: We [also] find him very learned in the customs, rites and manners of Antiquity' (Wormersley 1997: 270). In addition, Shakespeare showed 'a wonderful justness of distinction as well as extent of comprehension' in matters of politics and ethics, and he was well acquainted with ancient authors and the 'modern Italian writers of novels' (ibid.: 270). As if that were not enough, says Pope, we have Ben Jonson's endorsement of Shakespeare's genius. Did he not 'exalt him' above Chaucer and Spenser? And did he not 'challenge the names of Sophocles, Euripides and Aeschylus, nay all Greece and Rome at once to equal him' (ibid.: 271)? So yes, Shakespeare was learned.

Having saved the bard for neoclassicism, whose rules he also transcends, Pope then examines some of the problems the scholar of Shakespeare faces.

The list is long. It ranges from 'constant blunders in proper names of persons and places' to misattribution of plays. Shakespeare, snaps Pope, could never have been the author of such 'wretched' works as *Yorkshire Tragedy* and *London Prodigal* (Womersley 1997: 276). Sandwiched between these faults are any number of errors: spelling; the introduction of 'trifling and bombast passages'; the removal of 'beautiful passages' and the confounding of verse and prose (ibid.: 273, 274 and 275). None of these mistakes were Shakespeare's. They were the fault of the players changing the script and the printers not checking them. Even so we mustn't blame the players too much for we should remember that 'the Judgement, as well as the Condition, of that class of people was then far inferior to what it is in our days . . . the top of the profession were then meer Players, not Gentleman of the Stage' (ibid.: 275). Pope is none too confident about his ability as an editor and, indeed, sees it as a decline from his calling as a poet, telling his friend John Caryll, who provided him with the story for *The Rape of the Lock* (1712 and 1714), that 'I am become, by gradation of dullness, from a poet to a translator, and from a translator, a meer editor' (ibid.: 390). In that humble role he puts the various readings into the margin and 'those I have prefer'd into the Text . . . upon authority' (ibid.: 277). He is guided by Shakespeare's alterations and removes passages of doubtful origin to the foot of the page 'with an Asterisk referring to the places of their insertion' (ibid.: 277). Scenes are marked and obsolete or unusual terms explained. A catalogue of the first editions is also attached, 'by which the greater part of the various readings and of the corrected passages are authorised' (ibid.: 277). These editions, Pope continues, 'are the only materials left to repair the deficiencies or restore the corrupted sense of the Author' (ibid.: 277).

The work of a contemporary editor would be more sophisticated, but it would not be radically different. Except in one respect. He or she is unlikely to write anything like this: 'the most shining passages are distinguished by a comma in the margin; and where the beauty lay not in the particulars but the whole, a star is prefix'd to the scene' (Womersley 1997: 277). We are embarrassed by such bold declarations of beauty. Loveliness has no part in our response to literature. This is a problem of both culture and language. The brutal economism of British society, its instrumentalist mentality, relentless utilitarianism and endless audit trails leave little room for questions of beauty. It retreats to art but finds no refuge there for the dominant aesthetic seems to be a grotesque hybrid of banality, ugliness and sensation.[24] And even if beauty were acknowledged, there is still the problem of how to talk about it. The experience and the explanation of beauty are two different things. Addison says, 'there is nothing that makes its way more directly to the Soul than Beauty' (Steele and Addison 1988: 372), but it is very difficult to capture and convey that immediacy in the conventional language of criticism.

Consequently, critics tend to avoid discussion of the beautiful in art, which means they fail to deal with one of its most important attributes. We can look in vain from feminism to post-colonialism to find any acknowledgment that beauty is a component of literature. Not only does this diminish our experience of art, it also impoverishes our understanding of ethics. Why? Because of the historic connection between the beautiful and the good, a connection that has entirely slipped below the horizon of the contemporary critic.

We need to find a new way of speaking about art if we are to address this problem. One that seeks to communicate its total effect. The critic must try to evoke the particular impact a poem, or play or novel has on him or her. And this calls for a genuine response to the work, not one which relies on parroting the tenets of the prevailing orthodoxy. The assumptions behind most critical positions are rarely spelt out and subsist on vague moral justifications. For instance, it is wrong to exclude women from the canon – therefore we must seek to include them or construct a female canon. Aside from the historical inaccuracy of such claims, from Sappho to Zadie Smith women's achievements in literature have been acknowledged; there is no sense that one woman's writing is better than another's and, if we are to accept that there is no difference between one artwork and another, then why shouldn't we accept that there is no moral difference between one action and another? It is precisely these sorts of questions that contemporary criticism refuses to face.

Pope trusts his audience to appreciate beauty, when it is pointed out to them. The fact that he does not dwell on Shakespeare's moral message suggests that beauty and goodness are beginning to part company, leading to the situation described above where we have lost touch with both. 'A true critic' declares Addison, 'ought to discover the concealed Beauties of a Writer, and communicate to the World such Things as are worth their Observation' (Steele and Addison 1988: 423). The authority of the critic comes from his ability to see what others overlook. Lewis Theobald (1688–1744) makes the same point, that a critic should bring to light beauties 'that are less obvious to common Readers' (Womersley 1997: 288). But that is not as important for him as 'emend[ing] corrupt passages or explain[ing] obscure and difficult ones' (ibid.: 294). His 'Preface' to Shakespeare (1733/40) is an example of the growing distance between editorial and critical activity. Some of the corrections, writes Theobald, were guided by 'the Beauties and Defects of the Composition . . . but This was but occasional, and for the sake only of perfecting the other the two other Parts, which [are] the proper Objects of the Editor's Labour' (ibid.: 295). Theobald's 'Preface' takes issue with Pope on a number of points. There is a sense of old scores being settled because Pope had savaged Theobald in the first version of *The Dunciad*. He had made him king of the Dunces and dubbed him 'Tibbald', for which 'flagrant incivility', Theobald said, he was 'indebted' to Pope (ibid.: 292). He promised to 'return' the poet's 'civilities' but within the 'limits of common decency' for, as he is sure posterity will judge, it is far 'better to want *Wit* than to want *Humanity*' (ibid.: 292–3). Unfortunately for him, posterity is still undecided on the question.

Theobald's 'Preface' covers some of the same ground as Pope. He too marvels at Shakespeare's genius, defends his learning and blames the players for inconsistencies in the manuscript. But there the similarities end. Theobald very quickly begins to find fault with Pope's edition. He accuses him of not collating the old copies and of correcting Shakespeare's verse to its detriment. 'He has attacked him like an unhandy *Slaughterman*, and not lopp'd off the *Errors* but the poet' (Womersley 1997: 292). What delight Theobald takes in proving Pope wrong about the source of 'some Anachronisms' (ibid.: 299) we can only guess. And his joy visibly increases when he demonstrates Pope's ignorance of Homer. The poet who gave Theobald a provocation 'which a Man can never quite forget' is treated to a blast of sarcasm, as Theobald cries, 'see What a good Memory and sound Judgement in Conjunction can achieve!' (ibid.: 292 and 300).

There is no doubt that Pope was the better poet, but equally there is no doubt that Theobald was the better editor. His work on Shakespeare is far more extensive and elaborate than Pope's. In trying to restore 'to the Publick their greatest Poet in his Original Purity' Theobald scoured the sources, compared different manuscript versions and 'constantly endeavour'd to support my Corrections and Conjectures by parallel passages from Himself, the surest Means of expounding any Author whatsoever' (Wormersley 1997: 294 and 296). In addition, he explains his emendations, justifies his guesses, glosses difficult passages and elucidates references and allusions. Pope assumes the beauties of Shakespeare are more or less self-evident: Theobald knows that a great deal of work is required to make them shine through. His work heralds a move away from taste to scholarship in the study of literature. But it doesn't provide criticism with any more secure ground. It may have become a 'science' (ibid.: 294) but questions of literary use and the nature of literary significance remain. What criticism gains in editorial techniques, it loses in value.

Shakespeare was one of the reasons neoclassicism was never fully adopted in this country and, as the period wears on, he becomes the centre of an English canon. The historian Linda Colley argues that a British national identity emerges between the Act of Union in 1707[25] and the accession of Queen Victoria in 1837, based on constitutional monarchy, economic opportunity and empire. Above all, she continues, it rested on religion, specifically Protestantism, which was shared by the vast majority of Britons. Another historian, Gerald Newman, focuses not on a British, but on an English identity.[26] It was, he claims, the creation of an economically powerful but politically weak middle class impatient with aristocratic adulation of French culture which they believed was corrupting the manners and morals of native life. Traders, manufacturers, journalists and artists sought to combat the debilitating effects of continental fashion by forging an English identity whose central values were simplicity, sincerity, independence and hard work. Colley's suggestion that Protestantism formed the basis of national life is a powerful one. But it overlooks two things. First, as we saw in the last chapter, Protestantism could divide as well as unite and, second, late seventeenth- and eighteenth-century culture formed itself in reaction to religion. This makes Newman's focus on artists and writers as the source of English national identity initially more convincing but, as Krishan Kumar has shown, Newman 'fundamentally confuses English and British, Englishness and Britishness' (2003: 177). More seriously, he continues, Newman is not dealing with nationalism at all, but 'with the development of a strand of English moralism that has alternatively been seen as the source of the glories of the English literary tradition and the bane of its underdeveloped social science' (ibid.: 178). Kumar is right to distinguish between moralism and nationalism but it doesn't follow that the former has no part in the latter. The moral sense of 'fair play', for example, is one of the traditional ways in which the English identify themselves.

Whatever the precise details it is hard to deny that a sense of Britishness/Englishness began to permeate all aspects of the culture, from the codification of the rules of cricket in 1744 to English replacing Norman French as the language of the law. And this is the century that sees the appearance of that personification of Englishness, John Bull, created in 1712 by Dr John Arbuthnot (1667–1735), friend of Pope and physician to Queen Anne (1665–1714). Arbuthnot was a Scot. So too was James Thomson (1700–48), who wrote the words of England's unofficial anthem, *Rule Britannia*. The music was composed by an Englishman Thomas Augustine Arne (1710–78). We have already mentioned how the Scots practically invented modern English criticism and influenced its development. Now we find they have a hand in English iconography and patriotic lyrics. Scottish, English, British. National identity can be very confusing on these shores. But, as rule of thumb, Scottish and English are forms of ethnic identity and are expressed in cultural forms, while British is a form of political identity and is expressed by an acceptance of parliament and constitutional monarchy. The first stirrings of national identity began with the break up of Christendom and, from the beginning, was bound up with the consciousness of language. The power to determine correct usage in speech and writing lay with the court, but its influence diminished with the growth of the market, though language itself continues to remain vital to the sense of national identity.

After the Civil War, Thomas Sprat (1635–1713) suggested the creation of an English Academy which would not only 'weigh Words and Letters' but demonstrate that 'the Wits of our Nation are not inferior to any other' (Spingarn [1908] 1957: 114). His desire to purify the language was an essential to making England a great power for 'purity of Speech and greatness of Empire have in all Countries still met together' (ibid.: 113). Defoe also supported the idea of an academy 'to encourage Polite Learning, to polish and refine the English Tongue, and advance the so much neglected Faculty of Correct Language, to establish Purity and Propriety of Stile, to urge it from all Irregular Additions that Ignorance and Affectation have introduc'd' (in Crystal 2004: 377). Unlike the Renaissance writer John Hoskyns, Defoe felt that women prevented language from degenerating and so wanted them to play an active part in the academy which should also make it 'as Criminal to *Coin Words* as *Money*' (ibid.: 378). Jonathan Swift (1667–1745), too, considered the establishment of an academy to reform the language after the 'Corruptions' of the 'Usurpation' and the 'Licentiousness' of the Restoration (Mackie 1998: 404). Such an academy should 'have the example of the French before them, to imitate where these have proceeded right, and to avoid their Mistakes' (ibid.: 408). It would establish the rules of grammar, standardise spelling and find some method 'for Ascertaining and Fixing our Language for ever' (ibid.: 408).

The verb 'to fix' meant, in this period, both 'specify, determine' and 'give stability to, secure against change'. Johnson's *A Dictionary of the English Language* (1755) was intended to create order out of the 'confusion' and 'boundless variety' of the native tongue (Greene 1984: 305). But he warned that those who hoped his labours might 'fix the language and put a stop to those alterations which time and chance have hitherto been suffered to make in it without opposition' (ibid.: 324) were deluding themselves. 'May the lexicographer be derided', he writes, who imagines 'that his dictionary can embalm his language, and secure it from corruption and decay' (ibid.: 324). And the biggest source of corruption? Commerce, 'which however necessary, however lucrative, as it depraves the manners, corrupts the language' (ibid.: 325). Its 'jargon' of 'the exchange, the warehouse [and] the port' infects 'current speech' and swells the language, confounding distinction and overturning propriety (ibid.: 325 and 326).

We need to distinguish here between the idea that commerce is the enemy of culture and the idea that commerce supplies some of the terms and concepts we use to think about culture. This tension is apparent in Johnson who, on the one hand, announces that commerce corrupts the language and, on the other, famously states that 'No man but a blockhead ever wrote except for money' (O' Casey 1990: 30). It is this sort of tension that makes it difficult to set commerce and culture in conceptual opposition. There is some degree of dependency at the level of idioms and ideas as there is in the market between the writer, the publisher and the bookseller. Nevertheless, the next development in the history of criticism is to treat one aspect of culture, literature, as a standard by which to judge the depredations of, particularly, industry.

For now, we can note that the commerce has the same effect on language as it does on hierarchy; it dissolves distinctions, blurs boundaries and creates confusion. The demand for order in language is also a demand for order in society. Grammar was a way of organising speech and writing as manners were a way of organising society. The famed eighteenth-century culture of politeness 'promoted openness and accessibility, but at the same time set strict standards of decorum for merchants and manufacturers to live up to' (Vickery 1998: 38). 'Avoid proverbial expressions and trite sayings', Lord Chesterfield (1694–1773) wrote to his son, they are 'the rhetoric of a vulgar man . . . A man of fashion takes great care to speak very correctly and grammatically and to pronounce properly' (Roberts 1992: 162–3). There were more English grammars published between 1750 and 1800 than there were in the whole of the previous two centuries (Crystal 2004: 396). They covered such matters as spelling, pronunciation and what counted as correct or incorrect usage.

The two most influential were Robert Lowth's *Short Introduction to English Grammar* (1761) and Lindley Murray's *English Grammar* (1795). Murray's was the most popular but it also demonstrates just how hard it is to legislate on language use. For example, he tells us that 'Pronouns must always agree with their antecedents' which he then follows with the remark that 'of this rule there are many violations to be met with' (in Crystal 2004: 398). Many of these violations were committed by writers. 'The English language', Lowth thunders, 'as it stands in the writings of our most approved authors, oftentimes offends against every part of grammar' (ibid.: 397). What a change have we here. Once poetry was used to illustrate correct speech and writing, now it is so many errors. And yet what we have is only the appearance of change, for Lowth's remark is merely another example of the age-old tension between rhetoric and grammar, the former allowing more latitude in writing than the latter.

In general, though, the emphasis is less on literature as a form of rhetoric or grammar than as an expression of the nation. 'The chief glory of every people', states Johnson, 'arises from its authors' (Greene 1984: 327). True, there are still those who believe that literature has a role to play in shaping behaviour. Thomas Sheridan (1719–88), for example, father of the playwright Richard Sheridan (1751–1816) and a key figure in the elocution movement, argued in his *British Education: or the Source of Disorders in Great Britain* (1756) that the literary heritage could be the basis for polite instruction, but the trend is more towards constructing a canon that captures or rather creates, the national character. A common notion is that the canon is elitist, but this is not the case in the eighteenth century. Thomas Percy's *Reliques of Ancient English Poetry* (1765), for example, a three-volume collection of English ballads and popular songs dating back to the Middle Ages not only established the ballad as a valid literary form but also 'presented the case for a national literature with a long and illustrious history by means of a series of learned essays on a variety of English literary topics, such as medieval alliteration and metrical romances'.[27]

Addison's essays on Milton's *Paradise Lost* (1712) are an early example of canon-making. Addison does not use the term 'canon' but the fact that he thinks Milton should have a wider audience implies that *Paradise Lost* is relevant to the culture at large – which is one of the assumptions behind canon formation. The criteria for inclusion in the putative canon appear to be beauty and respect for the rules of classical writing. Addison's approach is to compare Milton's epic with Homer's *Iliad* and Virgil's *Aeneid*. He argues that the action of *Paradise Lost* has greater unity than either the *Iliad* or the *Aeneid* and that it is greater because 'it does not determine the Fate of single Persons or Nations, but of a whole Species' (Steele and Addison 1988: 415). Addison also claims that we find far more novelty and variety in the characters of *Paradise Lost* than in either of the ancient epics. But he is also aware of the faults of Milton's poem. The first is 'that the Event of it is unhappy' which, while that is 'most perfect for Tragedy, is not so proper for an Heroick Poem' (ibid.: 424–5). The second is that Adam is not a proper hero because he 'is unsuccessful and by no means a match for his Enemies' (ibid.: 425). In addition, Milton has offended against probability by including the allegorical figures of Sin and Death, a judgement more in the spirit of Edmund Spenser than Homer. He is also rather too fond of digressions and of displaying his considerable learning. Finally, his language is laboured and he uses too many 'technical words' (ibid.: 429).

Although Addison mentions Milton's faults, he believes that a critic should 'dwell rather upon Excellencies than Imperfections' (Steele and Addison 1988: 423). It is his job to 'discover the concealed Beauties of a Writer and communicate to the World such Things as are worth their Observation' (ibid.: 423). The critic is able to perceive more than the average person because he is acquainted with French and Italian critics and is well versed in the Greek and Latin poets. He is also has 'a logical head' and the ability to communicate clearly (ibid.: 422). Milton is judged by how well he conforms to the generic specifications of ancient literature and the emphasis falls on what is good rather than what is bad about his epic. Addison has little interest in the problems of editing *Paradise Lost*[28] and there is no attempt to place Milton in the context of his time or to consider his politics. But perhaps this was understandable since to do so would stir memories of the Civil War.

There is no suggestion of elitism in Addison's criticism. This is evident not only from him wanting to make the pleasures of Milton more widely available but also from his comments on the traditional ballad, *Chevy Chase*, which tells of the earl of Northumberland riding his men over the earl of Douglas's land in pursuit of game and the bloody battle that ensued. An 'ordinary Song or Ballad that is the delight of the common People, cannot fail please all such Readers . . . and the Reason is plain, because the same paintings of Nature which recommend it to the most ordinary Reader, will appear beautiful to the most refined' (Steele and Addison 1988: 350). An observation which suggests that truth to nature would appear to be another criterion for inclusion in the canon. The critic's learning does not set him apart from his audience. It is what enables him to give expression to the common experience. Anyone

> who brings with him any implicit Notions and Observations which he has made in his reading of the Poets, will find his own reflections methodised and explained, and perhaps several little Hints that had passed in his Mind, perfected and improved. (ibid.: 421)

This is a far cry from the situation today where experts talk over the heads of ordinary readers to other experts and where they discover not beauty but class, gender, ethnic or sexual bias.

Addison's interest in Milton is a reminder that the canon is based on the assumption that the literature of the past has a value. But what is that value? And is it relative to the period in which the work was written or is it relevant for all time? Addison appears to believe that Milton transcends the upheavals of the seventeenth century. The virtues of *Paradise Lost* are a more polished version of those found in the *Iliad* and the *Aeneid* and so Milton is part of a classical tradition that history cannot diminish. By the mid-century, a different attitude prevails. Thomas Warton (1728–90) who had a fondness for beer and was described by Fanny Burney's younger sister as 'the greatest clod I ever saw' made his name with *Observations on the Fairie Queen of Spenser* (1754). Warton begins by measuring Spenser's poem against the standard of the ancient epic. 'Sensible as he was of the importance of the unity of the hero and of his design', writes Warton, Spenser did 'not seem convinced of the necessity of that unity of action, by the means of which such a design should be properly accomplished' (Sigworth 1971: 358). For example, the poem is divided into twelve books, each one recounting a different adventure, which violates the epic requirement of unity of action.

But then comes the twist. Warton tells his readers that it is 'absurd' to judge Spenser 'by precepts which [he] did not attend to' (Sigworth 1971: 364). We must appreciate his work in the context of his time, which, unlike Warton's own, valued 'the various and the marvellous' (ibid.: 364). The difference from Addison is clear. He downplayed the context in which Milton wrote whereas Warton argues that we cannot understand the 'merits and manners' of Spenser without considering 'the customs and genius of his age' (ibid.: 366). So, too, Johnson who pronounces that 'to judge rightly of an author we must transport ourselves to his time, and examine what were the wants of his contemporaries and the means of supplying them' (Greene 1984: 717). Neither observation is new. The recognition that we can't read works from the past as if they were written in the present was very much a feature of Renaissance criticism, which itself was the culmination of a tendency, beginning in the thirteenth century, to read them historically rather than allegorically. Once more we are witness to a shift of emphasis rather than a radical departure. The history of criticism is like a pendulum that swings from the materiality of the text to the meaning of the text and back again. As in the eighteenth century, so in the Renaissance, the perception of the difference of the past spurred the development of editing techniques which, in turn, led to a more informed understanding of how the past *was* different, as we saw in the case of Theobald's Shakespeare.

Part of the value of a canon is that it has a meaning and significance for the present. A potential problem of scholarship is that it fixes the work too firmly in the past for it to speak to us. To which the response is that the work can only can speak to us if it has been properly edited. An obscure, fragmented one stutters, stammers, or remains silent. But this implies that the work speaks to us spontaneously, which of course it doesn't. We ventriloquise it. Yet that's not quite true either. The term 'conversation' better captures our relation to a Chaucer[29] or a Shakespeare. And we know we are in the presence of a canonical author when our conversation with him or her does not come to an end. This commonplace has its origins in the need to justify the study of literature once it had ceased to have a direct input into social life. That justification lay in the richness of its significations. The case of Shakespeare is instructive. Up to the mid-eighteenth century Shakespeare was staged according to the tenets of neoclassicism. But after the Seven Years War (1756–63) there was a patriotic turn away from performing Shakespeare according to the rules of French drama. Responsibility for interpreting his work now fell to editors who justified their existence by finding ever more meanings in his plays. The ability of readers to appreciate these was a sign of their cultivation and distance from the vulgar.

But to return to the metaphor of conversation. It brings out the human dimension of our relationship with literature, which was almost lost in the heady days of theory. And that human side comes out clearly in Johnson's *The Lives of the Most Eminent English Poets* (1779–81). The very title speaks of the selection process that is a feature of canon making. But Johnson is also interested in the lives of the poets whose work he describes. Thus we learn that Pope 'slumbered at his own table while the Prince of Wales was talking of poetry', that the 'great fault' of William Collins (1721–59) was his 'irresolution' and that Swift had 'a kind of muddy complexion' and 'practised a peculiar and offensive parsimony without disguise or apology' (Johnson 1984: 726 and 759; 1843?: 368). Johnson does not spell out the relation between art and life but it is fairly obvious he sees a connection between, for example, Akenside's 'unnecessary and outrageous zeal for what he called liberty' and a style where 'words are multiplied till the sense is hardly perceived' (Johnson 1843?: 493 and 495). And he encourages his readers to view poems as a reflection of the poet's 'mind and the complexion of [his] life' (ibid.: 482). Literature for Johnson is a transaction between writer and reader. The learning of the metaphysical poets instructs, 'but the reader commonly thinks his improvement dearly bought' (1984: 678, 1711). *Paradise Lost* has 'a want of human interest' while Shakespeare can cure the reader of 'the phantoms which other writers have raised up before him' because he gives 'human sentiments in human language' (ibid.: 422–3).

The common reader is the final arbiter of literary worth. This creature is largely a fictional creation used to boost the authority of Johnson's own opinions, but he embodies the principle of a cultural community in which everyone has a say and in which everyone has a responsibility for standards. The clearest expression of the relation between the critic and this community comes at the end of Johnson's essay on Thomas Gray (1716–71), author of the famous *Elegy Written in a Country Churchyard* (1751).

> In the character of his *Elegy* I rejoice to concur with the common reader; for by the common sense of readers uncorrupted by literary prejudices, after all the refinements of subtlety and the dogmatism of learning, must be finally decided all claim to poetical honours. The *Churchyard* abounds with images that find a mirror in every mind and with sentiments to which every bosom returns an echo. (Johnson 1984: 768–9)

The mirage we call the canon is here the product of a republic of readers. To regard it as a tool of oppression misses the historical point that literature might be seen as a source of unity for a divided nation, or even a middle class in search of its own identity. Being in trade does not make you a dictator, owning a shop does not make you an oppressor. We should try to follow Warton's and Johnson's advice and not impose our own way of seeing on the past.

Too much learning, a drawn-out analysis and an unthinking acceptance of the prevailing literary norms are all detrimental to true criticism. What, then, should a true critic seek? To be open and receptive and to give the work his or her full attention. Any attempt to legislate how literature should be is a denial of its nature and inevitably involves the critic in contradiction. Take the case of Johnson who stipulates that: the poet should 'gather his notions from reality, not from the copies of authors but the originals of Nature' (1984:

733); the reflections of the writer should be 'consonant with the general sense or experience of mankind'; poetic language should be close to 'common use'; the style should be 'well suited to the thought', diction should be 'elegant', verse should be 'measured' and rhyme 'correspondent' (1843?: 367, 452, 461, 500,). And yet these virtues did not prevent Johnson from praising those which were seemingly opposite. 'The highest praise of genius is original invention' (1984: 716); Young's *Night Thoughts* is 'excellent' because it is a 'wilderness . . . in which the fertility of fancy scatters flowers of every hue and every odour' (1843?: 489). Nor does Johnson object that the poem is written in blank verse.

Such contrary valuations are a reminder that criticism is an incurably pragmatic affair. But if we are to have an understanding of literature beyond the individual work – and how can we have an understanding of that without this wider vision? – we must classify and organise but always be prepared to adjust and even abandon our fond schemes. Joseph Warton divided English poetry into four categories. First was the sublime and the pathetic, second the moral and the ethical, third was poetry that used wit, taste and fancy in 'describing familiar life' and, finally there were 'mere versifiers' (Sigworth 1971: 293). With this classification we move away from the traditional hierarchy of genres to a new hierarchy of sensibility. But Warton's classification of poets does not command universal assent anymore than Johnson's list of eminent poets. To put this another way, there is no agreement about the canon or the criteria for inclusion. Contemporary attacks on the canon assume the existence of a fixed body of works that simply did not and does not exist. The real point is that, during the course of the eighteenth century, the view of literature changes from a body of writing that teaches to a body of writing that is taught.

## Conclusion

In the medieval period, commentators were concerned with the interpretation of literature and its effect on behaviour. In the Renaissance, there was less concern with the process of interpretation and more with how literature achieved its effects. In the late seventeenth and eighteenth century, attention shifts first to imitation and then to imagination and, throughout, there is a growing interest in the beauties of literature. At the same time, the term literature comes to be identified with imaginative writing more than a mere knowledge of letters. But, most important from our point of view, is that this is the period in which criticism is established as a discipline in its own right. It is charged with the task of justifying the study of literature now that literature has lost its social role of shaping behaviour. This role was limited to the court and now that literature is sold in the marketplace there is a danger that it will become one commodity among many. To prevent this literature is presented as a source of self-development, cultivation and refinement that separates it from other consumer goods (see Ross 2000: 2005). Those who are most likely to benefit from it are members of the middling sort who turn to things English in order to define themselves against a cosmopolitan aristocracy, which means that literature is also responsible for defining the spirit of the nation.

It is not just any literature that can fulfil these requirements. It has to be of a fairly complex nature. The fact that Shakespeare and Milton have to be annotated, glossed and referenced provides a justification for the study of imaginative writing and enhances its status as an intellectual discipline. Those authors who do not need to be edited do not enjoy the same high status as the Shakespeares and Miltons and we start to get a divide between high and low culture that will become an increasing concern of criticism. The relative democracy of taste gives way to the authority of the expert who has mastered the techniques of textual criticism (Patey 1997b: 11). The process of editing itself in some way parallels the development of capitalism. The idea that the work accumulates meaning sits well with an economy that accumulates wealth. The editor must manage meanings as the business man must manage his investments. This sounds far-fetched but for the links we have shown between literary and monetary language in our discussion of imitation and the imagination. These rhetorical connections suggest that culture and economics are not finally distinct. It is important to recognise this because much thinking about criticism and literature is based on a division, to put it crudely, between culture and cash that is simply not sustainable. Even the new interest in the imagination can be seen as the intensification of inner life as the integrated individual in a community gives way to the isolated individual of consumerism.

## Notes

1. An abridged version of this can be found online at <http://www.gutenberg.org/files/1564/1564-h/1564-h.htm>
2. See Marks 1968: 32–5.
3. For a good introduction to some of the magazines of the period, see Bond 1957. The collection includes an essay on *The Female Spectator*, showing that women's writing did not go entirely unnoticed until the 1970s.
4. The terms imagination and fancy were interchangeable until the end of the eighteenth century. Addison, for example, writes 'by the pleasures of imagination or Fancy (which I shall use promiscuously) . . . '. See Steele and Addison 1988: 368. But fancy wasn't the only term used for the imagination. Dryden defined 'wit' as 'the faculty of imagination in the writer' (in Sigworth 1971: 62).
5. Dryden sounds a different note. He says that the court is one reason for the improvement in the language. '[W]hence is it that our conversation is so much refined? I must freely and without flattery ascribe it to the court . . . At

[the king's] return, he found a nation lost as much in barbarism as in rebellion; and, as the excellency of his nature forgave the one, so the excellency of his manners reformed the other. The desire of imitating so great a pattern first awakened the dull and heavy spirits of the English from their natural reservedness; loosed them from their stiff forms of conversation, and made them easy and pliant to one another in discourse.' 'Dramatic Poetry of the Last Age', in Dryden 1954: 106.

6. For a brief history of the South Sea Stock Company, see Carswell 1960.

7. For an introduction to Grub Street, see Heaney 2006, from which these quotes are taken.

8. The key text here is Brewer 1997; but see too Bermingham and Brewer 1995.

9. For a comprehensive coverage of the topic, see Levine 1994. See also Patey 1997a.

10. See Roberts 1996.

11. One of Dennis's tragedies, a violent attack on the French in harmony with popular prejudice, entitled *Liberty Asserted,* was produced with great success at Lincoln's Inn Fields in 1704. His sense of his own importance approached mania, and he is said to have desired the Duke of Marlborough to have a special clause inserted into the Treaty of Utrecht (1713) to secure him from French vengeance. Marlborough pointed out that, although he himself had been a still greater enemy of the French nation, he had no fear for his own security. See <http://en. wikipedia.org/wiki/John_Dennis>.

12. See <http://encyclopedia.jrank.org/RON_SAC/RYMER_THOMAS_16411713_ .html>

13. See Kenneth Muir 1976.

14. See Bordieu 1984 and Day 2001.

15. Leo Boo was the second son of Abbe Thulle, chief of one of the Palau Islands, now known as the Republic of Belau. One captain Wilson and his crew were ship wrecked there and, in return for his help in providing materials for a new vessel, Wilson agreed to take Lee Boo back to England so he could become an Englishman. He died there of small pox in 1784. For further details see <http://www.stmary rotherhithe.org/prince-lee-boo.php>. For more details see Black 2005: 226–7 and Langford 1984: 414.

16. The quote is taken from the online text of *The Age of Reason* available at <http://www.ushistory.org/paine/reason/reason2.htm>.

17. Shaftesbury seems to have overlooked the fact that one of the favourite pastimes of the upper classes was, in the common phrase, for 'hunting, shooting and fishing'.

18. For a full discussion of the Scottish contribution to the study of English literature, see Crawford 2000 and Crawford 1998.

19. In one sense, though we are moving back; for the idea we experience poetry through the senses is reminiscent of Plutarch's comparison of reading with eating and drinking.

20. An online edition of *An Essay Concerning Human Understanding* can be found at <http://oregonstate.edu/instruct/phl302/texts/locke/locke1/Book2a.html#Chapter %20I>, from which this and the other quotes in this paragraph are taken.

21. See also Lord Chesterfield: 'There are wretches in this world profligate enough to explode all moral notions of good and evil; to maintain they are merely local, and depend entirely upon the customs and fashions of different countries'. Roberts 1992: 192–3.

22. For a full discussion of these terms, see Pocock 1985.

23. For an account of the misery many endured, see Thompson 1993.

24. On this point, see Dalrymple 'Trash, Violence and Versace: But is it Art?' in Dalrymple 2005: 140–52.

25. England and Scotland were united under one crown when James I, who was also James VI of Scotland, acceded to the throne in 1603. James called himself king of Great Britain. The Act of 1707 abolished the separate parliaments of England and Scotland and created one new parliament of Great Britain. The United Kingdom, as we tend to refer to Britain today, did not come into being until union with Ireland in 1801. However, in 1921, the greater part of Ireland gained independence leaving only northern Ireland still part of 'Great Britain'.

26. Newman 1987.

27. Nick Groom, 'Reliques of Ancient English Poetry', *The Literary Encyclopedia*, <http://www.litencyc.com/php/sworks.php?rec=true&UID=2420>.

28. For an example of the sort of problems encountered in editing Milton and the various views of editors of his work, see the section 'Editing Milton', in Womersley 1997.

29. Marcus Walsh examines how editorial techniques develop in the course of the century by comparing two different editions of Chaucer, one begun by John Urry (1666–1715) and finished by Timothy Thomas and one by Thomas Tyrwhitt (1730–86). See Walsh 2001.

# CHAPTER

## 5

# ENGLISH ROMANTIC, MORAL AND AESTHETIC CRITICISM

It was not unknown for book reviews in the nineteenth century to be 30,000 words long. We have to use far less than that to cover the entire period. Another difficulty is trying to balance comments about individual authors with an account of the wider context that helps determine the character of criticism in any given period. In previous chapters, we have glanced at how politics, the Church, schools, the court, the vernacular and the market have shaped the discussion of literature. In the nineteenth century, mechanistic conceptions of man and nature, social divisions, the growth of public opinion and the challenge to religious faith all have an impact on the nature of criticism. The decline of religious faith is particularly significant because it marks the end of the centuries old connection between the development of criticism and the study of the Bible and, in the process, it confers a new significance on literature itself. We need to sketch these various contexts if we are to have a better understanding of what critics have to say about literature. And we can sum up the development of literature in this period by saying that it moves from a concern with the self in romanticism to the condition of England in realism and back to the self again in aestheticism and decadence. Or, to put it more succinctly, we pass from literature as imagination to literature as impression.

## Some Contexts

In the seventeenth century, Thomas Hobbes described the body as a mechanism; in the nineteenth century, Thomas Carlyle (1795–1881) describes the entire age as 'mechanical' (Keating 1981: 47). 'Nothing is now done directly, or by hand; all is by rule and calculated contrivance' (ibid.: 47). The machine conditions not only our physical life but also our mental and spiritual one. There are machines for education, religion and politics. That is, the principles on which these institutions are conducted are becoming more mechanical in nature. Education, for example, 'that mysterious communing of Wisdom with Ignorance, is no longer an indefinable, tentative process, requiring a study of individual aptitudes, and a perpetual variation of means and methods, to attain the same end; but a secure, universal, straightforward business, to be conducted in the gross, by proper mechanism' (ibid.: 48). We can only wonder at what Carlyle would make of the paraphernalia of teaching and learning and quality assurance that characterises education today. In the early nineteenth century, criticism defines literature against mechanical conceptions of man and nature; a difficult task since, according to Samuel Taylor Coleridge (1772–1834), language itself has been 'mechanised' by the 'artificial state of society and social intercourse' (2006: 37). And if that was true then, how much more so is it now.

In the eighteenth century, Edmund Burke had declared that 'The age of chivalry is gone [and] that of sophisters, economists, and calculators, has succeeded' ([1790] 1986). In the nineteenth century, Karl Marx (1818–83) and Friedrich Engels (1820–95) announce that:

> The bourgeoisie, whenever it has got the upper hand, has put an end to all feudal, patriarchal, idyllic relations. It has pitilessly torn asunder the motley feudal ties that bound man to his natural superiors and has left remaining no other nexus between man and man than naked self-interest, than callous cash-payment. It has drowned the most heavenly ecstasies of religious fervour, of chivalrous enthusiasm, of philistine sentimentalism in the icy waters of egotistical calculation. (2002: 222)

The conservative philosopher and the communist revolutionaries both agree that there has been a profound change in the social order. The economy has become more important than society. Although we cannot separate the two, we can distinguish between them. In very crude terms, the economy is based on money and society on morality. The art of government is to find a balance between the two but, since 'the commercial revolution of the thirteenth century' (Kaye 1998: 15),[1] the need for profit has progressively eroded the claims of ethics, welfare and general happiness. Carlyle says that the pursuit of wealth has 'altered the old relations and increased the distance between the rich and the poor' (Keating 1981: 48). Marx and Engels go much further, declaring that Europe is going to split 'into two great hostile camps, into two great classes directly facing each other: Bourgeois and Proletariat' (2002: 220). The nineteenth century has woken up from the eighteenth-century dream that commerce would unify society. Trade has tried to make men realize the brotherhood of humanity, wrote Oscar Wilde (1854–1900), 'but it failed' (Small 1979: 96–7). Now we must look to criticism to 'make us cosmopolitan' (ibid.).

The various divisions of nineteenth-century Britain inform the criticism of this period if only because the novel, in particular, concerns itself with the problem of the 'two nations'.[2] But there is something else which we need to mention here. It is one of the arguments of this book that criticism draws increasingly on the idiom and imagery of money. This becomes a problem in the nineteenth century as commentators insist on the integrity of the human in the face of the dehumanising effects of industrialisation. It is a problem because the language of criticism borrows from that of commerce and therefore the two discourses cannot simply be opposed to one another. Matthew Arnold pitches the 'free play of mind' (Keating 1981: 196) against the practical man of business, but the very phrase chimes with the latter's cry of 'free trade'. Walter Bagehot (1826–77), author of some of the most exquisite criticism of the period, was responsible for a book on the workings of the money market, *Lombard Street* (1873) and he was also editor of the *Economist* magazine (f. 1843). Critics may define the values of literature against those of commerce but in doing so they fail to recognise not only the connection between the one and the other but also their own complicity in the discourse of trade. They thus participate in the very deformations of the human of which they complain. The relation between criticism and commerce is similar to the relation between one period of criticism and another; in both cases, there are similarities which we need to understand if we are better to appreciate the differences.

There was a positive perception of the public realm in the eighteenth century but this changes in the nineteenth. Largely the domain of the middle-class male, it was characterised by freedom, reason and self-cultivation. It was a space in which a particular kind of individual could flourish. Then two things happen. First, the growth of industrial society in which, says John Stuart Mill (1806–73), 'power passes from the individual to the masses and the weight and importance of an individual, as compared with the mass, sink into greater and greater insignificance' (Keating 1981: 78). Second, the public realm becomes public opinion, a term Charlotte Brontë (1816–55) struggles to understand, calling it a 'vague personification' (Faulkner 1989: 109). It is no longer the sphere where the individual grows but where he or she is controlled. At least according to Carlyle, who compares the role of public opinion to that of the 'Police' and, in words that resonate in our own surveillance society, he claims that it 'watches over us with its Argus eyes more keenly than ever' (Keating 1981: 64). Mill has a different view. Public opinion is a good thing but only in a small society where everyone knows everyone else. It is a body of wisdom that guides individuals in their choices. But, in mass society, where no-one knows anyone else, public opinion loses its authority, leaving individuals, the press and business to manipulate it to their advantage.

Mill gives the example of a trader in a small country town whose reputation has been tried and tested and compares him with a man setting up a business in a big city. If such a person trusted solely to 'the quality of his goods' then he may go for ten years 'without a customer' (Keating 1981: 86). In order to survive he has to give his commodities ' "a gloss, a saleable look" ' (ibid.: 87). It is all very well, says Mill, to complain about 'quackery' and 'puffing' but, in a crowded marketplace, 'any voice not pitched in an exaggerated key is lost in the hubbub' (ibid.: 87). Success, in such circumstances, depends not on what a person is, but on what he seems to be. The art of invention is no longer the preserve of the poet. The imagination is integrated into commercial life. It is the tool of the advertiser. Its powers are used, not to create new worlds, but to distort the facts of this one. Inspiration has become a selling technique.

The general effect of all this, says Mill, is the erosion of truth and standards and nowhere is this clearer than in literature. We have to read a great deal of material in order to know what is happening in the world, but this means that nothing is 'read slowly or twice over' (ibid.: 88). Authors are therefore content to dash their works off quickly. There is no point in labouring over their sentences if they are only going to be skimmed. 'Literature is becoming more and more ephemeral: books, of any solidity, are almost gone by; even reviews are not now considered sufficiently light; the attention cannot sustain itself on any serious subject, even for the space of a review-article' (ibid.: 89).[3] This is an early instance of the dumbing-down thesis and it is echoed later in the century by Bagehot when he writes that 'we live in the realm of the *half* educated' (1916: 350). The number of readers may be increasing, he notes, but not their quality. They are 'scattered', 'headless' and need guidance for, left to themselves, 'they take not pure art but showy art' (ibid.: 351). The concern is that mass society and increased literacy, in the words of Mill, 'weaken the influence of the more cultivated few over the many' (Keating 1981: 88). Of course we could put this the other way round, and say that, as more people learn to read and think for themselves, the less they need direction from their 'betters'.

Be that as it may, Mill's suggestion that the modern reader has no time to concentrate properly on any one work because there are so many he or she feels obliged to peruse has implications for both literature and criticism. Literature, he observes, has become 'a mere reflection of the current sentiments, and has almost entirely abandoned its mission as an enlightener and improver of them' (Keating 1981: 89). But those who wish to save literature from such a fate do have a choice. Instead of reflecting current sentiments, they can write about how literature reflects on itself, making that a principle of its construction. This leads to literature becoming complex, intricate and even obscure. The change begins towards the end of century. We can see it in Henry James's (1843–1916) reflections on the nature of form, 'the beginning and the end of the art of the novelist' (Hoffman and Hynes, 1966: 300), and in Arthur Symons's (1865–1945) characterisation of symbolist literature as being 'conscious of itself' (Guy 1998: 412). Such musings come to a head in modernism, the revenge of intellect on mass society.

The decline of religious faith also affects perceptions of art. It is true that the Victorian period was a great age of church building and restoration. It is also true that the evangelical movement (1789–1850) and the Oxford Movement (1833–45) kept Christianity at the forefront of public life.[4] In particular, the evangelicals – the term literally means of or pertaining to the gospel – were a significant presence in the campaigns against slavery and child labour but many found the passionate emphasis on original sin, hell and everlasting punishment morally repellent. One such was the inventor of the phrase 'the survival of the fittest', Herbert Spencer (1820–1903), who wrote in his *Autobiography* (1904) of his disdain for 'a deity who is pleased with the singing of his praises and angry with the beings he has made when they fail to tell him perpetually of his greatness' (in Gilmour 1993: 87). The criticism of Christian morality was not new nor, indeed, were the scientific objections to parts of the Bible. In the eighteenth century, there was a reaction against the rigours of Puritanism and doubts were cast on the accuracy of the Old Testament. The dimensions of Noah's ark seemed far too small to accommodate all the animals. What was new in the nineteenth century was geology and the theory of evolution.

The Geological Society was formed in 1807 and its most famous member was the extremely short-sighted Charles Lyell (1797–1875). His most influential work, *Principles of Geology* published in three volumes between 1830 and 1833, was a contribution to the debate between Catastrophists and Uniformitarians. The former believed that the earth was shaped by cataclysmic events, the latter that it was formed gradually over time. Lyell was on the side of the Uniformitarians and his intervention was decisive, despite some errors such as denying the existence of ice ages. Lyell built on the insights of James Hutton (1726–97) whom a biographer described as being 'almost entirely innocent of rhetorical accomplishments' (Bryson 2003: 90). Hutton explained that heat within the earth was responsible for thrusting up mountain ranges. Such processes required huge amounts of time and so the world must be far older than six thousand years, the number suggested by Archbishop James Ussher (1581–1656) who arrived at this figure after careful study of the Bible and other historical sources. The age of the earth, the changing character of the continents and, of course, the need to explain the existence of fossils all undermined the idea that God had made the world in seven days. 'If only the geologists would let me alone', cried the art critic John Ruskin (1819–1900), 'those dreadful hammers. I hear the clink of them at the end of every cadence of the Bible verses' (in Dawkins 2006: 118).

Lyell was a big influence on Charles Darwin (1809–82) who took a copy of the first volume of Lyell's *Principles of Geology* when he set out for the Galapagos islands on board the *Beagle* in 1831, and it was with Lyell's backing that Darwin read his first paper to the Geological Society on 4 January 1837. The theory of evolution, that species grow, develop and change into forms quite different from their initial state, did not originate with Darwin. A version of it can be traced back to the Greek philosopher Anaximander (610–546 BC) who believed that life began in warm mud or slime and that its development was characterised by conflict. But it wasn't until the eighteenth century that the theory was given scientific expression by the French naturalist, Jean-Baptiste Lamarck (1744–1829). Darwin's main contribution to the understanding of evolution was the idea of natural selection, whereby successful organisms, those with some advantage in the competition for food, passed on their genes to the next generation, leaving the unsuccessful ones to die out. The publication of *The Origin of Species* in 1859 was in part prompted by the work of a friend and admirer of Darwin, Alfred Russel Wallace (1823–1913), whose essay 'On the Tendency of Varieties to Depart Indefinitely from the Original Type' (1858) contained many of the same ideas. Lyell urged Darwin to publish first in case Wallace should be credited with the discovery. The book sparked a controversy which continues to this day. The claim that species evolve, that it is possible to trace human ancestry back to apes, clashed dramatically with the story of God's creation of Adam in his own image.

In 1856, R. H. Hutton (1826–97), one of the most influential critics of the second half of the nineteenth century, and assistant editor of the *Economist*, argued that theology, the study of God, and literature, the study of man, go hand in hand. Theology provides literature with a vision of what man is and what he might be, while literature provides theology with a concrete expression of its central truths (see Skilton 1993: 71). But it was difficult to maintain such thinking in the face of the findings of geology and the theory of evolution. Each cast doubt on the claims of Scripture. A world without religion seems cold and comfortless. Arnold describes it as one without 'certitude, nor peace, nor help for pain', while Alfred Tennyson (1809–92) shrinks at the thought that love is not 'Creation's final law' but 'Nature red in tooth and claw' (Ricks 1987: 27 and 305). One of the most haunting paintings of the period is William Dyce's *Pegwell Bay: A Recollection of October 5ᵗʰ 1858*. The area was particularly rich in fossils and Dyce's scattered figures suggest they are lost not just in the immensity of geological time but also, as a comet streaks faintly across the sky, in the vastness of the cosmos too. The decline of religious faith meant that art, which historically illustrated, interpreted or complemented doctrine itself, now became the source of meaning and significance in human existence – though in one sense this was a return to its roots. Had not drama grown out of ritual? Was not the poet the purveyor of celestial verities? By the end of the century Symons was proclaiming that literature had turned away from the real world and become 'a kind of religion, with all the duties and responsibilities of the sacred ritual' (Guy 1998: 413). The spiritual character of art changes the nature of criticism. Wilde says that, instead of explaining a work of art, criticism should 'deepen its mystery', that it should 'raise round it, and round its maker, that mist of wonder which is dear to both gods and worshippers alike' (Small 1979: 74).

Earlier in the century Arnold identified religion with culture because they share a common goal; 'the aim of setting ourselves to ascertain what perfection is and to make it prevail' and both 'seek determination of this question through all the voices of human experience . . . of art, science, poetry, philosophy, [and] history' (1993: 61). The kingdom of God and culture, says Arnold, are both 'internal conditions', for the quest for perfection is to do with thought and feeling 'as distinguished from our animality' (ibid.: 63). Once again we encounter the split between mind and body which runs through the history of criticism. In our time we favour the body over the mind as evidenced in our obsession with diet, exercise and cosmetic surgery, which may make it hard to sympathise with Arnold's idea of perfection. For him it was serenity of mind, for us it is a flat stomach. The part criticism plays in helping us to achieve Arnold's ideal is to establish an order of ideas which art can present 'in the most effective and attractive combinations' (Keating 1981: 189). The faith of the Christian allowed him or her to transcend mere worldly considerations and, while culture cannot compensate for the loss of heaven, it does provide a transcendence of its own. Criticism should resist all attempts to translate ideas into practice, while the notion of 'the free play of the mind upon all subjects', derived from the philosopher Immanuel Kant (1724–1804), temporarily releases the individual from the realm of practical affairs.

If criticism was part of the solution to the decline of religious faith, it was also part of the problem. Along with the Enlightenment critique of the truth content of the Old and New Testaments, the development of biblical scholarship undermined the sacred status of Scripture. Scholars examined such matters as authorship and dating, intention, inherent sense, the act of translation, the development of languages, the process of canon-formation, the linguistic and cultural contexts of the Scriptures and especially their roots in myth, legend and literary tradition. The 'lower' and 'higher' criticism of the nineteenth century further refine the process of textual investigation. The aim of 'lower' criticism is to establish the original version of the text while that of the 'higher' is to investigate the contexts in which it was written and read. The assumption is that the Bible is an historical work and should be approached in the same way as other ancient texts. If it is looked at as a statement of truth it is inconsistent and often absurd but, if it is looked at as literature, it has sense and coherence.

One of the pioneers in this field was Robert Lowth (1710–87), who showed that Hebrew poetry of the Old Testament depended on 'parallelism'[5] rather than the rhythm or rhyme of European poetry, and that it was best understood by becoming acquainted with 'the language of this people, their manners, discipline, rites and ceremonies . . . even their inmost sentiments and thoughts' (in Jasper and Prickett 2004: 26). Similar developments were occurring in Germany and the ideas of thinkers like Friedrich Schleiermacher (1768–1834), who argued that we can never know a work only interpret it, were introduced into England by Coleridge. The most notorious example of 'higher' criticism was David Strauss's (1808–74) *Life of Jesus* (1835),[6] translated into English in 1846 by Marian Evans, who did not yet call herself George Eliot (1819–80). Strauss repudiated the notion of Christ's divinity and said his miracles should be understood as myths not facts. If there were no miracles, there was no resurrection and human life ended at death.

### Romanticism: Mechanism, Mass Society and Political Economy

Like Carlyle, a number of romantic poets were worried about the impact of industrialism. Raymond Williams argues that William Blake (1757–1827), Percy Shelley (1792–1822) and William Wordsworth (1770–1850) used their art to 'uphold certain human values, capacities and energies which they felt industrialisation was threatening or even destroying' ([1958] 1975: 53). They emphasised the whole person against man as a specialised instrument of production, the importance of human relationships against competitive individualism and the eternal truths of the imagination against the transience of political economy. Blake declares that machines were 'destructive of humanity and art' (in Ackroyd 1996: 309), Coleridge bemoans 'political economy' and the 'general contagion of its mechanic philosophy' (Kitson 1989: 82) and Shelley says that its operations will 'exasperate the extremes of luxury and want' (Hoffman and Hynes 1966: 183). This hostile attitude to the emerging industrial society may explain two features of romantic poetry, its preoccupation with nature and the individual.

The process of art is seen as organic compared to the mechanical nature of production. John Keats (1795–1821) states that 'if Poetry come not as naturally as the Leaves to a tree, it had better not come at all' (Kitson 1989: 104) and Coleridge says that it recalls 'those products of the vegetable world where gorgeous blossoms rise out of the hard and thorny rind and shell within which the rich fruit was elaborating' (1986: 180), an image he elaborates in an essay on Shakespeare entitled 'Vital Genius and Mechanical Talent' (1818).[7] Nature, not divine inspiration, is becoming the new creative principle of poetry, though there are those like Blake and Shelley who continue to insist that it is the gift of God. The imagery of nature in romantic accounts of poetry stands for life and vitality and growth but it lends itself to appropriation by conservative thinkers who, by presenting the social order, as 'natural' imply that it cannot be changed. Indeed there is a close connection between Edmund Burke's idea of society and Coleridge's idea of poetry since both should balance and reconcile 'opposite or discordant qualities, sameness with difference [and] a sense of novelty and freshness with old or customary objects' (1986: 227).

The romantic idea of the individual is partly a reaction to the idea that only science can know the truth of things and partly to the growth of mass society which threatened to absorb the individual into the crowd. Blake opposes spiritual truth to the scientific kind in the lines:

The Atoms of Democritus
And Newton's Particles of Light
Are sands upon the Red sea shore
Where Israel's tents do shine so bright (1975: 67)

and he makes the idea that everyone sees differently the basis of his art, 'I see Everything I paint in this World, but Everybody does not see alike . . . As a man is, so he sees' (Kitson 1989: 37). The value placed on the individual is a new phenomenon in the history of literature. Historically, the purpose of art was not self-expression but to encourage readers to imitate models of excellence. Individuals have always existed, but the *idea* of the individual comes to prominence when commercial pressure causes hierarchies to crumble, forcing people to forge their own identity. The appearance of the individual is therefore tied to the development of capitalism. It isn't simply the invention of romanticism. Indeed some of the conceptions of the individual that we find in romanticism reveal the peculiarly empty nature of the individual in capitalism.

Blake's notion that every person sees differently validates the idea of the individual but it is also faintly disturbing. 'To the Eyes of a Miser a Guinea is far more beautiful than the Sun & a bag worn with the Use of Money has more beautiful proportions than a Vine filled with Grapes' and, to the question, '"When the Sun rises do you not see a round disk of fire somewhat like a Guinea?"' Blake's reply is 'O no, no, I see an Innumerable company of the Heavenly Host crying "Holy, Holy, Holy is the Lord God Almighty"' (Kitson 1989: 37 and 42–3). What is unsettling here is the hint of psychosis. There is no shared perception of reality just a projection of individual interests or imaginings. Unlikely as it may seem, Blake's understanding of how we see the world is not far removed from the fantasies of consumerism and celebrity culture. We have the same atomised consciousness, the same confusion of image and reality. The intensity of the inner life of Blake's individual is a direct result of his isolation. His mind may be vision filled but, not being part of any group or community, his social existence is empty. The problem is more radical in Keats who says the poet has 'no self' (ibid.: 111). This an extreme version of his doctrine of 'negative capability', the state 'when a man is capable of being in uncertainties, Mysteries, doubts, without any irritable reaching after fact & reason' (ibid.: 103). Having 'no identity' (ibid.: 111), the poet is able to assume the identity of whatever he describes: 'if a Sparrow come before my Window', writes Keats, 'I take part in its existence and pick about the Gravel' (Hoffman and Hynes 1966: 112).

The idea of the individual, as it appears in Blake and Keats, has some kinship with Arnold's view that 'our present unsettled state' is, at bottom, due to 'the notion of its being the prime right and happiness, for each of us, to affirm himself, and his ordinary self to be doing, and to be doing freely and as he likes' (1993: 138). Blake's concept of an hermetically sealed self is one element in the evolution of a society where it is perfectly acceptable to 'do as one likes', and there is an obvious connection between the empty self of Keats and the constant need for affirmation. The irony is that both Blake and Keats are repelled by industrial society and yet their view of the self contributes to the formation of an English middle-class mentality of which Arnold despairs. Its self-satisfaction impedes the work of culture which includes the free play of mind, seeing things as they are, the study of perfection, the exploration of the good and the moral and social passion for doing good, and the resistance to fanaticism and abstraction, the two plagues of our own time (1993: 59 and 76).

Blake also recoils from abstraction. 'To Generalise is to be an Idiot. To Particularise is the Alone Distinction of Merit' (Kitson 1989: 39). His statement overturns the neoclassical view that art should represent general nature, but it also resonates with Coleridge's criticism of political economy as 'an unenlivened, generalizing Understanding' (ibid.: 82). This in turn echoes Burke's observation, already mentioned, that the French Revolution ushered in the age of 'sophisters, economists, and calculators'. The conventional explanation for one of the characteristics of romantic poetry, its intensity, is that it grows out of the tradition of the sublime (Abrams 1976: 132–8). William Hazlitt (1778–1830) used the term 'gusto' to describe the 'power or passion' of art, and he made the point that criticism should not analyse a work, or inquire into its causes, but 'reflect [its] colours, light and shade, [its] soul and body' (1982: 201). It should, in other words, 'formulate a verbal equivalent for the aesthetic effect of the work under consideration' (ibid.: 201).

In this instance, the suggestion is that the romantic stress on sensation and, later in the century, the aesthetic demand for precision, are responses to the bloodless character of political economy, though George Steiner has also suggested that the events of the French Revolution bred a taste for drama and excitement (1971: 27) which underpinned such cries as Keats's 'Oh for a Life of Sensations rather than of Thoughts!' (Hoffman and Hynes 1966: 111) and George Gordon Noel Byron's (1788–1824) statement that 'the great object of life is sensation, to feel that we exist, even though in pain' (in Praz 1988: 74). If Burke is right in claiming that commerce and political philosophy banish habits, sentiments, affections, morality and manners from their account of the human, then all that is left is sensation and, in this, Keats and Byron anticipate the hedonistic and thrill-seeking nature of contemporary consumer culture. The rich emporium of sensory experience, which is an integral part of what it means to be an individual, is deformed not just by the abstractions of political economy but by the conditions of life in industrial society. The repetitive character of work in the factories numbs the senses while the destruction of traditional ties reduces the scope and variety of social interaction. Carlyle, for instance, writes that 'the moral, religious [and] spiritual condition of the people' has ceased to matter, what is important now is 'their physical, practical, economical condition' (Keating 1981: 54).

The most dramatic example of the reduction of persons to their 'economical condition' is the use of the term 'hands' to describe those who worked in factories. Marx makes the economic relation between those who own the means of production and those who do not the basis of his theory of class. Compared to the language of hierarchy, that of class is 'more mechanistic, less organic, connoting not a system of interrelations and interdependence but of separation and independence' (Himmelfarb 1984: 289). For the purpose of clarity we can say that what is important in hierarchical society is social status, what is important in class society is economic position. The former offers a greater potential for self-fashioning if only because the individual is part of a number of different groupings, but the latter consists of only two groups, the bourgeoisie and the proletariat, and the individual can only belong to one or the other; and, whichever one it is, his or her identity is exactly the same as that of every other member of the class. He or she is either an owner, or a non-owner.

The individual, then, becomes an abstraction by being defined in purely economic terms, either as a hand or as member of a class. But, as both Burke and Marx argue, there is something fundamentally abstract about the nature of commercial society itself. We can see why if we look at how money works. It provides a common measure by which commodities can be exchanged. It functions by representing commodities not as they are but by what they have in common, and what they have in common is the human labour that produced them. The difference in price between commodities expresses the different amounts of labour used to produce them. In order for money to represent what commodities have in common, it must ignore what is individual about them. Money, we might say, takes no account of the fact that one commodity is a shawl and another is a silk stocking; it is simply a measure of the amount of labour time necessary to produce these different items. Now if what Carlyle says is true, that cash payment is the sole nexus between people, then the principle of abstraction, that is the denial of the concrete, has been imported into the very heart of the social. And not just the social but the self too. For, as Shelley points out, money has become the 'visible incarnation' of its very 'principle' (Hoffman and Hynes 1966: 185).

Money is like language because both are forms of representation. Money represents commodities while language represents objects, thoughts and feelings. We use the word 'chair' for the object chair and the word 'love' for the feeling love. Money confers value on commodities while language confers value on objects, thoughts and feelings. And both signify in a similar way. Ferdinand Saussure (1857–1913), whose work on linguistics laid the foundation for the rise of literary theory, explains:

> To determine what a five franc piece is worth, one must know: (1) that it can be exchanged for a fixed quantity of a different thing, e.g. bread; and (2) that it can be compared with a similar value of the same system, e.g. a one franc piece, or with coins of another system (a dollar, etc.). In the same way, a word can be exchanged for something dissimilar, an idea; besides, it can be compared with something of the same nature, another word. Its value is therefore not fixed so long as one simply states that it can be 'exchanged' for a given concept, i.e. that it has this or that signification: one must also compare it with similar values, with other words that stand in opposition to it. (Saussure 1974: 83)

The connections between money and language – the poet Robert Southey (1774–1843) says that he 'endeavour[s] to write in such English as would bear the assay of Q. Elizabeth's mint' (in Morgan 1983: 95) – help to explain, in very general terms, the close association between the idioms of criticism and finance, particularly as criticism is concerned with the value of literary works as they compare with one another. Bagehot says that the business of criticism is an 'estimate' not a 'eulogy' (1916: 198).

But how do romantic and other writers respond to the generalising character of political economy? In the first place, they take an interest in the concrete and the particular, and in self-expression rather than truth to nature. In the second place, decorum finally ceases to be a criterion of literary judgement. The romantic emphasis on genius, which Coleridge defines as the ability to combine old and new, to contemplate the world as if it were seen for the first time, and to unite the feelings of childhood with the powers of manhood (1986: 182), undermines the idea of genre. Genius finds its own expression, it does not abide by the rules of epic or lyric. In any case, the whole system of genres is a reflection of the fine distinctions of feudal society and, when that passes, so do they. As industrialisation advances, the language of class increasingly comes to replace the language of status, making considerations of decorum largely irrelevant. Decorum belongs to a society of social gradations, not class polarisations. Poets and cultural commentators tend to express this division in the very broad terms of culture versus commerce. Shelley contrasts poetry, the realm of 'virtue, love, patriotism and friendship', with 'the selfish and calculating principle' (Hoffman and Hynes 1966: 185) of industry; Carlyle contrasts poetry, religion and morality, which form man's 'dynamical nature', with his 'mechanical contrivances' (Keating 1981: 59–60); while Arnold contrasts Hellenism, that is thinking, with Hebraism, that is doing (1993: 126–37). The implication is that literature, with the help of criticism, should heal man's divided nature, though we should stress that this division has been a constant throughout history. The form it takes now is between the rich inner world of the mind and an impoverished outer world of mechanism.

### Romanticism: Reviews, Criticism and Public Opinion

The eighteenth century was dominated by what is often called 'the republic of letters'. This included not just criticism but writing about history, philosophy and politics too. Starting in the seventeenth century, it originally consisted of scholars from the academies and learned societies of Europe, but soon spread out to embrace the salons, coffee shops and publishing houses of emerging civil society. The republic was independent of existing institutions of power and its most radical claim 'was that nearly anyone could be a critic' (Klancher 2003: 298). Such a view, encouraging people to think for themselves, was an important factor in undermining the authority of the rules of neoclassicism. The inclusive nature of the republic was reflected in the use of common speech. Magazines like the *Monthly Review* (1749) and *Critical Review* (1756) were written in a plain style to distinguish them from the increasingly professional discourse of specialists. The future, however, lay with the expert. The development of the various disciplines of knowledge made them difficult for the layman to comprehend and this was one of the factors leading to the demise of the republic.

Nationalism was also a factor in its fall. I mentioned a few examples of the English variety in the last chapter but the same stirrings were evident elsewhere in Europe. The cosmopolitan character of the republic therefore diminished as writers focused more on indigenous affairs. In England, at the end of the eighteenth century, there is a divide between the literary critical republic and a public opinion 'recognised as authoritative by Parliament, king, tailor and plebeian reformer' (Klancher 2003: 304). What we have here, effectively, is a split between the political and the cultural realm. Historically, various writers have claimed that poetry is political because it drew men into society and bound them together. As late as 1821 Shelley writes that 'poets are the unacknowledged legislators of the world' (Hoffman and Hynes 1966: 190). But this idea is, to use another phrase of Shelley's, 'a fading coal' (ibid.: 185); poetry is becoming ever more marginal to the business of the State.

Criticism was affected by these changes in at least two ways. It could either devote itself to moulding 'polite opinion which would be consistent with the aims and expansion of commercial society' (Klancher 2003: 313) or it could withdraw from this public role and become increasingly specialised, meditating on the nature of criticism itself. This was the path Coleridge chose. He was dismayed at what he saw as the decline of literature. In 'old times' books were 'religious oracles', then 'venerable preceptors' then 'instructive friends'; but now they are the vehicles of vanity and mere entertainment (2006: 59–60). Literature has become a 'trade', and poems are 'manufactured' (ibid.: 38). A huge increase in the number of books means they cease to benefit mankind, producing instead a sort of 'beggarly day dreaming' (ibid.: 50). But what Coleridge finds particularly mortifying is that 'all men being supposed able to read, and all readers able to judge, the multitudinous PUBLIC, shaped into unity by the magic of abstraction, sits nominal despot on the throne of criticism' (ibid.: 61). The 'ultimate end of criticism', for Coleridge, is 'to establish the principles of writing' not to formulate 'rules for passing judgement' (ibid.: 90). In seeking to give criticism rigour and purpose in an age where it has degenerated into 'arbitrary dictation and petulant sneers' (1986: 179), Coleridge at once looks back to the traditional idea of criticism as prescription and forward to the modern idea of criticism as method. And what I mean by 'method' here is a clearly identifiable approach to literature, feminist, post-colonialist and so on.

Coleridge wants to distinguish criticism from mere reviewing, to make it a vocation rather than a pastime. He thus initiates the process whereby it becomes a professional discourse, characterised by the use of a technique and specialised terminology. But there are two problems with this tactic. First, Coleridge's proposal for a 'fixed canon of criticism' is surely at odds with the 'organic' nature of literature, for what is fixed cannot grow. Second, the introduction of a method makes criticism seem like a mechanical operation. Formally at least, it begins to take on the character of an abstraction. Of course this has always been an element of criticism. We only have to think of the prologues to authors in the Middle Ages or the rules of neoclassicism in the late seventeenth century. But these were a means to an end, the greater understanding of the Bible or the proper staging of tragedy. What happens, though, when we get rid of the notion of literature? We are left with just the method, and that is more or less the state we are in today.

The arrival of theory in the late 1970s precipitated an attack on the very idea of literature. In one sense, those who led this charge were right. There was no such thing as 'literature'. The term has different meanings at different times. But, in another sense, they were wrong. Literature's richness of significentation makes it indispensable to our linguistically impoverished culture. By dismissing the idea of literature, critics severed their connection with an art devoted to the exploration, at the deepest level, of ideas, ends and values. As a result, criticism became an empty formalism, a means without an end. Or, to put it another way, it focused on itself rather than literature. Carlyle foresaw this danger as early as 1831 when he warned that the prevalence of reviewing would lead to 'all Literature' becoming 'one boundless, self-devouring review', which, 'like a sick thing, superabundantly "listens to itself" ' (in Skilton 1993: 7). This was certainly true of criticism in the 1980s and 90s. It adopted a self-referential posture, pondering on its own nature before degenerating into a technique of reading that uses 'literature' as a way of validating its own 'isms'. The study of English is now no more than a training in the application of a method, not 'an adventure among masterpieces', to use Anatole France's (1844–1924) magnificent phrase. And we can see the seeds of all this in Coleridge's desire to distinguish criticism from reviewing.

Coleridge's distaste for reviews is evident throughout his *Biographia Literaria* (1817) which is a mixture of autobiography, philosophy, psychology and literary criticism. In his opinion, reviewers are partisan, motivated by malignity and rarely read the works they criticise. The exceptions are the *Edinburgh Review* (1802–1929) and the *Quarterly Review* (1809–1967). The *Edinburgh* supported the Whig[8] or reform party and the *Quarterly* the Tory party. Despite their differences, the *Edinburgh* and the *Quarterly* appealed to a mainly middle-class readership. The *Edinburgh* may have claimed that the power of the state lay in 'the great body of the people' but it instantly qualified this dangerous notion by adding 'especially among the more wealthy and intelligent' (in Klancher 2003: 313). But neither of these magazines indulged in the kind of invective that could be found in *Blackwood's Magazine* (1817–1980). Under the editorship of its founder, William Blackwood (1776–1834), it ran a sustained campaign against the 'cockney school' of writers which included Keats and the essayist Leigh Hunt (1784–1859) who was described by the magazine as 'a little mincing boarding school mistress' (in Gross 1991: 21). The trading of insults could have deadly consequences. The first editor of the *London Magazine* (1820–9),

John Scott, was shot in a duel by a henchman of John Gibson Lockhart (1794–1854), one of the men who put *Blackwood's* on the map, and who is best remembered for his *Life of Sir Walter Scott* (1837–8 and 1839). Even in the so-called age of politeness, when writers could be equally rude to one another, nobody was actually killed.

### Responses to Romanticism

What, then, was the response to romantic poetry?[9] The first thing to say is that the very term 'romantic poetry' is misleading because it assumes that poets as different as Coleridge and Keats all shared a common agenda. They didn't. Blake's view of language was quite different to Wordsworth's. Blake, in his prophetic books, writes in the hieratic tradition that wants to protect religious truth from vulgar misunderstanding, 'That which can be made Explicit to the Idiot is not worth my care' (Kitson 1989: 37), while Wordsworth writes in the tradition of the plain style, wanting to convey the feelings and notions of rustic life 'in simple unelaborated expressions' (Hoffman and Hynes 1966: 15). And the picture has been further complicated by the reassessment of female romantics such as Mary Robinson (1757–1800) and Charlotte Smith (1749–1806). All the same, the publication of the *Lyrical Ballads* in 1798 had an immediate impact. 'Childish', 'vulgar', 'affected', 'artificial', 'perverse', 'plebeian', 'blasphemous' and 'diseased' were just some of the terms used to describe the poems. Coleridge was attacked for his 'babyish simplicity' and for his 'uncouth, pedantic and obscure diction'.[10]

What particularly caught the attention of a number of critics was Wordsworth's statement of purpose: 'to choose incidents from common life and to relate or describe them, throughout, as far as possible, in a selection of language really used by men' (Hoffman and Hynes 1966: 15). This appalled the editor of the *Edinburgh*, one Francis Jeffrey (1773–1850), who declared that poetry, like religion, had its standards 'fixed long ago by certain inspired writers whose authority it is no longer lawful to call in question' (in Morgan 1983: 2). We are back with the idea of a hierarchy of genres, and ballads come at the very bottom. Jeffrey is prepared to concede that 'the poor and vulgar may interest us' but he is not prepared to accept that their manner of expressing themselves can be used in poetry (ibid.: 4). We tend to think of romantic poetry as the poetry of feeling so it comes as a surprise to read that Jeffrey thought that this was precisely what Wordsworth's poetry lacked. 'The business of poetry', he wrote, is 'to please without any laborious exercise of the understanding' (ibid.: 6). And when Wordsworth does suspend his 'meddling intellect'[11] the feelings that he portrays are 'babyish and feeble rather than manly and strong' (ibid.: 6). This remark, together with the reference to Hunt as a boarding school mistress, underlines the tradition of poetry as a masculine activity which can be traced back to its praise of the warrior and its role in political oratory.

But Jeffrey has yet one more objection to Wordsworth and that is that he does not draw his inspiration from Shakespeare, Milton, Dryden, Pope or Johnson but from the continent, particularly France and Germany. In short, he should be more English. So, as on other occasions, we find that nationality is a factor in critical discourse. And for nationality we should read politics. Hazlitt makes the point that the French Revolution was the most direct influence on the 'Lake School', the name given to the work of Coleridge, Wordsworth and Southey because they all lived in what is now Cumbria which, incidentally, meant that their poetry could be dismissed as provincial. The ideas of the French Revolution, liberty, equality and fraternity, inspired English radicals and alarmed the government into passing the Combination Acts (1792–7) which prevented the growth of trade unions as well as working-class reading groups and debating clubs, and the Six Acts (1819) which made it illegal for any periodical costing less than sixpence to appear more than once every twenty-six days, or for it to comment on matters of Church or State.

One of the criticisms Burke made of the French Revolution was that it sought to break completely with the past and that, says Hazlitt, is what the Lake School aspired to do as well: 'all was to be natural and new. Nothing that was established was to be tolerated' (1982: 215). Hazlitt is referring to the way Wordsworth and Coleridge react against the followers of Pope and 'the old French school of poetry' but it is quite clear from his imagery that he is talking about more than literature: 'kings and queens were dethroned from their rank and station in legitimate tragedy or epic poetry, as they were decapitated elsewhere' (ibid.: 215–16). Furthermore, the Lake poets 'scorned degree, priority and place', claiming kindred with 'the commonest of the people' (ibid.: 217). The objection to Wordsworth and Coleridge, then, is not just that they wanted to make poetry anew but that, in the process, they threatened the social order. At the beginning of the eighteenth century, there was little difference between poets and critics in their attitude to literature. They both subscribed, more or less, to the doctrine of neoclassicism but now a gap has opened between them. Poetry aims at innovation, while criticism cleaves to tradition and approved standards. One of the features in the modern criticism is that it develops along separate lines from literature, becoming a discipline in its own right. It is also characterised by a somewhat authoritative tone which is a modified form of the dogmatism found in Victorian criticism. This was a response to the ignorance of the audience. The new reading public, claims Houghton (1957: 141), was far larger and much less knowledgeable than its eighteenth-century counterpart. In need of education, they lacked the means to appeal against the critic's judgement. Declaration replaced conversation.

### Romanticism and Religion

Blake saw angels in a tree on Peckham Rye. Coleridge was curious about the mental processes of such visions, an interest that can be traced back to Locke's *An Essay Concerning Human Understanding* (c. 1689). He and Wordsworth wanted to explore the psychological aspect of the supernatural in the *Lyrical Ballads* (1798). Their focus was 'the dramatic truth of such emotions, as would naturally accompany such situations, supposing them real. And real in this sense they have been to every human being who, from whatever source of delusion, has at any time believed himself to be under supernatural agency' (Coleridge 1986: 191–2). Why the curiosity about the psychology of the supernatural? Because the rational basis for believing in religion or a world of spirits was being undermined by science and philosophy. David Hume's *Dialogues Concerning Natural Religion* (1779) was one of many works purporting to show that reason and religion were incompatible.

The romantics were confronted with a paradoxical legacy. On the one hand, reason had demonstrated the problems of revealed religion but, on the other, it failed to acknowledge the role of feeling in human life and understanding. This opened the way to religious experience being validated emotionally if not epistemologically. The stories of the Old Testament could thus be valued for their poetic power instead of being dismissed as fictions or false history. The next step was to acknowledge that art could handle the profound questions about human existence that had previously been the exclusive preserve of religion. Or, to put this another way, art translates religious experience into secular terms which means it keeps the depth if not the doctrine of Christian theology. For example, the highest form of the sublime in the previous century was the deity, but, in the late eighteenth and early nineteenth century, it was nature. Similarly, the imagination. Traditionally, God created, humans imitated. But now the poet is seen to exercise that godlike power by bringing a poem into existence. 'The primary imagination', writes Coleridge, 'I hold to be the living power and prime agent of all human perception and as a repetition in the finite mind of the eternal act of creation in the infinite I AM' (1986: 190–1). The immortal soul becomes the immortal work of art, and morality is no longer based on doctrine so much as a reverence for life itself. Above all, art rescues the self from either dissolving in a Lockean stream of impressions or disappearing along with the idea of the soul.[12] The romantic self finds expression in its various creations. It is but a short step from this to saying that humans find fulfilment in their labour. Next to God, work was 'the most popular word in the Victorian vocabulary' (Houghton 1957: 242). The romantics may have defied industrialisation, but by identifying the self with production they underpin the Victorian ideology of the dignity and duty of work.

### The Legacy of Emotion

As we have already seen, not all critics were impressed with the centrality of emotion in romantic poetry. The civil servant and dramatist Henry Taylor (1800–86) said that while it 'may move the feelings and charm the fancy' it 'fails to satisfy the understanding' (Faulkner 1989: 71). Thomas Love Peacock (1785–1866) was more forthright: 'While the historian and the philosopher are advancing in, and accelerating the progress of knowledge, the poet is wallowing in the rubbish of departed ignorance' (Hoffman and Hynes 1966: 154). Peacock's argument, which prompted Shelley to write his *Defence of Poetry* (1821), is strictly utilitarian. Since poetry 'can never make a philosopher, nor a statesman' and since it 'cannot claim the slightest share in any one of the comforts and utilities of life', it should be discarded (ibid.: 156). Poetry's main audience is a 'reading public' who are not interested in learning anything; they just want to be 'excited by passion, which is the commotion of a weak and selfish mind, affected by pathos, which is the whining of an unmanly spirit, and exalted by sublimity, which is the inflation of an empty head' (ibid.: 157). Poetry has slipped from the highest expression of human achievement to a form of entertainment that gratifies our basest emotions. The divide between 'high' and 'popular' culture, which has always been a latent feature of the history of criticism, is beginning to manifest itself. The irony is that we would now regard the romantics as part of the 'high' culture of our own period.

And indeed they left an impressive legacy. For example, the imagination and fancy were no longer regarded as interchangeable once Coleridge distinguished between them. In very simple terms, one is the power of creation and the other is the manipulation of what already exists. The clarification of critical concepts was one achievement of the romantics, another was that they made emotion central to poetry. Poetry, said Wordsworth, 'is the spontaneous overflow of powerful feelings; it takes its origin from emotion recollected in tranquillity' (Hoffman and Hynes 1966: 30). Poetry is the 'expression of a feeling' (Mill 1963: 8). Or, as a writer in *Blackwood*'s declared, poetry is 'impassioned truth' (in ibid. 1963: 8). The problem with these definitions, says Mill, is that they also apply to eloquence. Mill therefore distinguishes eloquence which is 'heard' from poetry which is 'overheard' (ibid.: 8). Eloquence, he writes, 'supposes an audience' but the 'peculiarity of poetry appears to lie . . . in the poet's utter unconsciousness of a listener' (ibid.: 8). The ancient connection between poetry and rhetoric is finally broken with the result that poetry is now a mainly personal experience.

This creates problems for criticism. The idea that works have layers of meaning, or that they promote virtue, or that they are true to nature, or even that they help to cultivate taste seem irrelevant to the absorbed individual turning the pages by gaslight. These concepts belonged to a largely public conception of criticism which diminishes as literature is consumed in private. The challenge now facing criticism is how to connect these two realms, how to give the private experience a public resonance when the relation between them is in crisis. This problem, the split between the public and the private, is, of course, one of the major themes of the nineteenth-century novel, usually expressed as the conflict between duty and desire. Mill moves from defining poetry to defining the poet. He repeats the old idea of *poeta nascitur, non fit*, that poets are born, not made. The defining feature of a poet is that his ideas and insights are linked together by emotion and this distinguishes him from the scientist or man of business who compartmentalises things. They classify, the poet connects.

Southey, writing a little earlier than Mill, declared that the poet writes for self-expression and even the elevation of his own character, but Southey also believed that the most important ingredient of poetry was emotion. This didn't mean that the poet was to neglect morality, rather he created the habit of mind which induced it. Southey's own purpose was 'to diffuse through my poems a sense of the beautiful and the good . . . rather than to aim at the exemplification of any particular moral precept' (in Morgan 1983: 95). The expression of emotion, then, was not at the expense of morality. Poetry retains this ancient function but it has lost its didactic character. This is, of course, the contrary view to the one expounded by Peacock. He also thought that poetry detracted from the search for knowledge but Mill believed that it was a stimulus to the search for truth. In terms which could almost be seen to address Peacock directly, Mill writes 'that capacity for strong feeling which is supposed necessarily to disturb the judgement is also the material out of which all motives are made, the motives consequently which lead human beings to the pursuit of truth' (1963: 23).

Arthur Henry Hallam (1811–33), whose death inspired one of the major works of poetry in the nineteenth century, Tennyson's *In Memoriam* (1850), was closer to Peacock than Mill in thinking that sensation rather than emotion was the defining feature of romantic poetry. Since the senses of a Keats or Shelley told them 'a richer and ampler tale than most men could understand' (Faulkner 1989: 44), their work was difficult to understand. But some fault lay with the readers who were not prepared to make the effort to appreciate them. Such indolence, argues Hallam, encourages the publication of mediocre work whose subject is 'the *usual* passions of the heart' which are dealt with in a 'simple' style without 'the transforming powers of the imagination' (ibid.: 46). In addition to the distance between author and audience, English writing has itself declined from the splendours of the Elizabethan age. Like Jeffrey and Southey, Hallam holds the Puritan revolution and the introduction of French culture at the Restoration responsible for the decay of

English poetry. Prior to that time, a consciousness of its power 'became a part of national existence; it was ours as Englishmen; and amid the flux of generations and customs, we retain unimpaired this privilege of intercourse with greatness' (ibid.: 47). Until now. For we have 'undergone a period of degradation' (ibid.: 47). Anticipating T. S. Eliot's notion of the 'dissociation of sensibility', Hallam declares that one characteristic of poetry's degenerate state is that thought and feeling, 'which in former times were intermingled', are now 'restrained within separate spheres of agency' (ibid.: 48). We can have poetry of one or the other but not both together. Art now affirms that division in the conception of the human which runs through this history.

A particularly personal account of this division can be found in Mill's *Autobiography* (1873) where he describes how his education had developed his intellect but not his feelings. Mill's great goal in life was 'to be a reformer of the world' (Tennyson and Gray 1976: 578) but he realised that, should he succeed, it would not bring him happiness. The knowledge plunged him into depression. His analytic habit of mind had worn away his feelings, excluding him from that 'pleasure of sympathy with human beings' which is 'the greatest and surest source of happiness' (ibid.: 580). It was then he turned to literature, particularly Wordsworth, whose poems were a 'medicine' for his state of mind because they 'expressed not mere outward beauty, but states of feeling, and of thought coloured by feeling under the excitement of beauty' (ibid.: 582). He found in them 'a source of joy, of sympathetic and imaginative pleasure which could be shared in by all human beings' (ibid.: 582). Mill's experience shows that, as feeling, the value of poetry is more therapeutic than artistic. 'I value[d] Wordsworth less according to his intrinsic merits', writes Mill, 'than by the measure of what he had done for me' (ibid.: 583). But, as so often in the history of criticism, we find that, for each new perception, there is usually a precedent of some sort. Here it is Aristotle's notion of catharsis. Yes, Aristotle deals with the communal purging of emotion in relation to a particular literary form whereas Mill describes how he recovered his emotions by reading a particular poet. Nevertheless, both men recognise the importance of the emotions to art, either as a way of managing them or as a way of acknowledging and educating them.

And although Mill is writing about his own response to literature, his remarks do have a wider significance for he relates his own stunted, emotional growth to the English character in general which, in conjunction with 'English social circumstances, make it so seldom possible to derive happiness from the exercise of the sympathies, that it is not wonderful that they count for little in an Englishman's scheme of life' (Tennyson and Gray 1976: 584). Hallam bemoaned the fact that the decline of literature and the distance between the poet and the public meant that it could no longer play a part in shaping the national character but Mill clearly implies that this is not the case, that the purpose of literature is to make the English come to terms with their emotions. It is a theme taken up by E. M. Forster (1879–1970) whose novels explore the 'undeveloped heart' (1965: 13) of the English middle class.

## The Pathetic Fallacy

Ruskin was more cautious in his approach to the role of emotion in poetry. He began by challenging what he understood to be Coleridge's view of the relation between subject and object, namely, that it was hard to distinguish between them. In fact Coleridge does not quite make this claim, he merely notes that it is very difficult to *prove* that 'this sheet of paper is separate from the phenomenon or image in my perception' (2006: 188). But Ruskin was not concerned with nice distinctions, only with discrediting those philosophers who imagine 'that everything in the world depends upon [their] seeing or thinking it' (2004: 68). His desire to assert the existence of an independent reality perhaps explains his support for the Pre-Raphaelite Brotherhood (f. 1848), a group of painters committed to naturalism and truth in nature. The problem is inherent in the Lockean tradition. It does not allow us to distinguish clearly between the inner world of our impressions and the outer world of fact. The two are inextricably mixed. Ruskin takes on this tradition by altering its language: 'the word Blue does not mean the sensation caused by a gentian on the human eye; it means the power of producing that sensation' (ibid.: 69) – his point being that there is a clear divide between the subjective and the objective world. Indeed, he dislikes these 'sonorous' terms, preferring 'plain old English' (ibid.: 69) because phrases such as ' "it seems so" are more intelligible than "it is subjectively so" ' (ibid.: 69).

Once again, a critic extols the virtues of simplicity, embracing the elegant rather than the elaborate expression. No philosopher is going to be convinced that Ruskin, simply by a change of terminology, has drawn a clear boundary between observer and observed. And what is hard to separate in the realm of empirical reality becomes even more entangled in the realm of art. Although we can discriminate to a certain extent between our impression of an object and the object itself, we cannot do this with any degree of certainty when talking about literature. *King Lear* does not have the power to produce the sensation that it is a great work in the same way that a gentian has the power to produce the sensation of blueness. It takes familiarity with the language, a comparative knowledge of other works, an understanding of the culture in which it was written, a capacity to respond to its power and passion, an ability to uncover yet more dimensions of the play and to bring it to bear on the great questions of life. And this list is by no means exhaustive.

Ruskin's discussion of subject and object is a prelude to his discussion of the pathetic fallacy. This takes two forms. Either the poet deliberately describes something which is not the case in order to create a pleasurable effect, for instance, a crocus as a spendthrift, or else the poet's excited state of feeling produces a falseness in his impression of external things. Ruskin uses the difference between these two forms to discriminate between the 'greatest poets' and those of the 'second order' (2004: 71). Pope is repeatedly held up as an example of the second. His portrayal of Ulysses' encounter with the ghost of one of his men, Elpenor, whom he didn't realize was dead, fails to convey any sense of his shock or urgency. The lines ' "How could thy soul, by realms and seas disjoined, / Outfly the nimble sail and leave the lagging wind" . . . are put into the mouth of the wrong passion – a passion which could never have spoken them – agonized curiosity' (ibid.: 72–3). The old criterion of decorum is being invoked here. And Pope would have been most surprised to find himself accused of flouting it, since he prided himself on his adherence to poetic propriety. What is acceptable in one age is not so in another. But that implies we cannot be infused, moved, uplifted, animated, astonished or transported by the literature of previous ages. Yet we can. And so while fitness of expression is central to our experience of literature, it does not completely account for its effect. Literature doesn't just transcend history, it transcends itself.

One of the features of Ruskin's discussion of the pathetic fallacy is his urge to classify types of poet. First there are two, then three, then four kinds of poet. The classifications are based on the capacity for feeling and the power to command it. Ruskin preserves the principle of the sublime when he says that 'there are always some subjects which ought to throw a man off balance, some by which his poor human capacity of thought should be conquered' (2004: 74). But the emphasis is on the truth of the feeling and the ability to control it. The falseness of a feeling manifests itself in 'fanciful metaphorical expressions' (ibid.: 77), while Dante is the very model of a poet who receives all feelings 'to the full' but who also has 'a great centre of reflection and knowledge in which he stands serene, and watches the feeling, as it were, from afar off' (ibid.: 75). Accurate perception, ordered emotion, these are the qualities of the very best writing. We are moving away from the romantic aesthetics of imagination, sensation and feeling and back to those of neo-classicism. Keats is a second-order poet because he is 'generally subdued by the feelings under which [he] writes' which means some of his 'expressions and modes of thought are in some sort diseased or false' (ibid.: 75).

## Arnold and Poetry

Arnold also looked askance at Keats, sighing over the 'harm' he had done to English poetry (Faulkner 1989: 139). Ruskin thought that poets should see things clearly but Arnold thought they should 'begin with an Idea of the world in order not to be prevailed over by the world's multitudinousness' (ibid.: 139). Here was where critics could be of some service, not by reiterating the rules of good writing, but by establishing 'an order of ideas' and making the 'best ones prevail' (Keating 1981: 189). It was Arnold's contention that 'the elements with which the creative power works are ideas' and that 'the grand work of literary genius is a work of synthesis and exposition' (ibid.: 188–9). We have already mentioned the importance he attached to the free play of ideas, that they cannot be sufficiently valued in and for themselves, and that they should be free from all political and practical considerations, but perhaps what needs stressing now is how different Arnold's conception of criticism is from our own. We work with a much diminished sense of the term. We analyse works from the perspectives of gender, ethnicity and sexuality and, at the same time, teach transferable skills to make our students employable. The contradiction of this position – apparent cultural liberation and actual economic enslavement – is hardly noticed. We are therefore in sore need of a criticism that is alert to such tensions, a criticism that values the free play of ideas and the attempt 'to see the object as in itself it really is' (ibid.: 186) instead of as an example of a particular theory or approach. But that danger is potentially there in Arnold in as much as he tells us to start from 'the idea' which must surely prevent us from seeing the work in its true light.

Arnold values criticism because he values poetry and the reason he values poetry is because of the role it has to play in modern life. As we said earlier, this role is in part determined by the decline of religion and so 'we have to turn to poetry to interpret life for us, to console us, to sustain us' (Hoffman and Hynes 1966: 256). But only the best poetry can do that. And the best poetry, Arnold is quick to point out, is not necessarily English. Shakespeare, indeed, is compared unfavourably to the ancients because he was incapable of saying a thing 'plainly' (ibid.: 237). We have said that clarity is the ideal of English writing, but it was first a classical virtue. One feature which marks out the very best poetry is sincerity, or 'non-charlatanism' (ibid.: 256). This means that poetry forms a strong contrast with the world of commerce which, as Mill argued, is based on insincerity. Authenticity is precious to the extent that it is rare, a sentence that demonstrates how difficult it is to talk about art without drawing on economic concepts of some sort, a point made far more eloquently by Ruskin in his inaugural address to the Cambridge School of Art in 1858 (2004: 98). Another characteristic of the best poetry is that it focuses on 'excellent actions', that is those which appeal 'most powerfully . . . to the great primary human affections' (Hoffman and Hynes 1966: 231). But this characteristic cannot be found in the modern world, only the ancient one. In Greek poetry, the action 'predominated over the expression' but in modern poetry 'the expression predominates over the action' (ibid.: 232). The single action of a Greek epic or tragedy ensures 'clearness of arrangement, rigour of development and simplicity of style' (ibid.: 238), all qualities which modern poetry lacks. Moreover, the emphasis on action means that ancient poetry creates a far better 'moral impression' than 'the most striking single thought or . . . happiest image' (ibid.: 239).

The faults that Arnold finds with modern poetry and criticism, that poems seem to exist 'for the sake of single lines and passages' and that critics are only interested in 'detached expressions' (Hoffman and Hynes 1966: 234) are symptomatic of a divided society, the most dramatic manifestation of which is the split between the middle class and an industrial working one. Victorian Britain was also characterised by other tensions. It was a place of profound optimism and anxiety, of an interest in ideas and a virulent ant-intellectualism, an age in which, said Mill, 'mankind had outgrown old institutions and doctrines' but had not yet 'acquired new ones' (cited in Houghton 1957: 1). Arnold said that the 'the confusion of the present times is great' with many voices 'counselling different things' (Hoffman and Hynes 1966: 235). Is it any wonder, then, that the lack of social and political unity is reflected in its literature? The interest in the part rather than the whole mirrors a society deeply at odds with itself. 'There is no community in England', wrote the novelist and politician Benjamin Disraeli (1804–81), 'there is aggregation, but aggregation under circumstances which make it rather a dissociating than a uniting principle' (1985: 94). Mill thought poetry necessary to cultivate the feelings in order to make a person whole; Arnold agrees but adds that, by appealing to the primary human affections, poetry will also draw people together. It is one aspect of culture whose aim is to find the 'common basis of human nature' underneath class divisions (1993: 108). Men of culture, he writes, 'are the true apostles of equality' (ibid.: 108).

Truth and seriousness are two further qualities which constitute the best poetry, but it is not wholly clear what Arnold means by these terms. And his remark that they are 'inseparable from the superiority of diction and movement' (Hoffman and Hynes 1966: 265) does not particularly further our understanding. Arnold says that it is much easier to demonstrate them by pointing to particular examples than to theorise about them in critical discourse. The best guides to excellent poetry are 'the lines and expressions of the great masters' (ibid.: 262). These act as 'touchstones' for 'detecting the presence or absence of high poetic quality' (ibid.: 262). And, continues Arnold, 'short passages, even single lines will serve our turn quite sufficiently' (ibid.: 262). Can this be the same Arnold who objects to critics seizing on 'detached expressions' as a way of estimating a poem's worth? It is of course unfair to conflate remarks made in different contexts about different things but the inconsistency – if we can call it that – underlines the previous point that it is impossible for any one philosophy to account for all phenomena in a rapidly changing and an increasingly complex world.

The qualities that Arnold identifies as belonging to the very best poetry – truth, seriousness, sincerity and action – are not self-evident. Unless we read in the proper manner, we may not be able to recognise or appreciate them. In order to make sure that we do, we must avoid the historical fallacy and the personal fallacy. The historical fallacy is looking at a poem purely in terms of what it tells us about the progress of a nation's language, thought or art (Hoffman and Hynes 1966: 258). Arnold does not deny that a knowledge of a work's origins and its historical relationships adds to our understanding of a work but that is not our purpose in reading poetry. Always the aim is 'to feel and enjoy [the] work as deeply as ever we can, and to appreciate the wide difference between it and all work which has not the same high character' (ibid.: 259). The historical fallacy is most likely to affect us when reading works from a previous age while the personal fallacy is most likely to affect us when reading poets of our own age. If we are not careful our own ideas, feelings and preferences will prevent us from seeing 'the object as in itself it really is' and so we will not be able to know its true worth. As Arnold puts it: 'Our personal affinities, likings and circumstances, have great power to sway our estimate of this or that poet's work and to attach more importance to it as poetry than in itself it really possesses' (ibid.: 258). If we can avoid both these fallacies then we will truly be able 'to feel and enjoy the work' and this is 'what is salutary, this is what is formative' (ibid.: 259). That use of the word 'formative' suggests that Arnold still subscribes to the belief that poetry shapes character. As we have argued, the conditions that made this rhetorical conception of the art viable have long since passed away. But if poetry is no longer a means of preparing us for a public role, that does not mean it cannot help in fashioning our private selves. In the eighteenth century, literature was used as a form of self-cultivation but, in the nineteenth century, at least in Arnold's view, it has become a source of consolation.

But poetry doesn't just offer consolation. The poet's business, says Arnold, 'is not to praise the age, but to afford men who live in it the highest pleasure which they are capable of feeling' (Hoffman and Hynes 1966: 240), a remark that has obvious affinities with Pater's famous statement that 'art comes to you proposing frankly to give nothing but the highest quality to your moments as they pass' (1986: 153). Comfort, truth, authenticity and delight. These are the qualities that make poetry a 'criticism of life' (Hoffman and Hynes 1966: 257). By constant reading we get a sense of the 'really excellent, and of the strength and joy to be drawn from it' (ibid.: 257) and this will hopefully counteract the smugness, self-satisfaction and pride of the English middle class which imagines that nineteenth-century Britain is the most advanced and civilised nation the world has known. Arnold quotes John Roebuck (1802–79) who, incidentally, was a friend of Mill, though they fell out over their different attitudes to the emotions (Tennyson and Gray 1976: 584). 'What is the state of England?'

asks Roebuck. 'Is not property safe. Is not every man able to say what he likes? I ask you, whether the world over or in past history, there is anything like it? Nothing' (Keating 1981: 200). Arnold juxtaposes this boast, together with another by one Mr Adderley that the English are the best breed in the whole world' (Keating 1981: 199), with the following newspaper report.

> A shocking child murder has just been committed in Nottingham. A girl named Wragg left the workhouse there on Saturday morning with her young illegitimate child. The child was found soon afterwards dead on Mapperly Hills, having been strangled. Wragg is in custody. (ibid.: 201)[13]

The contrast between the rhetoric and the reality dramatises the role of poetry and indeed culture in the modern world. It is not simply the art of self-cultivation, as in part it was in the eighteenth century, but a standard by which to judge the shortcomings of society. Culture, in the widest sense, is, for Arnold, not merely the sheer desire to see things as they are, though that is crucial, but also 'the love of our neighbour, the impulses towards action, help and beneficence, the desire for removing human error, clearing human confusion, the noble aspiration to leave the world better and happier than we found it' (1993: 59). This view of culture seems to contradict Arnold's other claim that ideas should be valued in and for themselves, not translated into practice. But that refers mainly to criticism and, in any case, the free play of ideas is a prelude to the creation of a set of ideas that will eventually permeate the whole of society – though one weakness of Arnold's position is that he does not say how this happens. More positively, Arnold does not retreat to an ivory tower. He recognises the claims of industry, of the machine, of sports and of the Puritan conscience. But they develop only one part of a person, they do not perfect the whole which is the special responsibility of culture.[14] The divisions of society are mirrored in those of the self. Arnold looks to culture for the cure. And culture means not just England, in fact hardly England, not even Europe, though that is where the emphasis falls, but the great globe itself. Arnold's definition of criticism is, finally, 'a disinterested endeavour to learn and propagate the best that is known and thought *in the world*' (Keating 1981: 211. My italics). Unfortunately, criticism has fallen prey to the professionals and become yet one more specialism, wholly defeating its task of making us whole.

## Novel Criticism

The nineteenth century was the age of the novel. There were novels in the eighteenth century but, by and large, they were regarded more as forms of entertainment than instruction and so were deemed to be rather frivolous.

Suspicion of the genre continues into the nineteenth century with fiction being seen as a danger to a reader's moral and mental well-being, though its social usefulness was increasingly being acknowledged. Thomas Henry Lister (1800–42) who, as well as being the first registrar general of England and Wales, also found time to be a novelist and a dramatist, said that the tendency of Dickens's writings was 'to make us practically benevolent' (Skilton 1993: 41). This defence of literature is familiar from the ancient world. Even the appearance of new literary forms does little to alter the fundamental assumptions of criticism. The novelist Anthony Trollope (1815–82) sounds exactly like Horace when he says that the writers of stories must 'teach' and 'please' (ibid.: 57). And Edward Bulwer Lytton (1803–73) shows that the tradition of *grammatica* is not quite extinguished when he describes the various parts of the novel, how it achieves its effects and its differences from drama (Faulkner 1989: 78–96).

Nevertheless, the rise of the novel does throw these concerns into new relief. One motif of this history is the distinction between high and low literature which comes very much to the fore in discussion of the novel. Thomas de Quincey (1785–1859) best known for *Confessions of an Opium Eater* (1821) but also the author of a number of tracts on economics, including *The Logic of Political Economy* (1844), worried about what effects the demands of readers from 'the mechanic and provincial sections of our population' (Skilton 1993: 23) would have on literature. The audience for popular fiction 'are poor in capacities of thinking, and are passively resigned to the instinct of immediate pleasure' (ibid.: 23). They were only interested in stories, which is 'a function of literature neither very noble in itself, nor tending to permanence' (ibid.: 24). A writer who does not take this into account will fail to sell his or her work. The 'genius' of authors, writes Bagehot, 'is habitually sacrificed to the tastes of readers' (ibid.: 26). He distinguishes between high and low literature on the grounds that the former aims at describing 'the whole of human life in its spheres, in all its aspects, with all its interests, aims and objects' (ibid.: 26), while the latter focuses on only part of it. Bagehot gives the example of romance, which deals 'solely with the passion of love' and which regards all other parts of life as a distraction from the fantasy which 'charms it' (ibid.: 26).

An Oxford philosopher and later professor of Ecclesiastical History, Henry Mansel (1820–71), tried to put popular fiction into its social and economic context.[15] The aim of 'sensation novels', he declared, was 'excitement, and excitement alone' (Skilton 1993: 75). There were three principal causes that had given rise to this phenomenon: periodicals, circulating libraries and railway bookstalls. By its very nature a periodical contains a good deal that is ephemeral and, moreover, it 'belongs to that class of works which most men borrow and do not buy, and in which, therefore, they take only a transitory interest' (ibid.: 76). We should acknowledge that middle-class association between property and seriousness. The weekly or monthly instalments of stories eventually appear in book form on the shelves of the circulating libraries. Mansel is as dismissive of these itinerant dispensers of entertainment as he is of periodicals. They are 'the chief hot bed for forcing a crop of writers without talent and readers without discrimination'; they give us 'the latest fashion and no more' (ibid.: 76). And, once again, ownership is invoked as a mark of literary worth. The book that is worth buying is the good book. Railway travellers do not have a great deal of time to 'examine the merits of a book before purchasing it' and so booksellers 'find an advantage in offering something that may catch the eye of the hurried passenger, and promise temporary excitement to relieve the dullness of the journey' (ibid.: 77). The sensation novel, which deals with the more lurid aspects of contemporary life, such as crime, bigamy, blackmail, drug addiction and so forth, aims at electrifying the readers' nerves, not exercising their judgement. Literature has become a distraction, a relief from tedium, not a means of learning how to live. Since only the reader knows how well he or she is entertained by a particular novel, the need for criticism has practically ceased.

Certainly the centuries-old justification that literature influences behaviour comes under scrutiny in this period. An anonymous contributor to *Cope's Tobacco Plant*, the house journal of a Liverpool business, questioned the idea that 'low class literature' could corrupt a young person's morals. He or she makes the entirely reasonable point that the effect of a book depends as much, if not more, on the character of the reader, than on the work itself. A novel cannot be called good or bad 'by what is called its "effect" on those who read it; for this influence we find to arise from a quality in the reader rather in the book itself' (Skilton 1993: 84). So, then, what does make a good book? A 'competent and conscientious' author, one who puts 'the best power of his heart and brain' into his work (ibid.: 84). The excellence of such a book may not be evident at first, but the patient reader will eventually come to a true appreciation of its worth. Mass publications do not require sustained examination. They please easily but will not last because they lack the 'beauty which has its foundations in the deepest nature of man' (ibid.: 82). The contributor does not use this distinction to denigrate cheap fiction; on the contrary, he or she suggests that 'the second rate is what the ignorant require for catching the first gleam' (ibid.: 83). Rather touchingly, the writer declares that within 'fifty years the bad and the middling in literature will be unable to find a publisher because they will be unable to find a market' (ibid.: 83). His optimism is a reflection of the nineteenth-century belief in progress, that society moves from ignorance to knowledge, from repression to freedom and from feudalism to democracy. And yet, as one contemporary noted, in every face one saw 'the authentic signature of care and anxiety' (in Houghton 1957: 60).

## Realism: The 'Condition of England', Sensationalism and Idealism

The word 'realism' entered the language in the 1850s. The appearance of the term is related to what Carlyle called 'the condition of England' question (in Flint 1987: 1). This concerned the extent and likely effect of urban and rural poverty. Unless remedied, discontent could lead to revolution. Such fears haunted novels like Charlotte Brontë's *Shirley* (1849) and Dickens's *Barnaby Rudge* (1841). One way of addressing those fears was to find out exactly how the poor lived and then try to improve their lot. To that end the 1840s and 50s saw the publication of a vast number of government reports – the Blue books – as well as articles and newspaper reports describing the conditions in slums, factories and on the land. Mrs Gaskell's *North and South* (1855) was one of a number of works that sought to describe the reality of industrial life and to make suggestions on how to eliminate the conflict between masters and men. Mrs Gaskell's solution was to urge both factory owners and operatives to recognise their common humanity and mutual dependency.

The idea of 'realism' in short was, in part, a response to a social problem. In the eighteenth century, literature was an imitation of nature but, in the mid-nineteenth, it was trying to make sense of a new kind of society. This involved representing it as accurately as possible. Unfortunately, the novelist often found that he or she was restricted in what they could say by considerations of decency. Moreover, as the philosopher and literary critic G. H. Lewes (1817–78) noted, the artist's power to represent reality was limited by his or her chosen medium: 'the canvas of the painter, the marble of the sculpture, the chords of the musician, each bring with them peculiar laws' (Skilton 1993: 102) that refract whatever reality they aim to represent. The requirement that there should be a balanced relation between part and whole, that characters should be 'definite and well grouped', that 'their introduction should be justified by some sort of necessity' and that the work should 'excite' as well as 'leave an impression of beauty, completeness and repose' (ibid.: 100) means that a pattern is imposed on reality, perhaps falsifying it in the process.

Realism was often compared with sensationalism. The realist novel was concerned with character, 'the fundamental critical term in the period' (Skilton 1993: 118) while the sensation novel was concerned with plot. Eneas Sweetland Dallas (1828–79), whose *Gay Science* (1866) was an unsuccessful attempt to establish the first principles of criticism, refined this basic distinction by adding that, in the realist novel, characters determine their own lives while, in the sensation novel, they are 'ruled by circumstance' (ibid.: 136). In one of the favourite images of the time, they are 'puppets, dummies, and unnatural creations that grimace and jerk their way along the scenes' (ibid.: 123). How can we capture character? A critic in the *Spectator* (f. 1828) opined that it is 'through the construction of the little circumstances, the variations of the angles of the little mental and moral reflectors [that] we catch a new glimpse of [a character's] nature and essence' (Skilton 1993: 119). The best way to portray character was through interaction with other characters. The poet and essayist William Caldwell Roscoe (1823–59) said that the novelist studied not man 'the individual soul . . . but man the social animal, man considered with reference to the experiences, the aims, the affections, that find their field in his intercourse with his fellow-men' (ibid.: 146). Hence we find one critic praising Trollope's characters because they 'are more or less interesting almost exactly in proportion to the degree in which their mode of influencing or failing to influence other people is unique and characteristic' (ibid.: 134).

The appeal of the sensation novel was that it was exciting. A key figure in the development of British psychology, Alexander Bain (1818–1903), said that the rapid changes of plot keep readers in a state of 'thrilling expectation' while minor incidents 'serve to discharge at intervals' (ibid.: 127) their pent-up feelings and emotions. This is catharsis for the masses. Ruskin locates the appeal of the sensation novel in 'the monotony of life' found in 'any great modern city' (ibid.: 139). This stems from the absence of nature, the drudgery of work and the dullness of the environment. These and other privations give rise to a craving for stimulation which only sensation novels can satisfy. Trollope rejects these broad distinctions between realism and sensationalism, saying that 'a good novel should be both, and in the highest degree' (ibid.: 138).

Realism was contrasted with idealism as well as with sensationalism. David Masson (1822–1907), who was apparently the first person to write on the British novel for a university audience, saw Thackeray as a realist and Dickens as an idealist (see Skilton 1993: 112). As we saw above, realism, in the broadest sense, refers to 'actual life' (ibid.: 86). It is the novelist's equivalent of the critic's aim, which is 'to see the object as in itself it really is' (Keating 1981: 186). Realism deals with the present. If things happen in life, they should be portrayed in art. Wilkie Collins (1824–89), a hugely popular writer in his time, argued that 'the business of fiction is to exhibit human life' which, of necessity, includes 'scenes of misery and crime' (ibid.: 93). For some, this made realism a rather sordid affair while, for others, the photographic view of life seemed somewhat mechanical and lacking in imagination. Idealism is the assumption that, behind the familiar appearance of things, there is a deeper reality which can only be grasped by the imagination. This is not just a legacy of romantic thinking, it goes back to Sidney's defence of poetry as invention. Bulwer Lytton's response to those who said that only realism could advance the cause of reform was to argue that it was, in fact, the romantic strain in art that woke the audience from 'their chronic lethargy of contempt and compelled 'the Lawgiver 'to redress what the Poet had lifted into esteem' (ibid.: 88).

Lewes claimed that realism and idealism complemented one another. 'Realism is the basis of all art and its antithesis is not Idealism, but *Falsism*' (Skilton 1993: 102). Falsism romanticises reality. It presents us with a factory worker speaking 'refined sentiments in unexceptionable English, and children utter[ing] long speeches of religious and poetic enthusiasm' (ibid.: 102). Lewes evokes the old idea of decorum when he demands that writers should 'either keep people silent, or make them speak the idiom of their class' (ibid.: 102). The significance of idealism is that it adds emotion to reality, making the reader sympathise with the portrait of ordinary life. The debate between realism and idealism is a working out of some of the issues of romanticism. The imagination is viewed with some suspicion because it does not show things as they are, but the importance of emotion is recognised. Realism and idealism are eventually brought together in the Marxist conception of realism which claims that, by an accurate representation of the surface features of society, we are able to discern and, indeed, direct those forces underneath working for change.[16]

Collins claims that while we may recoil from a writer's description of a slum, or an industrial dispute, such scenes serve 'a moral purpose' (Skilton 1993: 102), which suggests that realism has a commitment to morality as well as truth. George Eliot muses on the relation between representation and ethics in 'The Natural History of German Life' (1856). She complains that those who talk or write about the working class know very little about them: 'our social novels profess to represent people as they are, and the unreality of their representations is a grave evil' (Hoffman and Hynes 1966: 222). Instead of relying on direct observation in their depiction of 'the people, the masses, the proletariat [and] the peasantry' (ibid.: 220), artists prefer to idealise them. As a result, we have pictures of peasant girls who 'look as if [they] knew the poems of Letitia Elizabeth Landon[17] (1802–38) by heart' (ibid.: 220). The purpose of art is to extend our sympathy but it cannot do this if that sympathy is turned towards a false object instead of a true one. 'We want to be taught to feel, not for the heroic artisan or the sentimental peasant, but for the peasant in all his coarse apathy, and the artisan in all his suspicious self-ishness' (ibid.: 223). Another version of this view appears in Eliot's novel *Adam Bede* (1859). It occurs in the chapter entitled 'In which the Story Pauses a Little'. Once more she reiterates her view that art should focus on real people, otherwise 'we may happen to leave them quite out of our religion and philosophy, and frame lofty theories which only fit a world of extremes' (Skilton 1993: 107).

Eliot's desire to include 'real breathing men and women' (ibid.: 106) in her art is not just a reaction to idealism. It is also a response to the merging of 'social questions' with 'economical science', the idea that 'the relations of men may be settled by algebraic equations' (Hoffman and Hynes 1966: 224). The desire to establish an exact likeness of, say, 'those old women scraping carrots with their work-worn hands' (Skilton 1993: 107) is a way of defying the reduction of human beings to economic abstractions. Art cherishes the particular; it promotes the integrity of the individual against idealism, mechanisation and market forces. There is also a political dimension to Eliot's philosophy of inclusion. The call for greater representation in art parallels the call for greater representation in Parliament. One of the major developments of the nineteenth century was the extension of the franchise but it was dependent on property and payment of the rates. The Reform Bill of 1832 gave the vote to £10 householders, that of 1867 to all urban householders, and that of 1884 to all county householders. The idea of representation and what it means is central to art and politics in the nineteenth century. But Eliot is no egalitarian. Her descriptions of, for want of a better phrase, labourers, are often condescending and occasionally dismissive. They are 'coarse, common people' and 'ugly, stupid and inconsistent' (ibid.: 105 and 107).

These terms are applied not to a person but a class, which seems to illustrate Thomas Docherty's point that 'to represent those who have not been represented, it is first necessary . . . to consider them *abstractly* as a homogenised class with shared qualities or properties' (2002: 132). Realism, in seeking to represent individuals hitherto excluded from the realms of art, only succeeds in classifying them. And there is one further irony. At the very moment the working class are made visible, the middle class become invisible. 'The most remarkable deficiency in modern fiction', Bagehot asserts, 'is the omission of the business . . . in most novels, money *grows*' (1916: 173). In the end, the claim that realism helps to heal the divisions of society cannot be sustained. It may, in contrast to idealism, appear to represent reality but, by avoiding the topic of how money is made, realism covers up the operations of capitalism which produce the divisions it offers to overcome. Yes, realism may bring the working class into focus but, since one of the great fears of the nineteenth century was revolution, that was a means of monitoring and controlling them. Novels like *North and South* and Dickens's *Hard Times* (1854) contain working-class characters who act as models for working-class readers. In the former, Nicholas Higgins is made to give up drink and take 'an interest in sacred things' (Gaskell 1993: 348) while, in the latter, we are made to admire Stephen Blackpool for refusing to join in strike action.

### Bagehot on Sterne and Thackeray

We have looked at some of the major concepts deployed in the criticism of the novel but what about discussion of individual authors? We get a flavour of this from Bagehot's comparative study of Laurence Sterne (1713–68) and William Makepeace Thackeray (1811–63), best known as the author of

*Vanity Fair* (1847–8) and Dickens's major rival for the allegiance of the early Victorian reading public. The comparison also allows us to see how at least one critic saw the differences between the eighteenth- and nineteenth-century novel. Bagehot's approach is partly biographical because he believes that we need to 'enliven the tedium of criticism with a little interest from human life' (1916: 95). Sadly, late twentieth-century critics did not agree and banished all biographical considerations from discussion of a writer's work, with predictable results: a surge in dullness without a corresponding rise in enlightenment.

Bagehot concentrates on Sterne's *Tristram Shandy* (1759–67) and the first thing he seizes on is its 'fantastic disorder of form' (1916: 105). A great writer such as George Eliot, says Bagehot, plots her story carefully. By 'first strokes and fitting preliminaries [she] should form and prepare [the reader's] mind for the due appreciation and the perfect enjoyment of high creations' (ibid.: 105). A second fault of *Tristram Shandy* is its 'indecency' (ibid.: 106). Bagehot's particular worry here is that the novel may fall into the hands of young ladies. Having just described George Eliot as 'the greatest living writer of fiction' (ibid.: 105), Bagehot then remarks that 'the indiscriminate study of human life is not desirable [for young ladies] either in fiction or reality' (ibid.: 107). He has a rhetorical conception of novels to the extent that he believes that they form a young woman's 'idea of the world, define her taste and modify her morality; not so much in explicit thought and direct act as unconsciously and in her floating fancy' (ibid.: 107). And all the more effective for that, we might add. Bagehot's idea of how novels influence their readers signals a shift of emphasis in the history of criticism. Traditionally, art made its audience conscious of virtue and vice so that they could behave accordingly. But the recognition of the key role of emotion in human psychology means that there is now a greater appreciation of its effect, of its power to insinuate ideas instead of merely promoting them. Similarly, there has been a shift in the attitude to women. In the Renaissance they were seen as a danger to literature, now literature is a danger to them. Once they threatened to subvert the language, now the language threatens to subvert them, principally because they are now defined more in terms of emotion than in terms of wit and intellect and it is to the feelings that novels appeal.

Bagehot's long discussion of what is and is not suitable for young ladies brings out yet another aspect of realism: that it was also a matter of gender. Bagehot's more general argument is that while we can put up with what is 'barbarous and animal in reality' we should not have to endure it in literature (1916: 109). The introduction of 'ugliness is always a sin in art' (ibid.: 109). The aesthetic of beauty and the ethic of decency are far more important than an accurate record of existence. This is not mere prissiness on Bagehot's part; it is a recognition of the transforming power of art. It is not a mirror, it is a form of alchemy, turning base metal into gold. The problem of criticism is that it turns it back again. Telling us what literature omits, dissolving it back into its context, or raiding it to illustrate this or that agenda dissipates its wealth instead of distributing it. The economic metaphor again. The vices that disfigure *Tristram Shandy* are bawdiness and lack of seriousness, grave defects in an age whose 'distinguishing characteristic' was its 'moral earnestness' (Houghton 1957: 220). Bagehot is careful not to dwell on these matters nor on those details of Sterne's life, such as his affair with a maid servant that drove his wife temporarily insane. They would have offended the Victorian conception of morality which, as any one with the faintest acquaintance of the period knows, was less a code of virtue than a cloak for vice.

Another defect of *Tristram Shandy* is that it 'contains eccentric characters only' (Bagehot 1916: 110). This is in part due to the final fault of the novel, that it is – and you can almost hear Bagehot spit out the word – *'provincial'* (ibid.: 112). The country town in the eighteenth century, he contends, 'abounded in odd characters, they were out of the way of the great opinion of the world and shaped themselves to little opinions of their own' (ibid.: 110). This changed with the growth of public opinion. The railway in particular brought from London 'a uniform creed to every cranny of the kingdom, north and south, east and west' (ibid.: 110). While this broadened the outlook of those unfortunate enough to live outside the capital it also crushed their individual spirit. For that reason, Bagehot is ultimately ambivalent about the provincial. It maybe quirky and closed minded but it testified to a variety in English life which was fast disappearing. We can fly to another city, he writes, 'but it is all the same Roman Empire; the one code of heavy law presses us down and makes us – the sensible part of us at least – as like other people as we can make ourselves' (ibid.: 110).

Bagehot is not against the portrayal of oddities as long as they have a degree of credibility. He cites the example of Hamlet, 'one of the most eccentric [characters] in literature', who 'enlarges our conception of human nature' because we are to understand that he is a 'vividly possible man' (1916: 111). The trouble with Sterne's characters is that, generally, they lack this degree of probability and so they appear unnatural. And even where they are shaded off into human nature, this 'society of originals' is not shaded off into the world, but 'is left to stand by itself, as if it were a natural and ordinary society, a society easily conceivable and needing no explanation' (ibid.: 111–12). But the great masters of literature do not work like that. They create 'a constant atmosphere of half commonplace personages [which] surrounds and shades off, illustrates and explains every central group of singular persons' (ibid.: 112).

Bagehot spends far more time on Sterne than he does on Thackeray, which suggests that the former intrigues him more despite or because of the flaws in his work. If Sterne was sensitive to the peculiarities of character, Thackeray was drawn to the scenes of society: 'the streets, the servants, the clubs, the gossip, the West End fastened upon his brain' (1916: 121). He was particularly alert to the feelings and point of view of those lower down the social scale than himself. Hazlitt said that Thackeray could not enjoy the company in the drawing room for wondering what the servants thought of him. As Bagehot puts it, 'the footman's view of life was never out of his head' (ibid.: 121). Bagehot believed that the 'duty of the critic' – and what are we to make of that word 'duty'? – was to 'explain, as far as we can, the nature and limits of genius, but never to deny or question for one moment its existence' (ibid.: 165). And with Thackeray, as with Sterne, the spotlight falls on his shortcomings. He fails to be a truly great artist because he 'could not help half accepting, half believing the common ordinary sensitive view of life, although he knew perfectly knew in his inner mind and deeper nature that this apparent and superficial view of life was misleading, inadequate and deceptive' (ibid.: 122). High art was more than low realism.

Thackeray's sympathy with 'humble persons' (1916: 124) forms part of the impulse behind *The Book of Snobs* (1848), his satire on social climbers. They 'go to rack and ruin from trying to ape their betters' (Tennyson and Gray 1976: 624). Bagehot argues that Thackeray's attack is too indiscriminate. Of course, 'striving after unpossessed distinction' (1916: 126) is to be condemned, but that is hardly the most heinous fault in our nature. Snobbery is one form of the desire to better ourselves and in

> a society like ours, in which there are prizes which every man may seek, degradations which everyone may erase, inequalities which everyone may remove, it is idle to suppose that there will not be all sorts of strivings to cease to be last and to begin to be first, and it is equally idle to imagine that all such strivings will be of the highest kind. (ibid.: 126)

Bagehot's disagreement with Thackeray is social rather than artistic although the two categories cannot finally be separated. As a banker, Bagehot belongs to a middle class that believes in self-improvement and that is why he objects to Thackeray's mockery of those who try to better themselves. Bagehot is therefore on the side of progress while Thackeray is attached to traditional hierarchies.

But it is not quite so simple as that. The apparently backward-looking Thackeray anticipates at least one aspect of modernist literature, the theme of self-consciousness. His worry about how the footman perceives him as he climbs the stairs is echoed in T. S. Eliot's 'The Love Song of Alfred J. Prufrock' (1917), in which the narrator imagines the women's comments on his thinning hair as he descends the stair. Even the line 'And I have seen the eternal Footman hold my coat, and snicker' (Eliot [1969] 1978: 15) recalls Thackeray's anxiety about what those in livery think of him. But it was his concern with the poor that made Bagehot so uncomfortable, not just with Thackeray but also with Charles Dickens (1812–70). The 'real tendency of their exhortations', he wrote, 'is to make men dissatisfied with their inevitable condition, and what is worse, to make them fancy that its irremediable evils can be remedied, and indulge in a succession of vague strivings and restless changes' (Bagehot 1916: 192). This seems to contradict Bagehot's earlier remark about not just the inevitability but the desirability of social mobility. A closer examination reveals a distinction – not always clear – between what individuals can do to better themselves and what can or cannot be done to correct the ills of society. The point, once again, is that Bagehot moves seamlessly from artistic to social considerations and back again. His musings on the respective styles of Thackeray and Dickens lead him to ponder the best forms of social organisation, and full democracy is not of them. The best art for Bagehot is like the political process: it does not concern itself too much with the provincial or the lower orders.

### Aestheticism, Ethics and Economics

In the late seventeenth and eighteenth century, English criticism was influenced by French neoclassicism. In the late nineteenth century, it was influenced by the French idea of art for art's sake. The phrase originated with the poet, novelist and art critic Théophile Gautier (1811–72). The heroine of his novel, *Mademoiselle de Maupin* (1835), justifies her various amours by arguing that the pursuit of sensation is a pleasure in itself. Charles Baudelaire (1821–67), dandy, opium addict and syphilitic, but also one of France's greatest erotic poets, was the antithesis of neoclassicism. Excess, artifice and vice were his watchwords, not restraint, nature and virtue. In his philosophy there was no contradiction between the beautiful and the ugly. What caused this transformation in the canon of criticism? In France, it was the redundancy of the artist. He or she 'no longer had a niche in society because no class existed which felt any need for their productions or identified itself with their interests' (Gaunt 1975: 11). Consequently, the artist was a sort of anarchist. He despised the bourgeoisie partly because they were only concerned with money but chiefly because they didn't believe the arts served any useful purpose. And since so few were interested in art, it must be preserved 'like a sacred mystery' (ibid.: 12).

It was for similar reasons that the doctrine of art for art's sake appealed to English writers and critics. As we have argued, the central problem of criticism since the Renaissance has been to find a justification for the study of poetry – later literature – once it has ceased to shape the vernacular and the values of the elite. The two most common were that it was a model of behaviour and an expression of the nation. Neither was finally convincing because they both depended on a rhetorical conception of poetry whose demise had given rise to the question to which they were supposed to be the answer. Despite the claims made for realism, the link between art and morality has been broken. Ethics had migrated to economics. Samuel Smiles declares in *Self-Help* (1859) that 'some of the finest qualities of human nature are intimately related to the right use of money' (Smiles 1958: 281). Saving is good, spending is bad. The discipline of work strengthens character, but a 'taste for dress, style, luxuries and amusements' (ibid.: 290) retards its development. Of course art can explore questions of right and wrong but it can only do so because of its distance from the sphere of action. Its exploratory idiom is not suited to commercial expediency and so it has little value in the marketplace except as a commodity or as a tool of training. Richard Olivier, for example, uses *Henry V* to teach business people leadership qualities,[18] a theme taken up by Norman Augustine and Kenneth Adelman in their book *Shakespeare in Charge: The Bard's Guide to Leading and Succeeding on the Business Stage* (1999) and John O. Whitney and Tina Packer in their *Power Plays: Shakespeare's Lessons in Leadership and Management* (2000).

It is as the moral idea of art is fading that the view of it as an expression of the nation's soul intensifies. Or, more accurately, we could say that ethics is re-energised as Englishness. 'For many people', writes Kumar, 'literature, not Parliament or the monarchy, *was* England, the noblest and most heartfelt expression (Kumar 2003: 220). The late nineteenth century saw the publication of a number of works that portrayed the nation. Most famous was Palgrave's *Golden Treasury of English Verse* which first appeared in 1861 and this was followed by Sir Arthur Quiller-Couch's *Oxford Book of English Verse* (1900). One job of a critic, it seems, was to assemble works that were representative of the national character. But why? Part of the answer was growing social unrest. The new unions, the suffragette movement, the agitation for Home Rule in Ireland and the spread of socialist ideas revived the fear of revolution, never far beneath the surface of the nineteenth-century middle-class consciousness. There was also anxiety about economic decline; about the industrial challenge of America and Germany; about the ambitions of Russia; about safeguarding trade routes to India; and about the European scramble for land in Africa. The promotion of the national literature was an attempt to unify different groups, to weld them into one nation. But an appreciation of Shakespeare was hardly going to mitigate the effects of poverty or powerlessness. In any case, the reading public preferred Sherlock Holmes.

Aestheticism is a recognition that the relation between art and ethics has been weakened. Indeed, Wilde declares that the link between them is completely broken. 'The sphere of art and the sphere of ethics', he writes, 'are absolutely distinct and separate' (Small 1979: 89). The doctrine of art for art's sake also militated against an interest in a national literature which, with its celebration of virtues such as sincerity, must have seemed narrowly moral as well as stuffily provincial to the aesthetic temperament. But it would be wrong to imply that aestheticism had no connection with the native tradition of thinking about literature. The stress on sensation can be traced back to romanticism while the attention to form, particularly in Wilde (ibid.: 92–3), follows on from the discussion about realism and idealism. The claim that art served no practical purpose derives from Arnold's insistence that 'the notion of the free play of the mind on all subjects [is] a pleasure in itself' (Keating 1981: 196). Pater acknowledges the continuity between his own position and Arnold's when he writes that:

> 'To see the object in itself as it really is' has been justly said to be the aim of all true criticism whatever; and in aesthetic criticism the first step to seeing one's object as it really is, is to know one's impression as it really is, to discriminate it, to realise it distinctly. (1986: xxix)

The ghost of Locke also lurks in that remark. But its significance for our history is that it shifts criticism from the public to the private sphere. To know precisely what one feels about a work, not what role it can play in the polity, has become the primary goal of criticism.

Or at least of aesthetic criticism. Which, of course, is not the only type. On the verge of its rise to prominence, many critics still took a highly moral view of art. The poet, novelist and playwright Robert Williams Buchanan (1841–1901) was outraged by Dante Gabriel Rossetti's description of a kiss.

> Here is a full-grown man, presumably intelligent and cultivated, putting on record for other full-grown men to read, the most secret mysteries of sexual connection, and that with so sickening a desire to reproduce the sensual mood, so careful a choice of epithet to convey mere animal sensations, that we merely shudder at the shameless nakedness.[19]

Algernon Swinburne (1837–1909) suffered a similar attack on the publication of his *Poems and Ballads* (1866). Dubbed 'the libidinous laureate of a pack of satyrs' (Guy 1998: 370) by the editor and Liberal Member of Parliament John Morley, Swinburne defended himself first by saying that an author's opinions are not necessarily those of his characters, second by claiming that it is the job of literature 'to deal with the full life of man and the whole nature of things' (ibid.: 381) and third by appealing to the classical tradition. One of the poems, the 'Ode to Anactoria', was a 'paraphrase' of Sappho. The authority of the ancients is summoned to sanction the sensuous side of life and to counter the narrow moralism of some Victorian critics.

There were also those who were concerned by the way poetry seemed to be losing its traditionally masculine character. In the words of Alfred Austin (1835–1913), who was appointed poet laureate after the death of Tennyson, it had become 'feminine, timorous, narrow and domesticated' (Bristow 1987: 124). Its soul, he announced, echoing Arnold, should be 'action, action, action' (ibid.: 124). W. H. Mallock (1849–1923), another critic who showed an interest in economics, agreed. Contemporary verse dealt in 'the weakest emotions' and 'the most tiresome platitudes' (Bristow 1987: 126). Mallock also wrote 'recipes' instructing readers how to write like a modern poet. To imitate Tennyson's *The Idylls of the King* (1859), one must have a 'prig' for a hero who 'must be set upright in the middle of a round table', next to 'a beautiful wife who cannot abide prigs', and they must be surrounded by 'a large number of men and women of the nineteenth century, in fairy-ball costume, flavoured with a great many possible vices, and a few impossible virtues' (ibid.: 129).

Despite the largely moral tone of his commentary, Austin did try to explain the nature of modern poetry partly in terms of the society in which it was written: 'great poetry is like everything else, an affair indispensably of external conditions' (Bristow 1987: 118), a remark that suggests criticism was moving away from the romantic idea of genius as the cause of art. But, at the same time, Austin sought to preserve art's special status which he thought was being eroded by its association with commerce. It is 'not like dry-goods, whatever some people may think' (ibid.: 119–20), and neither a patron nor the state nor the public nor the laws of supply and demand can call forth art. Only 'spontaneity, simplicity, faith, unconscious earnestness, and manly concentration' (ibid.: 120) can do that, a list that contains both romantic and Victorian characteristics. Criticism proceeds by accruing terms at first contrary and then complementary. But, as here, this can lead to confusion rather than clarity. Austin maintains that art is the product of external factors yet, at the same time, says this is not the case, it is the product of internal ones.

Bagehot believes that it is the job of the critic to make poetry something more than 'light amusement' (1916: 307). The poet should be encouraged to strive for 'exquisite thought', 'sublime feeling' and 'consummate description' (ibid.: 306). This recommendation occurs in the course of his discussion of Tennyson and Robert Browning (1812–89), the two major poets of the mid- to late nineteenth century. Bagehot echoes Samuel Johnson in his view that 'the business of the poet is with types' (Bagehot 1916: 311). He also states that criticism, if it is to judge literature wisely, should spend time 'among the simple principles of art' (ibid.: 317). Bagehot divides the art of poetry into three: the pure, the ornate and the grotesque which roughly correspond to the classical, the romantic and the medieval. Pure poetry describes the perfect type as economically as possible and Milton is the great exemplar. Tennyson is the chief representative of ornate poetry which makes the best of 'imperfect types' by covering up their defects and Bagehot compares this manoeuvre to the 'sudden millionaires of the present day [who] hope to disguise their social defects [by] hiding among aristocratic furniture' (1916: 337). Grotesque art deals not with normal types but 'abnormal specimens . . . not with what nature is striving to become, but by what with some lapse she has happened to become' (ibid.: 338). Browning is the great master of this art whose saving grace is that its 'ugliness' recalls 'the perfection, the beauty, from which it is a deviation' (ibid.: 345). The dominant forms of contemporary poetry are the ornate and the grotesque. They please the eye for a moment and then 'the hasty reader passes on to some new excitement' (ibid.: 351).

## Walter Pater (1839–94)

Bagehot disapproves of such restlessness, saying it is 'not favourable to the due appreciation of pure art, of that art which must be known before it can be admired' (1916: 351), but agitation is Pater's starting point. The tendency of modern thought, he writes in his famous 'Conclusion' to *Studies in the History of the Renaissance* (1873), is 'to regard all things and principles of things as inconstant modes of fashion' (Pater 1986: 150). This was not mere dilettantism on his part but a recognition of the dynamic nature of contemporary society. Pater was writing at the end of a century of change whose pace looked set to intensify. In every area, from evolution to the extension of the franchise, from industrialisation to the seaside excursion, British society was being transformed. The city, with its crowded streets, rapid changes of scene, and competing demands on the senses, played a big part in altering the conditions of perception. The packed pavements, the rattle of carriages and the glare of advertising trained consciousness to cope with simultaneous and fleeting impressions. 'Our physical life', writes Pater, is in 'perpetual motion' while our 'inward world of thought . . . is still more rapid' (ibid.: 151–2).

Pater's interest in impressions can be traced back to Locke, though it is also related to developments in the psychology of perception that were occurring in the late nineteenth century.[20] The beauty of Pater's writing almost transforms psychology into poetry. It also brings out what was darkly implicit in Locke; that we are alone and that our sense of self is highly unstable. Our experience, 'already reduced to a group of impressions, is ringed round . . . by that thick wall of personality' (1986: 151) which prevents us from reaching out to others or them from reaching out to us. And then these impressions, on which our sense of self depends, are so fast and fleeting that we are continually forming and reforming ourselves or, as Pater puts it, we are perpetually 'weaving and unweaving' (ibid.: 152) ourselves. The purpose of art is to 'give the highest quality to [our] moments as they pass, and simply for those moments' sake' (ibid.: 153). This represents another shift in the history of criticism. Literature is now esteemed for the passing sensation, not the lasting truth. But as always, what appears to be a radical change is often nothing more than a newly emphasised continuity. One of the aims of literature has always been to provoke delight. The context, though, is new. Literature should excite sensation to counter 'a society that seems able to deaden the senses and the spirit alike' (Freedman 1990: 2).

This means that the value of art is realised in the present. As late as the eighteenth century, Samuel Johnson declared that the only true test of a work was time, a belief partly based on the idea that history was largely continuous. The Enlightenment belief in universal human nature ensured Aristotle was still relevant to Dryden's conception of tragedy. But the central experience of the nineteenth century was change. What other period had known the transforming power of the machine, felt the age of the earth, sent God into exile? The idea that art should be permanent could not survive in a culture that had witnessed the crumbling of long-established truths and suffered the upheaval of the industrial revolution. Its value, for Pater, lay in the brilliance with which it crystallised our impressions of the present. Art helps us to make the most of time, not transcend it. And it doesn't teach us anything. 'Not the fruit of experience, but experience itself is the end' (1986: 152). The aesthetic critic is formed by the traditions of eighteenth-century sensibility and romantic individualism. He or she therefore does not work by rules but by temperament. Beauty is not absolute but relative. The key question is: 'What is this song or picture, this engaging personality presented in life or in a book to *me*?' (ibid.: xxix). We should note the continuity between art and existence in that quotation which suggests that aestheticism is more an attitude to life than a realm set apart, as has often been claimed. The aesthetic critic then has to 'distinguish, analyse, and separate from its adjuncts, the virtue by which a picture, a landscape, a fair personality in life or in a book, produces this special impression of beauty or pleasure' (ibid.: xxx). In searching for that elusive quality which makes something what it is and no other thing, he or she is part of the nineteenth-century revolt against abstraction.

But when Pater turns his attention to what constitutes literary value he deserts the particular for the general. What makes a work worth reading is the precision of the writing and the 'truth to bare fact' (Small 1979: 31), which makes literature sound like science. Indeed, Francis Palgrave (1824–97) declared that there was a scientific method for studying poetry. It consisted of finding the causes that produced the effect of pleasure. We are back with Aristotle, whose theory of causes revolutionised the reading of the Bible in the thirteenth century. The pleasure of poetry, says Palgrave, is 'the elevation and purification of the soul' and it is caused by 'formal or technical laws, unity, metrical structure and the like' (Dennis and Skilton 1987: 127). We have already alluded to the link between impressionism and the psychology of perception, but there is also a small thesis waiting to be written on the connection between theories of vitalism[21] and Pater's idea that criticism consists of identifying 'the strange, mystical sense of life' (1986: xxxi) that flows through a work.

The distinction between good art and great art depends 'not on its form, but on the matter' (Small 1979: 45), a claim which is hard to reconcile with the idea that all matter is nothing but our momentary impression of it. Great art, Pater observes, is also noted for 'its compass, its variety, its alliance to great ends, or the depth of the note of revolt, or the largeness of hope' (ibid.: 46). That is a much larger conception of art than the one found in his 'Conclusion'. It now has altogether loftier aims than making the most of the passing moment such as: the 'increase of happiness', the 'redemption of the oppressed', the 'enlargement of our sympathies' and the 'presentation of some new or old truth about ourselves' which 'may ennoble and fortify us in our sojourn here' (ibid.: 46). Pater even suggests that art may be for the glory of God, perhaps in contrition for the perceived immorality of endorsing experience for the sake of experience. The important point, though, is that Pater has moved away from aesthetics to ethics, from individual impressions of beauty to abstract ideas about art.

## Oscar Wilde

Wilde's discussion of criticism is partly rooted in romanticism. After all, he does say that 'emotion for the sake of emotion is the aim of art' (Small 1979: 78). But he is also reacting against that tradition. 'All bad poetry', he remarks flippantly, 'springs from genuine feeling' (ibid.: 92). He distrusts the emotions because they are a source of division. Only the intellect can discern what we have in common. One of the benefits of criticism is that it 'annihilate[s] race prejudices by insisting on the unity of the human mind in the variety of its forms' (ibid.: 97). The discipline of reading, the ability to distance oneself from emotive issues, is a necessity in a world 'dominate[d] by the fanatic whose worst vice is his sincerity' (ibid.: 98), a remark that applies equally to our own time with the resurgence of religious fundamentalism. Above all, Wilde rejects the romantic view that art is a form of self-expression. He claims that we can only express ourselves indirectly. 'Man is least himself when he talks in his own person. Give him a mask and he will tell you the truth' (ibid.: 85). This assertion partly relates to Wilde having to hide his sexuality, but it also relates to the increasingly mediated character of social experience. Mill wrote of how commerce erodes honest communication, forcing people to adopt poses in order to compete more successfully. And, at least since Carlyle, commentators were aware of the powerful new phenomenon of public opinion, which appears to mirror our core values but which in reality constructs them.

Wilde's criticism is, in many respects, similar to Pater's. The sole aim of the critic, for example, 'is to chronicle his own impressions' (Small 1979: 68) and, again like Pater, he values precision. 'To the aesthetic temperament', he writes, 'the vague is always repellent' (ibid.: 80). But Wilde goes further. The encounter with art is a form of autobiography or, as he puts it, 'the record of one's own soul' (ibid.: 68). This is another apparently new departure in the history of criticism. Seeing the object in itself as it really is, and knowing one's impression as it really is, are now absorbed into a conception of criticism as the narrative of the self.

There are at least three ways in which the critic uses literature as a form of self-fashioning. The first is 'to surrender absolutely to the work in question' (Small 1979: 88). This implies that the critic puts his or her own personality to one side, but this seems to be contradicted by the second approach which involves the critic 'intensifying' his or her personality since that is the only way he or she can give a true interpretation of the work. I say 'seems' because the contradiction is more apparent than real. It is only by suspending our sense of self that we can know the work, and it is only by knowing the work that we can know ourselves. The work gives us a new insight into ourselves and, as a result, we have a new insight into the work. The performance of a work provides the best illustration of what is meant. 'When Rubinstein plays . . . Beethoven', writes Wilde, 'he gives us not merely Beethoven, but also himself, and so gives us Beethoven absolutely reinterpreted through a rich artistic nature . . . made wonderful to us by . . . an intense personality' (ibid.: 76).

The third way in which the critic uses the work as a form of self-development hinges on the relationship between creative and critical writing and, here, Wilde clearly has Arnold in mind. Arnold notes that the distinction between the two is by no means clear-cut for criticism itself can be a creative activity. Would Johnson have better employed, he asks, in 'producing more *Irenes*[22] instead of writing his *Lives of the Poets*'? (Keating 1981: 188). The relationship between criticism and creativity is complementary, as when criticism codified the rules for good writing. Its main purpose now is to prepare, for the creative power, the best ideas of the age which the latter then presents 'in the most effective and attractive combinations' (ibid.: 189). But, despite the vital role he assigns to criticism, Arnold still believes that it 'is of a lower rank than the creative' (Keating 1981: 188).

Wilde also sees criticism and creation as mutually dependent but he refuses – at first – to place one above the other. He describes the critical faculty as 'the fine spirit of choice and delicate selection' without which the artist can neither 'realise life for us' nor 'give it momentary perfection' (Small 1979: 58). This perfection comes from form which, by giving shape to things, reveals their beauty. It also intensifies our experience of them. 'Find an expression for joy and you intensify its ecstasy' (ibid.: 92). Both the artist and the critic make use of form but it is the latter who uses it most creatively. He or she regards the art work as 'a suggestion for some new mood or thought or feeling which he can realise with equal or perhaps greater distinction of form' (ibid.: 84). The critic 'deals with materials' that have already been 'purified for him' (ibid.: 67). Gustave Flaubert (1821–80) may create, in *Madame Bovary* (1857), a classic from 'the sordid and sentimental amours of the silly wife of a country doctor' but his achievement is merely the starting point for the critic to produce work that will be 'flawless in beauty and instinct with intellectual subtlety' (Small 1979: 67–8). All of which is to say that the critic expresses him or herself through the creative use of art. We do not care whether his or her judgement is sound. We care about the quality of his or her response. And so we enjoy Ruskin's 'mighty and majestic prose . . . so fervid and fire-coloured' regardless of whether his view of Turner is right or not (ibid.: 68). Criticism does not justify art, art justifies criticism. Though, in the end, we cannot tell them apart.

Wilde's argument is an early instance of 'the death of the author, birth of the critic' thesis that held sway in literature departments in the 1980s and 90s. The difference is that Wilde is not entirely serious. In criticism, history occurs twice; the first time as irony, the second time as sincerity. Well, in this instance anyway. Wilde boosts the status of criticism at a time when its influence was declining. This was due to a number of factors, including the growth of popular literature, whose success did not depend on the opinions of a refined mind and the rise of the specialist. 'Where shall we look for the successors of the Mills and Ruskins', asked the historian G. M. Young (1882–1959), 'or of the public for which they wrote,? We 'go out into a Waste Land of Experts, each knowing so much about so little that he can be neither contradicted, nor is worth contradicting' (in Altick 1973: 268). Although Wilde tries to define criticism in general terms, his account makes it seem a highly specialised activity. To understand Shakespeare, for example, it is necessary to have a sound knowledge of history, of literary forms, of the conventions of theatre, of the canons of criticism, of the condition of the language and so on. The critic's aim is always to place the work 'in some new relation to the age' (ibid.: 76), which he does by casting it in a different form, that is, the critical idiom itself, so startling us into a fresh awareness of its significance. The greatness of art, the critic reminds us, springs from its ability to give shape to the chaos of life, thereby eternalising the passing emotion. The problem with life is that 'one can never repeat exactly the same emotion. How different it is in the world of art' (ibid.: 77).

The critic's ultimate goal is self-perfection but this doesn't mean he has nothing to contribute to the wider culture. Indeed, the desire to intensify his personality is a reminder of the importance of the individual in an age of increasing anonymity. And since the critic 'bears within himself the dreams and ideas and feelings of myriad ages' (Small 1979: 82) he forms a vital link between past and present which, in a society that felt itself quite different to all those which had preceded it, makes him an especially important figure. But the critic also looks to the future. Indeed, 'it is to criticism that the future belongs' for the necessity of imposing form on flux 'does not grow less as the world advances' (ibid.: 95). Art takes second place to criticism here because its subject matter 'is always diminishing' (ibid.: 95). The growth of mass society makes it difficult to innovate and therefore the 'tendency of creation is to repeat itself' (ibid.: 59). Poor Wilde. He wasn't to know that a great age of artistic experiment was just about to begin. Nor indeed that the emphasis he gives to form would be one of the sparks that ignited it.

Because it looks to the future, criticism is about growth. And the mind grows by contemplating the work of art. Like Arnold, who seems to have influenced him most, Wilde believes that criticism should be set apart from practical life or, as he terms it, action. Action, he writes, 'is limited and relative. Unlimited and absolute is the vision of him who sits at ease and watches' (Small 1979: 79). It would be easy to criticise Wilde by saying that this makes criticism the preserve of a leisured elite, as if it hadn't always been that. But he is right: time is one of the factors in our relationship with art, without it we can have no sense of the work's value. And academics, in whose hands the fate of criticism largely rests, suffer from a lack of time to read and reflect. The growing burden of administration, together with a huge increase in student numbers, has created a type of criticism that is easy to teach, simple to apply and convenient to mark. Which of course means it's not criticism, merely a technique of reading. Wilde makes contemplation central to the encounter with art. We must give ourselves wholly to the work and can 'think of nothing else' while we are involved with it (ibid.: 88). The aim of contemplation is 'not *doing* but *being*, not being merely but *becoming*' (ibid.: 82). And, in phrasing the matter in this way, Wilde is, of course, challenging the Victorian orthodoxy that 'work is the appointed calling of man on earth, the end for which his various faculties were given, the element in which his nature is ordained to develop itself, and in which his progressive advance to heaven is to lie' (Thomas Arnold, in Houghton 1957: 244). Similarly, his desire that the critic preserve the mystery of art is a reaction to the 'chill mathematics of thought' (Small 1979: 80) and the mechanical principle, a forerunner of the audit culture to the extent that it implies visibility and predictability.

But there is an irony here. Wilde may define the critic in opposition to the Victorian idea of work but that very definition itself contributes to the growth of professional culture. Gaunt suggests that the doctrine of 'art for art's sake' was a form of 'specialisation' because it '*defined* the artist as such' (1975: 17), while Freedman claims that:

the texts of aestheticism work as a form of specialised, esoteric knowledge, which is not only gathered, analysed, and ordered by aesthetic professionals in any number of fields but which also serves to mystify the authority of those professionals. As a result, the nature of the 'aesthetic' was itself transformed. Despite the overtly democratising tendencies evident in the earlier phases of aestheticism, the result of aestheticism's endeavours was that the perception of the beautiful was no longer held to be a universal or communal experience; rather it . . . serve[d] to define the expertise of the relevant authority, which that authority then imparts to an awed but appreciative public. (1990: 36)

Moreover, Wilde resorts to a monetary idiom that complicates the distinction he makes between criticism, which appeals to our highest instincts, and commerce, which appeals to our lowest. Criticism is seen as a matter of separating gold from silver, and silver from lead, and later he declares that the critic 'should lend as much as he borrows' (Small 1979: 59 and 76). Not only that, but Wilde was actively involved in the newly forming institutions of mass culture. He was, for example, an editor of *Woman's World*. Aestheticism was not a realm apart but deeply implicated in the formation of consumer society. Both the aesthetic critic and the consumer subscribe to the idea that pleasure is the greatest good. Pater's analysis of perception is a kind of training for consumerism which 'demands two different things of the self: endlessly mobile receptiveness to an infinitely eddying succession of sensual experiences, and a cognitive organization of that flux or welter of experiences' (Freedman 1990: 68). And Wilde's critic uses art in the same way as the consumer uses commodities: to fashion a series of identities that never come to an end. 'Criticism is always moving on', writes Wilde, 'and the critic is always developing' (Small 1979: 86).

## Conclusion

Nineteenth-century criticism has to deal with the legacy of romanticism and the place of literature in industrial society. Despite the introduction of new terms such as realism, much of the criticism of this period is similar in nature to that which we have encountered in earlier ages. Literature is still seen, for example, in largely moral terms. Even the novel's rise to prominence does not affect this most fundamental assumption about art. Nevertheless, we have noted how social changes have influenced the nature of criticism. Its focus on sensation, emotion and real life are a reaction to a whole host of factors ranging from the French Revolution to political economy. And literature has to fulfil some of the functions of religion, for example consolation, as belief in Christianity declines. There are other developments too. Since the late eighteenth century criticism had struggled to find an adequate response to the romantic notion that literature was the expression of feeling. For, if that were the case, who was to judge how adequate that expression was? Ruskin's discussion of the pathetic fallacy was an attempt to answer that question but the growth of mass society, the rise of literacy and the provision of popular reading undermined the critic's authority. Literature was becoming a matter of preference. It's not surprising then that Wilde tries to revive criticism by making it a means of self-development. As such, it seems to hold out different values to those of the surrounding society. But this opposition is more apparent than real not only because of the overlap between critical and commercial terms but also because the aestheticism of Wilde and Pater is deeply implicated in the emerging consumer society. In attempting to make criticism and creativity one, Wilde looks back to a time when the relationship between them was complementary. But the nineteenth century sees them start to develop along separate lines. As the study of literature moves into the universities, criticism surrenders what little is left of its public character and becomes part of the growing culture of professionalism, the domain of experts – which in a sense it always was.

## Notes

1. That is 'the rapid growth of trade, market and towns; the acceleration of agricultural and craft production; the evolution of specialised commercial enterprises and techniques; and the penetration of money and commercial values into all areas of social life' 1998: 15.

2. The phrase comes from the subtitle of Benjamin Disraeli's novel, *Sybil or the Two Nations* (1845).

3. Samuel Johnson, on a similar note, remarks that 'mankind may come, in time, to write all aphoristically . . . grow weary of preparation, and connection, and illustration, and all those arts by which a big book is made' Johnson 1990. Johnson's words seem on the verge of coming true in our own age, where so many things compete for our attention that we have to divide it into ever smaller parts.

4. For an excellent overview of the Victorian period, including a full discussion of the evangelical movement and the Oxford Movement, see Gilmour 1993.

5. 'The correspondence of one verse, or line with another, I call parallelism. When a proposition is delivered, and a second subjoined to it, or drawn under it, equivalent, or contrasted with it in a sense; or similar to it in the form of grammatical construction; these I call parallel lines; and the words or phrases answering to one another in the corresponding lines, parallel terms', in Jasper and Prickett 2004: 27.

6. For an overview of the work and Strauss's method, see <http://www.westarinstitute.org/Periodicals/4R_Articles/Strauss/strauss.html>.

7. For a full discussion of Coleridge's organic theory of art and indeed the character of romantic criticism generally, see Abrams 1976.

8. The word Whig derives from the word 'whiggam', a country term used to urge on a horse. It was first used to describe religious insurgents from the south of Scotland who marched on Edinburgh to purge it of ungodly elements. The term was used in England to describe those who tried to block Charles II's brother James from succeeding to the throne because he was a Catholic. 'Whig' was eventually dropped for that of 'liberal'.

9. For a comprehensive view of the relation between romanticism and reviewing, see: Morgan 1983; Klancher 1987; 1996; Demata and Wu 2002; and Wheatley 2003.

10. Cited in Cox 1999.

11. Ironically, the phrase is Wordsworth's. It comes from the poem 'The Tables Turned' (1798). The whole verse reads 'Sweet is the lore which Nature brings; / Our meddling intellect / Mis-shapes the beauteous form of things: – / We murder to dissect.'

12. For a more detailed discussion of these issues, see Shaffer 2003.

13. It has been noticed that Arnold seems more concerned with Wragg's name than her situation. 'If we are to talk of ideal perfection, of "the best in the whole world", has anyone reflected what a touch of grossness in our race, what an original shortcoming in the more delicate spiritual perceptions, is shown by the natural growth among us of such hideous names' (Keating 1981: 201). But this is to ignore Arnold's main point which is that the English middle class cannot afford to be so complacent when such tragedies occur in their midst. Nor can Arnold's recoil from the sound of certain English names be dismissed as snobbery for it is based on a sense that the beautiful, the good and the true are one, a view which has a long tradition in the history of criticism. Finally, we should remember that far from being an elitist Arnold believed that the final goal of culture is 'to do away with classes [and] make the best that has been known and thought in the world current everywhere' (1993: 79).

14. The one-dimensional nature of humans under capitalism is brilliantly captured in Dickens's method of characterisation. He takes one trait of a person and makes that their defining aspect.

15. The best starting point for an introduction to the variety of reading material in this period is Altick 1957.

16. The classic statement of this view can be found in Lukács 2006. For other Marxist theories of literature, see Eagleton and Milne 1996.

17. A very successful poet and novelist. For more detail of her life and work, see <http://www.litencyc.com/php/speople.php?rec=true&UID=5142>.

18. See <http://www.oliviermythodrama.com/800/store/books.cfm?o> for details.

19. The full text of the review is available at <http://www.victorianweb.org/authors/buchanan/fleshy.html>.

20. For a brief review of these developments, see <http://www.marxists.org/reference/subject/philosophy/help/percept.htm>. See also Reed 1998.

21. Vitalism is what distinguishes animate from non-animate matter. In its simplest form it states that matter is infused with a special fluid or spirit that gives it life

while in its more sophisticated version it refers to the organisation of living bodies. Although the theory can be traced back to Aristotle, it rose to prominence in the sixteenth and seventeenth centuries as a reaction to the mechanistic view of the body. Vitalism gradually lost its appeal towards the end of the nineteenth century, especially as the theory of evolution seemed to explain, in scientific terms, the nature of living matter. For a brief introduction to the history of vitalism, see <http://mechanism.ucsd.edu/~bill/teaching/philbio/vitalism.htm> and, for an account of vitalism in the nineteenth century see <http://www.bbk.ac.uk/english/skc/againstlife/>. Although the word 'vitalism' disappears, the idea lingers on. Critics as diverse as F. R. Leavis, William Empson, Roland Barthes and Jacques Derrida all discuss literature in terms of 'force' or 'intensity'.

22. The play concerns the fate of a Greek slave loved by the Emporer Mahomet.

CHAPTER

# 6

# INSTITUTIONALISING ENGLISH
# CRITICISM: MEN OF LETTERS,
# MODERNISM, TRADITION AND THEORY

Institutionalisation and proliferation are two words that spring to mind when looking at twentieth- and twenty-first-century criticism. As the study of literature is located ever more in schools and universities so we witness an explosion of theories about its nature, purpose and significance. Formalism, feminism, phenomenology, hermeneutics; it is all very exciting, especially when the French arrive in the late 1970s. But despite all the drama, despite all the exotic theorising, there is actually very little change in the fundamental approach to literature; it remains either rhetorical or grammatical. Moreover, we should not be fooled by those who claim that the study of literature is subversive. Not only is an English degree, like any other, used as a form of social classification, particularly if obtained from a traditional university but, as I shall argue, it is closely tied to market and management philosophies. In part, this has been imposed on English but it also arises from the long-standing connection between the idioms of criticism and money.

## Beginnings

The year 1900 was truly remarkable. Arthur Evans (1851–1941) discovered the first European civilisation; Sigmund Freud (1856–1939) published *The Interpretation of Dreams*; Max Plack (1858–1947) unveiled quantum theory; Hugo de Vries (1848–1935) identified what would later come to be called genes; Pablo Picasso (1881–1973) stepped off the Barcelona train at Gare d'Orsay, Paris; and Coca-Cola arrived in Britain.

Evans's excavations in Crete revealed a culture that was far older than either Attic Greece or Ancient Rome, one which had, in fact, given rise to both. He named it Minoan because Homer, Hesiod and Thucydides had all referred to a king Minos from Crete and because the people of that region had worshipped the bull, or Minotaur. The civilisation Evans had unearthed was contemporary with the biblical pharaohs and 'outshone even Solomon hundreds of years before his splendour would become a fable among Israelites' (Watson 2000: 17). Its roads, palaces, frescoes and the cursive writing on clay tablets, famously known as Linear A and Linear B, proved that Crete was the stepping stone between Egypt and Europe. It was a find of enormous significance, a civilisation that flourished nearly a thousand years before Homer was born. Despite years of research, much of it remains a mystery. Linear A has still not been deciphered. And so, with gaps in our knowledge, we continue to see classical Athens as the mother of the modern world. Evans's discovery has yet to be fully appreciated. But, in terms of criticism, it intensified interest in the idea that elements of myth, magic and ritual underlie all literary works, a notion that had its origins in James Frazer's *The Golden Bough* (1890). His main thesis, that ancient religions were fertility cults centred on the sacrifice of a sacred king, influenced Jessie L. Weston's *From Ritual to Romance* (1920). T. S. Eliot (1888–1965) said he drew on Frazer, but especially Weston, for *The Wasteland* (1922). 'Not only the title, but the plan and a good deal of the incidental symbolism of the poem were suggested by [her account] of the Grail Legend' (Eliot 1978: 76).

While Evans was uncovering the earliest stages of European civilisation, Freud was doing the same for the human mind, how it was fixed in infancy and childhood by the interaction between instincts and the wider environment. Indeed, he compared the new 'science' of psychoanalysis to archaeology. The various layers of the mind were analogous to the various layers of the Eternal City (Freud 1930: 6). Freud's claim, in his first major work, was that dreams were wish-fulfilments. He distinguished between the manifest content of dreams, those tumbling, broken images, and the dream thoughts – the repressed instincts, memories and desires which seek in sleep the expression they are denied in waking hours. The dream work is the process whereby these unruly impulses are disguised, enabling them to enter the conscious mind without activating its defences, which would otherwise hurl them back from whence they came. The clear implication of Freud's theory, which he elaborated in his later work on sexuality and the neuroses, was that humans – well men anyway – were dominated more by instincts than ideals.

Freud belongs to the romantic tradition which challenged the notion that reason was man's chief characteristic. He put into quasi-scientific language 'the burnt-out passions, the ghastly guilt and the melancholy habits' (Praz 1988: 61) of the Byronic figure who represented the dark side of the imagination. But his relevance for this history is his challenge to the long-established notion that what distinguishes humans from the animal kingdom, and what links them to the divine, is the power of speech. It was belief in that power which gave poetry its value, and so Freud's view of how the unconscious shapes communication has consequences for how we see literature. He would have agreed with Ben Jonson that 'no glass renders a man's form or likeness so true as his speech' (Vickers 1999: 578), but for different reasons. It is not the crafted sentence that reveals the essence of a person but a slip of the tongue, or pen. Literature is no longer a form of instruction or imitation or imagination or impression, but the record of an author's internal conflict. It is a compromise between the restraint and release of an instinct whose natural development was in some way retarded. After Freud, the critic is more interested in the accidental features of art than in its grand design, for it is those details which don't quite fit, which exist at the edge of a work that prove to be most revealing. The critic has once again become an interpreter not, as in the medieval period, of the work but of the author. Carefully studied, his or her writing betrays symptoms of their neurosis.

The promise of psychoanalysis was that human beings could be known and understood. More than that, it offered the possibility of redemption. The sinner confesses to the priest and the patient to the analyst and both are granted absolution, though one has to pay. The physical world, in contrast, was growing more mysterious. Nowhere was this more the case than with the atom. The old belief that the laws of physics applied to all objects, big or small, did not survive late nineteenth and early twentieth-century investigations of the atom. The discovery of the electron, for example, showed that it disappeared from one place and reappeared in another instantaneously. Then Max Planck's paper on radiation changed our conception of light. It was emitted from a heated object not in waves but in indivisible lumps or packets. Hence the Latin word 'quantum'. Planck also gave his name to the smallest possible measurements of length, mass and time. These are the points at which our conventional understanding of these terms breaks down. The Planck length, for instance, is $10^{-20}$ the diameter of a proton. An atom is made up of protons, neutrons and electrons, and half a million atoms lined up shoulder to shoulder could hide behind a human hair. With that in mind, try to imagine how much more tiny the Planck length is. It's impossible. And the quantum world is a strange place. Particles pop in and out of existence, events occur without causes, ghost images abound and, most strange of all, we create reality by observing it. The blurry world of sub-atomic particles only leaps into focus when we examine it. And we decide what to examine. If we look for its location, we get a particle at a place. If we look for its motion, we get a particle with a speed. But we can't have both. Werner Heisenberg (1901–76) called this the uncertainty principle because knowing either the position or motion of a particle means we can have only a partial understanding of how it will behave. Consequently, we are constrained to talk about probable outcomes in the sub-atomic realm, not certain ones.

And what's this got to do with criticism? There is a clear parallel between the quantum physicist and the reader for both create a reality by observing it. The one collapses all potential states of the atom by what he or she chooses to measure, while the other collapses all potential meanings of a book by what he or she chooses to interpret. Because we focus for personal, professional or ideological reasons on one part of a work rather than another, our versions of it will be slightly or even significantly different. Discussing the validity of these versions, comparing them, being able to appreciate what they add to our view of a poem, play or novel is what constitutes a good deal of critical activity. But, like the physicist, we never come to a complete understanding. Those who wanted to establish English as a university subject adapted the scientific paradigm to make the fledgling discipline more respectable. This, in part, was a reaction to the impressionism that dominated criticism in the late nineteenth century. They spoke of evidence, of sources, of criteria, of the need to be systematic in the approach to the study of texts.

At the time it seemed sensible but, in the long run, it has proved unhelpful, for English does not accumulate knowledge in the same way that physics or chemistry does. Nor can its effects be measured like the results of a scientific experiment. They are impossible to isolate and differ from one person to another, depending on age, education, and experience. Moreover, they are ongoing. There is no end product we can assess. Nor can the study of literature ever have a consistent methodology, for that would mean approaching each work in the same way. Real criticism is, in George Watson's memorable phrase, 'truly pragmatic' (1962: 104). Techniques may be useful when starting out but, like booster rockets, they must be discarded or else they will impede the reader's onward journey. If only those early pioneers had had the vision to adapt the quantum notion of reality for English, the subject may have looked very different today. Sadly, the owl of Minerva always takes wing at dusk.

Hugo de Vries differed from Evans, Freud and Planck in that he rediscovered what someone else had already discovered. That someone was Gregor Mendel (1822–84) a monk and a trained scientist. He bred peas and noticed that every seed contained two elements, one dominant, one recessive, which, when combined, produced predictable patterns of inheritance. Out of every four pea plants one was dominant, one was recessive and two were hybrid. Mendel's findings, published as *Experiments with Plant Hybrids* in 1866, did not receive the recognition they deserved, being cited only about three times over the next thirty-five years. De Vries had made similar discoveries. The character of a plant, for example, length of stem, was determined by 'a particular form of material bearer' (in Watson 2001: 17). And, in cross-breeding one plant with another, de Vries also realised that this 'bearer' took two forms, dominant and recessive. He was generous enough to acknowledge that the results of his work 'were, in essentials, formulated long ago by Mendel' (ibid.: 18) though he was careful to add that he had come to his own conclusions before he stumbled on the monk-scientist's neglected monograph. Darwin saw that all living things are connected, that ultimately they 'trace their ancestry to a single common source' (in Bryson 2003: 475–6) and Mendel provided the explanation for how that could happen.

What is the relevance of the discovery to criticism? There is none, at least not directly. If science has any value for criticism it lies in the metaphorical usefulness of its theories. What use, then, can critics make of evolution? Do literary forms adapt to the environment? Do they compete with one another? Do some have an advantage which enables them to triumph over their rivals? Not really. The rise of the novel and the corresponding decline of poetry are explained by developments in society rather than by natural processes. It is true that certain features of a genre, such as the death of the hero in tragedy, persist for centuries but this is no more to do with genes than collage has to do with cross-breeding. In other words, the metaphor of evolution is of strictly limited use, an imaginative way of bringing into focus the development of an author genre or literature in general. Edmund Gosse (1849–1928), who introduced Ibsen's work into Britain, declared that Milton was a 'complex instance of natural selection', adding that 'every producer of vital literature [contributes] an offshoot to the unrolling and unfolding organism of literary history in its ceaseless processes of growth' (1898: 391–2).

The critic's reliance on insights from other disciplines suggests that the study of literature produces few that are very useful to understanding either the nature or purpose of criticism. Why, it may not even be a proper subject. If the definition of a 'proper subject' is one with its own clearly demarcated field of knowledge, then criticism fails to qualify as one. It cannot even draw a boundary around what 'literature' is, though that may be the very reason why it is valuable; criticism, that is, compels us to think about what we mean by that most elusive term. But it doesn't just make us think, it also makes us think in a certain way. When we read novels, plays and poems we are inevitably led to consider a whole range of issues that, in academic terms, are the province of the specialist: psychology, history, social issues, science and so on. Criticism is, in part, an attempt to consider these in a holistic manner as they are realised in a work of art and, as such, it combats the compartmentalisation of intellectual life. 'Only connect', as E. M. Forster (1879–1970) famously said.

Picasso's arrival in Paris heralded a revolutionary new era in painting. His experiments were part of the more general ferment in art known as modernism, which, in very general terms, was characterised by an interest in form rather than content. The conventions of nineteenth-century realism, which depended on a transcendent point of view from which to survey, connect and comprehend the different parts of society, were ill-suited to convey the speed, crowds and machines of the modern world. Something else was needed, something that would evoke the swirling motions and multiple perspectives of contemporary life. Hence the attempt of Picasso and his fellow cubist Georges Braque (1882–1963) 'to represent the fact that our knowledge of an object is made up of all possible views of it: top, sides, front, back. They wanted to compress this inspection, which takes time, into one moment, one synthesised view' (Hughes 1991: 20). Picasso's *Les Demoiselles d'Avignon* (1907) was a major step towards cubism because its geometric figures and flat spaces broke with the painting conventions of the time. It also contained references to African art, reflecting a more general interest in the 'primitive' that was another characteristic of modernism. Changes in the nature of the artistic representation entailed changes in the nature of criticism. Art that was difficult needed to be explained and that was the critic's job. He or she was responsible for interpreting modern art for the benefit of a wider public.

And we mustn't forget Cocoa-Cola. The arrival of the soft drink from across the sea confirmed the existence of an emerging consumer culture, the major component of which was a literate but not particularly sophisticated public, the creation of the 1870 Education Act. 'Never before', declared H. G. Wells, 'had there been such reading masses' (in Carey 1992: 5). A number of writers deplored this development. D. H. Lawrence (1885–1930) demanded that 'all schools should be closed at once' adding that the 'great mass of humanity should never learn to read and write' (ibid.: 15), while Eliot contented himself with the observation that 'in our headlong rush to educate everybody, we are lowering our standards' (ibid.: 15), a sentiment that is often heard today. The masses did not want to read George Eliot or George Bernard Shaw 'but tales of adventure like Stevenson's *Treasure Island* and *Dr. Jekyll and Mr Hyde*' (ibid.: 6).[1] It was to cater for this public that Alfred Harmsworth (1865–1922), later Lord Northcliffe, launched the *Daily Mail* in 1896, which very quickly achieved a massive circulation. Four years later, Cyril Arthur Pearson (1866–1921) founded the *Daily Express* with a special focus on human-interest stories. Since these had formed the basis of literature since the time of Homer writers had to find a way of distinguishing their craft from that of the reporter. And so began the 'struggle between literature and journalism' which marked the early years of the century, literature being something you 'read twice', journalism being something you 'grasped at once' (Connolly 1988: 30).

It was a struggle, argues John Carey (1992), in which the self-appointed guardians of high culture quickly lost ground. A public confident in its reading habits, their tastes flattered – or manipulated – by the new media, no longer felt the need to defer to a cultural elite if, indeed, they ever had. In this brave new world, commerce trumped culture. 'Intellectuals', as Carey calls them, alarmed that their authority as cultural arbitrators was being under-mined, responded by making art too hard for the masses to understand. Out went human content, in came formal experiment. Technique ousted truth. Carey's thesis sounds plausible but for one thing. Why should intellectuals bother to put art beyond the reach of the masses when, by their own admission, the masses weren't interested in it anyway? Surely there are other explanations for the style of modernism other than that it was wilfully perverse?

We can find a version of Carey's argument in T. W. Heyck's claim that men of letters, in the mid-nineteenth century, lost faith in their role as 'preachers, prophets and teachers' who would save their fellow men from 'the social sins, the political catastrophes and the moral degradation that industrial life and values carried in their wake' (1982: 191). 'The tradition of cultural criticism', Heyck continues, 'began to flow in channels that led away from active involvement with the social, moral and spiritual needs of the reading public' (ibid.: 196). There were many reasons for this, including a suspicion of progress, a desire to depict society in a more realistic manner and a fear that art was being displaced by science. Carey simplifies this complex history and attributes the doctrine of artistic autonomy, which was in part a defensive reaction to the rise of science, to contempt for the masses.

His argument also conflates two contradictory traditions in the history of criticism. The first is that art should be restricted to an elite and the second is that the plain style is better than the artificial because it reaches more people. We found this preference in the Renaissance, after the Civil War, and again at the beginning of the nineteenth century, when Wordsworth dismissed the elaborate expressions conventionally used by poets, preferring to write 'in a selection of language really used by men' (Hoffman and Hynes 1966: 15). Cyril Connolly (1903–74) also resorts to this tradition in his characterisation of modernism, but he uses the terms 'mandarin' and 'vernacular'. The mandarin is

characterised by long sentences with many dependent clauses, by the use of the subjunctive and the conditional, by exclamations and interjections, quotations, allusions, metaphors and conceits. Its cardinal assumption is that neither the writer nor the reader is in a hurry, that both are in possession of a classical education and a private income. (1988: 29–30)

The vernacular style by contrast is 'always vigorous, thoughtful and alive, the enemy of elaboration and artifice, of moral hypocrisy and verbal falseness' (ibid.: 71).

Since at least the seventeenth century, the distinction between the two has been implicated in the class divisions of English society but, with the rise of mass culture, the plain style also comes to be identified with popular journalism and this complicates its traditional association with truth and sincerity. If the leader writers of the *Daily Express* use the vernacular to distort perceptions of current events, or to whip up emotion, then transparency in language appears only as another form of manipulation, another species of deception. Connolly makes a further point, that the colloquial idiom threatens to extinguish the individual voice. Compelled to write in simple, straightforward English, the diction and phrasing of one modern novelist sounds much the same as that of any other (ibid.: 83 and 86).

The centrality and longevity of the debate about which is better, natural or artificial writing, means that it is a convenient way of organising critical discussion. It predetermines, in part, the character of Carey's assault on modernist authors. But we also need to place the modernist style within its more immediate context. The 'stream of consciousness' novel, for example, can be viewed partly as an attempt to redefine what it means to be an individual in mass society. Its depiction of the freedom of the inner life stands in stark contrast to the outer one where the body is being redefined as a machine or part of a mechanism (Seltzer 1992). Connolly suggests that another reason for the particular style of modernist art, particularly after 1918, was that 'the world had lived too long under martial law to desire a socialised form of art, for human beings in the mass had proved but a union of slaughterers. There was more hope and interest in extreme individuality' (1988: 67). And there is one further argument we can consider. The intellectuals weren't just being snobs, as Carey claims, they were genuinely concerned about the fate of art in mass society. By insisting that it was difficult, by endowing with it a more esoteric character, they weren't merely shoring up cultural boundaries, they were reasserting art's value, one quite different to that found in the marketplace.

In doing so, they remind us that autonomy, depth and complexity are integral to our conception of the human. The sensationalism of cheap fiction and the certitudes of the popular press are not designed to cope with the intricacies of human nature. A debased realism is the idiom of both. As suggested above, newspapers and best sellers conspired to simplify life, to render it in bold strokes. The authentic artist could not compete with their version of realism and so was almost compelled to find another mode of expression. It wasn't just that modern reality proved too much for the conventions of realism, it was also that they had been appropriated by the publishing industry. What else, then, could the modernist artist do but experiment? From Igor Stravinsky's *Rite of Spring* (1913) to James Joyce's *Ulysses* (1922) innovation was rife. But though this impulse grows out of the aesthetic movement of the nineteenth century, its aim is much more serious. As the German polymath Theodor Adorno (1903–69) observed, it was the very subtlety and intricacy of artistic form which provided a refuge for a rounded conception of the human, and a resistance to the reductions of realism. It is now virtually in art alone, Adorno declared, 'that suffering can still find its own voice, consolation, without immediately being betrayed by it' (Adrorno, in Adorno et al.1990: 188). And he continues. 'It is not the office of art to spotlight alternatives but to resist, by form alone, the course of the world which permanently puts a pistol to men's heads' (ibid.: 180). In other words, art must ensure that its internal organisation acts as a check on the conventional ordering of experience found in the mass media. With Adorno we come to the end of one tradition of art: that it offers a model of how we might live.

We can, then, read modernist art in a number of ways. In part, it is the search for a form of representation adequate to a new kind of society, a search made all the more difficult because the idiom of realism has been commandeered by the institutions of mass culture.[2] In part, it is an attempt to keep the value of art separate from that of commerce. And, in part, it is a means of reversing the decline in the status of the elite. What does this mean for criticism? First, the notion of imitation, so long a part of its conceptual history, falls into abeyance. For now, the focus is on the formal nature of art. Second, critics begin to see their work in opposition to that of business. This has been going on since the nineteenth century, but the rise of the mass market intensifies consciousness of the problem. A. R. Orage (1873–1934), editor of *The New Age* (1907–22), complained that the 'doctrines of business' were seeping into art (1935: 118) and Sir Arthur Quiller-Couch (1863–1944), Professor of English at Cambridge, deliberately pitted the study of literature against demands that university subjects should be geared towards trade (1928: 8). Finally, criticism is complicit with making the appreciation of art a minority activity. It becomes part of the process of making literature mysterious. But how does this square with what we said earlier, that the critic's job was to explain it to the audience? It all depends on the size of the audience. A small, select one, the 800 subscribers to Eliot's cultural magazine the *Criterion* (1922–39), for example, can be flattered into the belief that it is being initiated into a secret knowledge denied the rest of society. There is nothing new here. Commentators throughout the ages have sought to restrict access to secular and sacred writings in order to maintain their power or position.

## The Man of Letters

The year 1900 may have been one of change in many areas but not in criticism. Not yet. Things continued there much as before. That is to say, there was no revolutionary transformation in the perception of literature. We can hear, in the work of Orage echoes from previous ages. Literature is a form of speech; it purifies the vernacular; it is an instrument of truth; the best kind is sublime. Even the old idea of decorum is still going strong. Orage argues that there is a hierarchy of subjects, and that writers must ensure they use appropriate styles for each. Nevertheless, there were straws in the wind. The rise of the mass market, the change in the perception and organisation of knowledge and the need to unify the nation all affected the development of literature and, consequently, criticism. In particular, they led to the decline of the amateur critic and the rise of the professional.

We have already touched on the mass market which, we should add here, is quite distinct from the Victorian public. That largely middle-class entity had begun to disintegrate in the late nineteenth century and, by the early twentieth, its great journals, weeklies and monthlies had 'lost their dynamism', or were even 'moribund' (Gross 1969: 243). The *Athenaeum* may have been in the doldrums, eventually folding in 1921, but *Tit-Bits* (1881–1984) and *Answers to Correspondents* were flying off the shelves. And all they contained, growled the novelist George Gissing (1857–1903), was 'the lightest and frothiest of chit-chatty information-bits of stories, bits of foolery, bits of statistics, [and] bits of jokes' (in Saunders 1964: 204). Yet what right had he to complain if that was the preferred reading matter of the majority? Surely they were entitled to some amusement since they worked so hard. 'Good God', cried an exasperated Charles Dickens (1812–70), 'what would you have of them?' (ibid.: 199). But Dickens was writing before 'give the public what it wants' had become the animating principle of the English media.

The whole effort of men like Harmsworth and Pearson was 'to relax the reader by entertainment which appeals to preconceptions, prejudices and tastes definable in advance' (Saunders 1964: 214). The genuine novelist, by contrast, demands that the reader make an effort to understand his or her work, that they make an imaginative leap into the unknown, that they open themselves to new experiences. Whether or not we agree with this distinction, and it is certainly problematic, contemporaries made it. Indeed, it is, in one form or another, a constant of the history of criticism. The difference is that, for the first time the majority taste now determines, or is made to determine, the character of the culture. If the minority wished to ponder the place and purpose of art they were perfectly free to do so in small circulation magazines such as the *English Review* (1908–23), *Poetry and Drama* and the *Freewoman/Egotist* (1914–19). Writing for such publications the critic had the satisfaction of knowing that his judgements were independent but also the frustration of knowing that they were almost entirely without influence. Exactly the reverse situation obtained in the world of journalism. There 'commercial necessity [meant] deferring choice of review books to the neighbouring columns of publishers' advertisements' (Rickwood and Garman 1966: 152). What Arnold called the highest function of the critic, 'to ascertain the master current in the literature of an epoch and to distinguish this from all minor currents' (Arnold 1925: 131) has degenerated into a puff for works that publishers were anxious to promote.

This may have been the view of those serious souls who populated *The Calendar of Modern Letters* (1925–7), whose mission was to maintain the 'apparatus of critical thought' and who deplored the 'shirt sleeve style of the popular University lecturer' (Rickwood and Garman 1966: 81–2). But if they wanted to restrict discussion of literary matters to the chosen few, there were others who wanted to spread the word more widely. One such was Arnold Bennett (1867–1931) whose brand of realism Virginia Woolf (1882–1941) politely rubbished in her famous essay 'Mr Bennett and Mrs Brown' (1966a).

'Mrs Brown' was the name Woolf gave to a woman she encountered on a train. She imagines how Bennett and his fellow novelists like John Galsworthy (1867–1933) would describe her. They would focus on Mrs Brown's brooch, or the carriage in which she sat. Woolf, by contrast, wants to convey something more subtle and, she would claim, more true: the fluid nature of Mrs Brown's inner life; 'scraps of talk', 'complexity of . . . feeling' and 'thousands of ideas', all meeting, colliding and disappearing 'in astonishing disorder' (ibid.: 336). Lawrence shared Woolf's dissatisfaction with the conventional understanding of character. Galsworthy, for example, deals only with man's social being and forgets about his 'naïve at-oneness with the living universe' (Lawrence 2002: 212). But Lawrence's solution is different to Woolf's. The novel should not show us the mind's jumble but should help us to live more fully, to set us 'trembling with life and the wisdom of life' and to reveal 'the changing rainbow of our living relationships' (ibid.: 175 and 196).

Woolf and Lawrence remind us that one of the staples of criticism is a discussion of form. They show how much that discussion has shifted over the centuries. The idea of decorum has given way to considerations of truth and life. Form is no longer decoration, but the articulation of being. At the same time, decorum is not quite dead, for both Woolf and Lawrence are searching for the right fit between form and content. Woolf finds the 'stream of consciousness' best reflects the change in human character that had occurred 'in or about December 1910' (Woolf 1966a: 320),[3] while Lawrence opts for lack of closure[4] to show the ongoing nature of our relationships.

Forster's conception of fiction is a compromise between these two positions. The novel is indeed concerned with the inner life but not to the point where it dissolves our traditional notions of character of which, Forster says, there are two types: 'flat' which tend to be comic and don't develop; and 'round' which tend to be serious and do develop. The development of character exists in some tension with the demands of plot: one is about thought, the other about action. Forster compares plot to 'a sort of higher government official' who wants 'individuals' to show more 'public spirit', to subordinate their own interests to those of the wider community (2000: 86-7). Like Lawrence, Forster is keen to see how his characters will grow but, unlike Lawrence, he accepts that events must be resolved even if that means our 'final impression' of character is one of 'deadness' (ibid.: 94). And speaking of 'deadness', that is precisely how Forster views criticism. It kills a work if it classifies it or relates to some 'tendency' (ibid.: 31).

Forster does not have a good deal to say about criticism and what he does say is often contradictory. On the one hand, it is a matter of affection, on the other hand, it is a matter of knowledge. This sort of confusion prevents him from 'establishing criticism on a higher basis than that of public utility' (1948: 403). It should aid us in our understanding of human nature but it can only do this if it adapts to the individual work of art. All too often, though, the critic, like the bureaucrat, betrays the particular by subsuming it under the general.

Perhaps it was these sorts of discussions that made people fear that literature was not for them. It all seemed so, well, abstract. Not so, said Bennett. Literature is 'the fundamental *sine qua non* of complete living' (1938: 13 and 15). Reading literature which, he said, cannot be defined, will make us more awake, more alive and intensify our capacity for pleasure. Speaking thus he sounds a bit like Lawrence. Less so when he says that to enjoy literature in this manner we must develop literary taste. And how exactly do we do that? First, set aside a time to read each day and stick to it. Second, surround ourselves with books, 'for the sense of owning must be flattered. Buy without any immediate reference to what you read. Buy! Surround yourself with volumes as handsome as you can afford' (ibid.: 31). But where to begin? Literature, as F. R. Leavis once remarked, is so desolatingly vast. And it's easy to be intimidated by the enormous effort needed to cultivate the right taste. Don't worry, says Bennett. 'Begin wherever the fancy takes you' (ibid.: 48). As long, he says, as 'you eschew modern works' (ibid.: 48). This is one of a number of inconsistencies in his argument. Literature is about life but we need taste to appreciate it properly. Do not pay any attention to critics but buy only what has 'received the imprimatur of critical authority' (ibid.: 31). Literature cannot be defined yet it is 'the expression of feeling, of passion, of emotion, caused by the sensation of the interestingness of life' (ibid.: 44).

That Bennett makes such contrary claims is a timely reminder that literature is many-sided, not that he has a cavalier disregard for consistency. But they are also a reflection of tensions in early twentieth-century English culture. The idea that literature is indivisible is a protest against the classifications of the collectivist state, but the division of literature into two kinds, that which informs and that which inspires, then into classic and modern and then into further 'divisions and sub-divisions *ad infinitum*' (1938: 43) shows that the literary was being mapped in the same way as the social.[5] Similarly, literature may be the space of the human, the place where we connect with others, but this involves submission to the critic's authority and learning the correct technique of reading. Bennett is a strong supporter of the Protestant work ethic. Yes, we may read for pleasure or to pass the time but these should not be the only reasons. We must also endeavour to learn about art, morality, politics, religion and science. Even enjoyment demands we exert ourselves. It can 'only be obtained by regular effort, and regular effort implies the organisation of that effort' (ibid.: 121).

Such remarks make Bennett sound as if he is trying to motivate his workforce. And indeed the very title of one chapter, 'How To Read A Classic', has the same prescriptive tone of scientific management,[6] which aimed to replace traditional practices with more efficient methods of working and so secure maximum prosperity for employer and employee. In practice, this meant devising a mechanical method of performing tasks which would then be imposed on the labourer. As Taylor puts it: 'When [the manager] tells you to pick up pig iron and walk, you pick it up and you walk, and when he tells you to sit down and rest, you sit down.'[7] Obviously, Bennett is not advocating anything like this. Nor would it be appropriate for literature. Nevertheless, some of his phrases would not be out of place in a management handbook. Another chapter is called 'System in Reading'. If literature is, in some way, a protest against the dehumanisation of modern society, its cause is not helped by a criticism that has rhetorical affinities with one part of that process, the manipulation of the workforce in the interests of profit.

What is most striking is the time Bennett spends on how much it will cost his reader to build a library. After nearly forty pages of listing books and their prices, Bennett has a chapter entitled 'Mental Stocktaking'. Readers are urged to 'make a valuation' of what they have gained from literature. 'Is it ethics – when did it influence your conduct? Is it a novel – when did it help you to understand all and forgive all? Is it poetry – when was it a magnifying glass to disclose beauty to you? (1938: 177). If they 'omit this mere business precaution' then their 'riches are not so vast as [they] thought them to be' (ibid.: 177) and the situation needs to be remedied, principally by meditating more on what they read. The by now familiar connection between critical and financial discourse suggests, in this instance, that we cannot divorce literature's promise of fulfilment from its place in the capitalist system of production and consumption. This is not so much a matter of it being a commodity that one can, or cannot, afford to buy, as of the dream of freedom being cast in the concepts of the market, a term which implies choice and self-determination but which masks the system of exploitation on which it operates.[8]

The relation between criticism and capitalist economics is neither one of complete contradiction nor complete collusion. There is a contradiction in that the freedom demanded by literature, to come into one's own being, is denied by the organisation of modern society. Or rather it is channelled in certain directions, such as consumption, which only help to maintain the system: to spend, one must work, mostly in jobs that stifle the spirit. There is also collusion in that critics use the idioms of money and, increasingly in the twentieth century, management when writing about literature, which has the effect of making finance and the factory[9] the very grounds of experience, giving it shape, meaning and significance. What if we look beyond contradiction and collusion? We can then see literature as a form of compensation: it gives us a sense of the life missed in our daily routines, a feeling of community in the midst of division and so on. Viewed in this way, literature can become, in Arnold's phrase, a criticism of life,[10] but only in so far as it is disconnected from it. The continuity between the concepts of criticism and capitalist economics re-establishes that connection and challenges the conventional view that the values of literature stand opposed to those of commerce. As we have shown throughout, the two converge. The task is to think of them together, to discover how they may critique and complement one another. What is happening, though, is that art's language of freedom and self-fulfilment is being increasingly appropriated by business for its own narrow ends.

One man who was alert to this danger in the early twentieth century was G. K. Chesterton (1874–1936). He attacked the idea of business education because it does not teach people to think, only to count. The purpose of education, he wrote, was 'that it should give a man abstract and eternal standards, by which he can judge material and fugitive conditions' (1953: 238). Why shouldn't those 'abstract and eternal standards' come from business though? They seem to. Everyday we find confirmation that profit comes before people and that ideas are judged by their contribution to enterprise. But Chesterton's point stands. By being able to compare, for example, our own society with those of others, both in the present and the past, we can appreciate that it is not the only kind and thus we are brought to a fresh sense of 'its beauties and virtues', and perhaps also a realisation that it 'may somewhere conceal a defect' (ibid.: 238). Making education *serve* the needs of the economy suggests that there is nothing wrong with a system based on exploitation, that vandalises the environment and that creates obscene inequalities of wealth. And it is a strange expression: to serve the economy. Shouldn't the economy serve us?

Bennett thought 'explanatory criticism very useful [because it] may throw one single gleam that lights up the entire subject' (1938: 88). Chesterton had a different view. By trying to explain things, by imposing 'a clear, hard and almost scientific method' (1964: 79) on an author, critics very often miss what is significant about him or her. Emotion is the key to art, writes Chesterton. And, in the end, Bennett would agree. A classic is a classic because 'it transmits to you, as to generations before you, distinguished emotion [and] because it makes you respond to the throb of life more intensely, more justly and more nobly' (1938: 60). Lawrence sounds a similar note: 'Literary

Criticism can be no more than a reasoned account of the feeling produced upon the critic by the book he is criticising' (2002: 209). This accent on feeling, a modified form of romanticism, may be a reaction to the mechanical nature of work and the escapism of the new art form of cinema. They, together with the syndrome of the 'lonely crowd',[11] speak of the atrophy of emotion that must be revived by art.

Chesterton states that emotion changes from age to age. 'Whole schools of art . . . can become merely mysterious and imbecile to the most enlightened generations if those generations do not cultivate the particular emotions by which those schools of art were inspired' (1964: 80). And so part of the critic's task is to tune us into the sentiments of bygone ages, not just for the sake of experiencing the sentiments themselves but also because they give rise to particular forms of expression. Understanding the link between feeling and expression will help us to better appreciate a Margery Kempe (1373–1438)[12] or a George Eliot. Chesterton was a great lover of Dickens and felt that modern critics were unfair to this most prolific of authors. Because they did not share his sentiments, they assumed that Dickens had 'absolutely no feeling for literature' (Chesterton 1964: 82). On the contrary, argues Chesterton, the so-called 'defects of Dickens are in a great many instances the proper and inevitable modes of expressing a certain gigantic conviviality and cordiality' (ibid.: 82).

The word 'sentiment' interests Chesterton. 'We shall never attain to a serious and complete criticism as long as the word "sentimental" is regarded as a term of depreciation' (1964: 11). He distinguishes passion from sentiment. The one looks at 'the central emotions of life' in a 'personal', the other in an 'impersonal', way (ibid.: 11). Sentiment is an acknowledgement of what we have in common, passion of what separates us. It 'is always a secret; it cannot be shared' (ibid.: 11).[13] Although Chesterton acknowledges that sentimental literature has its faults, it is nevertheless a source of harmless entertainment and is more sincere than the 'polished and cynical fiction fashionable among the educated class' (ibid.: 14). The modern novel has other - faults too. It is 'fragmented', 'formless' (Chesteron 1951: 135) and lacks purpose. The great authors of the nineteenth century always asked questions of human existence, even if they did not provide an answer, whereas contemporary writers dabble in 'the psychology of flirting and jilting and going to jazz dances' (ibid.: 133).

Chesterton also dislikes modern poetry. The problem with free verse, he complains, is that it is too like ordinary talk. Common parlance is 'tripped up by trivialities, tamed by conventions, [and] loaded with dead words' (ibid.: 247). A poet is supposed to transform language not reproduce it. The 'gold skins of undelirious wine' is so much more startling than 'grapes' (ibid.: 248). Chesterton sides with the popular artist against the one whose work is so rarefied it practically disintegrates if you pick it up. 'My taste is for the sensational novel, the detective story, the story about death [and] robbery; a taste which I share in common with at least the male population of this world' (1964: 34). How far the word 'taste' has travelled since the eighteenth century. Then it was a term which distinguished a person from the mass of mankind, now it is a sign of solidarity with them.

Chesterton was old fashioned for his time but, owing allegiance to no clique, he can always be counted on to say something new and startling. *Macbeth* (1605) is a portrait of a marriage; *Jane Eyre* (1847) is a detective story, while Browning was 'intellectually intricate because he was morally simple' (1951: 277). And bold statements such as 'the history of humour is simply the history of literature' (1964: 27) have an equally bracing effect. No critic can give us the truth of a work but the best can make it catch the light. Especially when they write as well as Chesterton. Dickens's characters 'live statically, in a perpetual summer of being themselves' (1951: 54); 'the fatal metaphor of progress, which means leaving things behind us, has utterly obscured the real idea of growth, which means leaving things inside us' (ibid.: 196).

Like a gallant knight, Chesterton takes up arms on behalf of the English language. He tilts his lance at the advertising industry with its tendency 'to reverse all that we mean, in order to get anyone to listen to what we say' (1951: 299).[14] He draws his sword against the abstractions of industrial capitalism, that dehumanising dragon which stands for everything that Chesterton most detests, the removal of a person's very self. Sociological generalisations flatten out 'all real types [and] real personalities' (ibid.: 259). Why he asks, can't we use the term workmen or even the working man? Why must always call them the workers? That awful appellation ignores 'the most important thing about a workman . . . that he is a man' (ibid.: 260). Respect for the individual is the guiding light of Chesterton's criticism. But he knows the battle is already lost. He is more Don Quixote than Sir Lancelot. The realisation is there in a wonderful essay on Thomas Gray's *Elegy Written in a Country Churchyard* (1751), where he observes that 'we see only the back of the ploughman as he plods away into the darkness' and when he returns we will see, not him, but 'a scientific works manager' (ibid.: 78).

This figure becomes the hero of the modern world. He evolves into the consultant of contemporary society, the expert errant, the person companies call when they are in trouble. The cult of manager reconciles culture and commerce. He fuses the values of the one with those of the other to create a corporate society. Everything must be measured by money. Big business restricts or even dictates the nature of research. Intellectual enquiry depends on the receipt of a grant; you won't get one if you wish to pursue truth, but you might if you can invent a new type of nail polish. Compared to designers, literary critics are at a severe disadvantage when it comes to demonstrating how their interpretation of Milton fills the national coffers; but the fact that we accept that the study of literature is justified only if it contributes to the gross domestic product is a sign of how thoroughly our thinking is dominated by finance. Whatever happened to the free play of thought? It became the free play of the market.

Orage was complaining about the decline of free intelligence in the early twentieth century. The main cause was 'the doctrines of business [which] have become the working rules of professed artists and writers' (1935: 119). And critics, he goes onto say, 'succumb to this deadening influence more easily than artists' (ibid.: 119). The scientific manager lurks behind John Middleton Murry's declaration that 'a system of laws or rules is necessary to the critic' (1924: 239), though so too does the spectre of neoclassicism. Commercial considerations are also blamed for narrowing the range of opinion in the press. Orage complains that newspapers and magazines cannot survive by the sale of free intelligence but must resort to 'bribes in the way of exclusive utilitarian information' (1935: 144). The 'reaction against the intellectualism of the nineteenth century' (ibid.: 145) is another reason for the decline of independent thought, as is the growth of religious scepticism, which is a little odd given the vigorous workout the brain usually receives in any dispute about the deity. But that's not what Orage has in mind. He agrees with Arnold that religion sustains a belief in the perfectibility of the human spirit, so when our faith in the former is shaken so too is it in the latter. That, combined with the sensationalism of mass culture, helps explain 'the diminution of our regard for one of the chief instruments of perfection, namely intelligence' (ibid.: 146).

The result of all this is that art, if it is not exactly dead, is certainly on a life-support machine. And if art is in a moribund state, then so too is criticism. But, as we have seen throughout this history, when are they not? How can art recover? Orage points to recent attempts 'to infuse into art the blood of savage cultures' (1935: 121). But primitivism is more about impulses than ideas which, for Arnold, are the very stuff of criticism. Orage says it is the job of literature to find the truth, which it does, not by copying nature, 'pretty well anybody' can do that, but by 'transfiguring' it (ibid.: 7). But, he sighs, few artists seem capable of that today.

If literature cannot flourish neither can criticism. And '[t]he price we pay for the absence of criticism', Orage writes, 'is monotony of production' (1935: 25). Given what he has said about commerce, it is strange he should use the idiom of an economist, even though it proves his point: business is all pervasive. It's there too in his remark that we need a 'literary policy' (ibid.: 117) which requires two things: 'first a good standard and second a perceptible drift and tendency in one's age' (ibid.: 117). But there are no good standards and there is no clearly discernable drift to the age. Industry has

collapsed the one and obscured the other. After examining a number of possible directions in which literature could develop Orage is forced to 'conclude
once more, that the age is really characterless' (ibid.: 117). Little did he know
that he was sitting atop the rumbling volcano of modernism.

Orage was not alone in fearing that criticism was on the wane. 'Is there
no guidance nowadays for a reader who yields to none in reverence for the
dead', asks Virginia Woolf, 'but who is tormented by a suspicion that reverence for the dead is vitally connected with understanding of the living?'
(1966b: 154). We have plenty of reviewers, she goes on to remark, but no
critics. And the reason for this, claims Murry, is 'economic necessity' (1924:
239). Criticism doesn't pay, reviewing does. Books are publicised but not
properly judged. There isn't the time. The reviewer, Woolf laments, 'has to
give us his opinion of a book that has been published two days, perhaps, with
the shell still sticking to its head' (1966b: 252). If criticism is a form of self-
expression, then the constraints of reviewing, the need to sum up a work
quickly, have debased it to a parade of 'prejudices', 'instincts' and 'fallacies'
(ibid.: 258).

T. S. Eliot advised that any critic worth the name must 'discipline his personal prejudices and cranks. . .and compose his differences with as many of
his fellows as possible, in the common pursuit of true judgement' (1976: 25).
The critic must not try to force his judgement on the reader; he must simply
elucidate the work and allow the reader to make up his or her own mind. Eliot
thought that the current 'degenerate'(1960: 2) state of criticism was owing
more to a failure to understand its true nature and purpose than to social or
economic factors. There was nothing stopping the play of 'free intelligence'
(ibid.: 12) except critics themselves. Eliot accused them of either aping scientific vocabulary or indulging in a form of impressionism that often amounted
to no more than retelling the stories of plays or novels.

Their greatest fault, however, was to judge works of art according to the
emotions they aroused because these emotions had more to do with their own
personal life than with the works of art themselves. So much for Chesterton
and his ilk, then. The reason why we judge works of art by the emotions is
because we cannot cope with the vast increase in knowledge that is characteristic of the modern age. '[W]hen we do not know', Eliot claims, 'or when
we do not know enough, we tend always to substitute emotions for thoughts'
(Eliot 1960: 10). Emotions are 'pernicious' (ibid.: 13). The end of reading
poetry is 'a pure contemplation from which all the accidents of personal
emotion are removed; [and] thus we see the object as it really is' (ibid.: 14–15).

In his emphasis on the importance of knowledge, Eliot sounds very much
like Arnold, but his campaign against emotion has a contemporary relevance,
and not just because his hostility to it is echoed in the work of I. A. Richards
(1893–1979), one of the first lecturers in the English School at Cambridge.

The declaration that poetry is 'an escape from emotion', that it is 'not the expression of personality but an escape from personality' (1976: 21), may be a reaction to the legacy of romanticism in English poetry but it is also an ideal credo for modern society with its Fordist methods of production and growing administrative apparatus that absorb the individual into the mass. The critic, Eliot stipulated, 'must have a highly developed sense of fact' (ibid.: 31), the very quality on which a man of business might pride himself.

At its simplest, criticism is speaking or writing about literature, but its idiom, tone, priorities and direction connect with wider ideas about the individual and society. Part of the force of Eliot's famous formulation, the 'dissociation of sensibility' (1976: 288), the split between intellect and feeling, derives as much from what it says about the early twentieth century as about the late seventeenth. It speaks of the cultural divide between the elite and the masses, of the occupational divide between those who work with their head and those who work with their hands, and it speaks, too, of the degraded condition of labour, of the man who must function like a machine without benefit of mind. Eliot's notion of the objective correlative, 'a set of objects, a situation, a chain of events which will be the formula of that *particular* emotion' (ibid.: 145) also has a contemporary resonance. It is about discipline, about finding the correct form for a feeling. The problem with *Hamlet*, Eliot argued, is that while the prince may be disgusted by his mother's behaviour, his feelings are out of proportion to anything she has actually done.

The fault Eliot finds with Shakespeare's play is similar to the fault that intellectuals find with popular culture: excess of feeling and its possible effects on wider society. In both *Hamlet* and discussion of mass society there is the same concern: that emotion or sensation may overwhelm the ability to order them. The objective correlative also partakes of the logic of scientific management. Frederic Winslow Taylor abhorred the idea of waste, of natural resources, of time but especially of human effort. And so he applauded the efforts of one Mr Frank B. Gilbreth, 'a member of our society'[15] for reducing the number of movements a bricklayer made from eighteen to five thus making him more efficient. Eliot's formulation is the critical equivalent of Mr Gilbreth's recommendations. It eliminates superfluity and streamlines expression.

The connections between criticism and commerce are not as clear as those between criticism and the wider culture. But they exist. And they need to be highlighted if we are to refine our understanding of how criticism is integrated into the social order. This is mostly a matter of its institutional location, but its rhetoric has affinities with the discourses of money and management. These may be faint but they have a cumulative effect which is to underwrite an economic conception of the human that may or may not be the same as the social conception found in literature. Eliot's remark that the artist's progress is 'a continual self-sacrifice, a continual extinction of personality'

(1976: 17) may be true but that is exactly what is demanded of the worker by the scientific manager. Taylor gives an example of how to talk to one. 'When this man tells you to walk, you walk; when he tells you to sit down, you sit down, and you don't talk back at him.'[16] And the idea that the artist should continually 'surrender himself to something more valuable' (ibid.: 17) is almost prophetic. Today, employees are expected to give their hearts and minds to the company. In return, it will 'make [their] job and life more mean-ingful' principally by meeting their 'need to participate in a purpose greater than the pursuit of [their] own interest' (Bunting 2005: 110 and 111).

Eliot's comments on sacrifice and surrender come from perhaps his best-known essay 'Tradition and the Individual Talent' (1919), which we can read in both social and economic terms. Eliot's interest in tradition is not simply that of a poet trying to find his place among his predecessors. It is also a response to the threat of mass culture and the devastation of the First World War. We discussed the shortcomings of Carey's argument earlier, but his claim that, in appealing to a broad public, the press and publishing industry under-mined the authority of tradition has some substance. The self-appointed guardians of tradition could only make it a part of social life if they were in contact with the wider society, but the rise of specialisation and the growth of the popular media had severed this connection. Eliot, then, had to reinvent tradition for a smaller and perhaps more appreciative audience. In the process, he gives it a new value, one which arises from the relation of works of art to each other rather than from their role in the wider community.

Not that Eliot's notion of tradition didn't address, albeit obliquely, the issues of his time. The biggest was the First World War. The use of gas, guns, bombs and aeroplanes resulted in an industrialised slaughter, the scale of which had not been seen before though it has been surpassed since. Who could any longer believe that history was progress when confronted with such carnage? The Great War was a rent in European consciousness. It marked a divide between the Edwardian age and the modern, between a world that had vanished and one of which all that could be said, for now, was that its birth was bloody and violent. Eliot's conception of tradition is an attempt to bridge that gap, to integrate past and present once more. 'The historical sense', he writes, involves a perception not only of the pastness of the past, but of its presence' (1976: 14).

His efforts recall those of John Leland and John Bale in the sixteenth century, whose makeshift English canon stood for a principle of continuity after the break with Rome. But they differ in one crucial respect. Eliot is almost going back to a medieval view of tradition, one based on a universal rather than a local identity. He stressed the 'mind of Europe' (1976: 16), not just because of the part national sentiments played in causing the War, but also because of his own position as an American in England, a representative of a cosmopolitan literary class whose only allegiance was to the Western heritage. And Eliot's argument has one other bearing on the contemporary cultural situation. His claim that the poet must understand the past if he is not to repeat it is similar to the psychoanalytic proposition that patients must remember their infant traumas if they are to be cured their adult ills. Eliot can sound very like Freud. 'The conscious present', he writes, 'is an awareness of the past in a way and to an extent which the past's awareness of itself cannot show' (ibid.: 16). That this awareness requires a good deal of 'erudition' is a reminder that neither literature nor criticism is simply a matter of 'sensibility'.

The commercial dimension of Eliot's essay is partly a matter of wording. He reaches for and rejects a number of words, 'development', 'refinement' and 'complication', as he tries to clarify the relation between the poet and the past. None will do. He cannot find the right expression – 'objective correlative' – for what he wants to say and peters out with the rather puzzling remark that this relation is 'perhaps only in the end based upon a complication in economics and machinery' (1976: 16). At the heart of Eliot's discussion, then, is the vague suggestion that a business metaphor might be the best way of imagining the poet's relation to his predecessors. More particularly, Eliot sees the poet as a producer. He can only obtain tradition by 'great labour' which involves the 'extinction' of his personality; his mind is 'a receptacle for seizing and storing up feelings, phrases [and] images' (ibid.: 14, 17 and 19), the raw material which he will make into art.

It is that labour, transforming the accidents of life into the necessities of literature, which gives a work its value relative to other works in the tradition. And that, in literary terms, is roughly Marx's theory of money. The price of a commodity represents the amount of labour used to make it and this forms the basis for comparing one commodity with another. To talk of commodities is to talk of consumption. Eliot makes no reference to the term but it has some relevance given that the essay focuses on how we process the new. Ezra Pound's call to 'make it new' could almost be the credo of capitalism. The latest Ford hatchback, though, carries the same message as the old: each model is a slight improvement on the last and consumption is a good. Far from opening up possibilities of change, the new simply strengthens the system, helping it to function more smoothly. A similar process operates in 'Tradition and the Individual Talent', where the new work is valuable to the extent that it fits into and renews what Eliot calls the 'ideal order' (1976: 15).

We have come a long way from Arnold. Eliot does not give us the best that is thought and said. Instead, we have a concept of criticism that functions like the economy. It stresses production, its values operate like those of money and its innovations refine and extend the order as whole. And it is based, just as the economy is, on the extinction of personality. Which, incidentally, opens the way for advertisers to transfer the idea of self-expression from literature and criticism to consumer goods, which is exactly what happens: we now define ourselves by the brands we buy. Finally, just as we cannot step outside the economy, neither can we step outside tradition. It has no boundaries. We can no more point to tradition than we can to the market. We can point to Baudelaire or BP but not to the whole of which they are a part.

The conventional view of 'men of letters' is that they were superseded by specialists and to a large extent this is true. But it is also true that men of letters could find themselves teaching in universities. This was the case with George Saintsbury (1845–1933) and Arthur Quiller-Couch, both of whom were journalists before becoming professors of English. And even if men of letters were not to be found in the lecture hall their ideas were often discussed there. Nor has the man, or indeed the woman of letters, entirely vanished. Melvyn Bragg and Clive James are two names that spring immediately to mind, while Germaine Greer comfortably straddles the two worlds of the academy and the media. What has not been noticed about the man of letters is the way that his work engages with or in some sense enacts the growth of corporate capitalism and the rise of the scientific manager. These developments are not central to their work by any means but they are there nevertheless and they reinforce that link between criticism and commerce which ultimately facilitates the incorporation of business practices into universities.

### The Discipline of English?

The establishment of English as an academic subject was part of the late nineteenth- and early twentieth-century reorganisation of knowledge. The only way to manage the many new discoveries in science and technology was to divide the disciplines into different parts, each one the province of specialists in the field. Chemistry, for example, was divided into four main branches: organic chemistry, inorganic chemistry, biochemistry and physical chemistry. Further subdivisions include astrochemistry, electrochemistry, petrochemistry and thermochemistry. A discipline not only requires an object of knowledge but also a methodology, a means of working with that knowledge based on the understanding of its fundamental principles and the practice appropriate to it. In order to become an expert in a discipline, a person has to demonstrate their knowledge and understanding of its material and methods. They therefore needed to study for a formal qualification, usually obtained by means of examination.

The growth of specialisation in the nineteenth century was accompanied by the increase in the number of professions. Three occupations were recognised as professions in the eighteenth century, the law, the church and medicine. To these were added, by the end of the nineteenth century, architecture, the civil service and engineering. Broadly speaking, a profession has four main features: systematic knowledge about a specific subject; a sense of service to the wider community; a code of ethics; and a progressive career structure. The growth of the professions reflects a profound change in English society. For example, the use of examinations for admission to the civil service 'marks the emergence of the bureaucratic state and a new means of attaining social status, one based not on family or money but on certification' (Martin 2000: 284). But since the candidates needed Latin and ideally Greek to get into university in the first place Britain's class system was in no immediate danger of collapse. The fact that 0.6 per cent of families own 69 per cent of the land (Cahill 2001) and the preponderance of those educated at public school and/or Oxbridge in politics, business, the media, academia and the arts suggest that it is still largely intact today.

A close relationship between the universities and the professions has existed from at least the medieval period when those destined for the Church took their degrees at one of the ancient institutions. By the time we reach the nineteenth century 'nearly every burgeoning profession sought to locate itself within a university structure' (Guy and Small 1993: 31). The organisation of disciplinary knowledge was very similar to the organisation of professional knowledge. In both, there are entry requirements, a body of knowledge to be mastered, a method of working, an examination leading to certification of competence and a clear sense of how the subject benefits the wider community. And, of course, university lecturers who teach and research in their disciplines are themselves part of the professional class. But when we look at English, the situation is more complicated. A literature lecturer is a professional. Applicants must meet certain entry requirements to be admitted to university, where they must study for at least six years before they can consider a career in the field. But what exactly constitutes disciplinary knowledge in English, what is its methodology and how does it serve the wider community?

We still have no proper answers to these questions and perhaps may never have. At the beginning of the century there were two views that dominated the discussion of whether or not English should become a university subject. The first was that it should be based on philology, which examines the history of the language, its grammar, orthography, etymology and parts of speech, and the second was that it should be an expression of national identity. The first solved the problem of disciplinary knowledge and the second that of social utility, but neither was complete in itself. Both answers, in fact, reflect the age-old divide in the study of literature between the grammatical and the rhetorical. Somehow, they never quite combine. But they do intertwine throughout the nineteenth century as momentum gathers to establish English as a university subject.

Contrary to the claims of a number of critics (Baldick 1987; Doyle 1989; Widdowson 1999), this does not proceed in a straightforward manner. As

Carol Atherton has shown, it was 'a piecemeal development that happened for different reasons, and at different stages, in different educational establishments' (2005: 14). New universities like Nottingham (f. 1881), for example, introduced English as part of a wider programme from the beginning whereas it had to wait a little longer before being included on the curriculum of older ones like Oxford. Another difference was that established institutions focused on language while the newer ones focused on literature. At Manchester (f. 1851) students learnt about the literary canon, while at London they were given such tasks as to 'make a list of Pope's chief works in chronological order, with brief descriptions' (ibid.: 31). But whether they were expected to know the Old English root of the word 'woman' or the significance of Stony Stratford to Shakespeare's *Richard III* (1600–1), the emphasis was on facts.[17]

It made sense to make a knowledge of facts central to the study of literature, partly because of the limited amount of time students had to spend on the subject and partly because knowledge of facts 'lent itself neatly to the demands of both teaching and assessment' (Atherton 2005: 31). Facts also served to guard the subject against the charge, in the famous phrase of the historian E. A. Freeman (1823–92), that it was 'mere chatter about Shelley'. Philology certainly and literature possibly looked more scientific if they dealt in verifiable claims. That certainly helped the case for establishing English as a discipline but it defined criticism in very narrow terms. Being able to give an outline of Chaucer's 'Merchant's Tale'? – was this all there was to criticism? What about analysis? Judgement? And, historically, wasn't literature supposed to shape behaviour in some way? Quiller-Couch certainly thought there was more to literature than knowing authors, dates and tendencies. The aim of the Cambridge English School was to 'train [the] understanding rather than test . . . memorised information' (1929: 161). We may get a better understanding of some of these issues if we explore how they developed during the nineteenth century.


### The Rise of English: Philology or Social Utility?

The origins of the literary discipline lay in the nineteenth century, in the utilitarian Mechanics' Institutes and the more Christian-orientated Working Men's Colleges. The purpose of the former was to teach 'the scientific principles underlying the new mechanical trades' (Palmer 1965: 32). Many also included English literature as part of their programme in the hope that it would make members less likely to resort to sensational fiction. The Working Men's Colleges, based on the belief that 'every man was a spiritual being' and that 'all institutions and history had a divine purpose' (ibid.: 36), had a complementary conception of literature. Books offered contact with great minds and 'a bond of fellowship between men regardless of class or epoch' (ibid.:

36). Literature was thus, to some extent, a substitute for the rupture with the past brought about by the industrial revolution. A way of life based on the village with its associated sports, fairs and shows was gradually coming to an end as people moved from the country to the towns.[18] The teaching of literature was, in part, viewed as a form of compensation for the loss of traditional culture by providing a 'new means of establishing connections with a national heritage' (ibid.: 39–40). The reality of community gave place to a representation of nation. These ideas inform discussions of English both inside and outside the university during the course of the nineteenth century but, since they are not forms of knowledge, they cannot provide the basis for a discipline. Philology will do that. Criticism, in the context of the Mechanics' Institutes and Working Men's Colleges is a rejection of popular literature and a form of reparation for a vanished culture. But once English begins to be taught in universities the focus falls on the facts of language rather than literature's evocation of a bygone age – though that, with modifications, will become an important ingredient in Leavis's criticism.

In 1800, England only had two universities, Oxford and Cambridge. University College London received its first students in 1828 and, later in the century, as we have seen, civic colleges were created in industrial cities such as Manchester, Birmingham and Liverpool.[19] The industrial revolution was the driving force behind the founding of these institutions, particularly in the late nineteenth century when it became necessary to compete with the new economic powers of Germany and America. Lord Henry Brougham (1778–1868), who was a key figure in setting up University College, supported an English literature course on the basis that it would promote an interest in the nature of government, the relation between labour and capital and 'the commercial prosperity of the country' (in Court 1992: 46).

The more the reading population knew about the nature of their society, the less likely they were to rebel against it. As with the Mechanics' Institutes, with which he was also involved, Brougham's course was designed as an antidote to sensation novels which would otherwise undermine the moral fibre of the labouring class, thus potentially endangering Britain's economic supremacy. Thomas Dale (1797–1870), Brougham's choice for the post of first professor of English in England, brought a distinctly Christian ethos to his duties, using literature to counter 'secular tendencies' and to 'inculcate lessons of Christian piety and virtue' (Court 1992: 62). But if English was to progress it had to do so on a more scientific and scholarly basis. That meant that 'it should be subordinated to philology' (ibid.: 66), the early practitioners of which compared the evolution of different European languages and assessed their contribution to a common civilisation.

T. W. Heyck has argued that the institutionalisation of philology was directly linked to theories of political economy. Academic specialisation was the intellectual equivalent of the division of labour. Both were driven by the same imperative: to demonstrate progress. A factory in which different people performed different tasks meant increased productivity; a university in which different departments focused on different subjects meant increased knowledge which, in turn, led to greater prosperity. More generally, as Atherton has argued, 'the growing emphasis on examinations reflected the wider ideals of industry and seriousness that were current in the nineteenth century, providing the student body with a measure of discipline and stressing the value of hard work' (2005: 34). Yet again we encounter a connection between conceptions of literature, ideas of criticism and market philosophy.

Henry Rogers (1806–77) carried philology forward at University College and included some literature on his course, which he divided into serious and non-serious. Although the term 'literature' had, since the late eighteenth century, come to be increasingly identified with imaginative writing, it could still be used to describe science, history, biography and oratory, which is what Rogers means by serious literature. The non-serious sort consists of novels, plays and poetry, from which we derive pleasure but not instruction. It is not clear whether Rogers thinks *Hamlet* (1603) is as trivial as *A Daughter of Heth* (1871), a sensation novel by William Black (1841–98), but it is certain that he has split Horace's conception of poetry in two. Literature either teaches or entertains, it cannot do both.

The study of English, Rogers declared, was the study 'of the history and structure of the English tongue' (in Court 1992: 73), particularly in its relation to Anglo-Saxon. The Teutonic vigour of Shakespeare or Milton made the literature of other countries seem 'faint and languid' (ibid.: 73), an observation that showed Rogers's opinion of native poetry and drama rose as soon as that of foreign countries was mentioned. We have heard such patriotic outbursts before. Sir Philip Sydney made a similar claim in the Renaissance when, as in the nineteenth century, England was in the process of building an empire. The interest in Anglo-Saxon raises the status of literature which, at least within the university context, enjoyed little prestige. After Rogers, English professors attend to those aspects of language which 'vividly recall the past greatness of the race', preserving those authors 'who best captured the Saxon essence, the political and spiritual essence of the nation' (ibid.: 74).

There are two consequences for criticism. The first is that it becomes a study of how a specific culture, rooted in race, reveals itself through its language and literature. This opens the way, as A. J. Scott (1805–66) observed in his inaugural lecture at University College in 1848, to using writers as an instrument for 'shaping national culture and political sympathies' (Court 1992: 103). Scott's emphasis on the potentially unifying powers of literature is understandable in that year of Chartist risings at home and revolution abroad. But Scott didn't view literature simply as a means to an end. Its essential value is 'the goodness of the thing in itself – the smell of a rose, the sweetness of music, the contemplation of truth or the communion of spirit with that of a great ancient [or] a great people' (in ibid.: 107).

It is worth emphasising that by an 'ancient' or 'great people', Scott did not simply mean the English. Like Matthew Arnold, with whom he corresponded, Scott believed that the student should steep himself in the classical works of other cultures. With the possible exception of the late nineteenth century, the study of English literature has never been the provincial affair that post-structuralists like Catherine Belsey (1980) and Anthony Easthope (1988) have claimed it is. Arnold wrote on several thinkers from different nations and believed that literature was 'but one more carrier of the rich and deep European cultural consciousness' (1925: 117), while Chesterton celebrated a range of writers from the Dominican friar Girolamo Savonarola (1452–98) to the Russian novelist Leo Tolstoy (1828–1910). It is only scholars who make one small period of history their special province and their labours potentially enrich all who are interested in literature and criticism.

Scott's claim that the scholar should be concerned with 'the good that is in [literature], not the good that it is for' (in Court 1992: 107) does not particularly strengthen the case for English as a university subject. That argument has to wait. A more immediate justification is the psychology of race, which is the second consequence for criticism of the improved status of literature. How does the mind of a people give language meaning? How does language express the mind of a people? J. F. D. Maurice (1805–72), who was dismissed from King's College in 1853 because he didn't believe in eternal damnation, argued that the best literary criticism draws out a work's power because 'the heart of the critic is in sympathy with the heart of the writer' (in ibid.: 90) and how much stronger that sympathy is likely to be if both are from the same race. In addition to cultivating feelings, literature is rich in insights that may support claims about human behaviour in general. But how exactly did it affect its readers? There had been an interest in the process of perception since Locke and literature was now seen 'as a linear form of the external order that determines the internal order of the perceiver' (ibid.: 90). Or, to put it another way, literature was one form of representation that helped constitute consciousness . Plato assumed that poetry influenced action, so too did Maurice. But he wanted to know the mechanisms by which that happens. His interest in psychology not only looks back to Locke but forward to I. A. Richards who was a moral philosopher before becoming a literary critic.

By mid-century, then, there were three possible reasons for establishing English as a university subject: the history of the language, the information it contained about race and culture and the psychological insights it offered into how behaviour was formed. The act of criticism was based on one or more of these ideas acting in concert. And we can add that, outside the university,

Arnold was busy considering two conceptions of man, one based on commerce the other on culture. Economic progress or spiritual perfection. Which would lead to a better society? It was a question that would also inform English studies.

It was philology that was to dominate the study of English from the mid-nineteenth century to the beginning of the twentieth, but it was of a slightly different kind to that which had gone before. There was a desire to make a distinctive contribution to the study of the English Language because the achievements of European scholars were threatening to eclipse native efforts. Who was the first to write an Anglo-Saxon grammar of any value? A Dane. Who wrote 'a really scientific grammar of the English Language?' A German. Who wrote a scientific treatise on English metre? An Austrian. 'Perhaps there is no greater reproach to the English Nation at large', wrote Walter Skeat (1835–1912), 'than the fact that the true value of our magnificent language should have been left in great measure for foreigners to discover' (1891: 18). Skeat immediately began remedying the problem, producing a four volume *Etymological English Dictionary* (1879–82). From now on the focus was to be on English itself rather than its relation to other languages.

And this was to be no mere linguistic exercise. Spelling, syntax and grammar were all scrutinised for what they could reveal of the history, social development and spirit of the English. David Masson (1822–1907), who began his career at University College before moving to Edinburgh, declared that philology should govern the teaching of literature. Its basic assumption, derived from German academics, was that Aryans were the true bearers of civilisation. Masson used the notion to promote English over Norman and Celtic culture, the latter being condemned for its 'promiscuity, hot-headedness and lack of self-control' (Court 1992: 155). Masson's belief in the superiority of Anglo-Saxon culture was reflected in his programme of lectures, which began with a survey of British geography and history and in which literature was conceived as a record of 'past thought' (in ibid.: 130). Only those works which bore the stamp of authentic Englishness received serious attention. Those written between 1400 and 1580, for instance, were dismissed for their lack of purity.

The promotion of Anglo-Saxon was yet another instance of the preference for the plain style that has been a constant in the history of English. Anglo-Saxon was prized above the classics just as the vernacular had been in the reign of Elizabeth. A thorough knowledge of it was the best preparation for a true appreciation of English authors. Anglo-Saxon also provided the requirements needed to establish English as a discipline. It was a body of knowledge, it had a method (the study of language) and it was socially useful. The fact that English literature was part of the civil service examinations ensured that Anglo-Saxon virtues would be spread abroad by those who went to administer the empire. They were also a means of promoting harmony at home. Masson suggested that literary men should mix with the working class in order to understand their condition 'appreciate and criticise their demands . . . and become their advocates, guardians and leaders' (in Court 1992: 128). It was a fanciful idea, never likely to happen. In the event it was the popular press which became the self-appointed voice of the people.

## Literature, History and the Nation

Masson was not alone in believing that literature could foster national unity. John Nichol (1833–94), who was chair of English Language and Literature at Glasgow University, argued that literature helped strengthen the social order by 'ton[ing] down our rancours [and] showing us the common grounds on which we may meet' (in Court 1992: 140). Most famously, Sir Henry Newbolt (1862–1938) in an address to the English Association (f. 1907) declared that literature should be used to create 'a bond of sympathy between members of society' (1928: 10). This is a restatement of one of the key recommendations of the report of the committee, chaired by Newbolt himself, into the teaching of English. The literary heritage, it stated, should act as 'an element of national unity, linking together the mental life of all classes by experiences which have hitherto been the privilege of a limited section' (1921: 10/15). An admirable sentiment: to make sure that everyone has the opportunity to enjoy high culture, formerly the preserve of a leisured elite. And while Newbolt may have written the most famous Imperialist poem in the language, *Vitai Lampada* (torch of life), he was no mere jingoist. He was, for example, a member of the Co-efficient Dining Club, founded in 1902, by Sidney and Beatrice Webb. This gathering of socialist reformers included the philosopher and later anti-nuclear campaigner Bertrand Russell (1872–1970) and the Liberal politician Richard Haldane (1856–1928) who moved more and more to the left during the course of his long career.

But there is no recognition of this in Chris Baldick's book, *The Social Mission of English Criticism: 1848–1932* (1987) where Newbolt and his committee are denounced for subverting the working class movement. All that talk about making literature more widely available was just a ruse to get the unions off Marx and onto Shakespeare. Brian Doyle takes a similar line, arguing that the Newbolt Report was a 'form of cultural intervention into popular linguistic practices with the overall purpose of generating subjective attachment to a particular sense of national identity' (1989: 51). If we take the long view, then neither Baldick nor Doyle are saying anything that hasn't been said before. The idea that literature should soften social divisions by promoting a sense of national unity goes back to at least the fourteenth century when John Lydgate created a native literary tradition to heal the rift in the kingdom caused by Henry Bolingbroke's usurpation of Richard II. But poetry did not bind the country together then anymore than it did at the end of the nineteenth and the beginning of the twentieth century, perhaps because it addresses itself more to the individual than to the group.

If anything, literature is a reflection of social disintegration. After Shakespeare's death, went the familiar story, there was a rift in the common consciousness.[20] Literature was either of the town or the country, never both. Its characteristic note was loneliness. The only time people turned to it in large numbers was during the First World War (1914–18). That event, writes C. F. E. Spurgeon, caused 'a certain liberation of the spirit, a realization that our ordinary material aims in life are no longer of prime importance, while the essential aims have increased in value' (1917: 5). As bullets ripped through the air, as shells pockmarked the landscape, as the heart was in danger of getting used to horror, poetry seemed a touchstone of truth, joy and vitality. For the poet is 'a lover of life, a lover of the glory and beauty of the world' (ibid.: 12). He makes us see how extraordinary is the ordinary and turns existence into essence. But nowhere does Spurgeon say that poetry is an expression of a common identity. People turn to it as individuals seeking hope, consolation and sustenance in a time of war. The implication of her argument is that they use culture almost as they use money, for their own ends not for the greater good. And this is a consequence of the economic organisation of capitalism. It encourages competition, not cooperation and therefore is more likely to breed selfishness than community spirit. Once the guns fell silent and the grass grew back, there was a return to 'money-getting' and 'fame-getting' (ibid.: 5). Profit, not poetry, was the normal state of affairs.

What Spurgeon seems to glimpse in her moving account of poetry and war is that, while art may give us an insight into what is most important in life, art itself is a minor activity compared to that of commerce. The most we can say of literature is that it is a private pleasure, not a public good. In its highest form poetry is, for Spurgeon, 'a state of mind, an experience of the spirit' (1917: 6). She was one of the members of the Newbolt committee and her resort to a religious idiom when talking of poetry was shared by others like J. Dover-Wilson who described literature as a 'means of grace' and as 'the chief temple of the human spirit in which all should worship' (in Baldick 1987: 97).

Others were repelled by this kind of speech. George Gordon (1881–1942), Merton Professor of Literature at Oxford 1922–8, criticised the 'growth of religious jargon about literature and history' and dismissed the Newbolt Report with the words 'Here at Oxford we have plenty to do without saving the State' (1946: 12). But at least he didn't burn the report as did Professor W. P. Ker (1855–1923) of University College London, a man much admired by J. R. R. Tolkein (1892–1973), not for his tendency to arson but for his

Anglo-Saxon scholarship. Walter Raleigh (1861–1922), the driving force behind the development of the Oxford English school, and its first professor, was another who did not share the reverent attitude to literature expressed by some of his contemporaries. 'I can't bear [it]' he declared (in Court 1992: 157). Consequently, he too was sceptical of poetry as a form of salvation. The response of these three men suggests that there was no consensus about the role of English in national life. Indeed Raleigh, far from seeing literature as a means of appeasing working-class grievances argued that the best writers were in sympathy with the masses and acted as their advocate. And, unlike some others, he thought that the teaching of literature should not be limited to the major authors. If students were to understand literary history, they needed to examine all aspects of it.

There is, then, some evidence to make us doubt the argument put forward by Baldick and Doyle that, by encouraging people to identify with their nation rather than class, literature would promote social harmony. So why have their claims been so widely accepted? Partly because the idea that literature integrates is in the cultural bloodstream but mainly because their analysis resonated with what was happening in Britain in the 1980s. Mrs Thatcher, for example, who was prime minister from 1979 to 1990, constantly appealed to the nation and the family while at the same dismantling union power (Hall and Jacques 1983). Baldick and Doyle project this rhetoric back into the past when its significance belongs in the present. This is not to criticise them, it is simply to restate the truism that we select from history what concerns us in the now.

My own arguments reflect anxieties about the nature and history of Englishness, the spread of market philosophy into higher education and the reduction of criticism to a method. Conveniently, I have discovered that these have always been a constant feature of critical debate, though not quite in the terms I have expressed them. The very persistence of these problems means they become a principle of continuity rather than a force of disruption, a mark of reassurance rather than a source of worry, perhaps even the constituents of critical identity rather than a means of undermining it. But all this is achieved, if indeed it is achieved, by giving the past a uniform character when it is, of course, marked by difference and disagreement and is always on the verge of disappearing.

We have seen that there are two basic arguments for establishing English as a university discipline: philology and literature as the spirit of the nation. The one was the study of the character of a people as it appeared in the development of their language, while the other was the expression of common values over time. Since both, in their different ways, are records of the past, we are reminded of the age-old link between literature and history. At the beginning of the twentieth century, it was generally believed that the historian gave us facts and dwelt on the drama of change while the literary artist gave us 'the mind and character of the people' and bore witness to 'the silent continuity of ordinary life' (Herford 1910: 4 and 8). History was thus a potential ally in the attempt to add English to the curriculum. Literary biography followed historiography in its assumption that the individual was the chief agent of change whether in art or politics. This notion lay behind the 'Great Writers Series' established by Eric S. Robertson in 1887 where, once again, close attention was paid to fact. Each book, wrote Robertson, 'will contain facts in such quantity as to be unrivalled text-books of literature' (in Guy and Small 1993: 114).

The influence of historiography was most clearly demonstrated in the attempt to establish authoritative editions of works. Scholars consulted sources and compared different versions of a work in order to recover the original version. Organisations such as the Early English Text Society and the Browning Society 'aimed to provide a literary archive of source material equivalent to that of the Rolls Series' (Guy and Small 1993: 113), a popular name for *The Chronicles and Memorials of Great Britain and Ireland during the Middle Ages* (1858–1911). Their efforts reflected the Whig belief that history was a record of progress. As did accounts of literature. The wine-loving George Saintsbury's *A Short History of English Literature* (1898) is a good example of how the literary past is seen as leading to the literary present.

But the narrative is not always one of progress. Edward Dowden (1843–1913), for example, who held the chair of English Literature at Trinity College Dublin, believed that the light of literature was being eclipsed by free-market economics and industrial progress. It seemed to have no place in the modern world; it was merely a record of departed things, thatched cottages, country churches and the village green, a land of lost content shining plain in Chaucer or Jane Austen. Court argues that this nostalgia for a rural, hierarchical England was the main ingredient of literary study in England. Perhaps. But it is possible, reading some of those he names, A. C. Bradley (1851–1935) and Quiller-Couch, to come to a different conclusion. Bradley's lectures on poetry are more concerned with understanding its nature than they are with looking back to supposedly better times. Indeed, he praises Keats for being on the side of progress (Bradley [1909] 1962: 229). Nor does Quiller-Couch seem unduly concerned by the disappearance of Merrie England. Anything can be the subject of English literature, he declared, as long as it is transformed into 'memorable speech' (1928: 17 and 91), and, unlike those intellectuals mentioned by Carey, he welcomed the 'New Reading Public' (1929: 211).

## The Argument in Schools

If there were those who were resigned to literature's marginal status in the new economic order, there were others who were determined to make it central to the experience of modern society. One such was George Sampson whose criticism of the curriculum in elementary schools, *English for the English* (1921), contrasts education with training. It is a work that is still relevant today for we too face what Sampson faced: a school and university system devoted to training instead of developing the whole person. And it seems that the early twentieth century had its own version of the current debate between education and teaching and learning. 'No-one is entitled', Sampson asserts, 'to lay down principles of teaching as if they were laws of mechanics' ([1921] 1970: 33). He attacks the obsession with measurement, declaring that if teachers 'abandon the art of teaching for the science of education, they may compile some ingenious and valuable statistics; but while the shepherds are thus dallying with the delights of mathematics, the hungry sheep look up and are not fed' (ibid.: 19).

Despite his use of the biblical idiom Sampson is not trying to promote Christianity. In fact he goes out of his way to say that we should look at the Bible simply as literature (1970: 116–17), something Baldick overlooks in his criticism of Sampson's 'confessional, if not apocalyptic' rhetoric (Baldick 1987: 101). It's important to distinguish here between religious doctrine and a desire to respect the depth of human experience. Darwin's theory of evolution may have may have made the Scriptures redundant but their age, the sanction of tradition, their poetry and their characteristic concern with the nature and purpose of life makes them a suitable idiom for raising the great questions of existence, if not for answering them. We cannot blame Sampson for falling back on religious language for no new one had yet been invented – indeed still hasn't – that confers such dignity and significance on our bid to make sense of ourselves and the world.

Education, Sampson writes,

> has nothing to do with trade, business or livelihood; it has no connection with rate of wages or increase of pay. Its scale is not the material scale of the market. Education is preparation for life, not merely for livelihood, for living, not for *a* living. (1970: 20)

The slip from education having 'nothing to do with trade' to it being, in part, 'a preparation for livelihood' underlines one of the main arguments of this history, that though we may wish to separate the realms of culture and commerce we cannot, in the end, do so. Nevertheless, Sampson does his best, declaring that the goal of education should not be to prepare children for their occupations, but to prepare them against them (ibid.: 27).

And what is the role of English in all this? Well, it is the 'medium of instruction, communication, the basis of knowledge, the condition upon which progress depends' (1970: 59). More than that, 'it covers the whole life of man from the cradle to the grave [and] is the sole means by which the people can be placed in contact with the embodied feeling, thought and experience of mankind' (ibid.: 59–60). English is 'by far the most important subject in elementary schools' and, as such, is charged with the supreme task of developing a child's 'mind and soul' (1970: 35). The high value placed on English, not just in schools but increasingly in universities too, raises the profile of criticism. It is a vital undertaking because it directs our attention to literature which Sampson views as the gateway to all life's glories. Certainly he has an exalted vision of English, his customary terms for it are 'beauty', 'love', 'joy' and 'laughter', but they are a good deal more uplifting than the mind-crushing terminology manufactured by the Quality Assurance Agency and the Higher Education Academy which have all but colonised the study of literature today.

Children, says Sampson, will need a systematic training in speaking and listening, reading and writing, together with an introduction to literature, if they are to have a rounded education, one that develops their intellect, their ethical sense and their emotions. Sampson is particularly critical of the way elementary schools fail to cultivate children's feelings. As a result, the English 'are ashamed of emotion and regard any approach to it as improper' (ibid.: 134). John Stuart Mill made the same complaint in the nineteenth century and, in the early twentieth, both E. M. Forster and D. H. Lawrence make it the subject of their art. Forster examines the 'undeveloped heart' (1965: 13) while Lawrence explores the nature of our sexual feelings.

Sampson's programme for elementary schools, which influences F. R. Leavis's conception of the university English department, is a combination of the two main traditions of thinking about literature, grammar and rhetoric. Learning to speak and write correctly belongs to the former, while the education of the emotions, belongs to the latter. Because he is utterly opposed to the notion that education 'is the process of fitting children to become factory hands or domestic servants' (1970: 137), Sampson emphasises the rhetorical aspect of teaching, that part which develops the whole person rather than the one which merely prepares them for employment. 'A humane education', he writes, 'has no material end in view. It aims at making men, not machines; it aims at giving every human creature the fullest development possible to it' (ibid.: 137).

## Commerce, Classics and Aestheticism

The fact that no government has seen fit to make this principle the basis of education shows that enterprise not self-expression is the priority of those in power. Secretaries of Education who insist that universities only teach skills which are directly relevant to the economy are the culmination of a trend that began in the sixteenth century with the migration of literature from the court to the marketplace. That marked the beginning of the end for the rhetorical conception of literature. It could hardly fulfil its function of forming character if there were no longer the rituals, ceremonies and elaborate systems of etiquette to reinforce it. Nevertheless, the idea that literature can shape behaviour persists long after the conditions which gave rise to it have disappeared. Sampson still believes that it can nurture 'the philosophic temper, the gentle judgement, the interest in knowledge and beauty for their own sake' (1970: 137).

Politicians and business leaders are impatient with such talk. What have Eliot's *Four Quartets* (1943) to do with modernisation? Here we encounter a contradiction that lies at the heart of contemporary life, that between economy and society. The one stands for change and dynamism, the dissolution of traditional hierarchies, while the other stands for stability and continuity, the importance of rank and gradation. Whether critics believe that literature is the memory of an old order or the foundation of the new, they are reacting to the impact of industrialism and technology. They see culture and commerce as embodying two completely different sets of values. The artist treats people as ends in themselves, the business man as means to an end. And yet this opposition, compelling as it first seems, will not bear scrutiny.

We only have to go back to Adam Smith, who argued that literary study developed the ethical sense that enabled people to perform more effectively in the marketplace. First, it presents a model of character, one of continuous growth, that complements an expanding economy. Second, by encouraging us to identify with a whole range of individuals and situations it improves our ability to negotiate, which is an essential skill in business. Being able to see a problem from someone else's point of view also enlarges our moral sympathies which then, ideally, act as a check on the greed and ambition of laissez-faire capitalism. And there's a political dimension in studying literature too. 'In prompting imaginative identification "with all sorts and conditions of men" it contributes to a sympathetic understanding relevant to democracy' (Martin 2000: 305).

And if we leap forward to the twentieth century what do we find? That the struggle to establish English as university discipline occurred at the same time as that to establish management theory. Perhaps this is just a coincidence. As may be the fact that the two subjects seem to develop in parallel. In the 1960s, for example, both were perceived as soft arts options that lacked a clearly defined body of knowledge. In response, criticism adopted the methods of structuralism, and business schools began training their students in specialisation, standardisation, efficiency, productivity and quantification. But the relationship between English and management theory may involve more than mere coincidence. That, at any rate, was the view of the Cambridge economist Alfred Marshall (1842–1924), who argued that the study of English enabled students to see a problem from the perspective of both workers and management making them better placed, if they entered industry, to deal with potential conflicts.

Grammar or rhetoric? Philology or social utility? Which of these would help establish English as a university discipline? Philology fell into disrepute after the First World War largely because of its connection with German scholarship. It therefore looked as if the study of literature would be justified in rhetorical terms. But, as we have seen, the context in which this conception flourished had long since vanished. Classics offered a possible model for English. It showed how the two parts of the subject, the study of language and the study of literature, could be brought together. Anglo-Saxon grammar was no less exacting than that of Greek or Latin while English literature opened a window onto the country, giving an insight into its sentiments, ethics and thoughts in the same way as Homer did for the Greeks and Horace did for the Romans. Furthermore, a knowledge of classics was essential to understanding a number of literary forms from Milton's epic to Pope's satires.

For all that, there was to be no rapprochement between the two subjects. There was, after all, a fundamental difference between them. The classics stood for the universal, English for the merely local. Scholars of Greek and Latin did not want their subject diluted by a comparison with English and hence the subject 'emerged as an alternative to the classical curriculum' (Martin 2000: 271). Literature enthusiasts were worried, in their turn, that English may seem just a pale reflection of the classics rather than a subject in its own right. To combat this perception they borrowed some of the methods of science and history. Thus they could claim that they were producing knowledge and culture in contrast to the classicists who were merely transmitting them. Finally, the study of classics was the mark of a gentleman, and its aristocratic overtones seemed out of place in the modern world. Like democracy, English was for everyone.

Psychology was a more promising ally in the quest to make English part of the curriculum. I. A. Richard's theory of practical criticism was rooted in an understanding of how the mind works. His writings were, in part, a reaction to Bradley's view that poetry was worth studying on its own account, that it had an intrinsic value. This goes back to Scott's idea about discerning the good that is *in* literature rather than the good that it is *for* and it receives its clearest expression at the end of the nineteenth century in the doctrine of art for art's sake. This was a defensive reaction to the philistine notion that, as art had no clearly discernible purpose, it was an essentially trivial activity.

Unlike Wilde, Bradley was prepared to concede that poetry may have 'an ulterior value as a means to culture or religion, because it conveys instruction, or softens the passions, or furthers a good cause', but that had no bearing on its intrinsic value 'as a satisfying imaginative experience' (1962: 4–5). Poetry was neither a part of the real world nor a copy of it. No, it was 'a world by itself, independent, complete, autonomous; and to possess it fully you must enter that world, conform to its laws, and ignore for the time the beliefs, aims and particular conditions which belong to you in the other world of reality' (ibid.: 5). Bradley was voicing a common view. W. H. Hudson, a university extension lecturer, made a similar point. The aim of literature, he wrote, 'whether it imparts knowledge or not, is to yield aesthetic satisfaction by the manner in which it handles its theme' (in Guy and Small 1993: 177). We are on the way to modernist formalism, to a perception of art as outside history. Arthur Symons, for example, in the introduction to his *The Romantic Movement in English Poetry* (1909), declares that the true critic should 'consider [poetry] in its essence, apart from the accidents of age in which it came into being' (in ibid.: 180).

The demand that we should look at the literary nature of a poem rather than its place in history or its purpose in society becomes another argument for making English an academic subject. In particular, it fulfilled one of the criteria for the creation of a discipline: a discrete object of study. But the definition of literature in aesthetic terms made it difficult to see how it could be of service to the wider community, which is also a requirement of disciplinary knowledge. Another is a clearly defined methodology which, again, English seemed to lack. There was no shortage of ideas about *why* students should study literature but precious few about *how* they should study it.

This is reflected in a collection of papers, 'The Teaching of English in Schools', published by the English Association in 1919. The teacher of English should cater to the moral, intellectual and aesthetic capacity of pupils. Children should be encouraged to seek truth for its own sake, to be 'braced and fortified' by their encounter with great writers, and to see that beauty is not merely a form of amusement but a sign of 'the glory of the universe' (Boas 1919: 7 and 9). In addition to promoting self-development, the English teacher is also concerned with 'the production of good citizens' (Morley 1919: 33). A right understanding of literature 'leads to an apprehension of the English mind and character'; from Chaucer to Dickens it is 'the open sesame to all that is best in [the people] and their history, the record of their achievements in the past, the clue to their unexpressed, often scarcely-realised hopes and aspirations for the future' (ibid.: 33).

But how are these ideals to be realised in practice? Much depends on the personality of the teacher. It is 'on what he or she has to give out from within, that in English work everything ultimately depends' (Boas 1919: 7). The teaching of English is divided, roughly, into composition and literature with some lessons on grammar. The method for teaching written composition is to choose topics wisely and give the children constructive criticism. That for oral composition is to make children act, read aloud, debate and deliver speeches. The general consensus is that there is no real method for teaching literature: whatever keeps 'the literature hour full of the "spirit of wonder" should be welcomed' (Chadwick 1919: 20). Another point on which the contributors agree is the need for a 'first-rate library in every classroom' (Sharwood-Smith 1919: 29). This would allow teachers to introduce children to the full range of English literature which they need if they are to develop a sense of its true value. At age 10 the girls at Clapham High School read Longfellow, by the age of 14 they are delving into Chaucer, Shakespeare and 'selections from great writers' (English Association 1909) and by 16 they are immersed in Milton, Burke and Wordsworth.

## Problems of Institutionalisation

There is a question mark over literature's status as a discipline because the sheer variety of methods used to teach it, from drawing pictures to learning poetry by heart, suggests that it has no distinct practice. But perhaps we are being a little hasty. Since English seems to have a number of different ends – good speech, the art of composition, aesthetic appreciation, the development of the person, the education of the citizen and so on – then it needs a number of different means to achieve them. Similarly, how can we discriminate between different kinds of literature if we approach them all in the same way? The manner of reading a morality play differs from that of reading a modern novel for we have to take into account differences of period, genre, belief, culture and language when reading *Everyman* (1485) which we don't have to do when reading Ian McEwan's *Saturday* (2005). Guy and Small make the point that is not enough to have a practice 'used to carry out the study of an object', there must also be 'a theory of that practice' (1993: 38). Certainly the contributors to 'The Teaching of English in Schools' consider how best to achieve their aims but it would be stretching the limits of charity to describe their efforts as a 'theory'.

There is also a problem with their conception of the ends of English. It is far too nebulous. For how do we assess the contribution of literature to a child's mental and spiritual growth or, indeed, to the cause of national unity? The short answer is we can't. As a result, it is difficult to be precise about the role of literature in social life. Guy and Small (1993) have criticised the work of Catherine Belsey and Terry Eagleton on precisely these grounds. Not only do they expand the definition of literature to include all forms of writing, thereby dissolving it as a specific object of study, they also charge it, at least in their early work, with the impossible task of eliminating discrimination and oppression. It is because there is so little agreement about what constitutes literature, what methods characterise literary study, and what literature contributes to society that its disciplinary status is so uncertain. As a result, it is very easy for government agencies to intervene in the subject and shape it to their own ends.

And this is exactly what is happening in schools and universities at the time of writing. More and more English must submit to the strictures of the Higher Education Academy and the Quality Assurance Agency. The concern of these organisations is not particularly with the nature of English but with such matters as widening participation, enhancing the learning experience and equipping students with skills which fit them for employment.[21] Gone is the idea of English as the medium of growth; gone is the idea of literature as the expression of national character. And gone too is the notion of literature as the best that has been thought and said in the world. Despite reassurances in the English Benchmark Statement that the nature of English 'means that any attempts at prescription should be avoided',[22] it contains, nevertheless, stipulations regarding what subject knowledge and skills a student should acquire, and what generic and graduate skills they ought to have on completing their degree. But it was ever thus. We only have to look back to ancient Rome where orators studied poetry to make them more effective speakers. And even then there were others, like Longinus, who believed it was much more than a form of instruction.

The English Subject Benchmark Statement does not solve the problem of whether or not English is a discipline. And if it is not, then in what way has it been institutionalised? This is a question addressed by Evan Watkins (1989) who argues that the concept of institutionalisation is an inadequate way of understanding how English functions in schools and universities. What we usually mean by institutionalisation is the process whereby commentary on literary texts has moved from the salon to the seminar room, from the newspaper to the specialist journal. This is true, but only up to a point. The focus on the critic's relationship with the work blinds us to all the other activities he or she must perform as part of their job. These include administration, appraisal, applying for grants, peer observation, teaching, marking, external examining, writing references, meetings, open days, staff development, consultancy and forging links with business. The list is by no means exhaustive but it is a reminder that an English lecturer spends more time on general duties than on interpreting literature.

It is this observation that leads Watkins to make an important distinction, drawn from Marx, between abstract and concrete labour. Marx was writing about the transformation of labour under capitalism. Workers, in the early stage of factory development, were still craftsmen, but they were no longer working for themselves – they had become wage earners. The arrival of the machine marked the next stage of development, transforming the character of labour from a skilled to an unskilled activity. Concrete labour, then, refers to the actual process of work, whether it is making a cabinet or feeding a conveyor belt, while abstract labour refers to the social organisation of work, 'the relations among people at the work location' (1989: 16). Watkins sees an analogy between factories and English departments. They are both environments in which work is increasingly systematised, monitored, regulated and controlled, and they are both concerned with production, the one with goods and the other with the values.

The values of English are usually expressed either through a respect for tradition or a celebration of the new, and both are forms of concrete labour. In crude terms, the critic engages with the work and shows how it is either radical or reactionary. But the abstract labour of the English department means that whatever values are discovered in particular work, whether they relate to its formal properties or its feminist politics, they are never circulated in that form. As Watkins puts it: 'you don't report to the registrar that *Paradise Lost* is a revolutionary fusion of contradictory ethical claims, or that John has a remarkable grasp of English history . . . You report that 60239 got [58] in Engl 322, which [will later] be circulated to the personnel office at Boeing as 60239's prospective employer' (1989: 18). It doesn't matter what John really thinks about Milton's role in the English Civil War; what matters is the grade he achieves, a grade that will tell the person considering John's application nothing about his attitude to history, but which will give some indication of his aptitude for the post.

Watkins's crucial point is that critics mistake the nature of their labour. They believe their readings of Shakespeare release insights and ideas that students will take with them into the wider world and which will, eventually, subvert the social order. In fact, argues Watkins, these insights and ideas are, in themselves, largely irrelevant. It is not the students' appreciation of the plurality of meaning in Alexander Pope that will impress prospective employers but their degree classification. Despite critics' claims to the contrary, the study of literature has a very minor role to play in promoting a culture's values. The media does that far more effectively. More people are familiar with the plot lines of *East Enders* than they are with the state of the contemporary English novel.

The real worth of literary studies is not in concrete but in abstract labour, understood as student grades. It is not values which emanate from English faculties, but evaluations. And that seems to be underlined by the recent proliferation of assessments in schools and universities and by the increasing emphasis on skills instead of subject knowledge. More words are devoted to these in the English Subject Benchmark Statement than to the nature of the subject or its content. Evaluations are circulated from the examination hall to the human resources departments of companies and corporations. And the very fact that they are circulated in this way underlines one of the main arguments of this book, namely, that there is, at the very least, a rhetorical affinity between the idioms of criticism and those of the market. For much of its history thinkers have tended to describe criticism in social terms, but it also has an underlying economic dimension which I have tried to trace during the course of this narrative.

We may be able to get a clearer understanding of this economic dimension if we consider Watkins's argument in a little more detail. He distinguishes between a restricted and a general economy in English. The restricted economy refers to conferences and journal articles whereas the general economy refers to the grading of students and, we might add, the salaries of academic superstars. Watkins suggests that the notion of evaluation in English is best understood as a form of surplus value. That is, since the study of literature is not directly related to a profession[23] and since it is not particularly necessary to the maintenance of the social order, it must provide something for society over and above any use value it may have, such as instruction in reading and writing or refining those arts. And what it provides, claims Watkins, is compensation. Education, he writes, 'does not simply reproduce existing social relations . . . In one way or another it adjusts [them] by adding something to them' (1989: 91).

But, in order for that to happen, 'education as a whole must be relatively free to construct its own *internal* organisation of work' (ibid.: 93). Watkins is describing academic autonomy or, in the case of English, the concrete labour of criticism. Whether we can still talk with any confidence about academic autonomy today is a matter of debate. Quality Assurance, Teaching and Learning, the system of grants and the demand that education be a form of social engineering have all undermined free inquiry. Universities, like schools, are becoming more and more functional. Anything that does not directly serve the economy is viewed with suspicion. Watkins was writing in the mid to late 1980s before government policy, both here and in the United States, demanded that higher education be more responsive to the market and so he was able to dwell more on how it 'compensated' for at least two shortcomings in the social order.

The first was the absence of an hereditary class for which education compensates by producing professionals. The second was the absence of that 'internal affective quality of life that passed along the stable conduits of traditional class society' (1989: 99), for which education compensates by allowing more people than ever before access to the arts. These provide the cultural skills which 'are increasingly made to appear interdependent with job skills' (ibid.: 111). The need for cultural skills has become more acute since the disappearance of the apprenticeship system which inculcated the virtues of responsibility, efficiency and self-discipline. There is, though, an argument for saying that the workplace has now become a training ground for cultural skills and that affective quality of life formerly supplied by education, particularly the study of literature.

Madeleine Bunting has explored this issue in her book *Willing Slaves: How the Overwork Culture Is Ruling Our Lives* (2005). Her main claim is that the old 'bureaucratic and hierarchical organisations which developed in industrial economies in the late nineteenth century' have all but crumbled and that we now live in a 'relationship economy' where consultants 'encourage team bonding, personal awareness and personal growth' (2004: 78 and 83). The supermarket chain Asda, for example, takes the emotional management of its employees very seriously. Staff must maintain a smile throughout their shift. Any slip is recorded on the surveillance system. The phone company Orange exhorts employees to live and breath the brand. In the words of one call centre manager, 'we encourage a sense of belonging so that people feel "I'm not just a number, this is my home"' (ibid.: 108).

If the workplace has changed its character so too has the university. Staff are service providers and students are customers. They pay for their education, they choose their courses and give feedback on their experience. Both in their subjects and in their structures universities refine the consumer mentality. In English, learning to discriminate between different works enhances the ability to choose between different goods. F. R. Leavis hoped that the discipline of close reading would protect the student from the siren calls of advertising, but he could not have foreseen how clever marketing would exploit a number of literary techniques to promote a product, how the use of irony or pastiche not only flatters the audience's intelligence but also suggests that there is no contradiction between culture and commerce. Why criticism itself, in the form of the review, approximates to the logic of advertising in as much as it promotes one book over another.

What, then, does all this mean? In the first place, it suggests that how we value a work is of little consequence to how we value the student, a process that is becoming ever more prescriptive: there must be clear assessment criteria; they must match learning outcomes; only certain words may be used when providing feedback. In the second place, the emphasis on student assessment locates the effects of criticism in the wider economy. We prepare young people for employment, not to intervene in the construction of meaning. In the third place, the exploration of human relationships is passing from literary authors to management theorists. Stories rather than scientific methods are now the preferred way of motivating the workforce. 'As we worked on research of our excellent companies', write Tom Peters and Robert Waterman in their hugely successful *In Search of Excellence* ([1982] 1995), 'we were struck by the dominant use of story, slogan and legend as people tried to explain the characteristics of their own institutions. All the companies we interviewed . . .were quite simply rich tapestries of anecdote, myth and fairy tale' (ibid.: 75). Whether that's true or not, the interest in fiction and, by implication, in emotion, imagination and relationships in part reflects the growing conflation of public and private space. The distinction between home and work diminishes as personal qualities become a requirement of business life. 'We ask employees to bring their humanness to work', says Mike Harris of the internet bank egg, while Anglia Water proudly announces that 'Friendship is part of our corporate culture' (Bunting 2004: 81 and 83).

These various developments cast some light on the current state of the institutional nature of English. The demand that each module teach transferable skills, for instance, is at the expense of subject knowledge. If we want to know the future in education we need only glance at the names of the various diplomas to be introduced into schools from 2008. Creative and Media, Engineering Construction and the Built Environment, and Society, Health and Development. None of the diplomas planned for 2009 or 2010, which include Hair and Beauty Studies and Retail, contain any of the traditional academic subjects. While not doubting the need for a curriculum that will appeal to many young people for whom the study of, say, history is a chore, what we have here is a cultural lobotomy.

The probable disappearance of literature from the curriculum of most schools will mean that there is less demand for it at university. Should literature vanish from institutions of higher education, there will be even fewer voices raised in its defence than there are now. Who will care about the integrity of the subject? Who will be able to put the case for scholarship, or to argue that its broad range of values should be brought to bear on the terrifyingly instrumentalist view of humans embedded in market economics? We have already noted how management theorists have begun to monopolise the human and the introduction of diplomas can only accelerate that trend. The Humanities diploma has not yet been written but it will not be compulsory and it must meet employers' needs.

Like literary critics, management theorists appropriate ideas from other disciplines for their own ends. The starting point of Peters and Waterman's book is Leavis's idea that we need to feel that life is significant. 'Our greatest need', they write, 'and most difficult achievement is to find meaning in our lives' ([1982] 1995: 75). Leavis believes we get this from art. ' "What for – what ultimately for?" is implicitly asked in all the greatest art, from which we get, not what we are likely to call an "answer", but the communication of a felt significance; something that confirms our sense of life as more than a mere linear succession of days, a matter of time as measured by the clock – "tomorrow and tomorrow and tomorrow. . ." ' (1973: 46). Peters and Waterman believe that we get it from being well managed at work. The good manager must acquire 'a sense of history, [and] perspectives from literature and art' ([1982] 1995: 35) if he or she is to make us feel our labours are worthwhile.

The erosion of subject knowledge or its appropriation by management theorists undermines English's disciplinary status. Furthermore, the conformist culture of higher education is hostile to the very idea of criticism, in all senses of the term. Criticism as a form of connection, of putting a work in context, or of placing it in a tradition does not fit well into an environment where the main unit of study is the individual module which results in a fragmented understanding of the subject. Neither does criticism as a form of judgement, of coming to a decision about how one work stands in relation to another for that involves a pronouncement on value whose discourse has been colonised by Quality Assurance and, as a result, has dwindled to mere process. There is no institutional support for criticism as a form of questioning or for criticism as the freedom to formulate an individual opinion. The one is viewed with suspicion while the other cannot be adequately assessed. If criticism is considered a method of studying literature, a method embodying a philosophy of the subject, then it has fallen into abeyance. With a weak sense of subject knowledge and a curtailed method of study, English is very much a discipline in crisis. Unless, that is, we recognise that its true function is to equip more and more people with skills to enable them to fit into the so-called knowledge economy and to evaluate them so they can be more easily sifted by potential employers. In which case, English is flourishing.

## Practical Criticism: Richards and Empson

Practical criticism, the close reading of words on the page, was once seen as a way of appreciating the power of literary language. Since the 1980s, though, it has suffered a bad press. Dismissed variously as narrow, a-historical and even fetishistic because it concentrates on part of a work rather the whole it has been more or less abandoned. But what English has discarded may prove rich pickings for practitioners in other disciplines. Contributors to a conference at Leicester University in January 2008 argued that drawing on the work I. A. Richards and F. R. Leavis would purge management theory of 'flat-earth empiricism and flatulent theory'.[24]

Richards, pioneered the use of practical criticism, which was to be the dominant approach to literature from the 1920s to the 1970s. It was developed partly in reaction to the rise of mass culture and partly in reaction to what Richards considered to be unsatisfactory theories of art, a term that he defined as the communication of a highly organised experience. The cinema and the best-seller were increasing the gulf between what was accepted by the majority and what was accepted by the minority and, if it continued to grow, then there was a danger that 'popular taste' would replace 'trained discrimination' ([1924] 2001: 31). The theory which irritated Richards most was Bradley's poetry-for-poetry's sake. In the first place, he didn't believe that poetry had a reality different to the rest of the world and, in the second place, he feared that such a theory dispensed with the need for critics. What possible use were they if all they could say was that poetry had no bearing on life? But Richards's biggest objection to Bradley was that, like many other commentators on literature, he spoke as though art possessed certain qualities 'when what we ought to say is that [it] cause[s] effects in us of one kind or another' (ibid.: 16). And what it causes us to do is bring what Richards calls our various 'impulses' into balance with one another.

He divides impulses into 'appetencies and aversions' ([1924] 2001: 42) and the aim of life is to ensure that the satisfaction of one appetency does not prevent the satisfaction of another. At the same time, Richards claims that some impulses have priority over others. We must, for example, attend to our bodily needs before we can attend to anything else. Then, as social beings, we must cultivate our faculties of communication and cooperation. The growing complexity of society calls more impulses into being and it is incumbent on us to order or, as Richards says, to 'systematise' them. Here is where art comes in. The value of painting, music and literature is that they excite, order and reconcile more impulses than any other activity. Cinema, by contrast, threatens to 'disorganise' our impulses because it appeals only to a very few, intensifying them rather than integrating them with others. Similarly, we are unlikely to enjoy the full benefit of art if we are not clear about its function. 'The. . .force of art', Richards declares, 'lies not in its capacity to present a timid imitation of our experiences, but in its power to go beyond our experience, satisfying and harmonising the unfulfilled activities of our nature' (ibid.: 218–19).

From what Richards says it is clear that the difference between good and bad art is that the former arouses, organises and fulfils many more impulses than the latter. The role of the critic, therefore, is to guide us to those works which achieve this effect and steer us away from those which do not. In addition, he must protect art against 'the crude moralities of the Puritan and the pervert' and try 'to narrow the interval' between 'accepted standards' and 'popular taste' ([1924] 2001: 32). The critic, for Richards, 'is as much concerned with the health of the mind as any doctor with the health of the body' (ibid.: 54). He is a ' judge of values' and the arts are 'an appraisal of existence' (ibid.: 54). To appreciate a work properly, the critic must adopt the frame of mind relevant to it; he must be able to distinguish between the different experiences the work offers and be a sound judge of values (ibid.: 104). In analysing the poem, for it is usually a poem, the critic will focus on different kinds of imagery, thoughts, emotions and attitudes. An understanding of these and other aspects of the poem, such as allusion, helps to organise our impulses into 'a systematised complex response' (ibid.: 166).

We have mentioned several times that Richards belongs to a psychological tradition of criticism that has its origins in Locke, but his discussion of the imagination is also influenced by Coleridge. Indeed, it could be said that one of the characteristics that Coleridge attributes to the imagination, its power to balance or reconcile opposite or discordant qualities (1997: 184–5), forms the basis of Richards's view of criticism. His most immediate predecessor is Pater. Both men were interested in how art affected consciousness. For Pater it enriched our fleeting impressions, for Richards it organised our impulses into a stable and satisfying hierarchy. The difference between Pater and Richards is not simply an intellectual one. Richards's approach to criticism, his desire to maximise our impulses and minimise waste ([1924] 2001: 46), is in line with the precepts of scientific management, as is his development of a method of reading, one that eschews emotion for a comprehensive grasp of 'the range, delicacy and freedom of the connections [the poet] is able to make between different elements of his experience' (ibid.: 166). Nor can the recurrence of terms like 'system' and 'organisation' be divorced from the shift from laissez-faire to corporate capitalism.

One consequence of that development was the growth of discourses of social control and classification which addressed the individual less as subject than as an object for state concern (Langan and Schwartz 1985). The regulation of impulses, in short, mirrored the regulation of the citizen. That may seem a dramatic statement and to a certain extent it is. But the purpose of education is to fit people for the society in which they live and we forget that at our peril, particularly in the present climate. Why do policy makers want to get rid of subject knowledge? Why do they say that there is no point in learning history? Who is going to benefit from the ignorance that will result if, as looks likely, they get their way?

In a famous experiment, Richards gave poems to his Cambridge students on which they were asked to comment freely. The results appear in *Practical Criticism: A Study of Literary Judgement* ([1929] 1973). What astonished Richards was the generally poor quality of the responses. The students had difficulty in construing meaning; they relied on stock responses; and they projected onto the poems ideas and attitudes that simply weren't there. Richards was shocked by what he found. Such insensitivity, 'poor discrimination and feeble capacity to understand poetry' ([1929] 1973: 319) made for a docile population which would be 'easy to control' (ibid.: 314). His warning is as relevant now as it was then as our civil liberties disappear one by one. Although Richards argued that we could take certain steps to try to improve reading ability, such as studying 'the psychology of the speech situation' (ibid.: 339), he accepted that misreadings were always likely to be the norm. 'The only proper attitude', he counselled, 'is to look upon a successful interpretation, a correct understanding, as a triumph against odds' (ibid.: 336).

It is a pity that practical criticism has been so derided in recent years. We need all the help we can get to read carefully, to respect what is there in front of us and not distort it for own purposes. We live in a world of spin. Practical criticism makes us feel the substance of things. It is a defence against those who would manipulate us by exploiting the emotive power of language. It is the scrupulous testing of words, the delicate sifting of their meanings and the due appreciation of their worth. It serves – or did once – to keep them clean and sharp; for words are the tools of thought; if they lose their edge so does our thinking. This is not a new idea. Nor is it confined to England. The Chinese philosopher Confucius (551–477 BC) observed that 'when the names of things are incorrect, speech does not sound reasonable; when speech does not sound reasonable, things are not done properly; when things are not done properly the structure of society is harmed' (Poole 2007: 1).

One of the people Richards influenced was William Empson (1906–84) who was sent down from Magdalene College, Cambridge, after contraceptives were discovered in his rooms. Richards was Empson's supervisor and was mightily impressed with his young student who 'seemed to have read more English literature than I had' (Empson [1930] 1995: x). The origin of Empson's most famous book, *Seven Types of Ambiguity* (1930), occurred in a tutorial. He and Richards were talking about one of Shakespeare's sonnets, beginning 'The expense of spirit in a waste of shame'. 'Taking the sonnet as a conjurer takes his hat', Richards recalls, Empson 'produced an endless swarm of lively rabbits from it and ended by "You could do that with any poetry, couldn't you" . . . so I said "You'd better go off and do it, hadn't you?" ' (ibid.: x). And so he did, producing a work that, according to one reviewer, 'was fraught with revolutionary consequences for the teaching of all literature and the future of literary history' (ibid.: xix).

In fact Empson's influence, in England at any rate, has turned out to be far less than that of another of Richards's students, F. R. Leavis. But why? Empson was continuing work pioneered by others, notably Freud and Eliot, and it may be that his contribution has been overshadowed by theirs. A more likely reason is that Empson's style of criticism, the teasing out of different meanings, runs contrary to the dominant form in English commentary which is more moral than intellectual. All literature is afflicted by ambiguity, which Empson defined as 'any verbal nuance, however slight, which gives room for alternative reactions to the same piece of language' (1995: 19). He identified seven kinds, ranging from two or more meanings being resolved into one to outright contradiction, 'marking a division in the author's mind' (ibid.: vi), each one being illustrated by examples from canonical English authors. The precision with which Empson analyses the various types of ambiguity stands in stark contrast to the vagueness with which he discusses how each one is ultimately a unity. What holds their various elements of ambiguity together is a 'force' (ibid.: 271). 'Forces', Empson writes, 'are essential to the totality of the poem and. . .cannot be discussed in terms of ambiguity because they are complementary to it' (ibid.: 272).

Empson's interest in the 'logical conflict' (1995: 271) between the literal meaning of words and the emotions, thoughts and attitudes they arouse in us looks forward to an aspect of deconstruction, namely, the tension between what is said and how it is said. Empson even anticipates one of the main objections to deconstruction, that it encourages us to believe words can mean anything at all. He cautions against 'a hedonism tending to kill language by dissipating . . . sense under a multiplicity of associations' (1995: 271). All the more puzzling, then, why he was ignored by English theorists, by which I mean those who sought to apply the ideas of, among others, Jacques Derrida (1930–2004), Michel Foucault (1926–84) and Jacques Lacan (1901–81) to literature. They sound so like Empson. Just listen to Catherine Belsey. The object of the critic, she writes, is to seek out 'the multiplicity and diversity of [a work's] possible meanings' (2001: 100). Perhaps Empson's belief that unity was important was what damned him in their eyes. But since they rarely mention his name it is hard to say. He doesn't even make the index of Belsey's highly influential *Critical Practice* (1980; 2nd edn 2001). Whether the omission is a genuine oversight or deliberate snub it argues a very poor knowledge of critical history.

More generally, Empson's analysis of ambiguity has isolated him from the mainstream of English critics who, by and large, adhere to a commonsense view of language. But why, then, should deconstruction have been so successful? After all, it too shows that we can never be certain about meaning. One answer lies in the way that deconstruction extends, amplifies and endorses management theory. For example, Gareth Morgan has seized on Derrida's idea that truth depends on metaphor, writing that 'metaphor offers a fresh way of thinking about organization' because it challenges existing realities to create new ones which 'can be lived on a daily basis' (1997: 143). Another management thinker, David C. Wilson, appropriates Derridean deconstruction to undermine the language of 'us and them' in corporations because 'binaries are not conducive to change' (1992: 56), while Roger Cooper (1987) believes Derrida's contribution to the enterprise culture lies in his notion of *différance* which, he argues, justifies endless improvement in quest of a reality that is always just out of reach. Empson has dropped below the critical horizon not just because he revealed the ambiguous nature of even the most innocent arrangement of words, but also because his work contains few metaphors that link literature and criticism with the economy or the workplace. The success of a critical discourse depends on how closely it is related to the many idioms of corporate capitalism. Even the plain style is allied with the entire managerial apparatus of transparency and accountability.

## Leavis, Criticism and English Theory

I said that the influence of F. R. Leavis proved to be more enduring than that of Empson. Why? Two reasons. First, Leavis's conception of criticism grows out of the tradition of cultural critique and, second, it contains ideas and idioms of scientific management.

Leavis believed that the scientific revolution of the seventeenth century, the growth of the press in the eighteenth, the urbanisation and industrial revolution of the nineteenth century had all but destroyed what he called the 'organic community',[25] by which he meant a society based on tradition, craft work, small trading and close personal relations, and which could flourish in either an urban or rural environment. Primarily, the organic community was the expression of the creative spirit which manifested itself in the all the activities of daily life from making a wheel to conversations in coffee houses. In the context of the city, the organic community took the form of a common culture where educated and popular taste were intertwined in a mutually beneficial relationship. Leavis argued, in his doctoral dissertation,[26] that the rise of journalism undermined this culture by creating different markets for different tastes. The constant reinforcement of these 'taste barriers' made it difficult for any one niche group to find common ground with any other niche group. Consequently, there was no agreement about what constituted 'standards' and, in this situation, the artist had little choice but to write for a particular market rather than 'an educated public'.

It is easy to see that Leavis was influenced by Eliot. His account of the organic community draws heavily on Eliot's notion of the dissociation of sensibility. Leavis does, however, have a slightly different understanding of tradition. Where Eliot identifies it with the great works of European literature, Leavis sees it more in terms of language, a language, moreover, which is the product of the people. It is 'the upshot or precipitate of immemorial human living, and embodies values, distinctions, identifications, conclusions, promptings, cartographical hints and tested potentialities' (1975: 44). It is the result of a creative collaboration by everyone in the community. It serves the dual purpose of preserving 'the picked experience of the ages' (Leavis and Thomson [1933] 1964: 81) and of preparing us for growth and change. But with the disappearance of the organic community and the disintegration of a common culture we lose contact with tradition. Without its moral, intellectual and spiritual resources we are unable to negotiate new experiences and, as human relations become ever more commodified and as technology continues to advance, our need to feel that life is significant becomes ever more acute.

This is where literature comes in. And here Leavis starts to sound like Eliot again. Literature links us to the past and is a source of new life in the present. It is that belief which underpins Leavis's idea of criticism. And it should be said that Leavis has a much more complex idea of criticism – which we will come to shortly – than his opponents allow. Take Catherine Belsey, the doyenne of English theory. She claims Leavis believes that literature 'reflects the reality of experience' (Leavis 1980: 6). Really? His repeated view is that literature is not a reflection of anything but an 'exploratory creation' (Leavis 1993: 130). Even the most casual reader of Leavis is forced to conclude that Belsey is either guilty of gross distortion or else has a very poor understanding of his work.

But we are dealing with the politics of criticism. Truth and fairness only get in the way when you have to discredit an opponent. English theory defines itself against Leavis. Its major premise, that all texts contain multiple meanings, does not extend to him. His work alone is immune from the plurality that characterises every other piece of writing. By such means do theorists like Belsey claim their work is a radical break with the past. But a closer inspection shows this to be a delusion. For example, Leavis, like Belsey, does not think that the author's intention is the key that unlocks his or her work. And, despite Belsey's claims to the contrary, Leavis shares with her the idea that language is not a reflection of reality. She says that 'language offers the possibility of distinguishing between a world of distinct individuals and things' (2001: 4); he says that 'the collaborative creation of a language has played a major part in creating the world we live in – the human world' (1986: 289).[27]

Belsey bases her 'critical practice' on the work of the Swiss linguist Ferdinand de Saussure (1857–1913) who, incidentally, claimed to be descended from Henry VII. He argued that language is a system of signs. Each sign is made up of the signifier, the sound or written form, and the signified, the concept. The relation between them is arbitrary. There is, for example, no necessary connection between the sound of the word 'tree' and the idea of a 'tree'. Words mean because they are different to one another, not because they name things in the world. If we cannot see or hear the difference between 'cat' and 'mat' then we have no way of communicating or conceptualising 'reality'. Belsey hails this as a 'new concept' (2001: 4). It's no such thing. Leavis had pointed out that 'pure reality *an sich* – reality not humanly created – is beyond our experience' (1986: 296); and, in the nineteenth century, John Stuart Mill stated that '[w]e only know anything as distinguished from something else; all consciousness is of difference . . . a thing is only seen to be what it is by contrast with what is not' (in Joseph 2007: 14). As in consumer culture, so in designer criticism. The new is often little more than the old in a fresh guise. It gives the impression of change when in fact things are pretty much the same. We are distracted, and power tightens its grip.

It is time to look a little more closely at Leavis's conception of criticism. 'The *utile* of criticism', he writes, 'is to see that the created work fulfils its *raison d'être*; that is that it is read, understood, and duly valued and has the influence it should have in the contemporary sensibility' (1986: 200). Reading, for Leavis, consists of a number of different elements. He makes a distinction between the poem and the black marks on the page, stressing that the poem has to be produced from those marks. 'I think', he says, when describing this process

> in terms of the ideal executant musician, the one who, knowing it rests with him to recreate in obedience to what lies in black print in the white sheet in front of him, devotes all his trained intelligence, sensitiveness, intuition and skill to recreating, reproducing faithfully what he divines his composer essentially conceived. (ibid.: 260)

The critic must understand the work. What the critic understands is the meaning or meanings of the work. The meaning is what the author intends and the reader understands the meaning as what the author intends: 'unless someone means and someone else takes the meaning, there is no meaning' (1986: 285). We should not assume from this that Leavis believes a work is simply the expression of an author's intention. As a true artist, the creative individual 'knows he does not belong to himself, he serves something [tradition] that is quite other to his selfhood, which is blind and blank to it' (1972: 172). Intention, therefore, is a more complicated idea than may at first appear. The main point, however, is that works do not need to be interpreted to make their meanings plain.

After understanding comes judgement and evaluation, though putting it like this simplifies what is essentially an integrated process. Judging a work of literature is both personal and public. It is personal because unless 'I judge for myself there is no judging' and it is public because 'our business is to establish the poem and meet in it' (Leavis 1986: 277 and 279). That is, we have to agree sufficiently about what the poem is in order to make differing about it profitable. Leavis used the term 'the third realm' (1975: 68) to describe this state where the poem is simultaneously public and private. The judgement of the poem takes the form of a question: 'this is so, is it not?' The question, writes Leavis, 'is an appeal for confirmation that the thing *is* so, implicitly that, though expecting, characteristically, an answer in the form of 'yes, but–' the "but" standing for qualifications, reserves, corrections' (1972: 62). 'This is so' represents the private part of the judgement, the 'yes', 'but' the public part.

The act of valuing is no simple matter. Leavis frequently pointed out that there was a 'treacherous confusingness' (1982: 190) between value and price, and he was at pains to insist that value judgements could never be proved. He believed that a literary work had a comparative rather than an inherent value. The critic compared it to other works by asking questions such as:

> How, as we come to appreciate it and to realise its significance, does it affect our sense of things that have determining significance for us? How does it

affect our total sense of relative value, our sense of direction, our sense of life?
(Leavis 1986: 246)

By these means the critic found a place for the work in the literary tradition
which was not a mere aggregate of works but their 'organic interrelatedness'
(Leavis 1972: 185).

The purpose of evaluating literature is to keep alive the tradition of the
human world, not by admiring its achievements but by bringing its values,
purpose and significance to bear on the present. The revaluation of literary
works revitalises the linguistic and conceptual resources for thinking about
human ends in a rapidly changing world. But the critic's duty is not only to
the past, it is also 'to establish where, in the age, is the real centre of significance, the centre of vital continuity. . .where we have the growth towards the
future of the finest life and consciousness of the past' (Leavis 1986: 283). He
or she looks at the work in terms of whether it 'makes for life' (ibid.: 281) or
against it. At the same time Leavis refused to define what he meant by life
except to say that, as it was about growth and change, the demand for a
precise formulation was neither relevant nor appropriate. There were two
ways in which literature 'made for life'; the first was by conferring a sense of
significance on routine existence and the second was by throwing into question our habitual judgements. 'Significant art', Leavis remarks, 'challenges us
in the most disturbing and inescapable way to a radical pondering, a new profound realization, of the grounds of our most important determinations and
choices' (ibid.: 281).

### Leavis, Theory and Management

Unlike Empson, Leavis engages explicitly with the notion of economy, which
may be one reason why his work has proved more central to literary study
than Empson's. Throughout his career, Leavis tells critics that they must
'wrest meaning from the economist' (1933b: 17) and 'discredit the clichés,
disturb the blank incuria and undermine the assurance' (1972: 107–8) of
those who would maintain that a society's health depends entirely on its Gross
Domestic Product: 'technological and material advance and fair distribution –
it's enough, it's the only true responsibility, to concentrate on them; that's the
attitude I confront' (ibid.: 78). In that case, why does he put a monetary
metaphor at the heart of his criticism? Literary values, he declares, 'are a kind
of paper currency based upon a very small proportion of gold' (1933b: 14).

It is strange. Leavis knows how hard it is to separate value from price; he
thinks that 'a society held together by communication in a language describ-
able as being of words that are the equivalents of a currency is unimaginable'
(1976: 148); and yet he slips easily into the idiom of finance. But when we

put this in the context of the history of criticism, it is perhaps not so odd after all. For we have seen that, from the fifth century BC, there has been, at the very least, an association between the language and working of criticism and that of money. And so it is not surprising, in the twentieth century, when market values infiltrate every aspect of life, to see an ever greater integration of the two, an integration that was considerably eased by the attack, particularly in the 1980s, on the concept of literature. What better way to ensure the spread of a brutal economism than to deride one of the few resources that could be deployed against it?

It's not just the idiom of money that disrupts Leavis's criticism, so too does the idiom of scientific management. It is about control, whereas literature is about creation. Scientific management is about adhering to a method, whereas criticism is about the free play of intelligence. On the surface, realising a complex experience in words and 'getting Schmidt to handle 47 tons of pig iron per day and making him glad to do it'[28] seem to be wholly unrelated activities. And so they are. Yet for all their obvious differences there are affinities between the Taylor's scientific management and Leavis's criticism.

Both men are concerned with production. For Taylor this means increasing output, for Leavis it means producing the work from 'the black marks on the page' which 'are not the same as the poem' (1975: 36). They are the printed letters and words, the raw material from which, in collaboration with others, we build up our idea of the poem. It is 'a product' (ibid.: 36). We find a similar view in Belsey, who proposes what she thinks is a new form of criticism, one which 'constructs its object, [which] produces the work' (1980: 138). But there's a difference. Leavis casts his argument in terms of human agency, of cooperative effort, whereas Belsey attributes the characteristics of intention and action to the term criticism itself.

Taylor places great emphasis on training, saying that only the scientific method would ensure that each man and each machine would yield maximum prosperity for the employer and the employee. Leavis too stresses the importance of training. The subtitle of *Culture and Environment* ([1933] 1964) is 'The Training of Critical Awareness', while in *How to Teach Reading: Or, A Primer for Ezra Pound* (1932), a title of which Taylor would have been proud, Leavis speaks of the need to 'improve one's apparatus, one's equipment as a reader' (1932: 73). And just as Taylor aimed to eliminate the 'rule-of-thumb' way of working because it was wasteful so too did Leavis endeavour to develop a more efficient technique of reading that would save students from 'profitless memorizing' leaving them 'better equipped to profit' from literature (ibid.: 26 and 42).

A key figure in ensuring optimum industrial output was the time-and-motion man, another of Taylor's innovations, and this same figure seems to inform Leavis's conception of the critics' 'surveying eye' of criticism (1936: 17).

Both belong to the age of Mass Observation (f. 1937), which aimed to record every aspect of life from cooking to the coronation of George VI (1937).[29] The demand that there be nothing hidden in the workplace or the poem dovetails perfectly with this project. The factory should be transparent and the poem self-evident; though how this relates to having to produce the poem from the black marks is unclear: it is one example of the tensions that characterise Leavis's writing and part of the task of reading him is to make sense of such apparently conflicting claims.

Finally, we should note that both Leavis and Taylor use the concept of the part and the whole to understand the literary work and the factory organisation respectively. The difference is that for Taylor this relation is mechanical whereas for Leavis it is organic. Taylor's view of the part and whole is predetermined. He advocates a strict division of labour to ensure maximum production. Leavis inclines to a more open-ended view, saying, in respect of tradition, that 'we are concerned with relations between works, between the creative achievements of different authors, between different pasts, and between the past and present' (1972: 111).

But this organic view of the relation between part and whole proves useful to later management theorists such as Peter Drucker who, in reaction to Taylorism, demanded that managers have a concept of the business organisation as 'a genuine whole, greater than the sum of its parts' ([1955] 1969: 24). The concept of the organisation has kept pace with conceptions of the literary work. The deconstructed text, for example, finds its counterpart in the 'flat' organisation. More specifically, Robert P. Gephart claims the meaning of modern business 'resides in [the] contexts and occasions where it is created and used by members, rather than [in] a specific, fixed, substantive form' (1996: 3). A similar point is made by R. Cooper and G. Burrell who argue that, since there is no objective standpoint from which to understand the postmodern enterprise, we should focus instead on 'the production of organizations rather than the organization of production' (1988: 106), a focus that requires the sort of discourse analysis practised by Foucault.

We can only speculate as to why there are these continuities between critical and management discourse. It may be that they are similar by nature – both involve the disciplining of emotion and techniques of production; it may be that the economic organisation of capitalism draws all the elements of a culture together; or it may be that critics found it useful to borrow management terms because it made the study of literature more professional. But that would mean they made conscious use of those terms which Leavis most certainly did not. What we can be sure of is that there is, in the late twentieth century, a shift from critics unwittingly absorbing the ideas and idioms of management to managers deliberately adopting the ideas and idioms of critics and cultural theorists. Paul Bate, for example, sounds like a post-structuralist when he writes that 'language structures thought', that the 'struggle for words is the struggle for meaning' and that managers are 'the manipulators of meaning' (1994: 9 and 11), while another management theorist, Tudor Rickards, tells the story of an expert in operations research who attended a conference on new thinking in management and was worried that he had missed meeting the most mentioned person there. 'Everyone kept talking about this bloke. I kept waiting for Foucault to turn up but I never met him. They say he's revolutionizing management thinking' (1999: 156).

And there are some striking similarities between theoretical ideas and market ideologies. The first wave of English theorists took Saussure as their inspiration and these likenesses may have their origin in his claim that language signifies in the same way as money (Saussure 1974: 83). It is puzzling that readers of Derrida, who was himself so scrupulous in bringing out the significance of casual metaphors, should have overlooked this image. Perhaps its ubiquity –'symbolic economy', 'libidinal economy', 'restricted economy', 'general economy' and so on – made it invisible. If the link with language sounds a bit tenuous, then how about the fact that the rise of theory coincided with the election of Mrs Thatcher's Conservative government? She came to power in 1979, Belsey's *Critical Practice* was published in 1980. The one advocated the free play of market forces, the other the free play of meaning.

Again tenuous. Let's look at the parallels with management. Belsey declares that language is a 'system of signs which signify by means of their relationship to each other rather than to entities in the world' (1980: 46). Fiona Czerniawska, a leading management consultant, claims that in the late 1970s the business person's distrust of language began to give way to an appreciation that language was in fact 'a coherent system of signs that determines the perception of reality' (1997: 8). Belsey further states that because language includes a range of discourses the construction of meaning will always involve 'contradictions and collisions' (1980: 54). Czerniawska agrees, for 'while language may be a system of signs', she writes, 'meaning is neither as consistent or coherent as is commonly assumed' (1997: 8). And just as Belsey believes that the critic's job is to contest meaning, so does Czerniawska believe that language is 'a truly competitive weapon in practical business (ibid.: 13).

It would need a separate book to explore the affinities between the rhetoric of criticism and market and management philosophies. The most we can say is that there is a great deal of circumstantial evidence connecting the two, evidence that, in the case of money, goes right back to Ancient Athens. One result of these connections is to make us doubt claims that theory is either a break with the past or more progressive than traditional criticism. What appears to be a radical reading turns out to complement new economic arrangements. For example, the conventional understanding of the idea of character in fiction was attacked because it took no account of the unconscious, ideology or gender (Belsey 1980: 13). But transformations in the culture of work were also undermining the idea of 'character'. According to Richard Sennett (1998), the demand for a multiskilled labour force on short-term contracts erodes qualities of loyalty, commitment and the ability to realise long-term goals which were integral to the old idea of character. The concept of character has now been replaced by that of 'identity' but this is hardly liberating since its attributes, plasticity, playfulness and 'performativity', are precisely what make it useful for a market where there are no 'jobs for life', where workers must be adaptable and accept the principle of performance-related pay.

The advent of theory in the late 1970s seemed to promise much. First, there was structuralism with its focus on the signifying properties of works. For a time it seemed as if it would unlock the secret not just of narrative but all social behaviour from hairstyles to haute cuisine. Structuralism was the last manifestation of the desire to make criticism a science. It crumbled in England along with the planned economy, and then came the various theories that made up post-structuralism, Lacanian psychoanalysis, Derridean deconstruction and so on. Nor must we forget Marxism and feminism which both saw literature as a form of oppression, distortion or a means of insight into the workings of ideology. Theory today (2008) is like a supermarket: there is so much to choose from. New humanism or cultural materialism? Post-colonialism or postmodernism? Eco-criticism or ethical criticism? The choice is yours. But the sheer variety should not distract us from one fundamental truth: that the demands of bodies like the Quality Assurance Agency are making the study of literature ever more prescriptive for students while the Research Assessment Exercise has distorted it for academics. Criticism is better off outside the academy.

## Conclusion

We have covered an enormous amount of material in this chapter, from modernism to management, from philology to the plurality of meaning, but there is one thread running through it all, namely, the rhetorical transactions between criticism and capitalism. It has been the argument of this book that these exchanges – and that does seem the appropriate word now – have eased the incorporation of business practices into the university. To say that suggests that the fate of higher education rested with literary critics; if only they had resisted the rise of theory things might have been different. They wouldn't. But a sense of how criticism is complicit in the discourse of economic modernisation might have made those radical souls of the 1980s and 90s hesitate before proclaiming how subversive their brand of criticism was and how it differed from everything that came before it didn't. In fact theory was the culmination of the trend to make criticism a career in academia rather than a conversation with art. It substituted doctrine for genuine engagement with the literary work, and its contempt for humanism played right into the hands of a system that viewed its subjects as nothing more than units of production and consumption.

And what of the future? If there is one thing writing a history has taught me it is that the past is too vast to grasp. We make falsifying patterns out of fragments that nevertheless have a small claim to truth. And if we can barely grasp the odd scraps behind us, how much less we can reach out to what may be in front of us. There are trends. The move towards vocational education is likely to mean that there will be less literature studied in most schools and universities. And there are those in higher education now who are calling for the abandonment of the essay as a means of assessment. Since that is one of the primary forms for elaborating a response to a work, its potential disappearance will change at least the medium of criticism as we know it.

Perhaps criticism will pass away and we will be left with just the review. The critic tries to relate a book to others, to assess its contribution to the culture, though what exactly the channels are for making that contribution felt is unclear. The reviewer mostly responds to the work itself and in fairly conventional terms at that. Of course the book itself may disappear. Or at least may only be available in electronic form. The internet, indeed, may create new possibilities for literature and criticism. The advantages for editing are already apparent. More generally, the blog, self-publishing and a potentially world-wide audience democratises the acts of writing and commentary. But there are problems. Not everyone who writes has something to say or can say it well and even the truly groundbreaking work may be lost in the clamour of cyberspace. Still, that is better than literature disappearing altogether, as happened in George Orwell's *1984* (1949). And as long as there is literature, there will be criticism in one of its many guises. For we must respond to whatever touches or moves us deeply. It is part of being human.

### Notes

1. Ironically, these books are now regarded in some quarters as 'literature'.
2. Is there a connection between increasing representation in politics, the growth of local democracy, the extension of the vote to women, and the retreat from representation in art?
3. Woolf is so often regarded as a saint by her devotees that they tend to overlook her contradictions and condescensions. She tells us that 'in or about December, 1910, human character changed', yet later, in the same essay, she declares that 'Mrs Brown is eternal, Mrs Brown is human nature [which] only changes on the

surface' (1966a: 330). And as for this great shift in human character, why, one can even see it 'in the character of one's cook' (ibid.: 320).

4. See, for example, *Women in Love* (1921).

5. For a good introduction to the growth of the collectivist state in the early twentieth century, see Langan and Schwarz 1985.

6. The key figure here is Frederic Winslow Taylor. His *Principles of Scientific Management* was published in 1911, the year after Virginia Woolf said that human character changed forever. Taylor's book is available online at <http://www. eldritchpress.org/fwt/ti.html>.

7. <http://www.eldritchpress.org/fwt/t2.html>.

8. We shouldn't forget, though, that there are people who cannot afford to buy books. A retired farmworker, speaking on *Newsnight*, 16 June 1993, said, 'My father looked forward to retiring so that he could read all the books he hadn't had the time to read when he was working; but when he retired he went blind. I looked forward to reading when I retired, but I can't afford to buy books. I pick them up in second hand shops but when I see the price, even if it's only a couple of pounds, I have to put them back.' Since then inequality has continued to grow in Britain and books, like everything else, have gone up in price. On the nature of markets, see Barber 2007; and Frank (2002).

9. Although we live in a post-factory age, the principles on which factories were run, discipline, monitoring, productivity, have been adopted by most corporations and professions, hence my use of the term in this context.

10. T. S. Eliot said this was 'a facile phrase and at most represents one aspect of great literature if it does not assign to the term "criticism" itself a generality that robs it of all precision' (1960: 11)

11. See Reisman, et al. 1953. The authors identified three personality types: tradition directed, inner directed and other directed. The first followed custom, the second relied on what they learned in childhood, while the third sought the approval of others, and it was these last that big organisations found most useful. It was not the authors who came up with the title but the publisher and the phrase was later used by Bob Dylan in his song 'I shall be released' which is on *Bob Dylan's Greatest Hits Volume 2* (1972).

12. Author of *The Book of Margery Kempe*, considered to be the first autobiography in the English language.

13. Chesterton's distinction between sentiment and passion derives in part from Burke's distinction between the beautiful and the sublime. Of course there is no exact correspondence but each distinction depends on one term being more related to the social and the other to the individual.

14. John Stuart Mill made a similar point when discussing how, in a crowded marketplace, traders had to resort to 'quackery' and 'puffing' in order to distinguish their commodities from those of their rivals. See previous chapter.

15. <http://www.eldritchpress.org/fwt/t2.html>.

16. <http://www.eldritchpress.org/fwt/t2.html>.

17. In Anglo-Saxon the word 'man' was gender neutral. The word 'wer' was placed before to signify a male, and the word 'wyf' to signify a female. Wyfman eventually evolved into the separate words 'woman' and 'wife'. Stony Stratford is where Richard III (then Duke of Gloucester) arrested prince Edward V. He and his brother Richard, Duke of York, were imprisoned in the tower of London and never seen again.

18. Raymond Williams points out that we can find these sentiments expressed much earlier, for example, in Thomas More's *Utopia* (1516). See Williams 1973. Each generation understands its own experience partly in terms of the loss of community, security and stability. It is the template for much historical writing from the enclosure movement to the destruction of working-class neighbourhoods. It is informed by the myth of Eden. It is history as tragedy.

19. I am drawing heavily in the following paragraphs from Franklin E. Court's highly readable *Institutionalizing English Literature* 1992.

20. Evan Watkins makes a good point on this matter. How can we talk about Shakespeare as symbol of a common culture? 'Most of the population of sixteenth century England had never even been to London, let alone heard of Shakespeare' see Watkins 1989: 148.

21. See, for example, the recent conferences 'Working It Out: Situated and Work-Related Learning in Humanities' (Preston, 16 March 2007), 'Here Be Dragons: Humanities, Enterprise and Education' (Leeds, 10 October 2007).

22. A copy of the Subject Benchmark Statement is available at <http:www.qaa.ac.uk/academicinfrastructure/benchmark/honours/english.asp#3>

23. The study of English is essential if the student wants to teach it but most will not, which means that there is an asymmetry between those who take the subject and those who go into the profession.

24. See <http://www.le.ac.uk/ulsm/doc/cjones_managerialsciences.pdf>.

25. Leavis's main source for the organic community is the work of George Sturt (1863-1927) who owned a wheelwright's shop in Farnham, Surrey. Sturt was the author of *Change in the Village* (London: Duckworth, 1912 and 1959) and *The Wheelwright's Shop* (Cambridge: Cambridge University Press, 1923 and 1993). Leavis's conception of the organic community is more complex than many critics have allowed. See Day 1996) 249–53.

26. 'The Relationship of Journalism to Literature: Studied in the Rise and Earlier Development of the Press in England' (1924). Quiller-Couch supervised Leavis's dissertation.

27. For details of these and other links between Leavis and Belsey see Day 1996.

28. <http://www.eldritchpress.org/fwt/t2.html>

29. For a good introduction to Mass Observation, see Hubble 2006.

# BIBLIOGRAPHY

## Polemical Introduction

Baldick, Chris (1987), *The Social Mission of English Criticism 1848–1932* (Oxford: Clarendon Press).

Barry, Peter (1995), *Beginning Theory: An Introduction to Literary and Cultural Theory* (Manchester: Manchester University Press).

Day, Gary (1996), *Re-Reading Leavis: 'Culture' and Literary Criticism* (Basingstoke: Macmillan).

Day, Gary (2001), *Class* (London: Routledge).

Day, Gary (2006), 'F. R. Leavis: Criticism and culture', in Waugh 2006: 130–9.

Eagleton, Terry (1990), *The Ideology of the Aesthetic* (Oxford: Blackwell).

Easthope, Antony (1991), *Literary into Cultural Studies* (London: Routledge).

Gordon, George (1946), *The Discipline of Letters* (Oxford: Clarendon Press).

Habib, M. A. R. (2005), *A History of Literary Criticism* (Oxford: Blackwell).

Smallwood, Philip (2003), *Reconstructing Criticism: Pope's Essay on Criticism and the Logic of Definition* (Lewisburg: Bucknell University Press).

Waugh, Patricia (ed.) (2006), *Literary Theory and Criticism: An Oxford Guide* (Oxford: Oxford University Press).

Widdowson, Peter (ed.) (1982), *Re-Reading English* (London: Methuen).

Williams, Raymond (1958), *Culture and Society 1780–1950* (Harmondsworth: Penguin).

Wimsatt, William K., and Cleanth Brooks (1957), *Literary Criticism: A Short History* (London: Routledge & Kegan Paul).

## Greeks and Romans

*Primary works*

Aristophanes (1964), *The Wasps, The Poet and the Women, The Frogs*, trans. David Barrett (Harmondsworth: Penguin).

Aristotle, *Politics* <http://classics.mit.edu/Aristotle/politics.html>.

Herodotus (1998), *The Histories*, trans. Robin Waterfield with an Introduction and Notes by Carolyn Dewald (Oxford: Oxford University Press).

Homer (2003), *The Odyssey*, trans. Robert Fagles (Bath: Bath Press).

Plato (1980), *The Symposium*, trans. Walter Hamilton (Harmondsworth: Penguin).

Russell, D. A., and M. Winterbottom (eds) (1972), *Ancient Literary Criticism: The Principal Texts in New Translations* (Oxford: Oxford University Press).

*Secondary works*

Barthes, Roland (1975), *The Pleasure of the Text*, trans. Richard Miller with a note on the text by Richard Howard (Oxford: Blackwell).

Bennett, Tony (1979), *Formalism and Marxism* (London: Methuen).

Bowie, Andrew (1990), *Aesthetics and Subjectivity: From Kant to Nietzsche* (Manchester: Manchester University Press).

Davis, Colin (2004), *After Post-Structuralism: Reading, Stories and Theory* (London: Routledge).

Dixon, Peter (1971), *Rhetoric* (London: Methuen).

Eliot, T. S. (1976), *Selected Essays* (London: Faber).

Finley, M. I. (1985), *The Ancient Economy* (Berkeley: University of California Press).

Ford, Andrew (2002), *The Origins of Criticism: Literary Culture and Poetic Theory in Classical Greece* (Princeton: Princeton University Press).

Gilbert, Allan H. (1940), *Literary Criticism: Plato to Dryden* (New York: American Book Company).

Goldhill, Simon (2004), *Love, Sex and Tragedy: Why Classics Matter* (London: John Murray).

Gorak, Jan (1991), *The Making of the Modern Canon: Genesis and Crisis of a Literary Idea* (London: Athlone).

Green, Peter (1998), *The Greco-Persian Wars* (Berkley: University of California Press).

Hallberg, Robert von (ed.) (1984), *Canons* (Chicago and London: University of Chicago Press).

Halliwell, Stephen (2006), 'Plato and Aristotle on the denial of tragedy', in Laird 2006: 115–41.

Jones, Peter (1999), *An Intelligent Person's Guide to the Classics* (London: Duckbacks).

Kagan, Donald (2003), *The Peloponnesian War: Athens and Sparta in Savage Conflict 431–404 B.C.* (London: Harper Collins).

Kennedy, George (ed.) (1997a), *The Cambridge History of Literary Criticism Volume 1: Classical Criticism* (Cambridge: Cambridge University Press).

Kennedy, George (1997b), 'Hellenistic literary and philosophical scholarship', in Kennedy 1997a: 200–19.

Kennedy, George (1997c), 'Language and meaning in Archaic and Classical Greece', in Kennedy 1997a: 78–91.

Kermode, Frank (2004), *Pleasure and Change: The Aesthetics of Canon* (Oxford: Oxford University Press).

Laird, Andrew (ed.) (2006), *Oxford Readings in Classical Studies: Ancient Literary Criticism* (Oxford: Oxford University Press).

Leavis, F. R. (1972), *Nor Shall My Sword: Discourses on Pluralism, Compassion and Social Hope* (London: Chatto & Windus).

Murray, Penelope (1981), 'Poetic inspiration in Early Greece', *Journal of Hellenic Studies* 101: 87–100.

Nagy, Gregory (1997), 'Early Greek views of poets and poetry', in Kennedy 1997a: 1–77.

Pope, Alexander (1978), *Poetical Works*, ed. Herbert Davies (Oxford: Oxford University Press).

Steiner, George (2003), *Lessons of the Masters* (Harvard: Harvard University Press).

Tate, J. (1927), 'The beginnings of Greek allegory', *Classical Review* 41: 214–15.

Tate, J. (1934), 'On the history of allegorism', *Classical Quarterly* 28: 105–14.

## Medieval Criticism

### Primary works

Macrobius (1990), *Commentary on the Dream of Scipio*, trans. with an introduction and notes William Harris Stahl (Columbia: Columbia University Press).

Minnis, A. J., and A. B. Scott (eds) ([1988] 2000), *Medieval Literary Theory and Criticism c.1100–c.1375: The Commentary Tradition* (Oxford: Clarendon Press).

Plato (1980), *The Symposium*, trans. Walter Hamilton (Harmondsworth: Penguin).

Preminger, Alex, O. B Hardison Jr. and Kevin Kerrane (eds) (1974), *Classical and Medieval Literary Criticism: Translations and Interpretations* (New York: Frederic Ungar).

Sigerson, George (trans.) (1922), *The Easter Song, by Sedulius* (Dublin and London: Talbot Press).

### Secondary works

Allen, Judson Boyce (1982), *The Ethical Poetic of the Later Middle Ages: A Decorum of Convenient Distinction* (Toronto and London: University of Toronto Press).

Atkins, J. W. H. (1943), *English Literary Criticism: The Medieval Phase* (Cambridge: Cambridge University Press).

Boitani, P. (ed.) (1993), *Interpretation Medieval and Modern: J. A. W. Bennett Memorial Lectures* (Cambridge: Cambridge University Press).

Copeland, Rita (1993), 'Rhetoric and politics of the literal sense in medieval literary theory: Aquinas, Wyclif, and the Lollards', in Boitani 1993: 334–57.

Copeland, Rita (1995), *Rhetoric, Hermeneutics, and Translation in the Middle Ages: Academic Traditions and Vernacular Texts* (Cambridge: Cambridge University Press).

Copeland, Rita (2005), 'Medieval criticism and theory', in Groden et al. 2005: 80–9.

Copleston, F. C. (1977), *Aquinas* (Harmondsworth: Penguin).

Delaney, Sheila (ed.), *Medieval Literary Politics: Shapes of Ideology* (Manchester: Manchester University Press).

Evans, R. J. (1997), *In Defence of History* (London: Granta).

Fischer, Steven Roger (2003), *A History of Reading* (London: Reaktion Books).

Fisher, John H. (1996), *The Emergence of Standard English* (Kentucky: University of Kentucky Press).

Gillespie, Vincent (2005), 'From the twelfth century to c. 1450', in Minnis and Johnson 2005: 145–238.

Grayson, Cecil (1965), 'Noblior est vulgaris: Latin and Vernacular in Dante's thought', in *Centenary Essays on Dante, by Members of the Oxford Dante Society* (Oxford: Clarendon Press): 67–80.

Green, Vivian (1996), *A New History of Christianity* (Bridgend: Sutton).

Groden, Michael, Martin Kreiswirth and Imre Szeman (eds) (2005), *The Johns Hopkins Guide to Literary Theory and Criticism* (Baltimore: Johns Hopkins University Press).

Hanna, Ralph, Tony Hunt, R. G. Keightley, Alistair Minnis and Nigel F. Palmer (2005), 'Latin commentary, tradition and vernacular literature', in Minnis and Johnson 2005: 363–421.

Hardison, O. B. (1976), 'Towards a history of medieval literary criticism', *Medievalia et humanistica* 7: 1–12.

Irvine, Martin (1994), *The Making of Textual Culture: 'Grammatica' and Literary Theory* (Cambridge: Cambridge University Press).

Jenkins, Keith (1991), *Rethinking History* (London and New York: Routledge).

Jones, Peter (2002), *An Intelligent Person's Guide to the Classics* (London: Duckbacks).

Kaster, Robert A. (1997), *Guardians of Language: The Grammarian and Society in Late Antiquity* (Berkley: University of California Press).

Kaye, Joel (1998), *Economy and Nature in the Fourteenth Century: Money, Market Exchange and the Emergence of Scientific Thought* (Cambridge: Cambridge University Press).

Kennedy, George (ed.) (1997a), *The Cambridge History of Literary Criticism: Volume 1 Classical Criticism* (Cambridge: Cambridge University Press).

Kennedy, George (1997b), 'Christianity and criticism', in Kennedy 1997a: 330–46.

Kennedy, George (1997c), 'Language and meaning in Archaic and Classical Greece', in Kennedy 1997a: 82–6.

Luscombe, David (1997), *Medieval Thought* (Oxford: Oxford University Press).

McGrath, Alistair E. (2001), *Christian Theology: An Introduction* (Oxford: Basil Blackwell).

Minnis, Alistair J. (1984), *Medieval Theory of Authorship* (London: Scholar Press).

Minnis, Alistair J., and Ian Johnson (eds) (2005), *The Cambridge History of Literary Criticism, Volume 2: The Middle Ages* (Cambridge: Cambridge University Press).

Murray, Penelope, and T. S. Dorch (2000), *Classical Literary Criticism* (Harmondsworth: Penguin).

Olson, Glending (2005), 'The profits of pleasure', in Minnis and Johnson 2005: 275–90.

Preminger, Alex, O. B Hardison Jr. and Kevin Kerrane (eds) (1974), *Classical and Medieval Literary Criticism: Translations and Interpretations* (New York: Frederic Ungar).

Russell, D. A. (1997), 'Greek criticism of the Empire', in Kennedy 1997a: 299–329.

Saul, Nigel (1997), *Medieval England* (Oxford: Oxford University Press).

Taylor, Andrew (1999), 'Authors, scribes, patrons and books', in Wogan-Browne et al. 1999: 353–65.

Watson, Nicholas (1999), 'The politics of Middle English writing', in Wogan-Browne et al. 1999: 331–52.

Wetherbee, Winthrop (2005), 'From Late Antiquity to the twelfth century', in Minnis and Johnson 2005: 99–144.

Williams, Raymond (1976), *Keywords: A Vocabulary of Culture and Society* (Harmondsworth: Penguin).

Wilson, N. G. (ed.) (1975), *Saint Basil on the Value of Greek Literature* (London: Routledge).

Wilson, N. G. (1996), *Scholars of Byzantium* (London: Duckworth).

Wimsatt, William K., and Cleanth Brooks (1957), *Literary Criticism: A Short History* (London: Routledge & Kegan Paul).

Wogan-Browne, Jocelyn, Nicholas Watson, Andrew Taylor and Ruth Evans (eds) (1999), *The Idea of the Vernacular: An Anthology of Middle English Literary Theory 1280–1520* (Exeter: Exeter University Press).

## English Renaissance Criticism

*Primary works*

Bacon, Francis (1997), *Essays* (Hertfordshire: Wordsworth).

Donne, John (1971), *The Complete Poems*, ed. A. J. Smith (Harmondsworth: Penguin).

Hobbes, Thomas (1985), *Leviathan* (Harmondsworth: Penguin).

Hobbes, Thomas (1996), *Leviathan*, ed. Peter Tuck, Cambridge Texts in the History of Political Thought (Cambridge: Cambridge University Press).

Locke, John (1988), *Two Treatises of Government*, ed. Peter Laslett, Cambridge Texts in the History of Political Thought (Cambridge: Cambridge University Press)

Montaigne, Michel de (1991), *The Complete Essays*, trans. M. A. Screech (Harmondsworth: Penguin).

Norbrook, David (2005), 'Introduction', in Woudhuysen 2005: 1–67.

Shakespeare, William (1991), *The Complete Works*, eds Stanley Wells and Gary Taylor (Oxford: Oxford University Press).

Vickers, Brian (1999), *English Renaissance Literary Criticism* (Oxford: Clarendon Press).

Woudhuysen, H. R. (ed.) (2005), *The Penguin Book of Renaissance Verse* (Harmondsworth: Penguin).

*Secondary works*

Baxandall, Michael (1988), *Painting and Experience in Fifteenth-Century Italy* (Oxford: Oxford University Press).

Blair, Ann (2001), 'Natural philosophy and the new science', in Norton 2001: 449–57.

Bragg, Melvyn (2004), *The Adventure of English 500 AD –2000: The Biography of a Language* (London: Sceptre).

Burrow, Colin, 'Jonson, Milton, and classical literary criticism in England', in Norton (2001): 487–99.

Cameron, Euan (1991), *The European Reformation* (Oxford: Oxford University Press).

Crystal, David (2004), *The Stories of English* (Harmondsworth: Penguin).

Damon, Philip (1967), 'History and idea in Renaissance literary criticism', in Philip Damon (ed.), *Literary Criticism and Historical Understanding: Selected Papers from the English Institute* (New York and London: Columbia University Press): 25–51.

Day, Gary (2001), *Class* (London: Routledge).

Dewar, Mary (1964), *Sir Thomas Smith: A Tudor Intellectual in Office* (London: Athlone Press).

Einstein, Elizabeth L. (1979), *The Printing Press as an Agent of Change*, Volume 1 (Cambridge: Cambridge University Press).

Elsky, Martin (2001), 'Reorganising the encyclopaedia: Vives and Ramus on Aristotle and the scholastics', in Norton 2001: 402–8.

Fischer, Steven Roger (2003), *A History of Reading* (London: Reaktion Books).

Gray, Floyd (2001), 'The essay as criticism', in Norton 2001: 271–7.

Greene, Roland (2001), 'The lyric', in Norton 2001: 216–28.

Hall, Vernon (1945), *Renaissance Literary Criticism: A Study of its Social Content* (New York: Columbia University Press).

Hallyn, Fernand (2001), 'Cosmography and poetics', in Norton 2001: 442–8.

Helgerson, Richard (1992), *Forms of Nationhood: The Elizabethan Writing of England* (Chicago and London: University of Chicago Press).

Jeanneret, Michel (2001), 'Renaissance exegesis', in Norton 2001: 36–43.

Hunter, George K. (2001), 'Elizabethan theatrical genres and literary theory', in Norton 2001: 248–58.

Kennedy, William J. (2001), 'Humanist classifications of poetry among the arts and sciences', in Norton 2001: 91–7.

Kumar, Krishan (2003), *The Making of English National Identity* (Cambridge: Cambridge University Press).

Liddell, Henry, and Robert Scott (1869), *A Greek English Lexicon* (Oxford: Clarendon Press).

Manley, Lawrence (2001), 'Criticism and the metropolis: Tudor-Stuart London', in Norton 2001: 339–47.

Minnis, A. J., and A. B. Scott (eds) (2000), *Medieval Literary Theory and Criticism c. 1100–c. 1375: The Commentary Tradition* (Oxford: Clarendon Press).

Moss, Ann (2001a), 'Humanist education', in Norton 2001a: 145–54.

Moss, Ann (2001b), 'Theories of Latin poetry', in Norton 2001b: 98–106.

Norbrook, David (2005), 'Introduction', in Woudhuysen 2005: 1–67.

Norton, Glynn P. (ed.) (2001), *The Cambridge History of Literary Criticism, Volume 3: The Renaissance* (Cambridge: Cambridge University Press).

O'Rourke Boyle, Marjorie (2001), 'Evangelism and Erasmus', in Norton 2001: 44–52.

Prescott, Anne Lake (2001), 'Humour and satire in the Renaissance', in Norton 2001: 284–94.

Reiss, Timothy J. (2001), 'Cartesian aesthetics', in Norton 2001: 511–21.

Ross, Trevor (2000), *The Making of the English Literary Canon: From the Middle Ages to the Late Eighteenth Century* (Montreal and Kingston: McGill-Queen's University Press).

Russell, D. A., and M. Winterbottom (eds) (1972), *Ancient Literary Criticism: The Principal Texts in New Translations* (Oxford: Oxford University Press).

Schoenfeldt, Michael (2001), 'Courts and patronage', in Norton 2001: 371–7.

Shuger, Debora (2001), 'Conceptions of style', in Norton 2001: 176–86.

Southall, Raymond (1973), *Literature and the Rise of Capitalism* (London: Lawrence and Wishart).

Vickers, Brian (1997), *In Defence of Rhetoric* (Oxford: Oxford University Press).

Ward, John O. (2001), 'Cicero and Quintilian', in Norton 2001: 77–90.

Waswo, Richard (2001), 'The rise of the vernaculars', in Norton 2001: 409–16.

Wheen, Francis (2004), *How Mumbo-Jumbo Conquered the World: A Short History of Modern Delusions* (London: Fourth Estate).

Williams, Raymond (1977), *Marxism and Literature* (Oxford: Oxford University Press).

Woudhuysen, H. R. (ed.) (2005), *The Penguin Book of Renaissance Verse* (Harmondsworth: Penguin).

Wrightson, Keith (2002), *Earthly Necessities: Economic Lives in Early Modern Britain* (Harmondsworth: Penguin).

## English Enlightenment and Early Romantic Criticism

*Primary works*

Arnold, Matthew (1991), *Selected Poems and Prose*, ed. Miriam Allott (London: Dent).

Beattie, James ([1783] 1996), *Dissertations Moral and Critical* (London: Routledge/Thoemmes).

Blair, Hugh (1911), *Lectures on Rhetoric* (New York and London: Funk and Wagnalls).

Boswell, James (1986), *The Life of Samuel Johnson* (Harmondsworth: Penguin).

Burke, Edmund (1986), *Reflections on the Revolution in France and on the proceedings in certain societies in London relative to that event*, with an introduction by Conor Cruise O'Brien (Harmondsworth: Penguin).

Burke, Edmund (1990), *A Philosophical Enquiry into the Origin of our Ideas of the Sublime and the Beautiful* (Oxford: Oxford University Press).

Dryden, John (1954), 'Dramatic Poetry of the Last Age', in John Dryden, *Essays*, with an introduction by W. H. Hudson (London: J. M. Dent): 95–107.

Fairer, David, and Christine Gerrard (eds) (1999), *Eighteenth-Century Poetry: An Annotated Anthology* (Oxford: Blackwell).

Greene, Donald (ed.) (1984), *Samuel Johnson: A Critical Edition of the Major Works* (Oxford: Oxford University Press).

Hobbes, Thomas (1985), *Leviathan* (Harmondsworth: Penguin).

Hoffman, Daniel G., and Samuel Hynes (eds) (1966), *English Literary Criticism: Romantic and Victorian* (London: Peter Owen).

Hume, David (1884), *Essays* (London: Ward, Lock & Co.).

Johnson, Samuel (1843?), *Lives of the Most Eminent English Poets: With Critical Observations of their Works*, with a sketch of the author's life by Sir Walter Scott (London: Frederick Warne).

Kames, Henry Home, Lord (2005), *Elements of Criticism Two Volumes*, edited and with an introduction by Peter Jones (Indianapolis: Liberty Fund).

Mackie, Erin (ed.) (1998), *The Commerce of Everyday Life: Selections from The Tatler and Spectator* (New York: Bedford/St. Martins).

Marx, Karl (1995), *Capital*, an abridged edition: edited with an introduction by David McLellan (Oxford: Oxford University Press).

Pope, Alexander (1978), *Poetical Works*, ed. Herbert Davies (Oxford: Oxford University Press).

Roberts, David (ed.) (1992), *Lord Chesterfield's Letters* (Oxford: Oxford University Press).

Russell, D. A., and M. Winterbottom (eds) (1972), *Ancient Literary Criticism: The Principal Texts in New Translations* (Oxford: Oxford University Press).

Shaftesbury, Anthony Ashley Cooper, Third Earl (1999), *Characteristics of Men, Manners, Opinions, Times*, ed. Lawrence E. Klein (Cambridge: Cambridge University Press).

Sigworth, Oliver F. (ed.) (1971), *Criticism and Aesthetics: 1660–1800* (San Francisco: Rinehart Press).

Singer, Alan, and Allen Dunn (eds) (2000), *Literary Aesthetics: A Reader* (Oxford: Blackwell).

Smith, Adam (1986), *The Wealth of Nations* (Harmondsworth: Penguin).

Smollett, Tobias (1985), *Humphry Clinker* (Harmondsworth: Penguin).

Spingarn, J. E. (ed.) ([1908] 1957), *Critical Essays of the Seventeenth Century Volume 2: 1650–1685* (Oxford: Oxford University Press).

Spingarn, J. E. (ed.) ([1957] 1968), *Critical Essays of the Seventeenth Century Volume 3: 1685–1700* (Bloomington and London: Indiana University Press).

Steele, Richard, and Joseph Addison (1988), *Selections from* The Tatler *and the* Spectator, ed. with an introduction by Angus Ross (Harmondsworth: Penguin).

Womersley, David (ed.) (1997), *Augustan Critical Writing* (Harmondsworth: Penguin).

*Secondary works*

Atkins, J. W. H. (1966), *English Literary Criticism: 17ᵗʰ and 18ᵗʰ Centuries* (London: Methuen).

Baridon, Michel (1997), 'Literature and science', in Nisbet and Rawson 1997: 778–97.

Black, Jeremy (2005), *A Subject for Taste: Culture in the Eighteenth Century* (London: Hambledon).

Bermingham, Ann, and John Brewer (eds) (1995), *The Consumption of Culture 1600–1800: Image, Object, Text* (London: Routledge).

Bond, Richmond P. (ed.) (1957), *Studies in the Early English Periodical* (Westport, CT: Greenwood Press).

Bordieu, Pierre (1984), *Distinction: A Social Critique of the Judgement of Taste*, trans. Richard Nice (London: Routledge).

Brewer, John (1997), *The Pleasures of the Imagination: English Culture in the Eighteenth Century* (London: Harper Collins).

Carswell, John (1960), *The South Sea Bubble* (California: Stanford University Press).

Colley, Linda (1992), *Britons: Forging the Nation 1707–1837* (New Haven: Yale University Press).

Crawford, Robert (ed.) (1998), *The Scottish Invention of English Literature* (Cambridge: Cambridge University Press).

Crawford, Robert (2000), *Devolving English Literature*, 2nd edn (Edinburgh: Edinburgh University Press).

Dalrymple, Theodore (2005), 'Trash, violence and Versace: But is it art?', in Theodore Dalrymple, *Our Culture, What's Left of It* (Chicago: Chicago): 140–52.

Day, Gary (2001), *Class* (London: Routledge).

Derrida, Jacques (1976), *Of Grammatology*, trans. Gayatri Chakravorty Spivak (Baltimore and London: Johns Hopkins University Press).

Donoghue, Denis (2003), *Speaking of Beauty* (New Haven and London: Yale University Press).

Fraser, Rebecca (2003), *A People's History of Britain* (London: Chatto & Windus).

Gelber, Michael Werth (2002), *The Just and the Lively: The Literary Criticism of John Dryden* (Manchester: Manchester University Press).

Gigante, Denise (2005), *Taste: A Literary History* (New Haven, CT, and London: Yale University Press).

Greene, Donald (ed.) (1984), *Samuel Johnson: A Critical Edition of the Major Works* (Oxford: Oxford University Press).

Heaney, Peter (2006), 'Grub Street', *Literary Encyclopedia* (22 April 2006) (The Literary Dictionary Company: 20 November 2006) <http://www.litencyc.com/php/stopics.php? >.

Hirschman, Albert O. (1977), *The Passions and the Interests: Political Arguments for Capitalism before Its Triumph* (Princeton, NJ: Princeton University Press).

Kennedy, George A. (ed.) (1997a), *The Cambridge History of Literary Criticism: Volume 1: Classical Criticism* (Cambridge: Cambridge University Press).

Kennedy, George A. (1997b), 'The criticism of the Stoics', in Kennedy 1997a: 210–13.

Kivy, Peter ([1976] 2003), *The Seventh Sense: Francis Hutcheson and Eighteenth-Century British Aesthetics* (Oxford: Clarendon Press).

Kumar, Krishan (2003), *The Making of English National Identity* (Cambridge: Cambridge University Press).

Langford, Paul (1984), 'The eighteenth century', in Morgan 1984: 352–418.

Levine, Joseph M. (1994), *The Battle of the Books: History and Literature in the Augustan Age* (Ithaca and London: Cornell University Press).

Lipson, E. (1964), *The Economic History of England Volume 3: The Age of Mercantilism* (London: Adam and Charles Black).

McKeon, Michael (1988), *The Origins of the English Novel: 1600–1740* (Baltimore, MD: Johns Hopkins University Press).

Mackie, Erin (ed.) (1998), *The Commerce of Everyday Life: Selections from The Tatler and Spectator* (New York: Bedford/St. Martins).

Marks, Emerson R. (1968), *The Poetics of Reason: English Neo-Classical Criticism* (New York: Random House).

Morgan, Kenneth O. (ed.) (1984), *The Oxford Illustrated History of Britain* (Oxford: Oxford University Press).

Muir, Kenneth (1976), 'Introduction', in William Shakespeare, *Othello* (Harmondsworth: Penguin).

Newman, Gerald (1987), *The Rise of English Nationalism: A Cultural History 1740–1830* (London: Weidenfeld and Nicholson).

Nicholson, Colin (1996), *Writing and the Rise of Finance: Capital Satires of the Early Eighteenth Century* (Cambridge: Cambridge University Press).

Nisbet, H. B., and Claude Rawson (eds) (1997), *The Cambridge History of Literary Criticism: Volume 4: The Eighteenth Century* (Cambridge: Cambridge University Press).

O'Casey, Brenda (ed.) (1990), *The Sayings of Dr. Johnson* (London: Duckworth).

Patey, Douglas Lane (1997a), 'Ancients and moderns', in Nisbet and Rawson 1997: 32–74.

Patey, Douglas Lane (1997b), 'The institution of criticism in the eighteenth century', in Nisbet and Rawson 1997: 3–31.

Pocock, J. G. A. (1985), *Virtue, Commerce and History* (Cambridge: Cambridge University Press).

Rivers, Isobel (ed.) (2001), *Books and Their Readers in Eighteenth-Century England* (London: Continuum).

Roberts, William (1996), *A Dawn of Imaginative Feeling: The Contribution of John Brown (1715–66) to Eighteenth-Century Thought and Literature* (Carlisle: Northern Academic Press).

Ross, Trevor (2000), *The Making of the English Literary Canon from the Middle Ages to the Late Eighteenth Century* (Montreal and Kingston: McGill-Queen's University Press).

Thirsk, J. (1978), *Economic Policy and Projects: The Development of a Consumer Society in Early Modern England* (Oxford: Clarendon Press).

Thompson, E. P. (1993), *Customs in Common* (Harmondsworth: Penguin).

Thompson, James (1996), *Models of Value: Eighteenth-Century Political Economy and the Novel* (Durham, NC: Duke University Press).

Vickery, Amanda (1998), *The Gentleman's Daughter: Women's Lives in Georgian England* (New Haven, CT: Yale University Press).

Walsh, Marcus (2001), 'Literary scholarship and the life of editing', in Rivers 2001: 191–215.

Williams, Raymond (1976), *Keywords: A Vocabulary of Culture and Society* (Harmondsworth: Penguin).

Womersley, David (ed.) (1997), *Augustan Critical Writing* (Harmondsworth: Penguin).

Wood, Ellen Meiksins (2002), *The Origin of Capitalism: A Longer View* (London: Verso).

Wrightson, Keith (2002), *Earthly Necessities: Economic Lives in Early Modern Britain 1470–1750* (Harmondsworth: Penguin).

## English Romantic, Moral and Aesthetic Criticism

### Primary works

Arnold, Matthew (1993), *Culture and Anarchy and Other Writings*, edited and with an introduction by Stefan Collini (Cambridge: Cambridge University Press).

Bagehot, Walter (1916), *Literary Studies* (London: J. M. Dent).

Blake, William (1975), *A Selection of Poems and Letters*, edited and with an introduction by J. Bronowski (Harmondsworth: Penguin).

Bristow, Joseph (ed.) (1987), *The Victorian Poet: Poetics and Persona* (London: Croom Helm).

Burke, Edmund (1986), *Reflections on the Revolution in France and on the proceedings in certain societies in London relative to that event*, with an introduction by Conor Cruise O'Brien (Harmondsworth: Penguin).

Coleridge, S. T. (1986), *Poems and Prose* selected with an introduction by Kathleen Raine (Harmondsworth: Penguin).

Coleridge, S. T. (2006), *Biographia Literaria* (Whitefish: Kessinger).

Dennis, Barbara, and David Skilton (eds) (1987), *Reform and Intellectual Debate in Victorian England* (London: Croom Helm).

Disraeli, Benjamin (1985), *Sybil: Or, The Two Nations* (Harmondsworth: Penguin).

Eliot, T. S. ([1969] 1978), *The Complete Poems and Plays of T. S. Eliot* (London: Faber).

Faulkner, Peter (ed.) (1989), *Key Documents in Literary Criticism: A Victorian Reader* (London: Batsford).

Flint, Kate (ed.) (1987), *The Victorian Novelist: Social Problems and Social Change* (London: Croom Helm).

Forster, E. M. (1965), 'Notes on the English character', in E. M. Forster, *Abinger Harvest* (London: Edward Arnold): 11–24.

Gaskell, Elizabeth (1993), *North and South* (London: Everyman).

Guy, Josephine (ed.) (1998), *The Victorian Age: An Anthology of Sources and Documents* (London: Routledge).

Hazlitt, William (1982), *Selected Essays*, ed. Ronald Blythe (Harmondsworth: Penguin).

Hoffman, Daniel G., and Samuel Hynes (eds) (1966), *English Literary Criticism: Romantic and Victorian* (London: Peter Owen).

Johnson, Samuel (1990), *The Sayings of Dr. Johnson*, ed. Brenda O'Casey (London: Duckworth).

Keating, Peter (ed.) (1981), *The Victorian Prophets: A Reader from Carlyle to Wells* (London: Fontana).

Kitson, Peter (ed.) (1989), *Key Documents in Literary Criticism: Romantic Criticism 1800–1825* (London: Batsford).

Marx, Karl, and Friedrich Engels (2002), *The Communist Manifesto*, with an introduction and notes by Gareth Stedman Jones (Harmondsworth: Penguin).

Mill, John Stuart (1963), *The Six Great Humanistic Essays*, with an introduction by Albert William Levi (New York: Washington Square Press).

Pater, Walter (1986), *The Renaissance* (Oxford: Oxford University Press).

Ricks, Christopher (ed.) (1987), *The New Oxford Book of Victorian Verse* (Oxford: Oxford University Press).

Ruskin, John (2004), *Selected Writings*, edited with an introduction and notes by Dinah Birch (Oxford: Oxford University Press).

Saussure, Ferdinand (1974), *Course in General Linguistics*, trans. Wade Baskin (London: Fontana).

Skilton, David (ed.) (1993), *The Early and Mid Victorian Novel* (London: Routledge).

Small, Ian (ed.) (1979), *The Aesthetes: A Sourcebook* (London: Routledge & Kegan Paul).

Smiles, Samuel (1958), *Self Help: The Art of Achievement Illustrated by Accounts of the Lives of Great Men* (London: John Murray).

Tennyson, G. B., and Donald J. Gray (eds) (1976), *Victorian Literature: Prose* (New York: Macmillan).

*Secondary works*

Abrams, M. H. (1976), *The Mirror and the Lamp: Romantic Theory and the Critical Tradition* (Oxford: Oxford University Press).

Ackroyd, Peter (1996), *Blake* (London: Minerva).

Altick, Richard D. (1957), *The English Common Reader: A Social History of the Mass Reading Public 1800–1900* (Chicago: University of Chicago Press).

Altick, Richard D. (1973), *Victorian People and Ideas* (New York: Norton).

Bissell, Elizabeth Beaumont (ed.) (2002), *The Question of Literature: The Place of the Literary in Contemporary Theory* (Manchester: Manchester University Press).

Brown, Marshall (ed.) (2003), *The Cambridge History of Literary Criticism: Volume 5: Romanticism* (Cambridge: Cambridge University Press).

Bryson, Bill (2003), *A Short History of Nearly Everything* (London: Black Swan).

Cox, Jeffrey N. (1999), 'Leigh Hunt's Cockney School: The Lakers' "Other"', *Romanticism on the Net* 14 (May 1999) at <http://users.ox.ac.uk/~scato385/hunt-lakers.html>.

Dawkins, Richard (2006), *The God Delusion* (London: Bantam Press).

Demata, Massimilian, and Duncan Wu (eds) (2002), *British Romanticism and the "Edinburgh Review"* (Basingstoke: Palgrave, now Palgrave Macmillan).

Docherty, Thomas (2002), 'The question concerning literature', in Bissell 2002: 126–41.

Eagleton, Terry, and Drew Milne (eds) (1996), *Marxist Literary Theory* (Oxford: Blackwell).

Freedman, Jonathan (1990), *Professions of Taste: Henry James, British Aestheticism and Commodity Culture* (Stanford: Stanford University Press).

Gaunt, William (1975), *The Aesthetic Adventure* (London: Cardinal).

Gilmartin, Kevin (1996), *Print Politics: The Press and Radical Opposition in Early Nineteenth-Century England*, Cambridge Studies in Romanticism, no. 21, <http://www/cup.org> (Cambridge: Cambridge University Press).

Gilmour, Robin (1003), *The Victorian Period: The Intellectual and Cultural Context of English Literature* (London: Longman).

Gross, John (1991), *The Rise and Fall of the Man of Letters: English Literary Life since 1800* (Harmondsworth: Penguin).

Himmelfarb, Gertrude (1984), *The Idea of Poverty: England in the Early Industrial Age* (London: Faber).

Houghton, Walter (1957), *The Victorian Frame of Mind 1830–1870* (New Haven and London: Yale University Press).

Jasper, David, and Stephen Prickett (eds) (2004), *The Bible and Literature: A Reader* (Oxford: Blackwell).

Kaye, Joel (1998), *Economy and Nature in the Fourteenth Century* (Cambridge: Cambridge University Press).

Klancher, Jon (1987), *The Making of English Reading Audiences, 1790–1832* (University of Wisconsin Press).

Klancher, Jon (2003), 'The vocation of criticism and the crisis of the republic of letters', in Brown 2003: 296–320.

Kumar, Krishan (2003), *The Making of English National Identity* (Cambridge: Cambridge University Press).

Lukács, Georg (2006), *The Meaning of Contemporary Realism* (London: Merlin Press).

Morgan, Peter F. (1983), *Literary Critics and Reviewers in Early 19th-Century Britain* (London: Croom Helm).

Praz, Mario (1988), *The Romantic Agony*, trans. Angus Davidson (Oxford: Oxford University Press).

Reed, Edward S. (1998), *From Soul to Mind: The Emergence of Psychology, from Erasmus Darwin to William James* (Yale: Yale University Press).

Shaffer, E. S. (2003), 'Religion and literature', in Brown 2003: 138–61.

Steiner, George (1971), *In Bluebeard's Castle: Some Notes towards the Redefinition of Culture* (London: Faber).

Wheatley, Kim (ed.) (2003), *Romantic Periodicals and Print Culture* (London: Frank Cass).

Williams, Raymond ([1958] 1975), *Culture and Society 1750–1950* (Harmondsworth: Penguin).

## Institutionalising English Criticism: Men of Letters, Modernism, Tradition and Theory

*Primary works*

Adorno, T., W. Benjamin, E. Bloch, B. Brecht and G. Lukács (1990), *Aesthetics and Politics*, trans R. Taylor (London: Verso).

Arnold, Matthew (1925), *Essays* (Oxford: Oxford University Press).

Bate, Paul (1994), *Strategies for Cultural Change* (London: Heinemann).

Bennett, Arnold (1938), *Literary Taste* (Harmondsworth: Penguin).

Bojie, David M., Robert P. Gephart and Tojo Joseph Thatchenkery (eds) (1996), *Postmodern Management and Organization Theory* (London: Sage).

Bradley, A. C. ([1909] 1962), *Oxford Lectures on Poetry* (London: Macmillan).

Chesterton, G. K. (1951), *Selected Essays* (London: Methuen).

Chesterton, G. K. (1953), *Selected Essays* (London and Glasgow: Collins).

Chesterton, G. K. (1964), *The Spice of Life* (Beaconsfield: Darwin Finlayson).

Coleridge, S. T. (1997), *Biographia Literaria* (London: Dent).

Connolly, Cyril (1988), *Enemies of Promise* (London: Andre Deutsch).

Cooper, R. (1987), 'Information, communication, and organization: A post-structural revision', *Journal of Mind and Behaviour* 8, 3: 395–416.

Czerniawska, Fiona (1997), *Corporate Speak: The Use of Language in Business* (Basingstoke: Macmillan, now Palgrave Macmillan).

Drucker, Peter ([1955] 1969), *The Practice of Management* (London: Heinemann).

Eliot, T. S. (1978), *The Complete Poems and Plays* (London: Faber).

Eliot, T. S. (1960), *The Sacred Wood: Essays on Poetry and Criticism* (London: Methuen).

Eliot, T. S. (1976), *Selected Essays* (London: Faber).

Forster, E. M. (1948), 'The raison d'être of criticism', *Horizon* 28: 37–411.

Forster, E. M. (1965), *Abinger Harvest* (London: Edward Arnold).

Forster, E. M. (2000), *Aspects of the Novel* (Harmondsworth: Penguin).

Frazer, James ([1890] 2004), *The Golden Bough* (London: Canongate).

Freud, Sigmund (1930), *Civilisation and Its Discontents*, trans. Joan Riviere (London: Hogarth Press).

Freud, Sigmund ([1900] 1976), *The Interpretation of Dreams*, trans. James Strachey (Harmondsworth: Penguin).

Gephart, Robert P., David M. Bojie and Tojo Joseph Thatchenkery (1996), 'Postmodern management and the coming crises of organizational analysis', in David M. Bojie, Robert P. Gephart Jr. and Tojo Joseph Thatchenkery (eds), *Postmodern Management and Organization Theory* (London: Sage): 1–11.

Gordon, George (1946), *The Discipline of Letters* (Oxford: Clarendon Press).

Gosse, Edmund (1898), *A Short History of English Literature* (London: Cassell).

Herford, C. H. (1910), *The Bearing of English Studies on National Life*, English Association Leaflet No. 16 (Oxford: Oxford University Press).

Lawrence, D. H. (2002), *Study of Thomas Hardy and Other Essays*, ed. Bruce Steele (Cambridge: Cambridge University Press).

Leavis, F. R. (1932), *How to Teach Reading: Or, A Primer for Ezra Pound* (Cambridge: Minority Press).

Leavis, F. R. (1933a), *For Continuity* (Cambridge: Minority Press).

Leavis, F. R. (1933b), *Mass Civilization and Minority Culture* (Cambridge: Minority Press).

Leavis, F. R. (1936), *Revaluation: Tradition and Development in English Poetry* (London: Chatto & Windus).

Leavis, F. R. (1972), *Nor Shall My Sword: Discourse on Pluralism, Compassion and Social Hope* (London: Chatto & Windus).

Leavis, F. R. (1973), *Anna Karenina and Other Essays* (London: Chatto & Windus).

Leavis, F. R. (1975), *The Living Principle: 'English' as a Discipline of Thought* (London: Chatto & Windus).

Leavis, F. R. (1976), *Thought, Words and Creativity: Art and Thought in Lawrence* (London: Chatto & Windus).

Leavis, F. R. (1982), *The Critic as Anti-Philosopher: Essays and Papers*, ed. G. Singh (London: Chatto & Windus).

Leavis, F. R. (1986), *Valuation in Criticism and Other Essays*, ed. G. Singh (Cambridge: Cambridge University Press).

Leavis, F. R. (1993), *The Common Pursuit* (Harmondsworth: Penguin).

Leavis, F. R., and Denys Thompson ([1933] 1964), *Culture and Environment: The Training of Critical Awareness* (London: Chatto & Windus).

Morely, Edith J. (1919), *The Teaching of English in Schools: A Series of Papers*, English Association Pamphlet No. 43 (Oxford: Oxford University Press).

Morgan, Gareth (1997), *Imagin. i. Zation: New Mindsets for Seeing, Organizing, and Managing* (London: Sage).

Murry, John Middleton (1924), *Countries of the Mind: Essays in Literary Criticism* (London: W. Collins).

Newbolt, Henry (1928), *The Idea of an English Association*, English Association Pamphlet No. 70 (Oxford: Oxford University Press).

Orage, A. R. (1935), *Selected Essays and Critical Writings* (London: Stanley Nott).

Peters, Tom and Robert Waterman (1995), *In Search of Excellence* (London: Harper Collins).

Quiller-Couch, Arthur (1928), *On the Art of Reading* (Cambridge: Cambridge University Press).

Quiller-Couch, Arthur (1929), *Studies in Literature* (Cambridge: Cambridge University Press).

Richards, I. A. ([1924] 2001), *Principles of Literary Criticism* (London and New York: Routledge).

Richards, I. A. ([1929] 1973), *Practical Criticism: A Study in Literary Judgement* (London: Routledge & Kegan Paul).

Rickards, Tudor (1999), *Creativity and the Management of Change* (Oxford: Blackwell Business).

Rickword, Edgell, and Douglas Garman (eds) (1966), *The Calendar of Modern Letters March 1925–July 1927* (London: Frank Cass).

Saussure, Ferdinand de (1974), *Course in General Linguistics*, trans. Wade Baskin (London: Fontana).

Skeat, Walter (1891), 'The educational value of English', *Educational Review* 1 November: 10–23.

Spurgeon, C. F. E. (1917), *Poetry in the Light of War*, English Association Pamphlet No. 36 (Oxford: Oxford University Press).

Sturt, George ([1912] 1959), *Change in the Village* (London: Duckworth).

Sturt, George ([1923] 1993), *The Wheelwright's Shop* (Cambridge: Cambridge University Press).

Weston, Jessie L. (1921), *From Ritual to Romance* (Cambridge: Cambridge University Press).

Wilson, David C. (1992), *A Strategy of Change: Concepts and Controversies in the Management of Change* (London: Routledge).

Woolf, Virginia (1966a), *Collected Essays Volume 1* (London: Hogarth Press).

Woolf, Virginia (1966b), *Collected Essays Volume 2* (London: Hogarth Press).

*Secondary works*

Atherton, Carol (2005), *Defining Literary Criticism: Scholarship, Authority and the Possession of Literary Knowledge, 1880–2002* (Basingstoke: Palgrave Macmillan).

Baldick, Chris (1987), *The Social Mission of English Criticism 1848–1932* (Oxford: Clarendon Press).

Barber, Benjamin (2007), *Consumed: How Markets Corrupt Children, Infantilize Adults and Swallow Citizens Whole* (New York: Norton).

Belsey, Catherine (1980), *Critical Practice* (London: Methuen; 2nd edn 2001).

Bryson, Bill (2003), *A Short History of Nearly Everything* (London: Black Swan).

Bunting, Madeleine (2005), *Willing Slaves: How the Overwork Culture Is Ruling Our Lives* (London and New York: Harper Perennial).

Cahill, K. (2001), *Who Owns Britain?* (London: Canongate).

Carey, John (1992), *The Intellectuals and the Masses: Pride and Prejudice among the Literary Intelligensia 1880–1930* (London: Faber).

Cooper, R., and G. Burrell (1988), 'Modernism, postmodernism and organizational analysis', *Organizational Studies* 9, 1: 89–111.

Court, Franklin E. (1992), *Institutionalising English Literature: The Culture and Politics of Literary Study 1750–1900* (Stanford: Stanford University Press).

Day, Gary (1996), *Re-Reading Leavis: 'Culture' and Literary Criticism* (Basingstoke: Macmillan, now Palgrave Macmillan).

Doyle, Brian (1989), *English and Englishness* (London: Routledge).

Easthope, Antony (1988), *British Post-Structuralism since 1968* (London: Routledge).

Empson, William ([1930] 1995), *Seven Types of Ambiguity* (Harmondsworth: Penguin).

English Association (1909), *Types of Curricula in Girls' Secondary Schools*, English Association Leaflet No. 8 (Oxford: Oxford University Press).

Frank, Thomas ([2000] 2002), *One Market under God: Extreme Capitalism, Market Populism and the End of Economic Democracy* (London: Vintage).

Gross, John (1969), *The Rise and Fall of the Man of Letters: English Literary Life since 1800* (Harmondsworth: Penguin).

Guy, Josephine, and Ian Small (1993), *Politics and Value in English Studies: A Discipline in Crisis?* (Cambridge: Cambridge University Press).

Hall, Stuart, and Martin Jacques (eds) (1983), *The Politics of Thatcherism* (London: Lawrence and Wishart).

Heyck, T. W. (1982), *The Transformation of Intellectual Life in Victorian England* (London: Croom Helm).

Hoffman, Daniel Gerard, and Samuel Lynn Hynes (1966), *English Literary Criticism: Romantic and Victorian* (London: Owen).

Hubble, Nick (2006), *Mass-Observation and Everyday Life* (Basingstoke: Palgrave Macmillan).

Hughes, Robert (1991), *The Shock of the New: Art and the Century of Change* (London: Thames and Hudson).

Hyman, Stanley (1948), *The Armed Vision: A Study in the Methods of Modern Literary Criticism* (New York: Alfred A. Knopf).

Joseph, John E. (2007), 'He was an Englishman', *Times Literary Supplement* 16 November: 14–15.

Langan, M., and B. Schwartz (eds) (1985), *Crises in the British State 1880–1930* (London: Hutchinson).

Litz, Walton A., Louis Menand and Lawrence Rainey (eds), *The Cambridge History of Literary Criticism Volume 7: Modernism and the New Criticism* (Cambridge: Cambridge University Press).

Martin, Wallace (2000), 'Criticism and the academy', in Litz et al. 2000: 269–321.

Palmer, D. J. (1965), *The Rise of English Studies: An Account of the Study of English Language and Literature from Its Origins to the Making of the Oxford English School* (Oxford: Oxford University Press).

Poole, Steven (2007), *Unspeak: Words Are Weapons* (London: Abacus).

Praz, Mario (1988), *The Romantic Agony*, trans. Angus Davidson (Oxford: Oxford University Press).

Reisman, David, Nathan Glazer and Paul Denney (1953), *The Lonely Crowd* (New York: Doubleday Anchor).

Sampson, George ([1921] 1970), *English for the English: A Chapter on National Education* (Cambridge: Cambridge University Press).

Saunders, J. W. (1964), *The Profession of English Letters* (London: Routledge & Kegan Paul).

Seltzer, Mark (1992), *Bodies and Machines* (London: Routledge).

Sennett, Richard (1998), *The Corrosion of Character: The Personal Consequences of Work in the New Capitalism* (New York: Norton).

Symons, Arthur (1909), *The Romantic Movement in English Poetry* (London: Archibald Constable).

Vickers, Brian (1999), *English Renaissance Literary Criticism* (Oxford: Clarendon Press).

Watkins, Evan (1989), *Work Time: English Departments and the Circulation of Cultural Value* (Stanford: Stanford University Press).

Watson, George (1962), *The Literary Critics* (Harmondsworth: Penguin).

Watson, Peter (2000), *A Terrible Beauty: The People and Ideas That Shaped the Modern Mind* (London: Phoenix).

Widdowson, Peter (1999), *Literature* (London: Routledge).

Williams, Raymond (1973), *The Country and the City* (London: Chatto & Windus).

# INDEX